Two Faces of South Asian Art:
Textiles and Paintings

Textiles from the Helen L. Allen Textile Collection
Blenda Femenias with a chapter by Cynthia Cunningham Cort

Paintings from the Earnest C. and Jane Werner Watson Collection
Joan A. Raducha

Elvehjem Museum of Art
4 February–18 March 1984

This exhibition was organized by the School of Family Resources and Consumer Sciences and by the Elvehjem Museum of Art, University of Wisconsin–Madison

The exhibition and catalogue were supported by grants from the Wisconsin Humanities Committee on behalf of the National Endowment for the Humanities, the Wisconsin Arts Board with funds from the National Endowment for the Arts, and the University of Wisconsin–Madison Consortium for the Arts, and Knapp Bequest Committees.

ISBN: 0-932900-06-2

Design by Tara Christopherson

Photo credits: All photographs by Laura Vanderploeg, except the following: Plate 1.5, Elsa Sreenivasam; 1.10, India Office, British Library, 1.22, John E. Cort; 1.35, 1.43, 1.51, Vickie C. Elson; 1.60, 1.62, Christoph von Furer-Haimendorf.

Map design by the University of Wisconsin–Madison Cartography Laboratory.

Table of Contents

Notes on the catalogue

Diacritical marks have been avoided in the text, as unnecessary for the English pronunciation of the many names and titles which label the objects. The palatal and the retroflex "s" have been transliterated as "sh," the pronunciation of which approximates the Indic sound in the names Shiva and Krishna.

The textile entries are numbered 1.1, 1.2, etc.; the paintings are numbered 2.1, 2.2, etc.

For the textiles, the dimensions of the warp precede those of the weft.

Textile terminology follows that in Irene Emery, *The Primary Structures of Fabrics* (Washington: The Textile Museum, 1966).

Each entry in the painting section ends with a reference to the number in Pramod Chandra's catalogue of the paintings in the Watson Collection at the Elvehjem Museum of Art. Any inquiries should refer to these numbers.

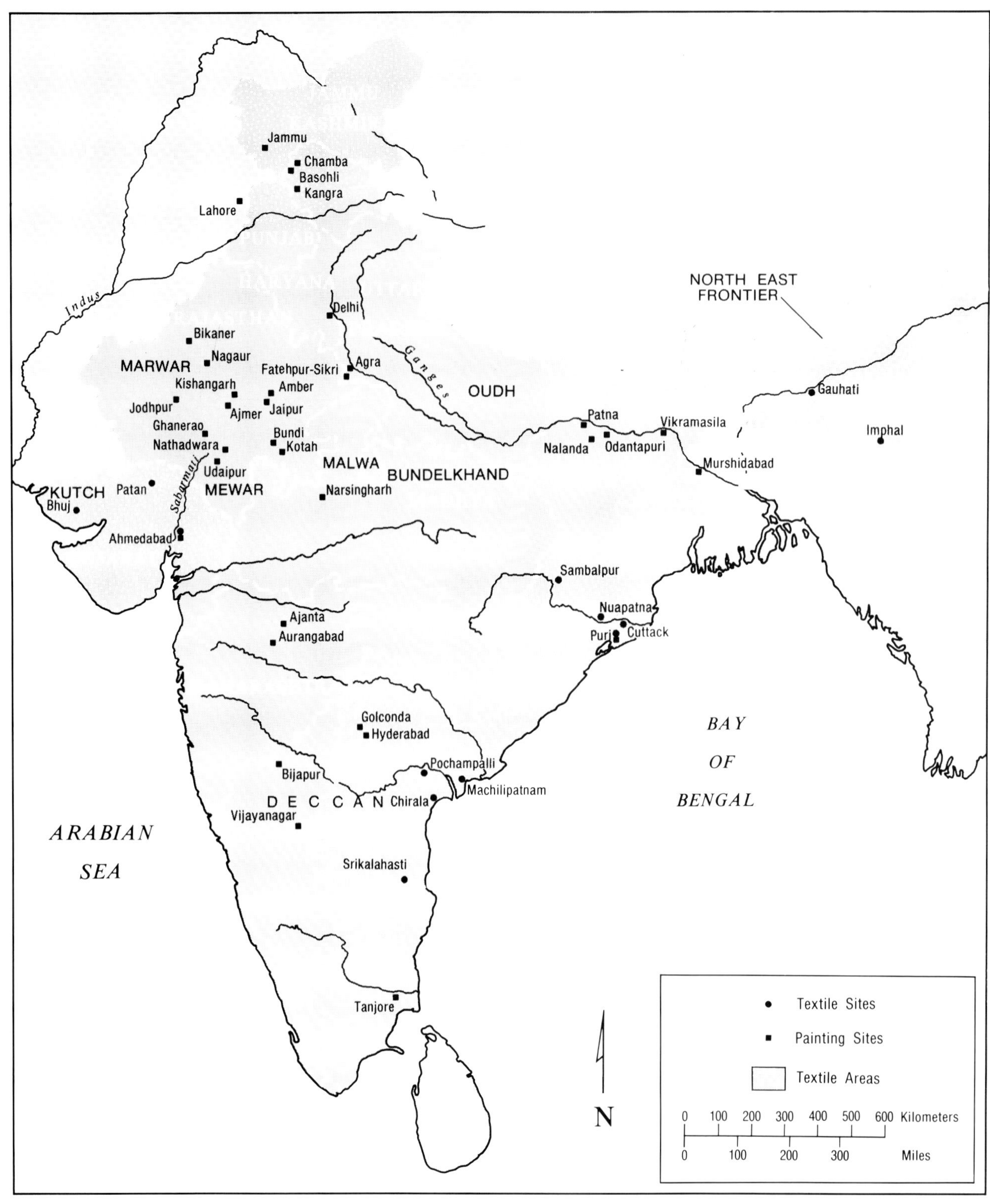

Jammu
Chamba
Basohli
Kangra
Lahore
Indus
NORTH EAST FRONTIER
Delhi
Bikaner
Nagaur
MARWAR
Fatehpur-Sikri
Agra
Ganges
OUDH
Kishangarh
Amber
Gauhati
Jodhpur
Ajmer
Jaipur
Patna
Vikramasila
Imphal
Ghanerao
Bundi
Nathadwara
Kotah
Nalanda
Odantapuri
Murshidabad
Saburmati
Udaipur
MALWA
BUNDELKHAND
KUTCH
Patan
MEWAR
Bhuj
Narsingharh
Ahmedabad
Sambalpur
Nuapatna
Ajanta
Puri
Cuttack
Aurangabad
Golconda
BAY
Hyderabad
OF
Bijapur
Pochampalli
BENGAL
DECCAN
Chirala
Machilipatnam
ARABIAN
Vijayanagar
SEA
Srikalahasti
Tanjore
N
Textile Sites
Painting Sites
Textile Areas
0   100   200   300   400   500   600   Kilometers
0   100   200   300   Miles

Foreword

The University of Wisconsin–Madison is fortunate to have two significant resources through
which to study and enjoy South Asian art—the South Asian Collection of the Helen L. Allen Textile
Collection in the School of Family Resources and Consumer Sciences, and the Earnest C. and Jane
Werner Watson Collection of Indian Miniature Paintings at the Elvehjem Museum of Art.

It is indeed a pleasure, therefore, to have the opportunity to exhibit portions of both collections
together and to benefit from the comparisons to be made in examining the two art forms. Most will
know these textiles and paintings as "Indian." In adopting the nomenclature "South Asian" we have
attempted to recognize the contributions of nations located in the Subcontinent outside of the modern political boundaries of India. Specifically, some of the objects in this catalogue are from within
areas of Pakistan and Nepal.

The Elvehjem is indebted to Blenda Femenias, Curator of the Helen L. Allen Textile Collection,
and Dr. Joan A. Raducha of the University of Wisconsin–Madison Department of South Asian
Studies for organizing, respectively, the textile and painting sections of the exhibition and catalogue.
In addition, we wish to thank Cynthia Cunningham Cort for her essay on *ikat* textiles. Ms. Femenias,
as project director, has devoted tireless efforts to many aspects of the exhibition and the concurrent
symposium.

The exhibition and catalogue were supported by a generous grant from the Wisconsin Humanities Committee on behalf of the National Endowment for the Humanities, the Wisconsin Arts Board
with funds from the National Endowment for the Arts, and the University of Wisconsin–Madison
Consortium for the Arts and Knapp Bequest Committees. We gratefully acknowledge this support.

The idea of exhibiting paintings from the Watson Collection with textiles from the Allen Collection
was the conception of the Elvehjem's late director, Katherine Harper Mead. Her enthusiasm for
collaborative projects involving other University of Wisconsin collections became well known during
her brief tenure here, and—as the visitor to this exhibition will testify—continues to enrich us all.

Stephen C. McGough
Acting Director

A Note on the Allen Collection

The Helen L. Allen Textile Collection is composed of over 10,000 textiles and related objects representing many areas of the world, time periods, designs, and techniques. This includes over four hundred South Asian textiles and costumes, some of which have been donated to the university by generous alumni and friends or purchased by Helen Allen and subsequent curators from collectors who had spent time in India. The vast majority, more than three hundred objects, represent the collecting efforts of one woman, Ruth Reeves.

Reeves was an American textile designer active as early as the 1930s in the Works Project Administration. The Allen Collection includes some of her WPA pieces. Always interested in the role of textiles in other cultures, and possibilities for adapting foreign designs to American tastes, she traveled to South America. Her first visit to India was in 1956 when she went there as one of the first Fulbright scholars. Becoming interested in *cire perdue*, she wrote the definitive book on Indian *cire perdue* in the late 1950s. She continued her studies in India under a Ford Foundation Grant and worked with the All-India Handicrafts Board and as honorary handicraft advisor in the office of the Registrar of India. She also aided the Census of India in recording the native crafts as practiced in individual villages, and assembled her textile collection.

In 1963, Reeves agreed to collect Indian ceramic, wood and metal crafts for Syracuse University; the first of the pieces were sent from India in 1966. Syracuse did not acquire her textile collection.

Ruth Reeves' goal in assembling the collection was apparently to construct a representative collection of the state of the arts in the 1950s and '60s. The collection is wide ranging in terms of provenance, technique, and quality. She collected not only the work that seemed best to her Western eyes, but also the most typical products then being produced by Indian craftsmen. Unfortunately, in 1966 Reeves died of cancer in New Delhi.

In 1976, the staff of the Allen Collection learned of the availability of Ruth Reeves' entire collection of South Asian textiles. Through the efforts of Ruth Harris, then curator, and the Allen Collection Committee, then chaired by Patricia Mansfield, Reeves' collection was purchased from her daughters, the executors of her estate. A stated goal at that time in regards this acquisition, the largest single acquisition for the Allen Collection up until that time, was its ultimate suitability for a substantial exhibition, such as this catalogue documents.

Given the tremendous diversity of the Reeves material, which was further expanded when added to material previously in the Allen Collection and collected since 1976 by curators, my task when beginning to formulate this exhibition was to select a small percentage of this material to represent some salient features of South Asian textiles, and at the same time to relate these selections to visual traditions represented by some of the miniature paintings in the Watson Collection. Ultimately, five different types of textiles were chosen, each representing a different region, theme, lifestyle, or technique significant in Indian art and culture. To represent each type most accurately, the holdings of the Allen Collection have been supplemented by generous loans from the following institutions and individuals: Joyce Carey, Cynthia Cunningham Cort, Joan Severa of the State Historical Society of Wisconsin, and Patricia Altman of the Museum of Cultural History.

Blenda Femenias

The Watson Painting Collection

The Elvehjem Museum of Art is fortunate to house the Earnest C. and Jane Werner Watson Collection of Indian Miniature Paintings. This collection of nearly 300 paintings was assembled by the Watsons in a two-and-one-half-year period, during which the late Earnest C. Watson served as the scientific attache to the United States Embassy in New Delhi, India. Represented among the array of miniatures are all of the major stylistic groupings of Indian painting, covering a period of nearly nine-hundred years. Thus, the collection is a treasure for the general museum audience as well as for the serious student of Oriental art.

A detailed catalogue of the collection was published by the Museum in 1971, accompanying the first exhibition of the entire collection. At that time, Jane Watson, an alumna of the University of Wisconsin–Madison, wrote a delightful history of the process involved in acquiring the collection. She also provided "Some Notes for Viewers," in which she shared many of the insights she had gained about Indian painting through her collecting experiences. Pramod Chandra, an expert in the field of miniature painting who currently holds the chair of Indian Art at Harvard University, wrote an essay on "Indian Painting" as well as the catalogue of this collection. He identified the major stylistic group-ings and described the salient characteristics of each. In all matters of attribution, this catalogue has deferred to his knowledgeable decisions. The reader is encouraged to consult the first catalogue for a more complete overview of the collection.

Since the first showing of the paintings in 1971, the Watson collection has been the subject of two other large exhibitions at the Elvehjem Museum of Art (in 1976 and 1981), and somewhat smaller exhibitions have been lent to other institutions, including the University of Minnesota. In each case, the selections were made according to the stylistic scheme of Professor Chandra's catalogue. In the current exhibition, which includes one hundred and two of the paintings, the arrangement is by theme, within which chronology is a secondary consideration. Thus, the viewer will have several opportunities to see a subject treated by more than one school, with markedly different results. It is hoped that this thematic arrangement of the paintings, and their exhibition in conjunction with textiles, some of which echo patterns found in the earlier paintings, will provide an interesting view of "two faces of South Asian art."

Joan A. Raducha

Acknowledgments

For their assistance in preparing this catalogue and exhibition, the efforts of the following people on my behalf are deeply appreciated:

First, the contributions of the faculty and staff of the Environment, Textiles and Design Department and the School of Family Resources and Consumer Sciences were invaluable. Dean Elizabeth Simpson provided administrative support. The members of the Helen Allen Textile Collection Committee were unflagging in their encouragement, empathy and good humor: Virginia T. Boyd, Joyce Carey, Patricia Mansfield, Betty Wass, and Manfred Wentz.

Linda Merz spent countless patient hours typing and revising the manuscript while she pioneered the new word-processor, with emergency assistance and proofreading ably provided by Marjorie Pfeifer.

The student assistants in the Allen Collection performed innumerable demanding tasks ranging from mounting and conservation to marathon photography sessions to steering me through the maze of computerization: Elizabeth Bard, Caitlin Callahan, Patricia Garone, Joan Kolodziej, Ann Hiltner-Skodje and Suzanne Quigley.

Much-needed conservation and cleaning were carried out by Lori Houg and Martha Tate, under guidance of Manfred Wentz. Students of museum techniques assisted with mounting textiles; Joan Bonow, Joan Borgwardt and Diana Dicus continued these efforts beyond the class requirements.

Beyond the School of Family Resources and Consumer Sciences assistance of various types was offered by many people. Sincere thanks go to Cynthia Cunningham Cort for her contributed essay on ikat as well for sharing her knowledge on other aspects of Indian textiles. She also, along with Vickie Elson, Christoph von Fürer-Haimendorf, and Elsa Sreenivasam generously shared rare field photographs, some published here for the first time.

Speakers at the symposium coinciding with the exhibition opening are thanked for their scholarly contributions and their willingness to brave the Wisconsin winter in February to participate in this collaborative endeavor: Milo C. Beach, Daniel J. Ehnbom, Mattiebelle Gittinger, Nina Gwatkin, Suman Shenoi, Elsa Sreenivasam.

Finally, I owe a very special debt of gratitude to Mattiebelle Gittinger, who first acquainted me with the tremendous beauty and power of South Asian textiles, an acquaintance which deepened with her guidance into respect and admiration for the exceptional objects produced over centuries by anonymous craftsmen. Moreover, her constant availability for information or advice has been a matchless contribution to this endeavor.

BF

The Elvehjem Museum of Art staff has provided me with valuable assistance at every stage of this project. Katherine Mead, the late director, initiated the idea of the catalogue and symposium and invited me to select and write about the paintings. Stephen C. McGough provided organizational energy and arranged for unlimited access to the print room so that I could become fully acquainted with the collection. Carlton Overland helped at several stages, but especially in editorial assistance and in the design of the show. Timothy Quigley, Lisa Calden, and Shirley Scheier made access to the paintings and file information an easy process. Typing and administrative matters were efficiently handled by Ruth Struve, Jeanne Niederklopfer, and Sandra Paske.

JAR

Part I: Textiles of South Asia

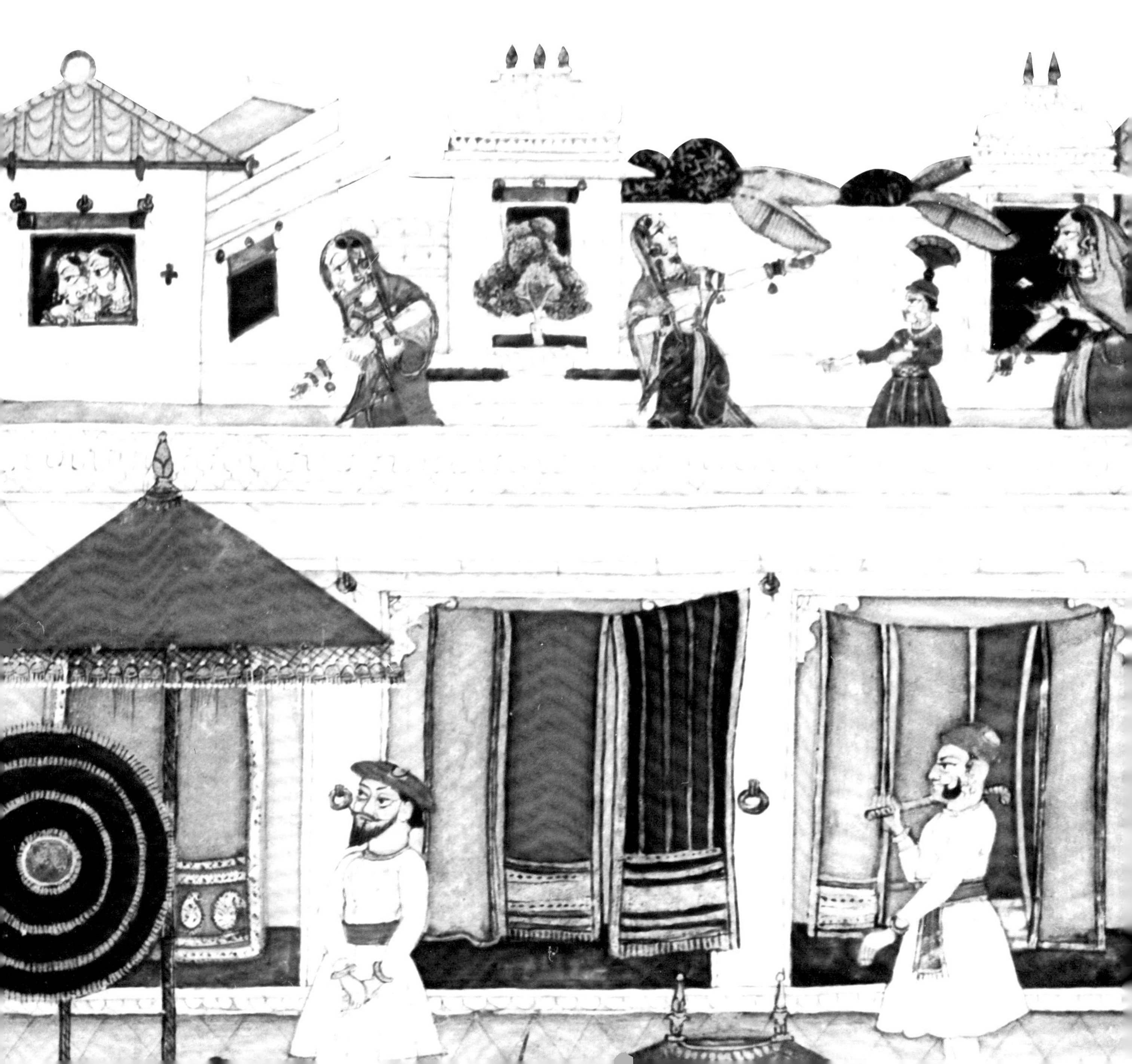

Introduction

The textile arts of South Asia have a rich and ancient heritage. In this catalog certain aspects of this heritage are examined, with particular emphasis on recently produced objects. These represent the skills of only a few areas; no attempt has been made here to catalogue the development of many centuries of production, for no such attempt could approach comprehension. The achievements of modern South Asian craftsmen reflect the importance textiles have long held in their culture. The emphasis in this catalogue is on textiles made in India for use by Indian people. The textiles are notable for the wide range of designs that appear on them and of skills used to create them, by textile artisans working in many different areas. In many cases both designs and skills are rooted in the traditional past, however, the transfer of skills from one area to another is a constant in South Asian history. Craftsmen have migrated for economic, political or religious reason, bringing their products, talents and materials on such journeys. Certain designs may be thought of as typically Indian, but it is probably more enlightening to examine typical themes and ideas presented in the textiles than to confine our examination to the designs themselves. For although the fabrics and costumes do have decorative and functional qualities, the value of many textiles goes far deeper. The use of certain motives, techniques or materials may render a fabric special in ways that are difficult to translate, even objects with basically secular associations. An Indian brocade weaver has described the discernment of these special qualities as

> the art of *pehcan* . . . our direct encounter with the fabric, its count, weight, feel. There is the telling detail. There is restraint and understatement. There is the abandonment in modulations of colour, lustre, sheen. . . . Pehcan indicates understanding of when and how the fabric surpasses its kind; where exactly it falls short of itself and why. It signifies a sense of proportion and of purpose. It implies the ability to visualize the fabric lavished, draped, accented; at its most subtle—to foresee the grace or lack of grace with which it will yield itself like a woman to the softening and maturing of the aging process. (Devi *et al.* 1982: 12).

Other objects are created with intrinsic and specific religious significance. The temple cloths discussed in Chapter 1 are examples of this latter type. In much the manner of wall paintings, temple carvings or manuscript illustrations, these cloths have a narrative function, telling the story of events or sacred texts. Both the *kalamkari* of Andhra Pradesh and the *matano chandarvo* of Gujarat originally had explicit uses for particular ceremonies; the chandarvo carry on this tradition, as well as being commercial commodities in recent times, while the kalamkari seem to have lost religious significance in terms of usage but not of iconography. The present needs of Indian craftsmen to market their works are as great as ever in the past.

Indian textiles have rarely been confined to the Subcontinent. Almost as early as there are written records, we can read of Indian textiles being used and worn in other parts of the world. After Alexander the Great's campaign to India, fine muslins brought back to Greece were much admired. Our earliest fragments of Indian printed cotton were found not in India, but in Egypt, remnants of trade west by the fifteenth century. This trend continued through the great age of trade and empire, when British, Dutch and Portuguese merchants vied for positions in important trade centers in Asia. Textiles were one of the main commodities exported all over the world. Indian craftsmen responded to this demand with amazing flexibility, creating textiles well suited to each particular market, whose desire for Indian textiles was based on local notions of the exotic.

What were these textiles that so excited first the admiration and later the imitation of so many parts of the world? The products of South Asian weavers, dyers, and embroiderers were astonishing in their diversity and quality. Magnificently colored painted cottons were hung on European walls like the finest tapestries, or cut up and made into dresses. Precisely patterned ikat saris made their way to Indonesia, where their designs were interpreted and incorporated into the Balinese weaving repertory. Floral prints were received in Japanese homes as fitting objects to use in the tea ceremony.

The Kashmir shawl, discussed in Chapter 2, is a splendid example of the adaptation of a South Asian garment to a necessary item of European fashion and commerce. Fine shawls, both warm and lightweight, with delicate floral clusters were coveted by the empress of France. Made of lustrous goat fleece, these might be woven, embroidered, or later a convoluted combination of both.

But for every textile that left India for foreign markets, many more remained at home, to be worn and used by South Asia's many peoples in their daily lives, for ceremonial occasions, or offerings to the deities. Even today, in many areas, domestic or cottage industry production of textiles for local needs is a reality. More often the case is that textiles produced in one area are marketed in the surrounding region, or on a national level. Enterprising weavers have endeavored to create less costly versions of popular and expensive cloths. The relationship between patola and other types of ikat saris, discussed in Chapter 3, is an excellent case in point of this phenomenon.

The sari is as close to national dress as any one garment can be in a nation made up of so many diverse cultural groups as is India. Only in Chapter 3 is the sari discussed to any length, for although the sari is worn by millions of South Asian women today, one objective of this discussion is to point out that the diversity present in South Asian culture and language is without a doubt manifested in its costume and textiles. Forms of dress unique to India and to certain regions of India persist. Today, increasing urbanization is drawing many villagers and rural people into the large cities, where their ethnic identity is often subsumed under a disguise of western garb. But in some areas, traditional clothing is still worn, traditional sacred hangings are still made, in an effort to continue the ancient heritage of textile arts of which many Indians are rightly proud. This continuity has sometimes resulted because geographical isolation allowed the local peoples to continue their traditions almost unhindered. The Kutch area of Gujarat, a peninsula rendered virtually an island by floods for much of the year, is an example, discussed in Chapter 4. Women there do not wear the sari, but rather blouses and skirts or dresses. The hill tribes of the North East frontier, discussed in Chapter 5, are another large group whose fiercely independent stance and close relations with Southeast Asia and China have greatly influenced the development of their costume and weaving traditions. It is the only area of India where the backstrap loom is commonly used, and the wrapped garments created on it are likewise unique.

However, for a large part of India, the contemporary trend toward increased production of quality handmade textiles and garments is the result of concerted efforts by the government of India to revive skills that had all but vanished under British rule. The British colonial domination of the Indian subcontinent and the developments of the Industrial Revolution combined to produce a disastrous effect on the livelihood of textile artisans, most of whom have historically been "professionals" by reason of caste. When the demand for the type of textile they produced declined, and then was all but eliminated, they suffered because they could not adopt alternative employment. "The bones of cotton weavers are bleaching the plains of India," British Governor-General Lord Bentinck stated dramatically in the late nineteenth century. This assessment is perhaps too pat to convey the complexity of the situation, yet there can be no doubt that thousands of weavers did starve because of lack of work. Although during the final years of British colonial rule the amount of handloomed fabric produced annually in fact increased, it did so at a much slower rate than the amount of millcloth imported from Britain or produced in India in British owned factories. The quantity produced was strictly controlled by law, and handloomed fabric was subject to excessive tariffs from which British millcloth was exempt, so weavers could not sell their products competitively. Ownership of textile mills was also forbidden to Indians.

The *swadeshi*, or independence, movement that began during the early twentieth century, culminating in independence in 1947 followed by the partition of Pakistan and India, had an equally dramatic and, for a time, equally devastating impact on South Asian textile production. With self-sufficiency a primary stated goal of Mohandas K. Gandhi and his followers, autonomous Indian production of its internal textiles needs was seen as a primary method by which to achieve this goal, and thereby break the British economic stranglehold on India. Stated in oversimplified terms, the argument ran that once it was no longer commercially profitable for the British to remain in India, they would leave. Rather than purchase British millcloth, whether made in England or India, all Indians, regardless of caste or occupation, were urged to take up spinning and weaving of plain cotton cloth, called *khadi*. This was a major tenet of the swadeshi movement, and the *charka* or spinning wheel was Gandhi's symbol, with which he was frequently photographed. In this way, with only a few hours of work per week, each Indian would in theory produce enough fabric to clothe himself in a simple manner, resisting all temptation toward fashionable dress, and eliminating all necessity to purchase cloth.

As a symbolic movement, the production of *khadi*, in which Gandhi always dressed, was no doubt successful. However, in practical terms, the ultimate effect on reviving the Indian handloom industry is difficult to assess. Today, textile production is the second largest source of employment in India, after agriculture. Many people thus employed, however, are laborers in textile mills, while others may work in their own homes, performing one of dozens of mundane tasks required to produce a single garment. Few if any of these workers can be considered craftsmen, and only a handful, artists. Even an artisan capable of creating a handmade textile masterwork may be deterred

1.1 Wall hanging in temple cloth style
(kalamkari)
Srikalahasti, Andhra Pradesh, 1966
66 x 49 in.

Plain weave; mordant and dye painted,
dyed
Cotton; offwhite, black, tan, brown,
blue, olive green
1965.9.98/PDI 1426

from doing so by economic reality. The All-India Handloom Board was set up by the government of India to promote the production and sale of handloomed fabrics. It is a counterpart to the larger All-India Handicrafts Board which is concerned with all other crafts. In 1961 the Census of India endeavored not just to obtain demographic information on all the people of India, no small feat within itself, but to do a complete survey of the processes and techniques of all occupations and crafts. Its findings run to the hundreds of volumes, several of which have been extremely useful to this study. Ruth Reeves was involved in this research and authored several volumes of this census. In recent years, a renewed emphasis on quality rather than quantity of material for export is a stated goal of the All-India Handloom Board. Its representatives have traveled to the workshops of many fine artisans, presenting ancient textiles preserved in museums, and challenging them to duplicate the quality contained therein, while using their own creativity to modernize the designs and themes. For this attention to quality, there is no substitute.

1.1

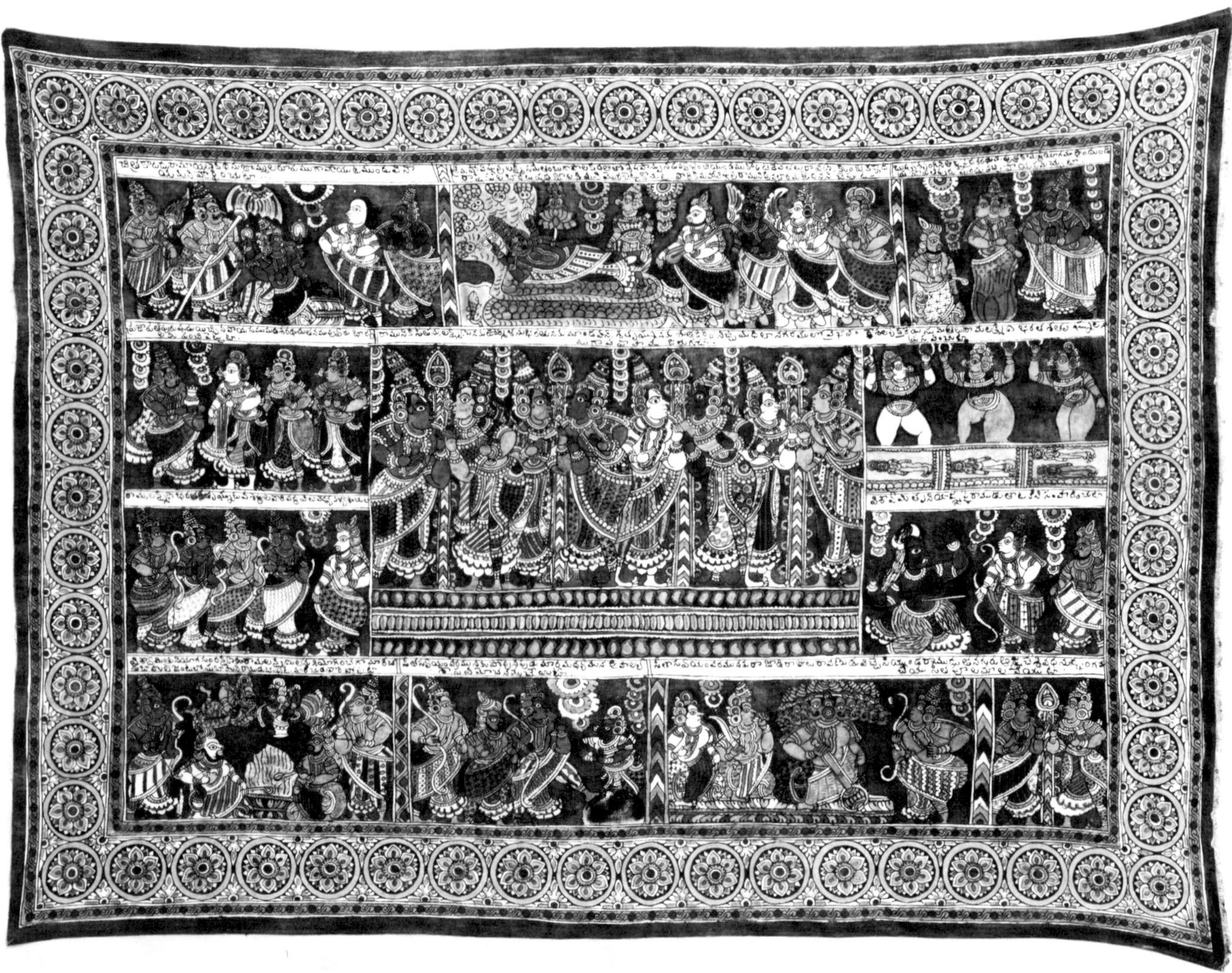

4

Temple Cloths of Srikalahasti and Ahmedabad

In view of the importance of religion in the daily life of many South Asian peoples, well-developed traditions of representative art, and the exemplary skills of cotton dyers known through history, it comes as no surprise that religious images provide the subject matter for several types of cotton cloths made originally for devotional purposes. Two major types, the *kalamkari* and the *matano chandarvo* are discussed in this chapter. A third type, the picchwai, is discussed in the painting section (see Pl. 2.33).

Kalamkari

Kalamkari are dye-painted cloths made in the town of Srikalahasti (sometimes called simply Kalahasti) in Andhra Pradesh. The name derives from the *kalam*, a specially made pen-like tool used to draw the outlines on the cloth, and *kari*, meaning work. Although a number of other painted or even printed cloths, such as those from the nearby town of Machilipatnam, are frequently referred to as kalamkari, the term is used here only for the hangings made in Skrikalahasti.

In recent years the production of kalamkari has been actively promoted by the government of India, in an attempt to make the cloths viable commercial items. Originally, however, the cloths were made by very few artisans, who produced them on commission for use within the temple of Skrikalahasti or to decorate carts during festivals.

It is generally assumed that South Indian temple hangings have their origins in mural paintings on temple walls and ceilings. Irwin and Hall (1971: 66) cite paintings at the Vijayanagar temple of Pampapati at Hampi as sources for comparison of both formula and detail, stating: "Costume, attributes and gesture are closely bound to a formula of express still living in South Indian temple dancing and drama—a formula which makes an immediate impact of communication for all Hindus." However, despite this connection with the Hampi paintings, which date before 1565, no cloths prior to the seventeenth century survive in this format of series of small panels, and there are no written records before the late nineteenth century. In 1889 Havell described "painted cloths used in Hindu sacred ceremonies . . . produced at Kalahasti" (quoted, *ibid.*: 67).

Kalamkari cloths often have a strong narrative character. Stories from Hindu mythology that are well known to the viewer are usually depicted, one favorite subject being the events of the *Ramayana* epic. The active quality of dance and drama that Irwin and Hall mention continues to be expressed in kalamkari, although with varying degrees of success depending on the artist's skill. Stylistic and iconographic detail make the individual characters readily recognizable. Two kalamkari with the same subject matter, but executed in different styles, are shown in Plates 1.1 and 1.2/Color Plate 1.1. They depict the events of the Ramayana from the conception of Rama through the hero's marriage to Sita. The following interpretation of the events shown in Plates 1.1 and 1.2 is based on information provided by Ramesh Jain (1968) and Irwin and Hall's description of a similar cloth in the Calico Museum of Textiles (1971: 78-79, no. 65, pl. 53).

In the large central panel, a multiple marriage is depicted. Rama is marrying Sita, and his three brothers Lakshmana, Bharat, and Shatrughan are marrying their lovers Urmila, Mandari and Shrut Kirti. The ten smaller panels depict the events leading up to this marriage, beginning in the upper left corner and moving in rows from left to right. The first panel shows the cloth's artist invoking the blessing of Ganesh for the success of his work, as is traditional. Ganesh is recognizable by his elephant head. In the second panel, Vishnu is pictured reclining on the multi-headed serpent Adishesha. He assures Indra and several other gods that he will aid them in eliminating the *rakshasas* (demons) who cause harm to gods and men. Ravana is the chief demon. To accomplish this, Vishnu agrees to be incarnated as the son of King Dasaratha, namely Rama. The third panel shows Dasaratha receiving the Santan Phal, a fruit, from a sage. In the fourth panel (second row, far left) Dasaratha shares his fruit with his three queens, Kausalya, Kaikeyi and Sumitra. The queens are next seen rejoicing, having given birth to four sons: Rama is the son of Kausalya, the Queen Eminent; Bharata of Kaikeyi; and the twins Lakshmana and Satrughna of Sumitra. The sixth panel then shows the princes learning the skill of archery from a great sage. In panel seven, Rama is shown killing the rakshasa Thataki, as he has been advised to do by this sage. In the bottom row on the left, the eighth panel shows the rakshasas Maricha and Subashu intent on destroying Koshik Yajna and Rama. Lakshmana kills Subashu, and Maricha runs away. The ninth panel details further exploits of Rama, who redeems Ahalya from the curse put on her by her husband Gautama for infidelity. In the tenth and final small panel, Rama has broken the Shiv Dhanush, the bow of Shiva, in the presence of the many-headed Ravana, a test of his power and integrity. He then arrives in Mithila Nagar and marries Sita. In the context of all these preceding events we can understand the rejoicing that takes place in the large

1.2 Wall hanging in temple cloth style *(kalamkari)*
Detail of central panel
Srikalahasti, Andhra Pradesh, 1966
67 x 47½ in.

Color illustration

Plain weave; mordant and dye painted, dyed
Cotton; offwhite, black, tan, brown, blue, green

1976.9.97/PDI 1425

central panel. The events are also written out above the panels in Telegu, the language spoken in Andhra Pradesh.

Not all kalamkari portray myths. The kalamkari shown in Plate 1.3 is a much simpler piece thematically. It lacks the narrative quality of the other two. The central character pictured under the temple dome is Krishna. He is embracing his consort Rukmani, who stands to his right, and his beloved Radha, to his left (R. Jain 1968). On either side of the temple dome we see angels blowing horns, and beneath the central figures are temple dancers and musicians. The layout of the cloth is somewhat reminiscent of the picchwais used in north India. This cloth may have served a similar function, hung behind the in-house altar.

1.3 Wall hanging *(kalamkari)*
Srikalahasti, Andhra Pradesh, 1966
68 x 50 in.

Plain weave; mordant and dye painted, dyed
Cotton; offwhite, black, tan, blue, green

1976.9.99/PDI 1413

1.3

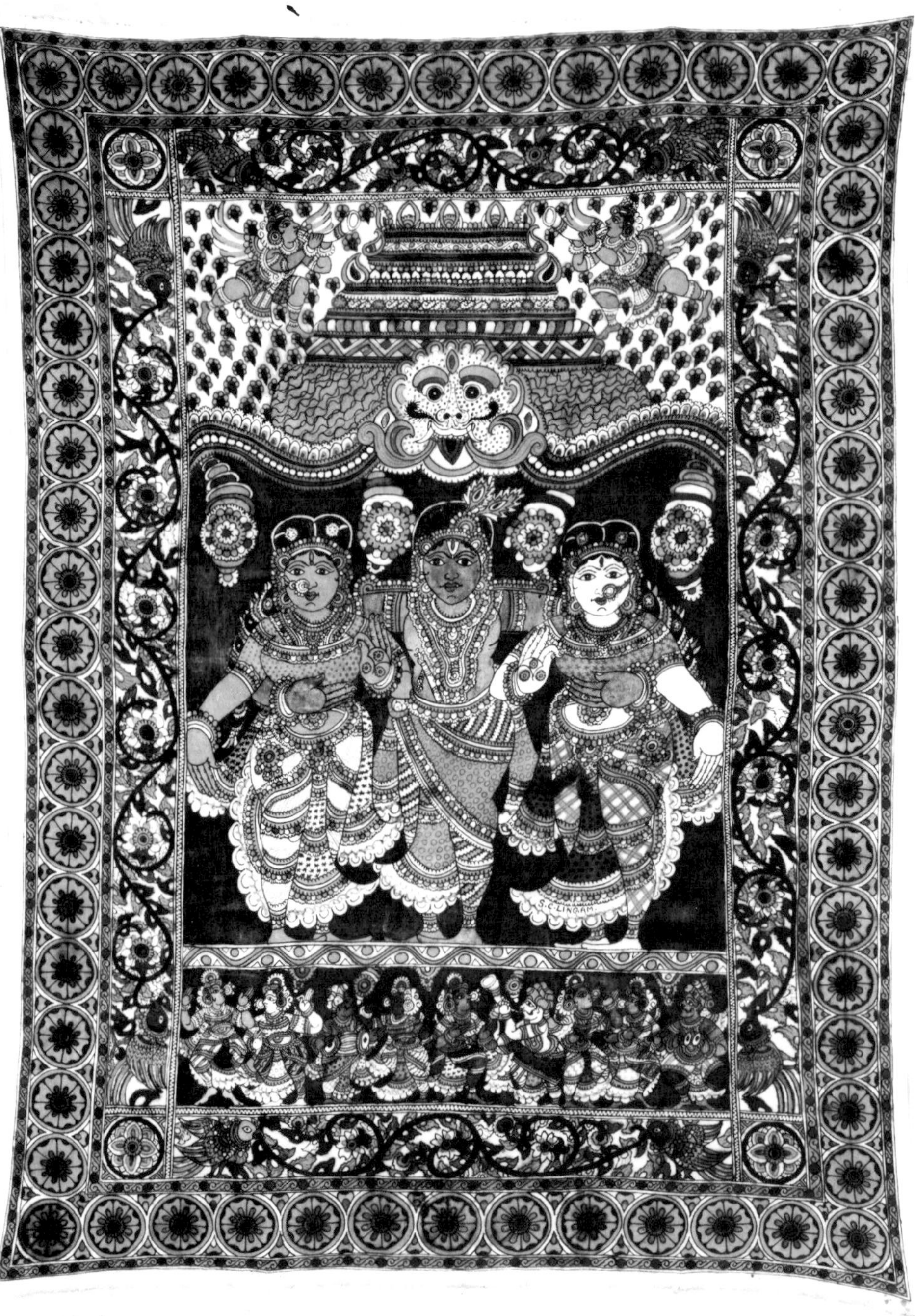

Nor are all kalamkari made to be used on walls. The layout of the cloth shown in Plate 1.4 indicates that it was intended for use as a canopy. The shape is nearly square, with the outermost figures organized around a central medallion, rather than in linear registers. The major figure here is Hanuman, the monkey-headed god. Each of the four women in the corners holds a baby monkey in her lap. Around the lotus-shaped medallion is Hanuman's army, the Baner Sena; in its center, more monkey gods stand at the edge of a lake or stream with fish. This piece also differs from the other three discussed here in that it has a large amount of white space, filled only with small leaves, and its outer border is a simple multicolor chevron design, rather than ornate flowers that appear on the others. This cloth is dated to 1957, and may represent commercially oriented innovations from the early years of the Pilot Training Center in Srikalahasti where it was made.

The predominant colors used in kalamkari are blue, dark red, tan, yellow, green, and black and white (see Col. Pl. 1.1). They are the result of the various natural dyes applied in a complex sequence. The techniques of painting and dyeing kalamkari have been the subject of several publications in recent years (Irwin and Hall 1971: 66-86, 173-74; All India Handicrafts Board n.d.); the findings of these studies are summarized here. The kalam which gives the cloth its name is a type of pen used only in India, and specially designed for painting with dyes. It is made with a stick or piece of bamboo, one end of which is trimmed to a point. Around this wool or hair is wound to create a porous wad which acts as a reservoir for the dye. Slight pressure on this wad causes the dye to run down through the tip. The kalam is used for painting on both mordants and dyes, following a design drawn in charcoal (see Pl. 1.5).

The mordants and dyes are applied in a specific sequence to give the exact colors desired. Very little immersion dyeing is actually done, primarily for red. Most of the dyes are painted on, and the combination of the dye with the mordant already applied gives the color. In some cases, the mordant is re-applied after the dye to intensify the color. The sequence is discussed in detail in the All India Handicrafts Board Publication, *Indian Kalamkari*. The following dyes are traditionally used: indigo (*Indigofera tintoria*) for blue; madder (*rubia cordifolia*) with suruli and pobbaku (*Narigama alta*) and alum mordant, for red; tannin-yielding myrobolam with iron acetate for black; myrobolam mordanted with alum and overpainted with mango bark (*Mangifera Indica*) for yellow; and indigo blue overpainted on this yellow for green. Repeated washing, rinsing, soaking, and bleaching of the cloth at numerous points during the painting process is necessary for the proper shade and intensity of colors to be achieved.

1.4   Canopy or table cover *(kalamkari)*
Srikalahasti, Andhra Pradesh, 1957
51 x 49 in.

Plain weave; mordant and dye painted, dyed
Cotton; offwhite, black, tan, brown, gray, green

1976.9.58/PDI 1440

1.5   Young woman using kalam and mordant to outline figures of Ganesh, Chetty workshop, Srikalahasti

1.4

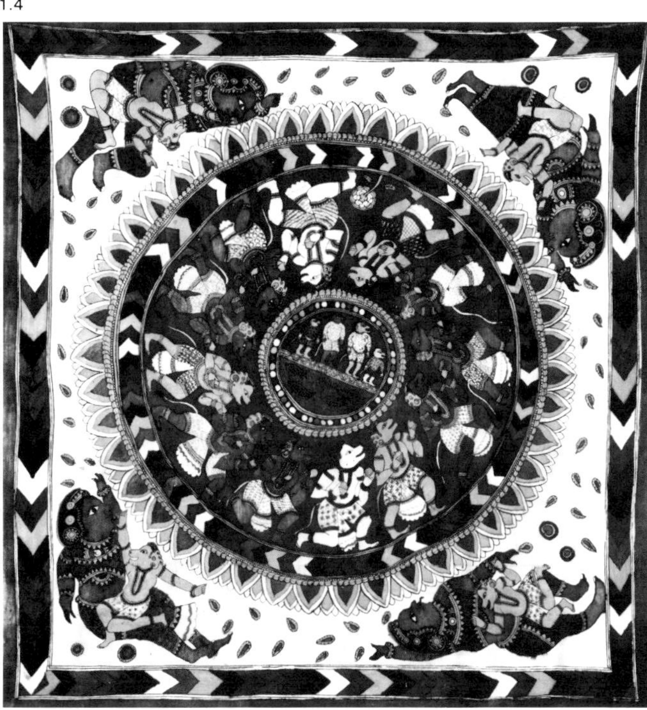

1.5

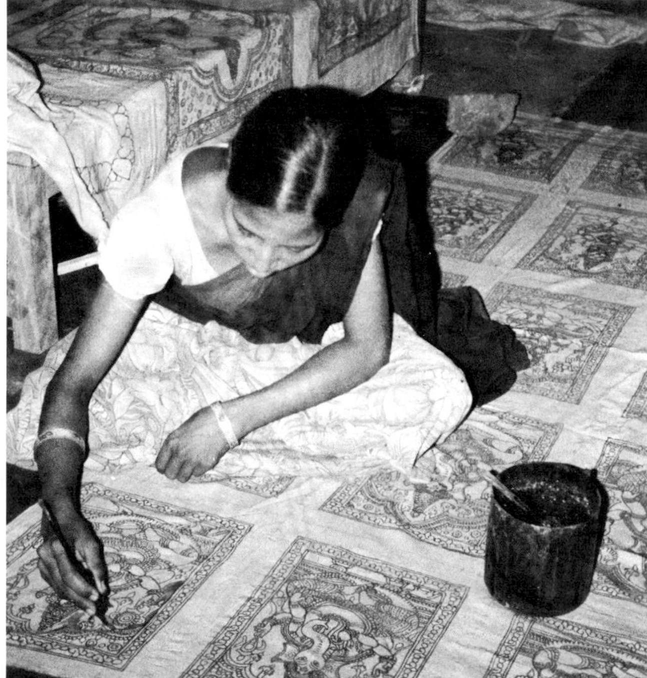

The creation of one cloth involves the labor of several people. The tasks are divided by the skill required to perform each one. Drawing the designs and painting in the small color areas and lines is more demanding than is washing or bleaching. These skills were formerly handed down within families of craftsmen. According to research done by anthropologist Sharon Wallace (personal communication, July 1983), by mid-twentieth century, however, only one craftsman was actually practicing. In the 1950s, the Indian government set up the Pilot Training Center at Srikalahasti in an effort to revive and revitalize these traditions. Young men were accepted who wished to come and study with this Master Craftsman and learn the skills of the kalamkari painters. The program has trained about sixty men, and, more recently, ten women (Pl. 1.5). The financial rewards of this profession are low, and not all the artists trained stay in the field. Also, the uses of kalamkari are increasingly secular. Today they are more of a fashionable home or hotel decorating item than a devotional object. Certain artists have responded to the challenge of making their work more viable commercially by creating kalamkari based on themes from other religions, such as a group of hangings recently produced based on Christian biblical or Buddhist themes (Devi *et al.* 1982: nos. 6-9) but laid out using the same format as traditional Hindu narratives.

Matano Chandarvo

In northwestern India, in the state of Gujarat, another sort of religious cloth is made, which is very different in appearance from kalamkari. The *matano chandarvo* is made in the city of Ahmedabad, and its iconography is limited to associations with the cult of the Mata, or the Mother Goddess. Like the kalamkari, the chandarvo have recently become a commercial item, but they are still used in devotional ceremonies as well. The cloths are created by a combination of block printing, mordant painting and dyeing.

The Mata is an aspect of the Devi, the most ancient goddess of India. The Devi has over one hundred manifestations throughout India, including Shiva's consort and Kali, and incorporates both creative and destructive qualities. The Mata aspect worshipped in Gujarat has seven different manifestations, identifiable by the mount on which she is seated, and by the objects she holds in her many hands. The Mata and the cloths on which she is painted are associated with rites and offerings

1.6 Temple cloth for Mother Goddess
(*matano chandarvo*)
a, overall view; b, center detail of Mata
Ahmedabad, Gujarat, before 1956
102 x 56 in.

Plain weave; mordant and dye block
printed and painted, dyed
Cotton; offwhite, black, dark red

1976.9.96/PDI 1350

1.6a

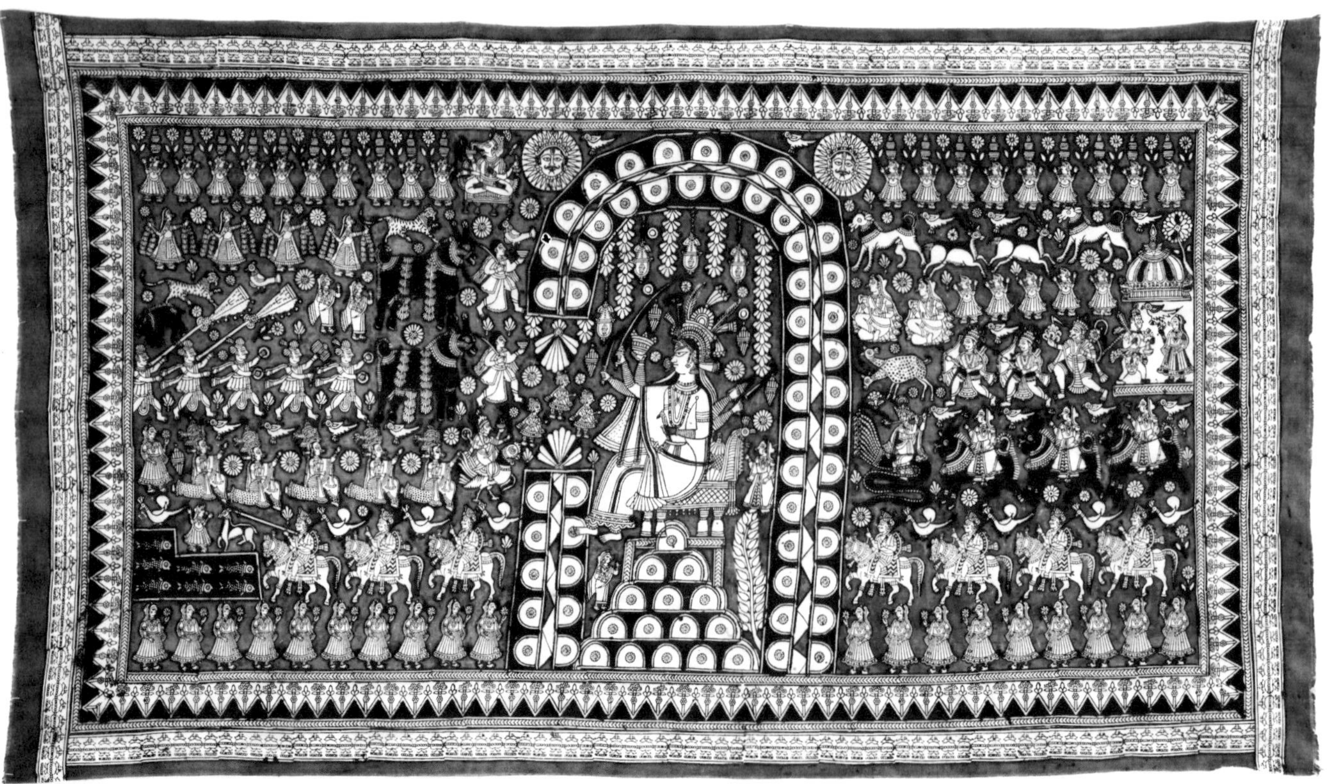

1.6b

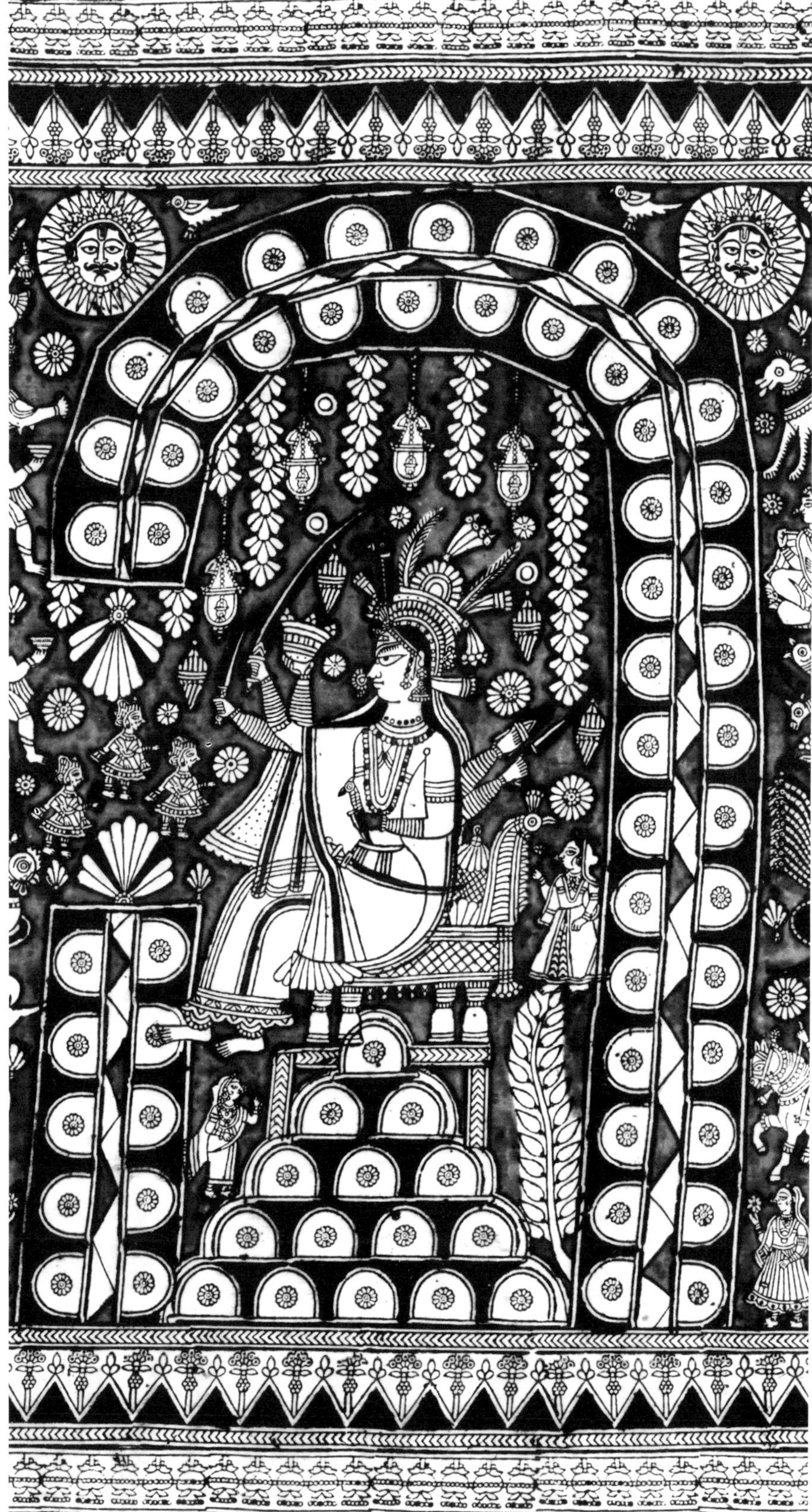

of supplication or thanks that include animal sacrifice. The story depicted on the cloths almost always centers around a large figure of the Mata, to whom a buffalo is being presented for sacrifice. The origins of the story are in the classical tale of the triumph of the Devi over a demon in buffalo form (Irwin and Hall 1971: 69), but the local version in Gujarat contains certain modifications.

The chandarvo are used as hangings and canopies to create a temple structure out of doors, around the shrine to the Mata, or as floor cloths for offerings, or as garments by the *bhuvo*, the shaman who addresses the Mata. The cult of the Mata is largely confined to the lower castes of Hindu society, and worshippers typically are street sweepers, leather workers, farm workers, or the Vaghris who make the cloths (Fischer, Jain and Shah in *Marg* 1978: 62). The Vaghris themselves were formerly nomadic peoples, or lived in rural villages near Ahmedabad. In their profession as chandarvo printers, they are now settled within the city itself. The close proximity of an artisan's home-workshop to the Sabarmati River is imperative, for the cloth is rinsed in the river and dried on its sandy banks (Erikson 1968).

Several related crafts and jobs are involved in the production of the chandarvo: washing the cloth to prepare for dyeing, carving the blocks used for printing mordants, the actual printing and painting of outlines, painting in larger mordanted areas, dyeing the cloth, and washing and drying the cloth to fix the dyes. The actual dyeing is done by Muslim dyers rather than by the Hindu Vaghris. In order to create the red background and black outline colors used in the chandarvo, two mordants and one alizarin dyebath are needed. The white of the figures is not reserved from dye; rather it is not mordanted so does not take the dye as well, and is further whitened by bleaching and washing in the river, the final step before the cloth is sold. The Vaghris work out of small home workshops and many members of the family become involved. The carving of the wooden blocks with which the outlines are printed on the cloth and the actual printing are considered the two most exacting jobs, and may be the province of master craftsmen. The block makers live in villages outside

1.7a

1.7 Temple cloth for Mother Goddess
(matano chandarvo)
a, left side; b, center; c, right side
Ahmedabad, Gujarat, before 1958
168 x 82 in.

Plain weave; mordant and dye block printed and painted, dyed
Cotton; offwhite, black, dark red

1976.9.281/PDI 1339

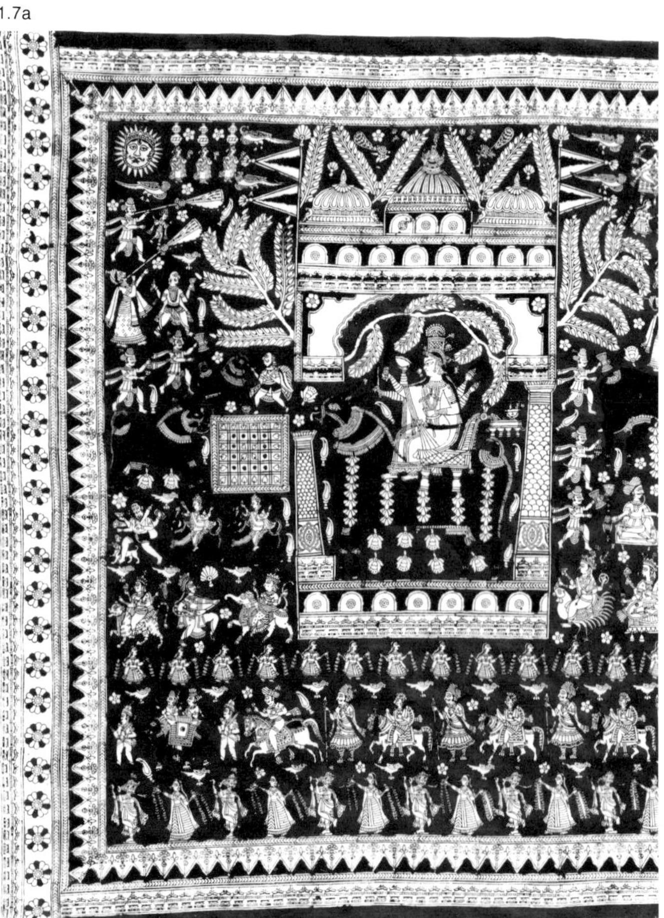

Ahmedabad. Despite the skill and time required to create the chandarvo, it is not a lucrative profession. One artisan engaged in this work maintained that success depends on the blessing of the Mata; working with his wife and children, he could make up to about ten hangings a month, while a very fine hanging might take an entire month. The speed depends not only overall quality but the amount of handpainting done, used especially for the large central figure of the Mata or the buffalo demon (Lakhmanbhai interviewed in Devi *et al.* 1982: 13-14).

Until recent years, not only the cloths themselves but also the blocks were considered sacred items. Once they had become worn through constant use, they were destroyed (Irwin and Hall 1971: 84). It has therefore been quite difficult for researchers to trace the history of this art. However, fragments of a stamped and mordant and dyed cloth, made in Gujarat in the fifteenth to seventeenth century, but excavated at Fostat, Egypt, appear to contain representations of the Khodiar aspect of the Mother Goddess, indicating that the same types of techniques were used for such themes as much as four centuries ago (Gittinger 1982: 46-47, figs. 31-32; Fischer, Jain and Shah 1982: 176-177, figs. 369-370). Large fragments or complete chandarvo extant date no earlier than the nineteenth century. The chandarvo discussed and illustrated here are mid- to late-twentieth century examples; two are wall hangings or enclosures and one is a canopy.

The hangings used to create the walls of the sacred enclosure around the shrine to the Goddess have a fairly standard format. In the center is one form of the Goddess, seated within a wooded bower or a pavilion. The remainder of the cloth is divided into numerous horizontal registers, filled with figures and scenes from Hindu mythology, attendants, dancers, soldiers, etc. A priest is always present, leading the buffalo to present as a sacrifice to the Goddess; sometimes the buffalo is presented with a demon form in place of its normal head. The Goddess always holds at least one type of weapon in one of her hands; she is depicted with as many as twenty arms. Sometimes other aspects of the Goddess also appear. The entire composition is framed with floral and geometric borders. The cloths are generally quite large, the smallest size being about four by six feet.

1.7b

1.7c

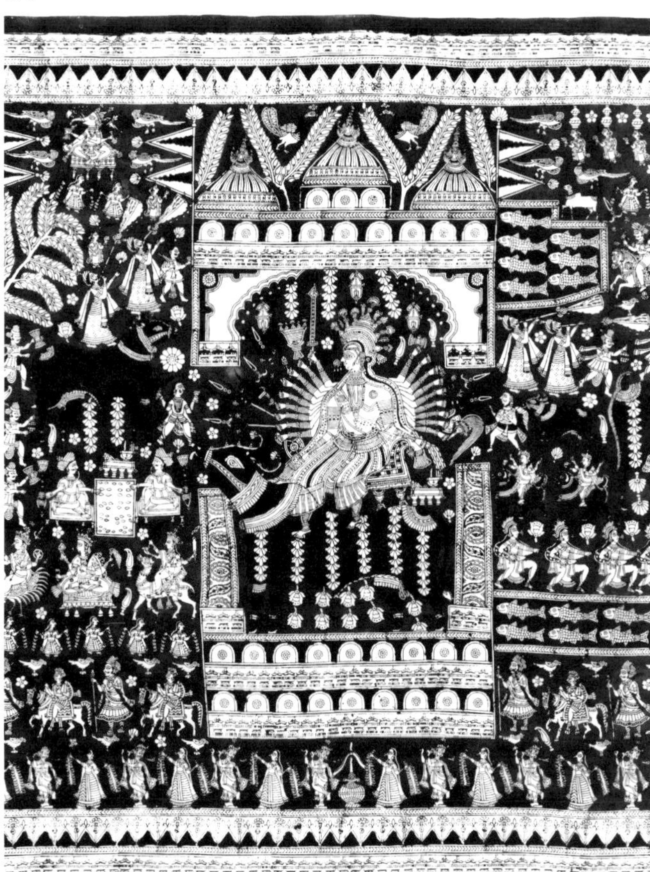

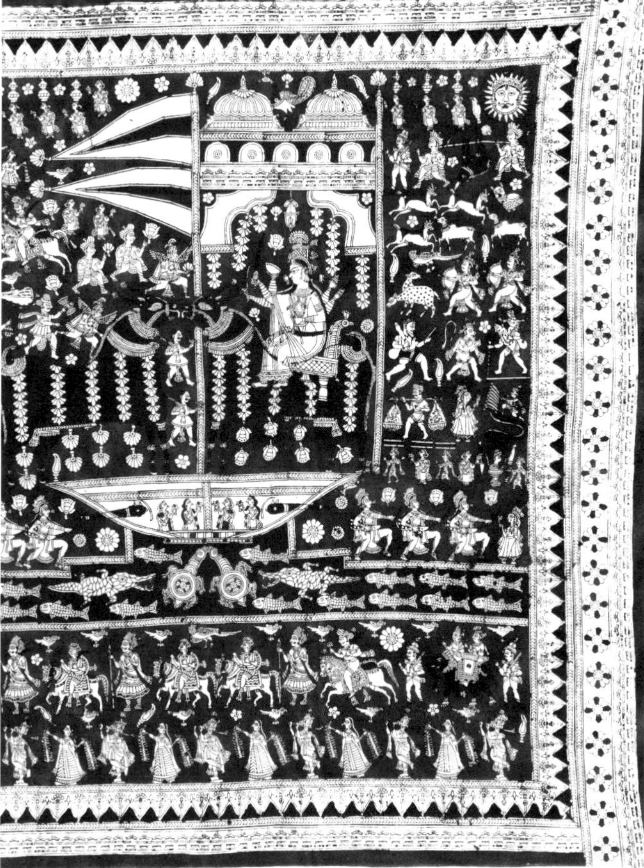

The Mata is depicted seated on her peacock throne atop a mountain in the chandarvo in Plate 6a-b. She appears in a woodland setting, with garlands hanging from an arch. In her six arms are held a bowl, a sword, a knife, and several long and short daggers; at her waist is another sword. Above the arch are the sun and moon, at the upper left is Ganesh. To the left of the arch, approaching the goddess, are two bhuva, or priests, each leading a buffalo, and holding a sword with which to kill it and a bowl in which to catch the blood. Beneath the bhuva is another aspect of the goddess, Bahuchara, riding the cockerel. To her left are kneeling devotees. Beneath them are soldiers on horseback hunting an antelope and a row of girls carrying flowers. Above them and to the left is a river or lake with seven fish. The whole left side of the cloth has an atmosphere of pageantry or a devotional procession, featuring trumpeters, musicians with cymbals, as well as an upper row of gopis or milkmaids. On the right side the row of gopis continues across the top, and horsemen and flowergirls along the bottom. To the goddess's right are figures from Hindu mythology. (The following attributions are based on the work of Fischer, Jain and Shah 1982, as interpreted and translated from the German by Joan Raducha.) Just outside the archway we see Krishna, recognizable by his flute, in triumph over Kaliya, the many-headed serpent. The row of figures above him represents an episode from the *Ramayana*: Rama and his brother Lakshmana have gone hunting, with bows and arrows, after the two-headed golden antelope, leaving his wife Sita at home. There she will be safe from demons if she remains within a sacred circular enclosure. However, the demon Ravana presents himself in the form of an ascetic to whom custom compels her to give food, thus allowing him access inside the circle. Ravana thereupon abducts her, and many of the subsequent events of the *Ramayana* deal with Rama's ultimately successful efforts to rescue her.

The other rectangular chandarvo illustrated here (Pl. 1.7a-c) deals with similar themes, but is larger and more complex. The goddess appears in three different major manifestations: On the left (Pl. 1.7a) she is the six-armed Meladi, mounted on a bull (Ziegenbock). In the center (Pl. 1.7b) she is Vihat, the twenty-armed goddess mounted on a water buffalo. On the right (Pl. 1.7c) she is Shikotar, also with six arms and mounted on a bull, but identified more closely with the ship in which she is afloat on a lake. Similar attendants, the priest and buffalo, dancers, and so forth, appear as in the smaller cloth discussed above; likewise, the story of the abduction of Sita is also told. However, there are additional scenes and figures.

The format of a square cloth with a large central medallion is also common for chandarvo (Pl. 1.8) and is reminiscent of the kalamkari discussed above and illustrated in Plate 1.4. This format indicates the cloth was used as a canopy, in conjunction with several of the rectangular cloths, to enclose the sacred space around the goddess's shrine. (See Erikson 1968: 52-53; Fischer, Jain and Shah 1982; pls. 257, 261ff for illustrations of completed enclosures.) The manifestation of the Mata presented here is probably the same as in the smaller rectangular cloth discussed above (Pl. 1.6a-b), for she too has six arms and is seated on a two-tiered platform which probably represents a mountain; however, in place of a sword, she holds a trident, and in place of one short knife, an axe. The trident is one of the most common symbols of the goddess in many of her manifestations. She is surrounded by an inner ring in which, a procession of two alternating male figures takes place, one on foot carrying a sword and staff, the other mounted and holding banners. A second ring surrounds this; at its top we find Ganesh, and under him are two devotees holding banners. Next to Ganesh are milkmaids. Around the ring we see four forms of the goddess: as Ambika, she rides a tiger; as Momai, a camel; as Bhahuchara, a cockerel; and as Shikotar, in a ship (Fischer, Jain and Shah 1982: 59-84). In addition, we see the now familiar bhuvo holding blood bowl, lake filled with fish, Ravana abducting Sita, Rama and Lakshmana hunting the golden antelope, Krishna conquering the Kaliya, and the usual garland bearers, attendants and trumpeters. Also featured on this cloth are Hanuman, the monkey god; Shiva in the form of Bhairava; Shravana, who carries his blind parents suspended from a yoke across his shoulders; and Sagalsha hiding her lover from her husband in a basket in the garden.

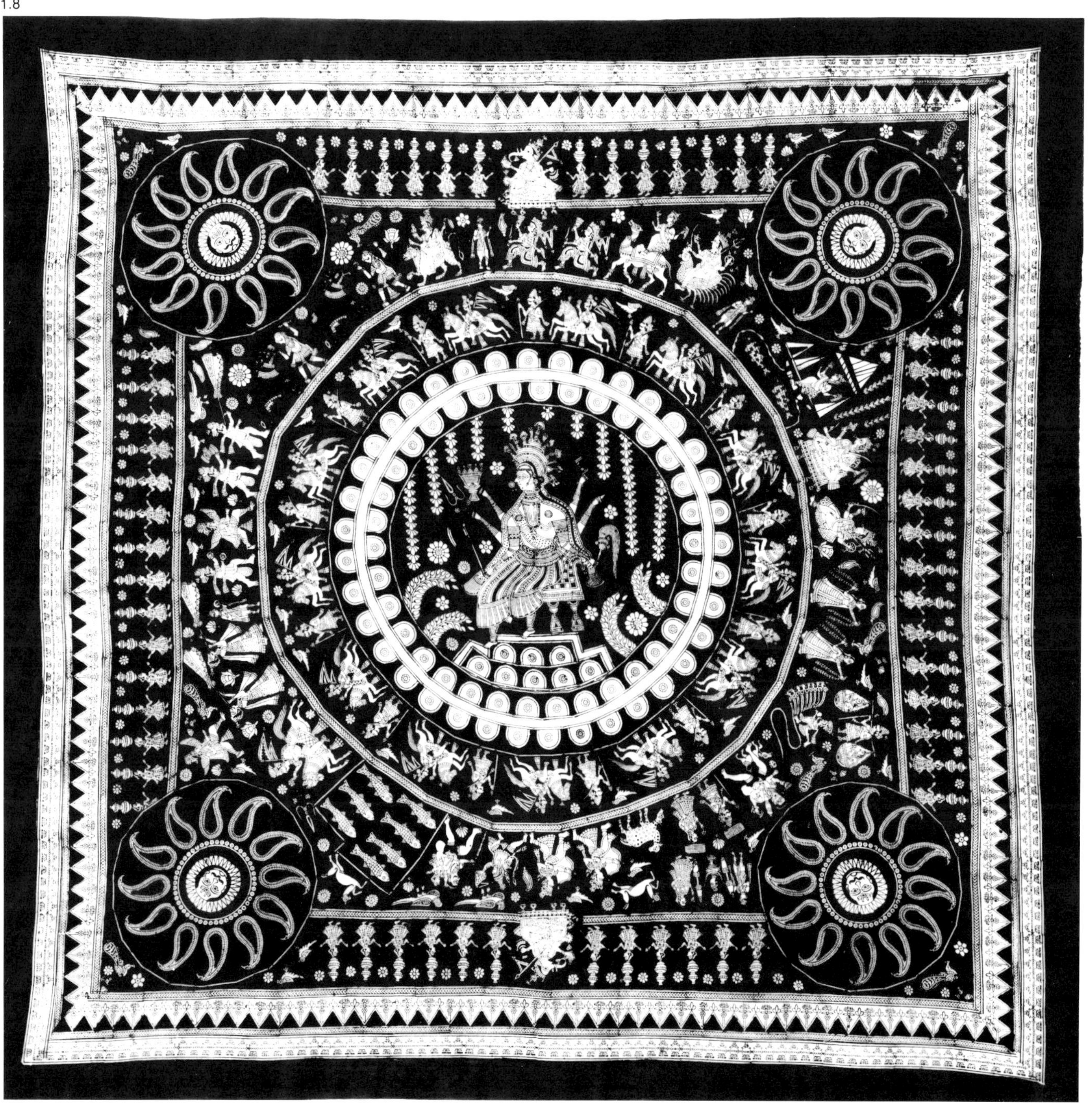

1.8 Canopy for temple for Mother
Goddess *(matano chandarvo)*
Ahmedabad, Gujarat, 1970s
106 x 106 in.

Plain weave, mordant and dye block
printed and painted, dyed
Cotton; offwhite, black, dark red

Collection of Cynthia Cunningham Cort

The Kashmir Shawl:
Indian Fashion Reaches Europe

For centuries fine wool shawls were woven in the far northwestern mountain area called Kashmir (now the state of Jammu and Kashmir). The shawl weaving industry for all of India was centered there. The shawl was a vital component of properly costumed men and women, reaching its apogee as a fashion in India during the Mughal empire. Apparent expert shawl weavers were brought to Kashmir from Turkestan by the ruler Zain-ul-'Abidin in the fifteenth century although wool shawls may have been woven there in earlier centuries (Irwin 1955: 2; Pauly in Yale 1975: 8). The design of the shawl, and the word *shal* from which it is derived, are of Persian origin. Originally the word applied more to the type of fabric used than to a specific garment. Shal meant any garment made of fine wool, especially goat wool. The best Kashmir shawls were made of *pashmina*, wool spun from the fleece of a goat that lives high in the mountains of Central Asia and Tibet, but not in Kashmir. This goat's fleece fabric or a sheep's wool fabric of similar texture has come to be known in English as cashmere because of its association with shawls produced there.

The saga of the shawl's evolution and eventual decline over centuries is a fascinating one, linking fashion, art, and economics in a complex network of international trade. Originally a man's garment, by the mid-nineteenth century, the shawl had been transformed into an enormous square draped over their gown by European women, its surface a riot of abstract floral patterning. Changes in design, form, and method of manufacture have been the subject of much scrutiny in recent years. John Irwin's unearthing of William Moorcroft's investigation of the weaving industry in the early nineteenth century has proved especially valuable (Irwin 1955, 1973).

The Mughal presence in India persisted for about four hundred years, and several emperors were famed as patrons of the arts. Akbar (r. 1556-1605) and Jahangir (r. 1605-1627) were especially competitive with the Persian courts for outstanding artistic displays. Indian arts subsequently became more divergent from those of Persia. The first European influences are attributable to herbals circulated among the courts, an idea noticed by Basil Gray as early as 1957 (cited by Pauly in Yale 1975: 27). This tendency toward increased naturalism solidified during the reign of Aurangzeb (r. 1658-1707). By the eighteenth century, Mughal decorative design had become a model of restrained, delicate ornament, verging on the static. Architecture, textile design, and metalwork commonly employ floral motifs, reflecting the Islamic love of gardens. Flowers typical of early eighteenth century patterning appear in an Ajmer painting in the Watson Collection (see Pl. 2.41): it shows Krishna leading Radha through a garden depicted as a number of individual, isolated plants arranged in tidy rows. Krishna's *patka* (sash) features a similar motif on its border.

Several other paintings in the Watson Collection express the use of this type of ornamental design in garments and other textiles. Indeed, Mughal society was a particularly cloth-conscious group, and correspondence of ornamentation between textiles and other arts is frequently apparent. The basic garment forms for men were a fitted coat with full skirt worn over long trousers, with a *patka* around the waist, a shawl draped over the shoulders, and a turban wound around the head in one of a variety of fashions. These garments are depicted in a late eighteenth century manuscript illustration from the *Alamgir-nama* (Pl. 2.80) depicting Aurangzeb and his courtiers. The regular placement of small floral forms on the courtiers' coats, for example, is quite clear. This painting also shows the Mughal penchant for using textiles in numerous contexts—canopy covering Aurangzeb's throne, carpet, covers on the throne's front, elephant and horse trappings, etc.

In a mid-eighteenth century Marwar painting, also in the Watson Collection (Pl. 2.45), we see similarly lavish use of textiles as canopies and awnings, as well as the elaborate use of intertwined floral design on what are apparent tiled or painted walls. The nobleman wears a turban, patka and shawl but rather than coat and pants he seems to be wearing two coats, the outer one shorter than the inner. It is interesting to note that while the border of his shawl features individual flowering plants in a single row, similar to the border of the patka worn by Krishna in Plate 2.41 discussed above, here the patka border is more complex, being deeper than that of the shawl and featuring more extensive floral ornamentation.

This delicate floral design is called *buta* (sometimes written *boteh*), literally, ''flower.'' In the early eighteenth century this slender form of flowering plant began to change to a denser form, with many flowers on one plant. The bright red shawl worn in a Kangra style painting of Raja Bir Singh (Pl. 2.86) is indicative of this trend, although the painting dates to the late eighteenth century. The buta design, often referred to as the ''cone'' or ''pine'' in the literature, cannot be a precise indicator of date, for ''because a certain form came into vogue at a certain period, it did not necessarily follow that earlier types were superseded. In fact, it often happened that the older well-tried motives and patterns outlived the new'' (Irwin 1955: 12). That is probably the situation here, for by the late eighteenth century,

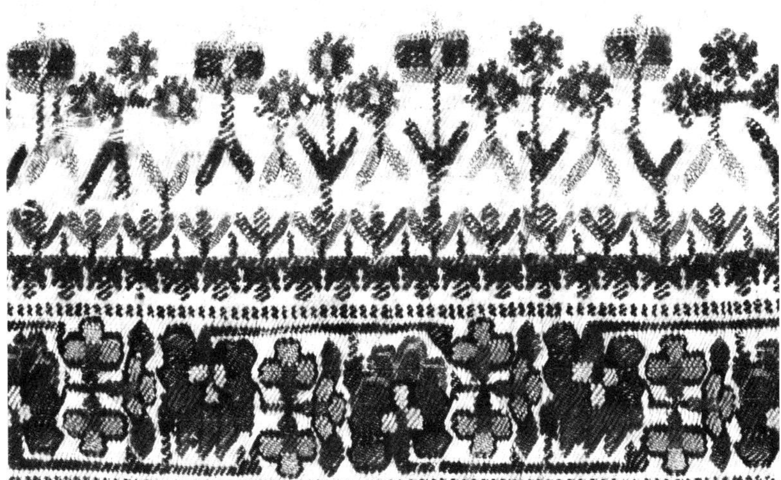

1.9

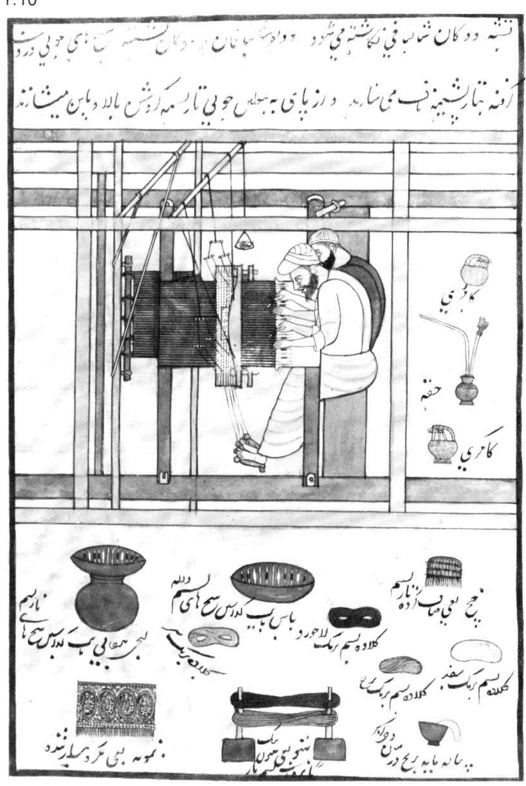

1.10

the Kashmiri buta form had been heavily influenced by a form also called the cone, but more closely linked to a leaf or tree design common to Persian art.

Textiles dating before 1700 are extremely rare, and the Allen Collection owns no complete shawls that can be dated reliably to the eighteenth century. A small fragment with very narrow borders (Pl. 1.9) is the oldest Kashmiri piece in the collection. It is complete from selvedge to selvedge; its four-foot width and the delicate small flowers and leaves on the vine correspond to the side borders of shawls dated to the mid eighteenth century by Irwin (1973: Pls. 5-9). It is woven in twill tapestry, a discontinuous-weft technique with wefts inserted using *tojli* or bobbins. The nineteenth century Kashmiri painting in Plate 1.10 shows the shawl loom in operation.

By the turn of the nineteenth century, the shawl was established as a fashionable garment in Europe. Numerous portraits by Ingres from the first decades of the century depict fashionable French women, their fine muslin empire style gowns the ideal background for the long, graceful shawl. Legend credits its introduction to Napoleon, who purchased Kashmiri shawls during his Egyptian campaign and brought them as gifts to his empress, Josephine. However, they were probably introduced several years earlier (Rossbach 1980: 17).

According to one of Josephine's ladies-in waiting, Mme. de Remusat, the empress "had from three to four hundred shawls. . .[which] she draped over her shoulders more gracefully than anyone else that I have ever seen." Her opinion is visually substantiated by Prud'hon's portrait, now in the Louvre. Whether possessing so many shawls was due to her own extravagance or her husband's capricious habits is difficult to say; Mme. de Remusat goes on: "Bonaparte who thought she was too much covered by these shawls, would pull them off and sometimes threw them into the fire" (cited in Waugh 1968: 214).

From about 1820 on, the fashion for shawls in Europe began to affect shawl design, at first somewhat subtly and later with increasing abandon. Two fine shawls in the State Historical Society of Wisconsin collection effectively illustrate this trend. One of the shawls, while still restrained in its designs and amount of color, nonetheless differs significantly from earlier shawl types (Pl. 1.11). Executed primarily in twill tapestry technique, it also includes embroidered cone motifs. Irwin dates similar shawls to about 1830 (1973: Pls. 32, 33); Pauly and Corrie date an almost identical piece to early nineteenth century and point up the parallel in design to "the shape of the Sasanian double-wing

1.9 Shawl fragment
Detail of side border
Kashmir, late eighteenth century
5½ x 51 in.

Twill tapestry
Wool or goat fleece; undyed, blue and red

WFI 2370

1.10 Kashmir shawl weavers at loom, nineteenth century painting

motif'' (Yale 1975: Pl. 11). This piece is an exceptional fine shawl, probably the only complete shawl discussed here that is made of *asli tus pashmina*, wild goat fleece. Rectangular in form, the soft undyed off-white of the field shimmers, outlined by delicately drawn borders of medium blue cones accented with red, green and tiny flecks of yellow. The large cones in the border face one direction, above these a row of smaller cones facing the opposite direction, which continues onto the side borders, creates a lyrical rhythmic quality which would be marvelous seen on a moving figure. Within each large cone are numerous plant forms, a star shape, and a flowering branch. The outline of the form is made up of tiny blossoms which come together to create a curved tip of four tendrils. The fineness of the wool and weaving, and the sensitive use of color and placement of motives make this shawl an example of a successful interrelation of design and weaving skills.

The other shawl from the State Historical Society of Wisconsin may date as early as 1820 (Pl. 1.12). It is similar in format to the earlier Mughal shawls, being rectangular, with end borders much deeper than the side borders; the field is undyed creamy white. However, the motives used are clearly divergent from previous tendencies in Kashmir shawl art. Rather than neatly defined cones of floral clusters or leaf forms, this shawl has pale green stylized cones with deeply bent tips, arranged in pairs. From within these long green cones, red cones emerge, their tips bent in the opposite direction and overlapping those of the green cones. Overlaying this already complex interaction of forms are vines, arabesques and meanders in pink, blue and yellow, all on a red and purple ground. Every form is outlined in another color, and each contains many smaller floral elements. This main border design is set off by bands of an arabesque and palmette design, and an inside border of shorter, bent overlapping cones continues around the sides. The outside border was woven separately and sewn on, perhaps at a later date. This careful arrangement of positive and negative spaces, to the point that ground and motive become almost indistinguishable, is clearly a new direction in Kashmir shawl design, and is almost certainly the result of foreign demands. Color renderings brought back to England by William Moorcroft in 1823 show that specific shawl patterns were created not only for the European market but for Russia and Persia as well (Irwin 1973: figs. 6-13; Karpinski 1963). The increased depth of the borders on all four sides, the degree of penetration of design into the center

1.11

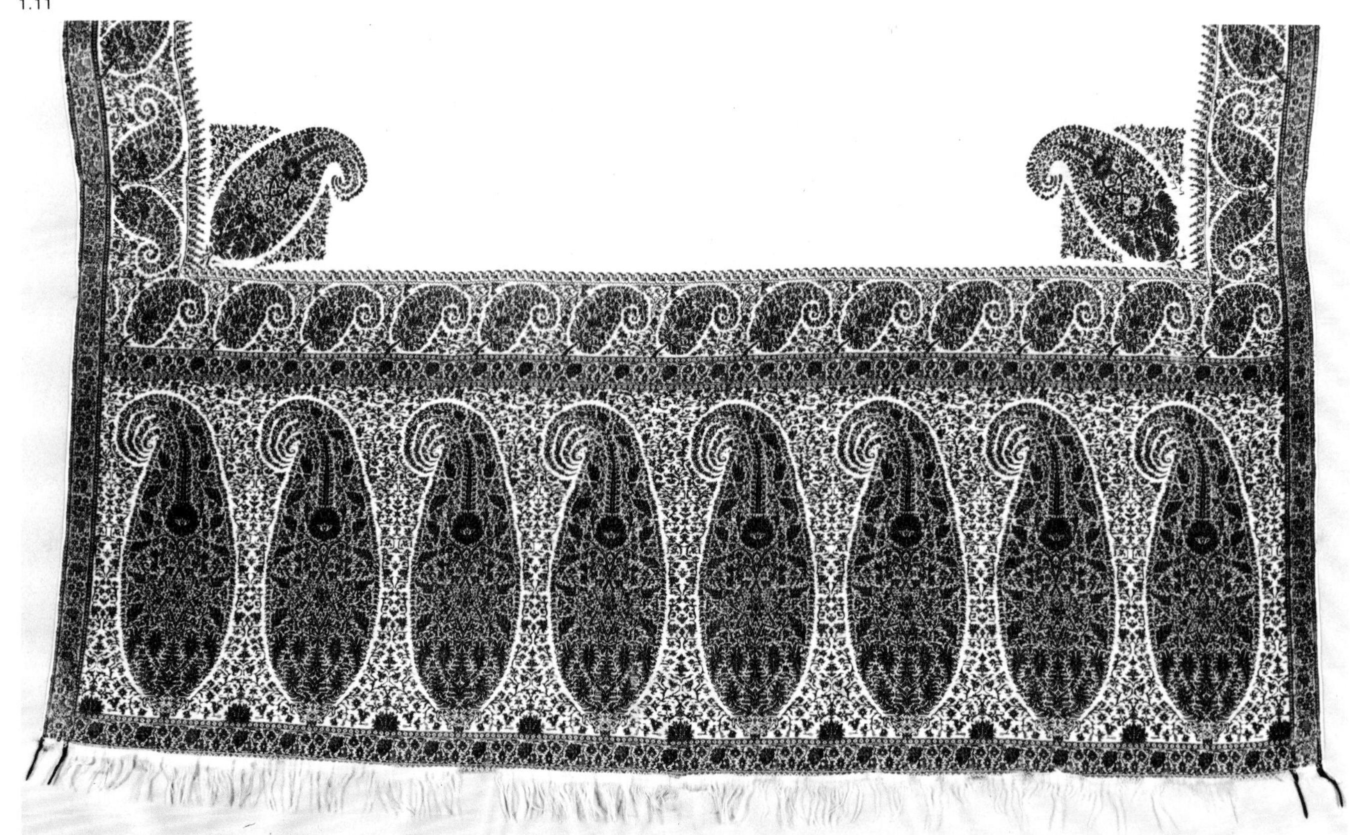

field, and the addition of tabs of solid color at the ends all point toward trends that continued to develop in shawls made for export throughout the century (Irwin 1973: pls. 24, 25; Yale 1975: pl. 16).

A twill tapestry shawl from the Watson Collection in the Elvehjem Museum of Art may have been woven for the Persian market in the mid nineteenth century or even woven in Persia (Pl. 1.13). Except for its rectangular shape, it bears little resemblance to the Mughal-inspired designs of the shawls in Plates 1.9, 1.11 and 1.12 above. The field is densely patterned and the end borders are apparent very shallow. (These borders, however, have been cut and originally may have been a great deal deeper.) The layout is a multicolor warp-striped field in which wide light aqua, pink and offwhite stripes alternate with narrower red ones. This field is overlaid with diagonal, interlinking tan vines to which are appended red and blue flowers; in each corner is a quarter circle. Stripes, quarter circles, and vines are all filled with different small floral and leaf motives. This shawl is a complex variation or combination of several, more standard shawl types made for foreign, non-European markets.

Pauly and Corrie illustrate a Kashmir shawl with quarter circles at the corners, dating it to the early nineteenth century (Yale 1975: Pl. 13). However, that shawl is square in shape and features a circle in the center of the field which the Watson shawl lacks. That format is known as *chand-dar*, 'moon' shawl (Irwin 1973: 15). Nor does the Yale shawl have a striped ground, but it does have a diagonal allover vine pattern; the interstices of the connecting vines are filled with curved cone motives, not blossoms, as on the Elvehjem shawl. Irwin illustrates a detail of a moon shawl in the Victoria and Albert Musuem, which has a striped ground but no vine pattern (1973: Pl. 15); the borders and infill of the circular sections are very similar to the Yale shawl. He further states, citing Moorcroft, that a densely patterned ground, ''in which the pattern 'almost completely covers and conceals the colour of the ground' '' (*ibid*.: 15) sometimes with a trellised field and central and corner medallions, was favored by Persian consumers. He illustrates such a fabric used to make up a man's coat (*ibid*.: Pl. 38).

A striped shawl illustrated by Pauly and Corrie furthers the idea of the Elvehjem shawl's Persian flavor. In this Yale shawl, which they identify as ''for the Persian market, or of Persian origin, late 18th

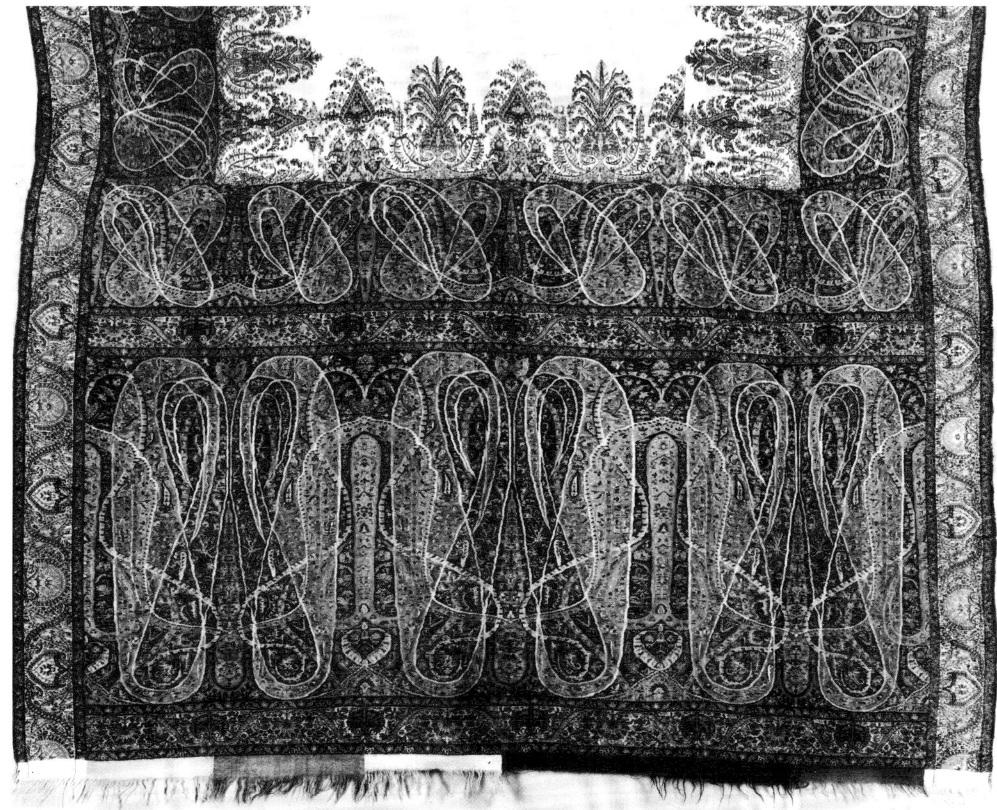

1.12

1.12 Shawl
Detail of border
Kashmir, 1820-1830
127 x 56 in.

Twill tapestry
Wool; undyed, red, green, with pink, blue, yellow and purple

State Historical Society of Wisconsin
49.217

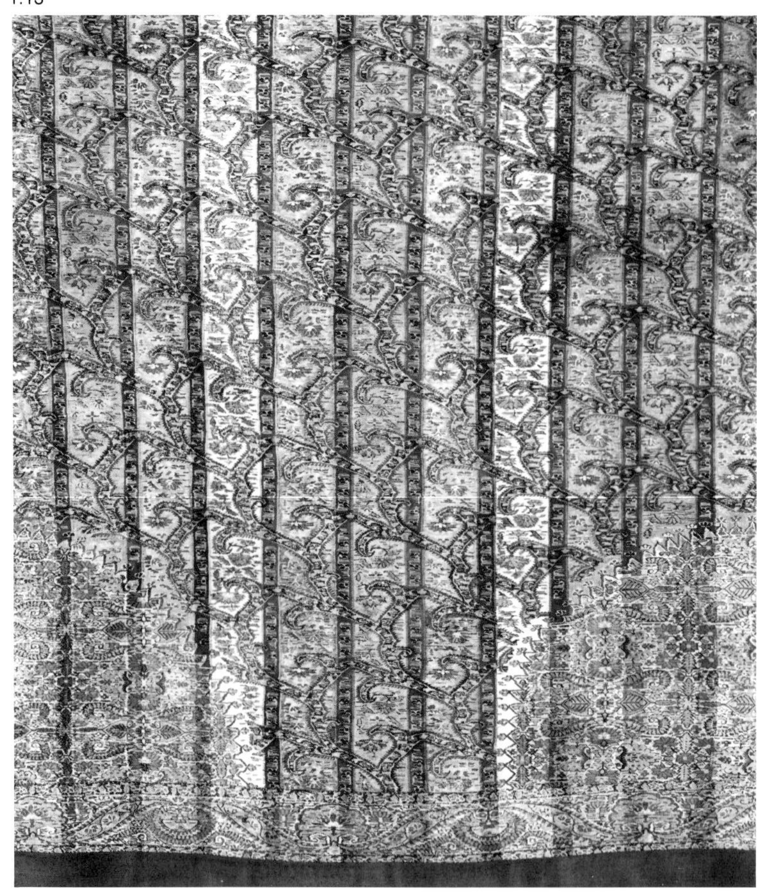

1.13 Shawl
Detail of one half
Kashmir, probably for Persian market,
mid-nineteenth century
86½ x 35½ in.

Twill tapestry
Wool; undyed, light blue-green, pink
and red stripes with multicolor patterning

Elvehjem Museum of Art

century'' (Yale 1975: Pl. 9), each stripe is filled with floral patterning that is quite similar to that in the quarter circles of the Watson shawl. The stripes themselves are of one broad width, however, and are not separated by narrower stripes as they are in the Watson piece.

Two pieces discussed by Rossbach in *The Art of Paisley*, both in the collection of the University of California, Berkeley, resemble the Elvehjem piece rather closely. He associates a striped layout with Turkish rather than Persian influence. One shawl, he calls ''Near Eastern. . .described as a Cashmere'' and dates it to the nineteenth century (Rossbach 1980: 88). It has the same striped format of alternating wide and narrow stripes as does the Elvehjem piece; in it, too, ''scroll-like motives are superimposed over the stripes, with secondary motives adjusting to both the stripes and the scrolls'' (*ibid.*). Since only a detail is illustrated, it is not known whether it features circles in the corners. However, Rossbach illustrates another shawl with multi-color striped layout, meandering vine, corner quarter circles and central circle, and an end border of the same serrated leaf and carnation design as the Elvehjem piece (*ibid.*: 90-91). It is identified only as a ''Cashmere-type shawl'' and not dated.

Whether the introduction of the square as a common shape is linked to the European market or to Islamic custom is difficult to establish with certainty. As fashionable European women's dress moved toward a fuller silhouette, it provided a suitable backdrop over which to display a large, square shape. Rather than the former four by ten feet size, after the 1830s six feet square increasingly became a standard. Pauly's attribution of the square format to seventeenth century Mughal canopies (see Pl. 2.80) cannot be discounted (Yale 1975: Pl. 17), but she offers it only as one theory, nor does she try to explain why this should not become a garment form until two centuries later. The square format has persisted into modern times for canopies (see Pl. 1.8) but the common shape of Indian shawls is still rectangular. We witness from this time forward many and more drastic changes in shawl design as well. The early square shawls made for Europe have a relatively shallow border on all four sides (Pls. 1.14/Col. Pl. 1.2, 1.15, and 1.18), about fifteen to twenty-four inches deep, leaving a large expanse of plain solid color area in the central field. The motives used on these shawls resemble those of the shawls of the 1820s only slightly. The cone form is present, but rather than repeated routinely across the border or interspersed with smaller motives, its presence is all but obscured by prominent arabesques and curving tendrils. The cone motif by the 1840s has become clearly of secondary importance.

There can be little doubt that the drastic change in design sensibilities of Kashmiri weavers was not of their own doing. Numerous travelers to Kashmir in the mid-nineteenth century report on the presence there of foreign agents, particularly French, who commissioned more marketable designs. As Irwin has pointed out (1973: 15, 16), rather than being "designed for eternity in the unchanging East" as an 1852 English magazine article would have it, almost all nineteenth century Kashmir shawls were designed in direct response to foreign tastes. In 1850, Simpson reported that "the French design patterns and send them out to Cashmere for execution" (*ibid*.).

It should be noted here that the Kashmiri shawl weavers had little say not only in the design of the garments, but even in their choice of vocation. They were weavers not just by trade or profession, but by caste. Throughout the nineteenth century, the shawl weaving industry was increasingly dominated by middlemen, both Indian and foreign; the weavers themselves made very little profit. In the 1830s the Jacquard loom was adopted in Paisley, Scotland for shawl production (Pauly in Yale 1975: 19). After the onslaught of mechanized shawl weaving in Britain and France, the Kashmir shawls had to be custom-made for the European market if they were to compete with the mass produced goods.

Kashmiri weavers invented a means to produce complex patterns more quickly. *Tilikar* or pieced shawls date from about 1830 on. Rather than weaving an entire shawl in one piece, building up the pattern by minute degrees as required in twill-tapestry, weavers wove smaller plain or patterned segments. These were then cut apart and pieced together in a sequence deemed aesthetically pleasing and economically viable by the design agent. After that step was completed, the shawl was turned over to an embroiderer (*rafugar*) who carefully outlined or disguised the joins with ornamental stitching, or even created entire pattern areas.

The shawl in Plate 1.14/Color Plate 1.2 is a good example of *tilikar* technique. It features a plain red field, surrounded by a delicate wavy inner border of solid color areas embroidered with tiny flowers and cones. Sewn to this is a second, six-inch wide border woven in twill tapestry where undulating vines intertwine with small curved cones and leaf shapes. The multicolored motives and white background alike are filled with tiny flecks of colors. Periodically, cone shapes cut from fabric of similar design but with different color background are inset. Finally, the outer border features the multiple niches common from this time on, with multicolored embroidery on various solid color grounds. This border is in turn split by an undulating solid black line.

1.15

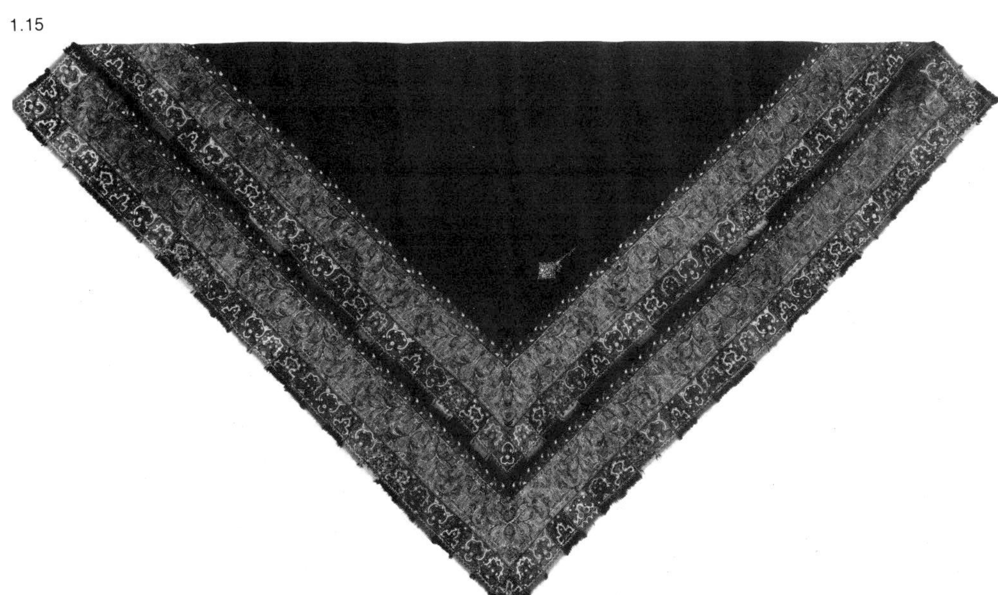

1.14 Shawl
Detail of corners
Kashmir, 1840-50
72 x 72 in.

Color illustration

Twill weave, twill tapestry cut and reassembled (*tilikar*); embroidered
Wool; red center, multicolor borders

WFI 1050

1.15 Shawl
Kashmir, 1840-50
68 x 67 in.

Twill weave, twill tapestry cut and reassembled (*tilikar*); embroidered
Wool; black center, multicolor borders

WFI 1045

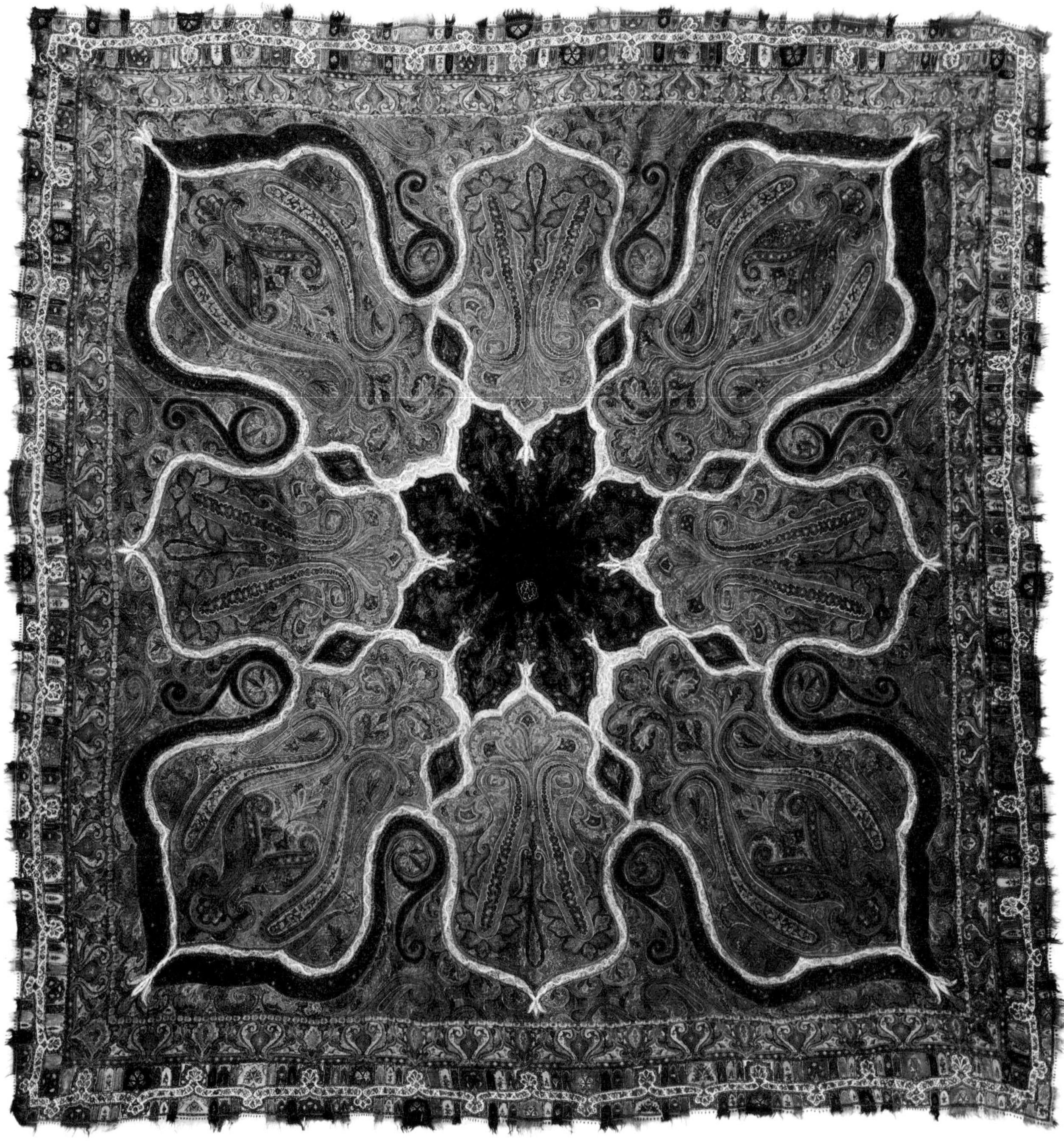

1.16 Shawl
Kashmir, 1850-70
77 x 74 in.

Twill tapestry cut and reassembled
(*tilikar*); embroidered
Wool; black center, multicolor

State Historical Society of Wisconsin
49.215

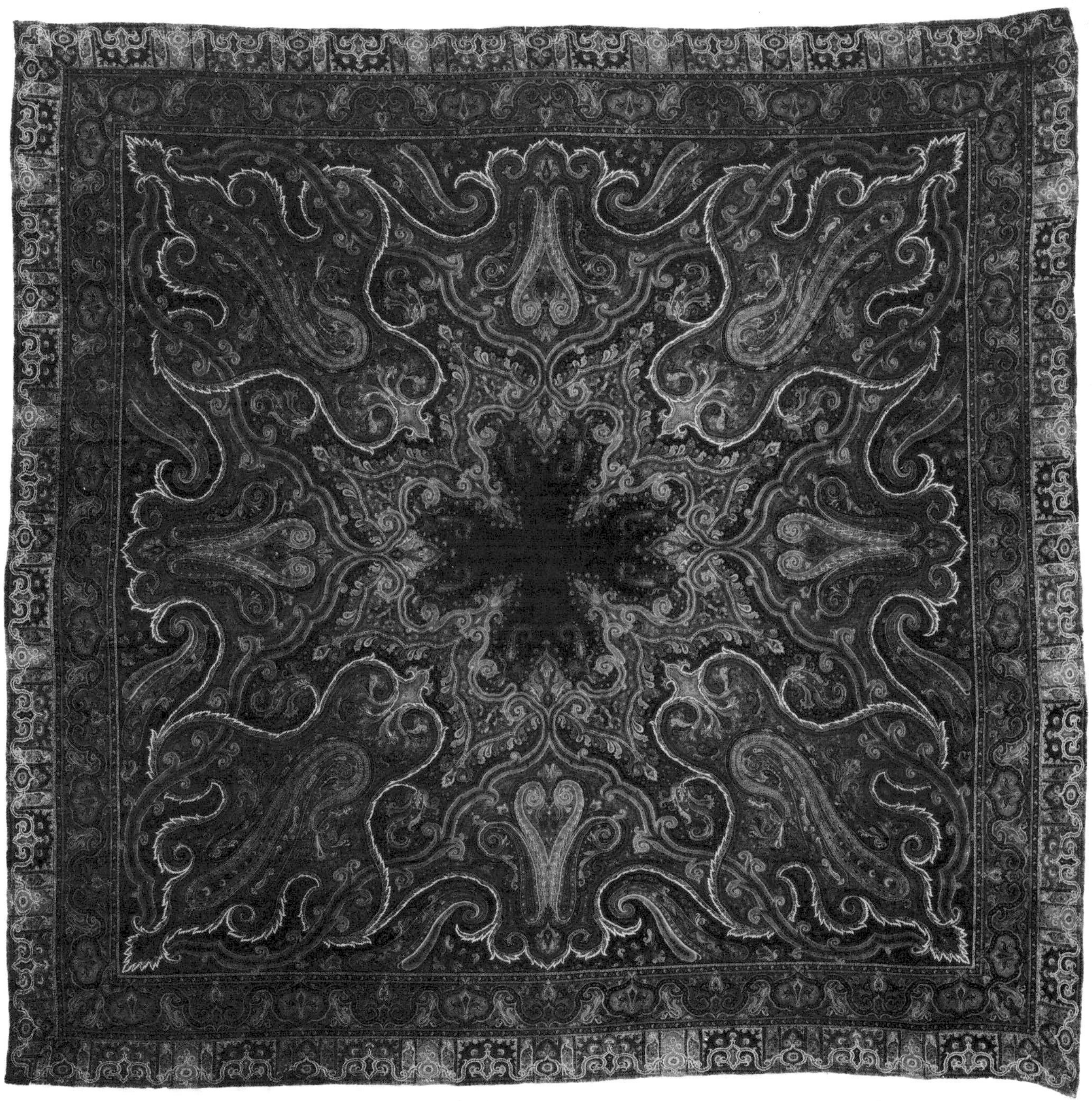

1.17 Shawl
Paisley style, probably Paisley,
Scotland, 1850-70
69 x 67½ in.

Supplementary weft, woven with
Jacquard mechanism
Wool; black center, multicolor

WJGB 2254

There is another design feature that indicates the shawls in Plate 1.14/Color Plate 1.2 and Plate 1.15 were produced to cater to European fashionable tastes. When the entire shawl is viewed flat, one sees the right side of two adjoining borders and the wrong side of the other two. The shawl was constructed to be worn folded roughly in half along the diagonal; thus folded, the wrong side of the top half becomes the right side, with two borders visible one above the other, to be draped over the shoulders and down the back of a crinoline-skirted lady of fashion. The size of the shawl and the depth of the border expand with the fullness of the skirt into mid-century.

Plate 1.16 shows a shawl dating from 1850-70. Shawls made after mid-century show increasingly deep borders, to the extent that the field practically disappears. The limit to which the use of tilikar patchwork technique is extended also increases. Other shawls have more minute areas cut from different loom pieces, but the long, curved undulating white and black arcs that unify this shawl's patterns must have been difficult for even a skilled embroiderer to control.

A comparison of this shawl with one woven on a Jacquard loom, shown in Plate 1.17, serves to point up the close relationship between the designs of Kashmiri hand looms and European mechanized looms. Both shawls feature an elaborate, convoluted interplay of motives symmetrically arrayed around the small black center, yet one was made on a simple frame loom with no labor-saving aids, and the other on a complex mechanized loom which then represented the vanguard of weaving technology. This design represents what has come to be considered typical Paisley design named for the weaving center at Paisley, Scotland. In some cases, the designs are copied so exactly from one type to another that only by using technical criteria can one tell them apart easily.

1.18

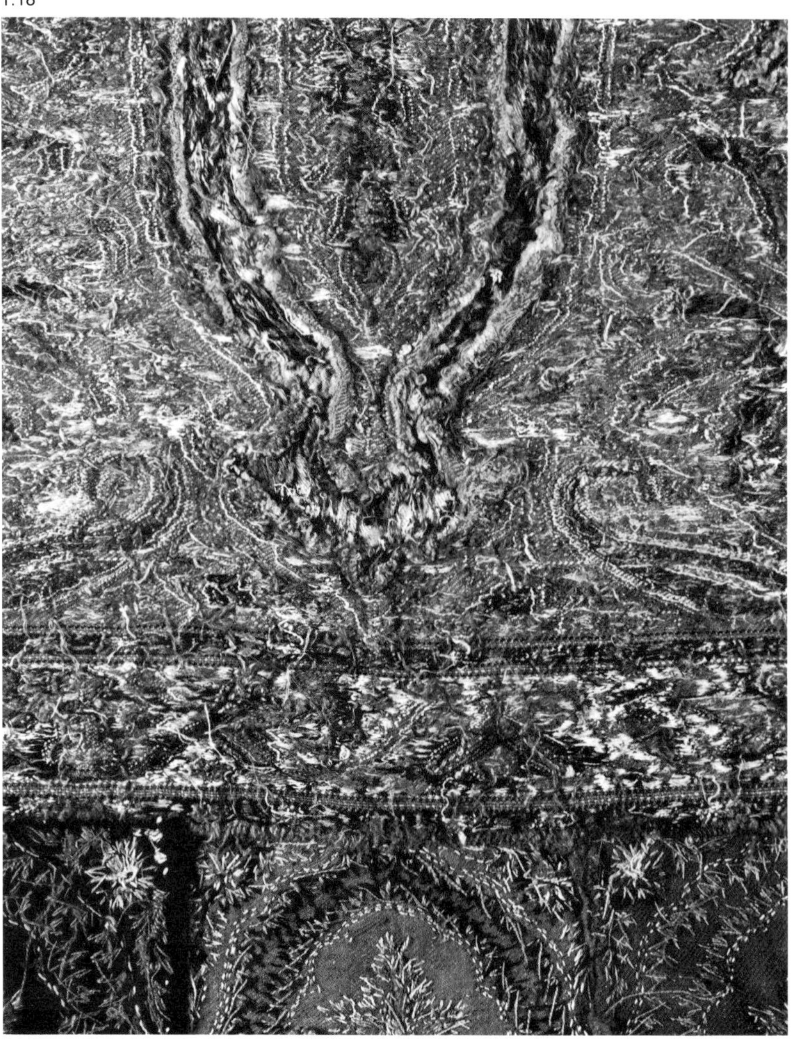

1.18 Shawl fragment
Detail of reverse
Kashmir, 1840-50
25 x 17½ in.

Twill tapestry cut and reassembled
(*tilikar*); embroidered
Wool; multicolor

WFI 1056

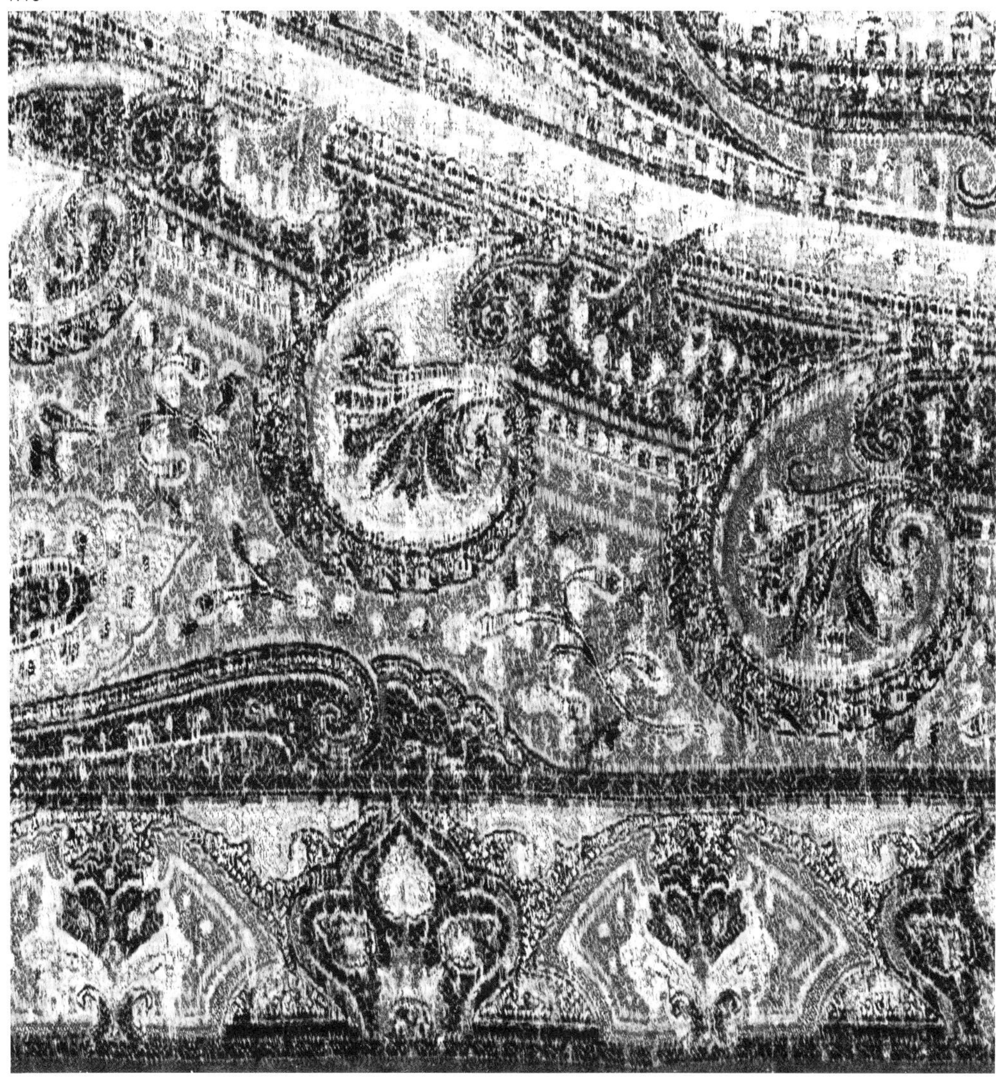

1.19 Shawl fragment
Detail of reverse
Paisley style, probably Paisley,
Scotland, 1860-70
32 x 32 in.

Supplementary weft, trimmed, woven
with Jacquard mechanism
Wool and silk; brown gold, multicolor

WJGB 1051b

Plate 1.18 shows the reverse of a tilikar shawl fragment. The long bent tips of the cones, together with the complexity of that motif's interaction with symmetrical, foliate forms, accentuated by the introduction of several shades of violet date it to about 1850-60. By looking at the reverse, we can see all the hallmarks of tilikar shawls: the tiny ridges created by the double-interlock that is characteristic of twill tapestry, the floats confined to pattern areas, the pieced construction, and the added embroidery.

These features can be contrasted with the floats that transverse the back of the Jacquard woven shawl shown in Plate 1.19. Each weft runs the full selvedge to selvedge distance, being pulled to the surface only where needed for the design. In some cases extremely long floats would be left on the reverse. If a large number of colors were used infrequently, this would also result in considerable bulk on the reverse and additional weight. For that reason the weft floats were usually clipped between pattern areas, leaving the ends exposed. They are held in place only by the tightly beaten wefts around them. The decline of the Kashmir hand-loom industry and the rise of the British industry went hand in hand. Ed Rossbach's recent investigation led him to wonder (1980:65):

> How could so many painfully laborious Cashmere shawls have been woven? . . . How could Europeans have demanded this of the Asians? . . . Since weavers of India were well acquainted with drawlooms and were highly skilled in their operation, why did they not turn to hand looms to compete with the Europe drawloom shawls? The Cashmeres remain as awesome accomplishments of the human hand, forever expressing Europe's enchantment with its new machines and India's desperate, feverish will to compete using its ancient hand methods.

Ikat Fabrics

Cynthia Cunningham Cort

Ikat fabrics are those which have had a pattern tie-dyed into their component yarns before weaving. This Malay word, which literally means "tied" or "bound," is used commonly in the West to describe such a fabric. It is distinguished from *plangi*, the other tie-and-dye technique, in which the woven fabric is tied and dyed. Both ikat and plangi are called resist techniques because the item to be dyed is tied in a predetermined pattern, usually with a thread, to block out or resist any dye that would otherwise penetrate the fabric or yarn being dyed. A succession of tyings in different places and dyebaths of different colors will increase the complexity of the design.

There are four types of ikat technique. In warp ikat, only the warp or lengthwise yarns are dyed in a pattern and the weft or crosswise yarns are a solid color. Weft ikat is the opposite of warp ikat. In mixed or warp and weft ikat, both sets of yarns are patterned with tie and dye but no specific pattern is produced in the areas where the dyeings coincide. Finally, there is double ikat, in which both warp and weft are dyed in the same pattern so that the patterns come into alignment when woven. An example of this final, extremely complicated technique is the *patola* sari woven in Gujarat in western India.

Ikat fabrics are woven in a number of weaving areas of the world, including Japan, Southeast Asia, India, Uzbekistan, Guatemala, and Ecuador. Patterns and techniques vary considerably from one location to another, but there are a few technical requirements and design characteristics that are similar throughout the world.

Ikat weaving is done in several centers in India: the Sambalpur region of Orissa, the Hyderabad area of Andhra Pradesh, and Patan in Gujarat in western India (see Map). Each of these three areas produces fabrics that are characteristic and easily identifiable. Ikat is also produced in the region around Pune in Maharashtra, and in Tamil Nadu, but the traditions of these areas are not longstanding, and so will not be discussed here.

Within India, the term "ikat" has no meaning. Both ikat and plangi fabrics are called by the Hindi word *bandhani*, which also means "tied". In the last ten years, ikat saris and shirting fabrics have become very fashionable within middle class society in urban areas far removed from the traditional local markets for these fabrics. As a result of this popularity, many weavers in other areas are consciously imitating patola designs, since these are the most complex and highly regarded of the ikat fabrics of India. Therefore, it has become common to call all ikat fabrics "patola," with more specific designations, such as Sambalpuri, added as needed. This is particularly true outside of the areas where the weaving is done, because the distinctions between saris woven in different areas are less important to the urban consumer than they are to the manufacturers. An indication of the current popularity of these fabrics is the fact that the large textile mills are turning out printed textiles, with the same designs and the blurred design outlines characteristic of ikat weaving but which are far less costly than authentic ikat textiles.

In this chapter saris are discussed more than yardage or other types of garments because most of the handloom fabrics produced in India are saris. *Khadi* fabric and Kashmir shawls are a few notable exceptions. Saris have their own design requirements because of the ways in which they are worn. Many of the designs in use for saris do not appear on other fabrics.

Every type of sari in India has a name which refers to its region of origin, technique of production, or characteristic appearance; sometimes the original meaning of the name is lost, but it is always applied to one specific type of sari or other fabric. For example, a Sambalpur sari is one from Sambalpur District, a bandhani sari is tied and dyed, a *dhup-chamh* (literally meaning sun and shade) sari is shot woven with one color for the warp and another for the weft creating an iridescent effect, and patola are the special double ikat wedding saris of Gujarat. Many of these names are used in everyday conversation between consumer and shopkeepers just as terms like denim and muslin are widely understood in the United States.

One of the major characteristics of ikat fabrics is that the outlines of each motif appear to be indistinct or out of focus in the direction of the ikat dyed yarns. That is, in warp ikat the lengthwise direction of the pattern will have blurred edges and the crosswise will have sharp outlines. The opposite is true for weft ikat and in double ikat the motifs will have blurred outlines on all sides.

This blurred appearance is caused by the dyes seeping in under the tying threads. This happens no matter how tightly they are tied. In addition, the yarns tend to become misaligned during the weaving process. The degree of imprecision in the alignment of yarns can be manipulated to produce different effects. In its most precise form, the patola of Gujarat, where the dyeing and weaving

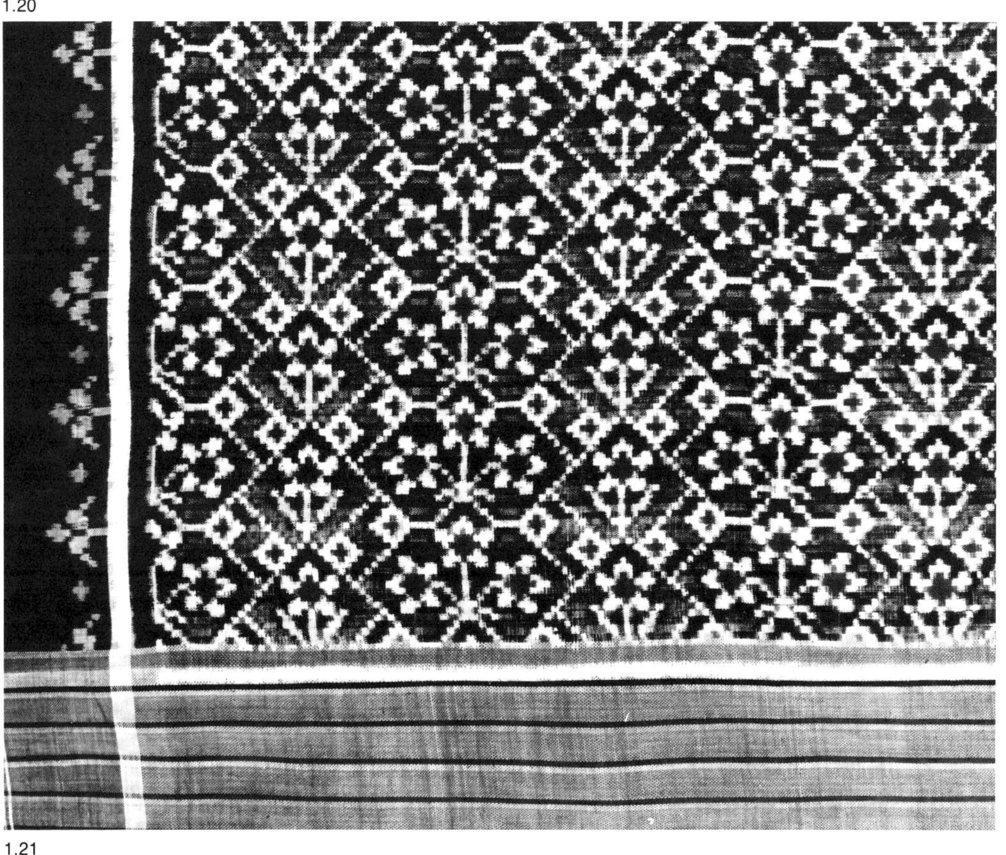

1.20 Sari with *Teen-Phul*
(three flowers) design
Detail of corner
Patan, Gujarat, before 1958
177½ x 47 in.;
weft repeat motif: 2½ in.

Patolu double ikat
Silk; purple with red, white, yellow

1976.9.115/WRel 2825

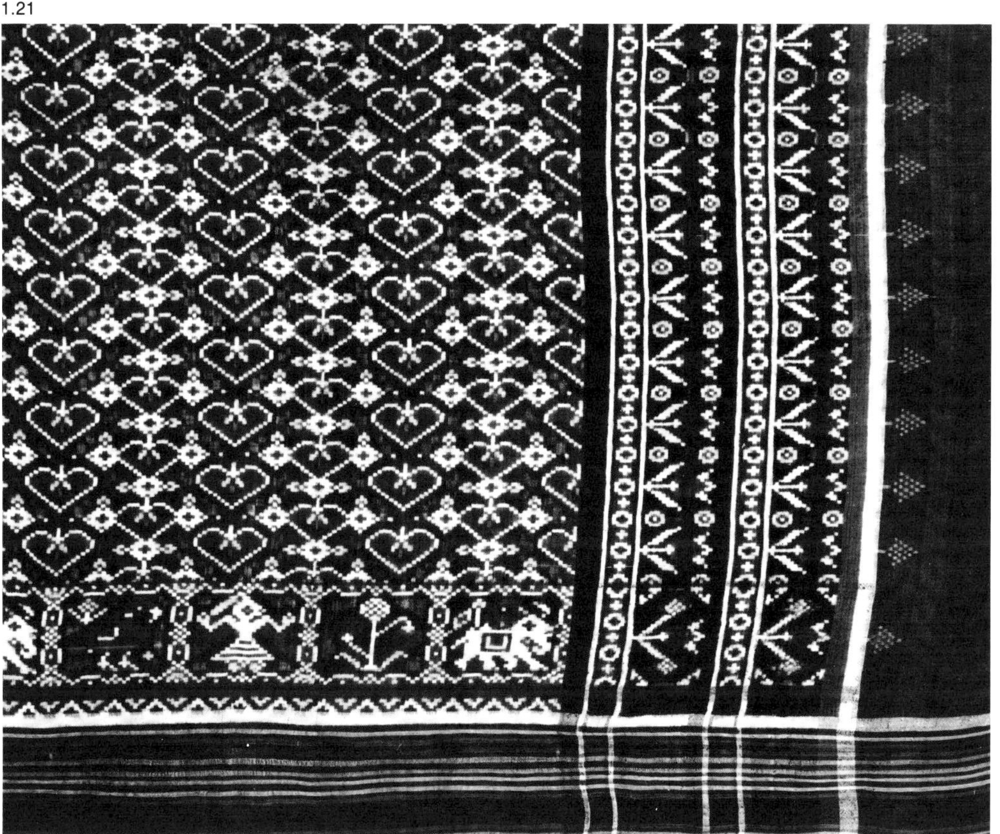

1.21 Sari with *Pan Bhat*
(betel leaf) motif
Detail of pallu, border and body
Patan, Gujarat, early twentieth century
150 x 53 in.

Patolu double ikat
Silk; deep red with blue, red, white and
yellow

Collection of Joyce Carey

are controlled to the maximum extent possible, the outlines are almost as sharp as if they had been printed. Such precision means that it takes months to produce a sari. In addition, a large part of the time-consuming aspect of patola production is the fact that it is double ikat, not single ikat as are most Indian ikat fabrics, and the alignment in both directions must be precise to make the pattern coincide. This exponentially increases the need for mathematical precision in measuring, marking, tying, and weaving over that needed for the fabrics patterned in either warp or weft alone. Most ikats, however, are produced in a few days or weeks, so the designs appear less precise in outline. In many places, the effect thus created is highly prized as a distinctive characteristic of these fabrics.

Another common characteristic of warp or weft ikat is a tinge of the solid-colored yarn overlaying the dyed colors of the pattern. This happens because the pattern is only tied and dyed in its various colors in one direction and the yarns in the other direction are a plain, solid color. If the warp is ikat-dyed white, red, yellow and blue, and the weft thread is blue, the pattern will have the appearance of being pale blue, purple, green and deep blue. This is particularly true for balanced, plain weave fabrics where warp and weft show equally on both sides. Most of the ikat fabrics of India are woven in a balanced, plain weave.

Double ikat does not have this color variation with its intersecting yarns. Instead, because both warp and weft yarns are dyed to create the same patterns and colors in the same areas, the colors are bright and clear except at the edges of motives, where they may bleed out into the surrounding color.

Gujarat

The most famous of the ikat fabrics woven in India is the *patolu* (plural: *patola*) or silk double ikat sari used on ceremonial occasions by certain Gujarati castes. Its fame is well deserved, for it is the most precisely measured, tied, and woven ikat fabric in the world.

From the end of the nineteenth century, craft historians have asserted that the quality of the patolu being produced is not as high as it was formerly (Watt 1903:256-259). Since the 1930s, when modern chemical dyes replaced vegetable ones, patola have looked quite different (Pls. 1.20, 1.21). More colors have been introduced (purple, orange, and several shades of blue and green), and the precise outlines of the old patola have not quite been achieved in the modern ones. This is partly a function of skill, but owes more to the time it takes to make a patolu in relation to the price it can bring.

At present only two families in the town of Patan, north of Ahmedabad in Gujarat, are weaving patola. In the largest of these two families fifteen working members support a total of forty-five people. Chhotalal Salvi, the head of the family, is acutely aware of how much time the weavers can afford to spend on each item to produce a quality product which will provide an adequate income for the family. In contrast to other weavers throughout India, who tend to be poor, the patola weavers are middle class and well-educated.

The patola weavers are also aware that their skills are valuable, and that they are the last people doing the technique in its traditional form. They have a great sense of pride and preservation of tradition. The Salvi family has twice been awarded the Master Craftsman Award by the Indian national government. (In 1981 an Orissi ikat weaver was also given this award, but the *tussah* silk sari he wove was very original in design and he was, in effect, starting a new tradition rather than restoring or preserving an old one.)

These national awards for excellence and skill are important for the preservation and revitalization of traditional Indian crafts. Between the First and Second World Wars, many of the traditional crafts, including patola weaving, very nearly died out as styles and markets changed. The Master Craftsman Awards have made the growing urbanized middle class which has the money to support such hand work aware that there is such a strong heritage of beautiful craftsmanship in India.

There was a large traditional market for patola in Indonesia, where they were valued in the courts of Java as symbols of royalty possessing magical powers (Gittinger 1979:30-31). Throughout Indonesia, the motives and arrangement of motives in patola have been copied and adapted by many of the local textile traditions. To this day, a piece of a patolu, used as a kind of long scarf, is an integral part of a Javanese dancer's costume. Since these old Indian fragments are rare and expensive, there has grown up in Indonesia an industry for reproducing the designs as exactly as possible in other techniques, such as *batik*, specifically for dancers' costumes.

In appearance, the patola saris are quite easily identified. The older ones usually have a deep cherry red or maroon for the background color, and motives of red, white, yellow, blue and black. Previously, people of one caste (to which the Salvis belong) did the tying and the weaving, while people of a different caste did the dyeing. Even among the dyers, those who did the indigo dyeing were distinguished from those who did all other kinds of dyeing.

Since the 1930s, through the efforts of Laherchand Kasturchand Salvi (Chhotalal's grandfather) and his family, techniques which were no longer being practiced have been relearned and consolidated, so that the weavers are now also the dyers. The use of naphthol dyes has simplified the dyeing and reduced the time required for it. These dyes have broadened the color scheme considerably, and today one can see saris with a main color of purple (Pl. 1.20), or bright golden yellow. Throughout India, the traditional color for ceremonial occasions, particularly weddings, is red. Many of these newer saris are clearly being made for customers with other uses in mind than the traditional occasions when a patolu would be given to a daughter or an in-law.

The motives of the patola are mostly geometric diamonds and squares or abstracted flowers and animals. The outlines of the motives are always made of small squares. Plate 1.20 shows a motif which involves the repetition of a group of three flowers. Plate 1.21 shows a dark red *pan bhat*, which is modeled after the heartshaped *pan* or betel leaf. The border of Plate 1.21 is also a very popular motif of an elephant, a parrot, a flower and a dancing girl. This is often used all over the ground of a sari rather than merely as the border. Outside of the decorated border, there is always a plainer border of stripes. The pallus, or decorated ends, are usually composed of two rows of flowers. These saris have two decorated ends. This results from the fact that the warp is folded before the motives are tied, and repeats of the same motif are grouped together to minimize the amount of tying needed. The second *pallu* of the patola is concealed when the sari is worn.

The process of patola production is shown in Plate 1.22a-i. It is important to measure warp and weft for any ikat fabric precisely, although this is obviously more crucial in a double ikat fabric where the motives must line up.

Warp is measured on a wall with pegs in it (Pl. 1.22a). It is approximately twenty yards long, or the length of three saris plus some loom wastage at the ends and between them. As the person warping walks back and forth between the pegs, a helper is seated at the bottom end crossing the individual yarns over and under more brass poles so that they retain their exact order throughout the tying, dyeing and weaving. The warp is then folded in such a way that the same motives are grouped together for economy of time and effort in tying (Pl. 1.22b). The folded warp is one-sixth as long as its full length.

The weft is measured on a board with a peg at each end (Pl. 1.22c). As the weft yarns are counted out they are also grouped according to motif repeats by dropping a cord into the yarns at specific intervals (Pl. 1.22d). This sectioning is also done to the warp after it has been removed from the wall but before it is folded.

Warp and weft are stretched on separate frames and marked with charcoal lines (Pl. 1.22e). Then they are tied off with cotton thread wrapped tightly around the bundles in the predetermined pattern (Pl. 1.22f). This cotton thread is the resist which will prevent the dye from penetrating in areas of the pattern where it is not required. For large areas strips of cotton cloth are also used.

After the first tying, the yarns are removed from their frames and dyed red. Then they are put back on their frames and areas which will be dyed the next color, yellow, have their ties removed while areas to remain red are covered up. This continues until all of the colors have been applied. When the ties are finally removed, the warp is stretched out to its full length and put onto the loom and the weft is wound onto bobbins to be woven across it.

Two people weave at one time on a loom which is stretched between concrete supports at the front and a pole at the back of the room, tilted at a sharp angle (Pl. 1.22g,h). The loom is simple and only has one set of heddles and a shed rod to create the spaces needed to pass the shuttle between alternate warp yarns in a plain weave.

Each afternoon, after about nine or ten inches have been woven, the weavers adjust the pattern by pulling the warp yarns individually into place to make the squares of design as precise as possible (Pl. 1.22i). It is for this reason that this sari must be made of silk which is very elastic and will not break as cotton would.

When the weaving of one sari is completed, it is removed from the loom and sold with no additional finishing.

Orissa

The state of Orissa, on the eastern coast of India, is bisected by a range of low but rugged mountains. To the east is the fertile coastal plain, and to the west a dry, underdeveloped area which

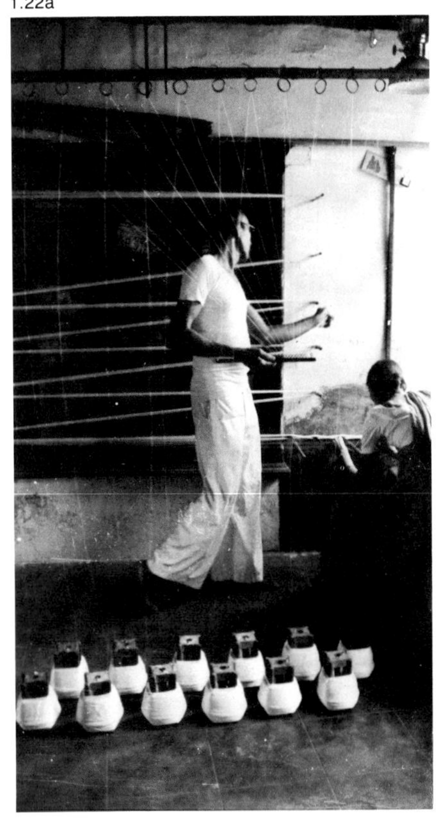

1.22a

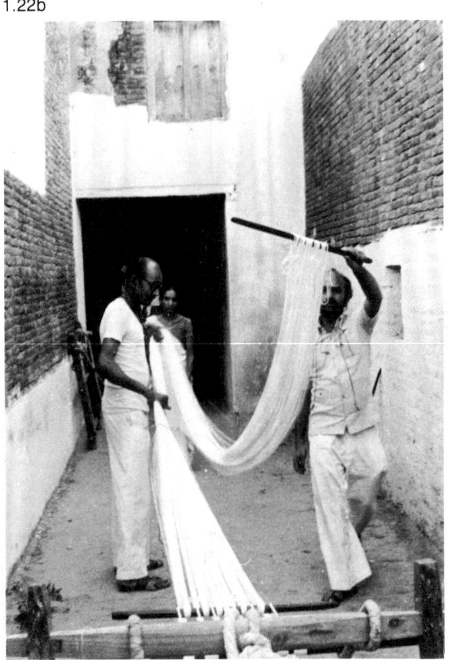

1.22b

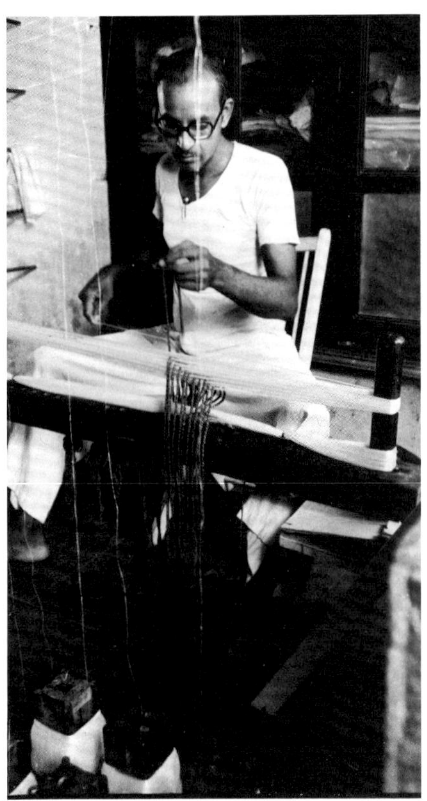

1.22c

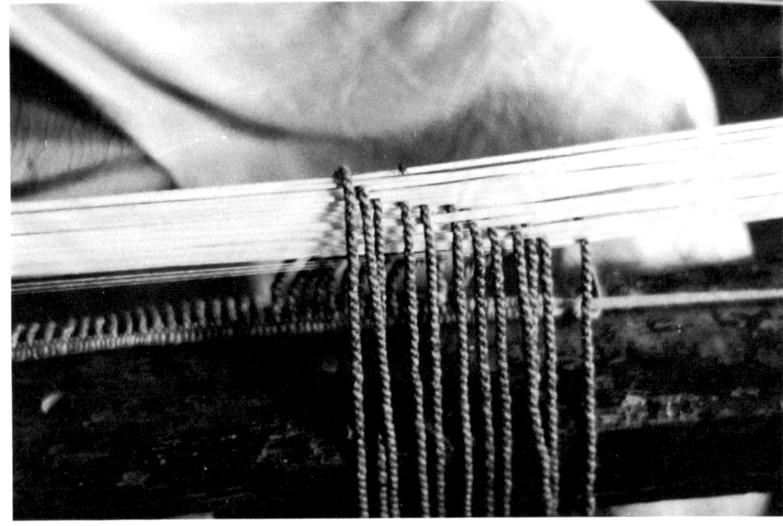

1.22d

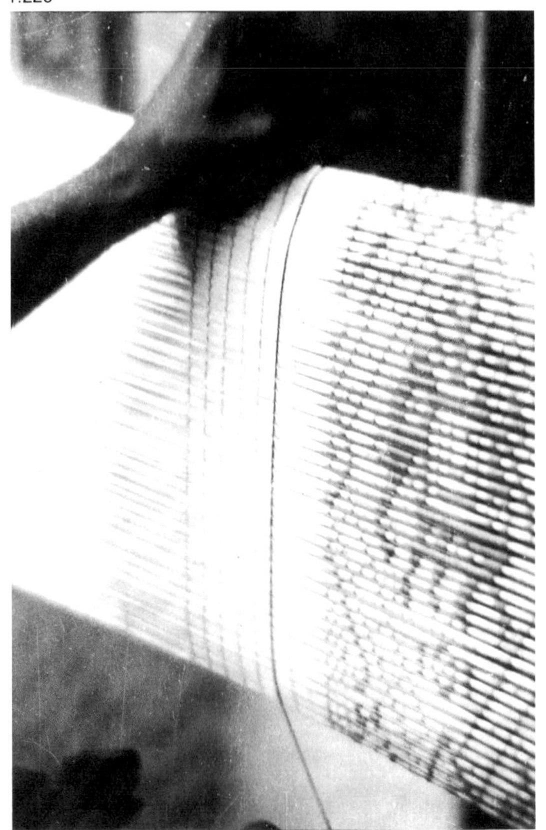

1.22e

1.22f

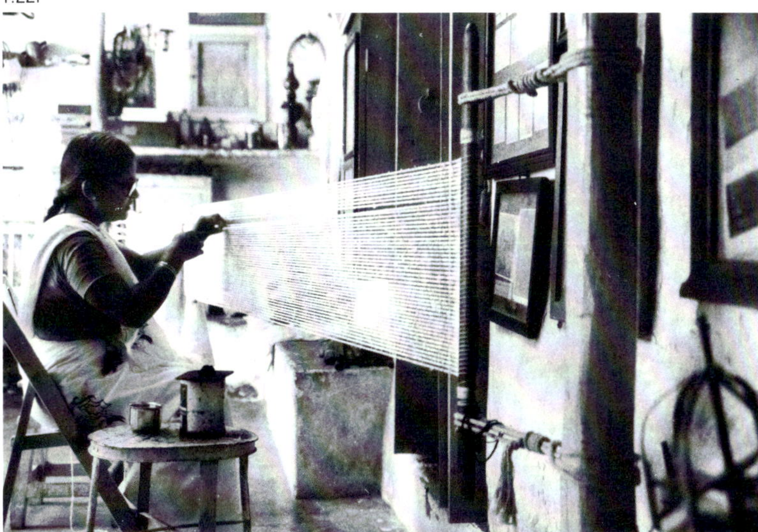

1.22g

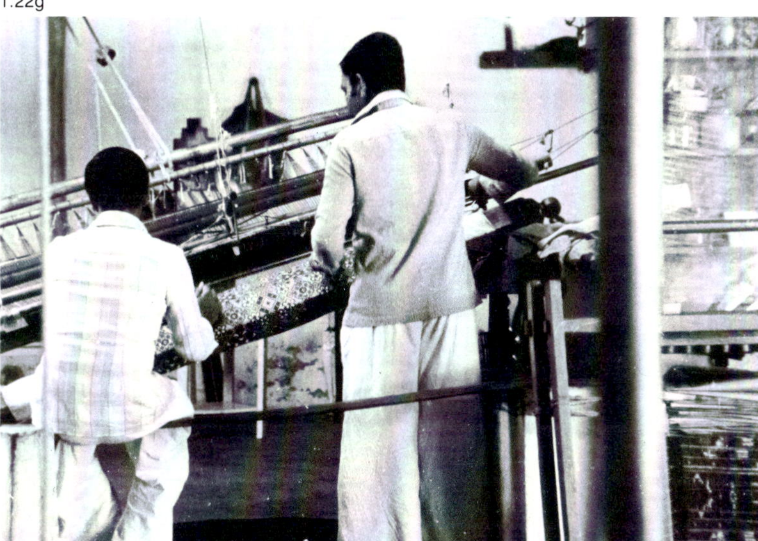

1.22h

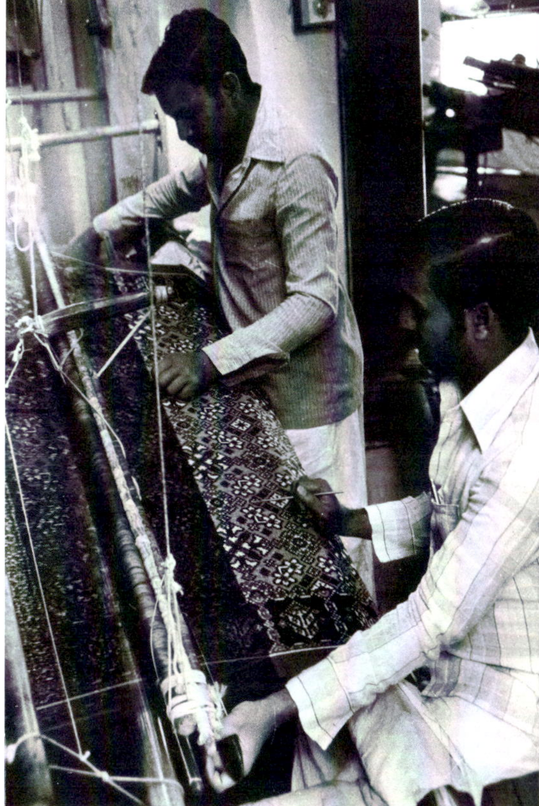

1.22i

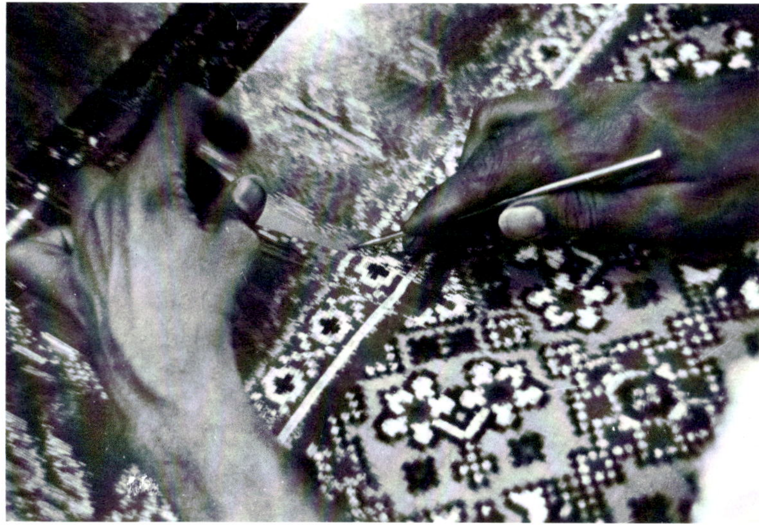

1.22 Patola production in the Salvi
workshop, Patan, Gujarat

a, measuring warp on wall
b, folding 20 yard warp to 10 feet
c, measuring weft
d, sectioning cords for grouping
repeats of one motif
e, marking yarns for tying. Area to the
right has already been tied with
elephant motif.
f, tying a warp as it is stretched across
the workroom
g, weaving
h, weaving
i, adjusting alignment of woven yarns in
pattern. Even in the unwoven area the
motives are visible.

extends into the central state of Madhya Pradesh. It is in this western area of the state, in the district of Sambalpur, that most ikat weaving is done, in small towns such as Bargarh, Barpali, and Sonpur. Several types of saris as well as men's shirting and household fabrics such as bed covers and table cloths are produced there.

The style of sari woven and worn locally is know as a *kapta*. It is somewhat shorter in both length and width than the standard sari available throughout most of India, which is six yards by forty-five inches. A kapta is also distinctive for its heavy, coarse texture, its limited color range (blue, green or purple, as well as the traditional white for widows), and the fact that is has two pallus and very narrow, plain side borders (Pl. 1.23). The borders, the body or central area, and the pallu (sometimes also called the *pallav* or *anchal*) are the three major areas of a sari to be decorated.

Traditionally, the design of a kapta includes very little ikat and relies heavily on supplementary warp and weft patterning. This is made using a dobby loom attachment (which facilitates weaving complex patterns), or a complicated set of flat wooden boards which are inserted into the warp lifting specific warp yarns in succession. What ikat there is usually takes the form of narrow rows of colored dots, simple fish, and flowers in the pallu. These motives alternate with rows of supplementary weft dotted lines while the border design is often composed entirely of small, dobby-controlled motives such as diamonds, flowers and fish. Thus, the small flower and fish motives often appear in both ikat weaving (as in the pallu of the sari in Plate 1.28/Color Plate 1.3) and in supplementary warp and weft patterning. Plates 1.25 and 1.26 show two pieces which are from the same area as the ikat patterned saris but which very entirely on elaborate rows of supplementary weft (and, in the border, warp) motives including the fish and flower as well as a turtle in Pl. 1.25.

Kaptas are worn only within a limited geographical area of western Orissa and eastern Madhya Pradesh. They are worn without either a blouse or a petticoat, and are wrapped in such a way that both ends show and the garment does not extend much below the knee. This method of wrapping is very functional in a rural area where many women work in the fields and require the ability to move freely. Most saris are worn so that they reach the floor. It is largely in urban areas where women work at less physically demanding jobs that the modesty requirements include covering the lower legs and arms. Styles of sari wrapping are also greatly dictated by regional cultural variations and are one way in which Indians can tell where a woman is from and what her status is.

Another Sambalpur sari is more modern in design than the kapta. It is woven in the same colors as the kapta for the local market, and in a larger range of colors for an urban middle class audience in other areas of Orissa. While the kapta includes limited ikat designs, the designs for this second, less traditional type of sari rely much less on dobby work and much more on ikat designs (as in the shawl, Pl. 1.24). They include warp ikat borders, a single weft ikat pallu and sometimes large double ikat checked or star motives in the body of the sari.

A third type of sari made in the same area has a much finer yarn count and uses a mill spun rather than a hand spun cotton yarn. These saris are highly decorated with ikat, using warp ikat in the border and weft ikat in the pallu and body, and are characterized by complex, new designs of animals parading up and down, sunsets behind mountains, large lotuses, and an occasional airplane. The ground is often shot woven and has rows of flower pots or butterflies growing up from the border (Pl. 1.27). These colorful saris are sent exclusively to large shops in the westernized cities such as Delhi and Calcutta. They are not worn locally at all, largely because they cost about six to eight times as much as the kapta.

In addition to the three major types of sari described above, there is the *vichitra* ("special" or "extraordinary") sari. This traditional sari is the oldest design currently being produced in the area. The colors of the vichitra design are maroon, black and white. It includes rows of ducks, fish, abstracted lions, and waves in ikat which run lengthwise down the body of the sari and across the pallu. The border has small supplementary warp designs of flowers and fish. In the body, between the other animals, there is often a pattern called *saktapar* which consists of a checkerboard of one inch squares in double ikat. Although it is common for an Orissi sari to have both warp and weft ikat in it, it is unusual for the warp and weft to line up into even the most simple double ikat motif. (For a more lengthy discussion of the history of all of the common Orissa and Andhra Pradesh motives, see also Mohanty and Krishna 1974.)

Some of the other ikat fabrics produced in the Sambalpur area include household fabrics such as placemats and bedcovers, *rumals* (handkerchiefs), and men's shirting fabrics. Many designs used for the shirting fabrics and rumals are the same checks and stars as are found in the second type of sari described above. There are also stripes of flowers and fish as are found in a pallu. The

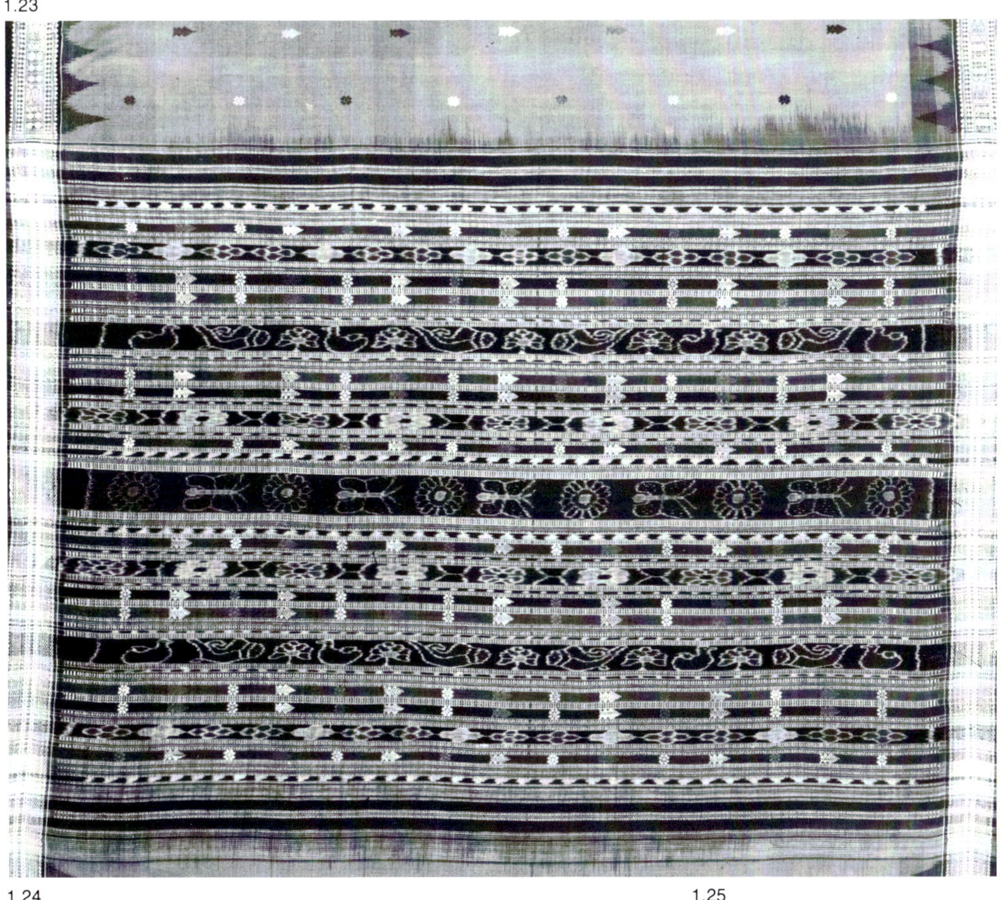

1.23 Sari
Detail of pallu
Sambalpur, Orissa, before 1958
172 x 43½ in.

Weft ikat, plain, supplementary warp
and weft weave
Cotton; blue-green, multicolored

1976.9.261/WRel 2833

1.24 Shawl
Detail of border
Orissa, 1960-70
65 x 32½ in.

Weft ikat, plain and supplementary weft
weave
Tussah silk; undyed, multicolor

WRel 2419

1.25 Sari
Detail of pallu
Barpali, Orissa, before 1958
212 x 45½ in.

Warp and weft ikat, plain, supplementary warp and weft weave
Cotton; undyed, red, multicolor

1976.9.260/WLFI 2859

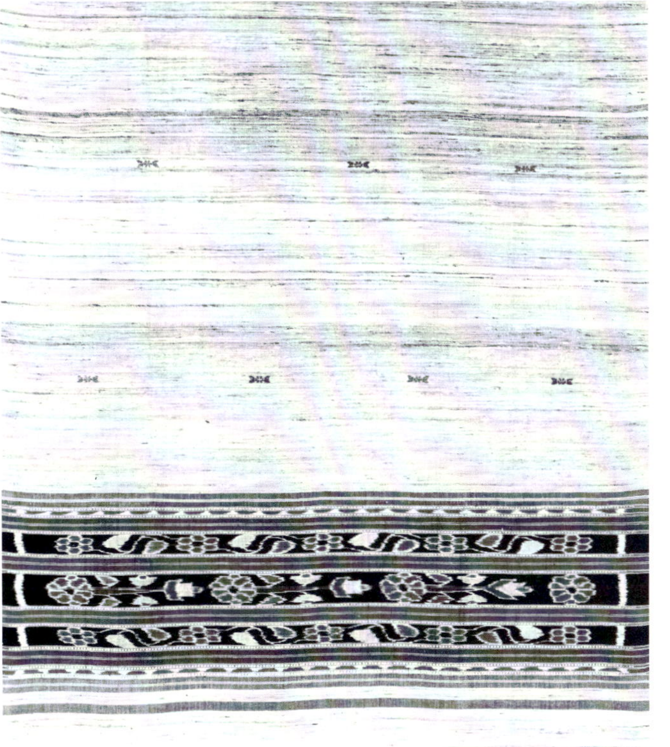

1.24

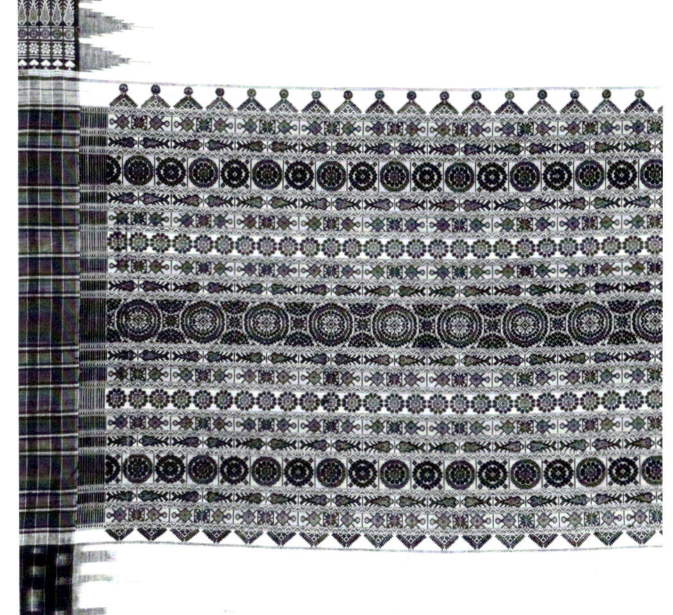

1.25

rumal usually has a simple border on all four sides, which involves both warp and weft ikat. At the corners where the ikat lines meet there is no attempt to make them create any particular pattern. In the center there may be a weft ikat flower, a simple double ikat star or, in older examples, the sakta-par design. Sometimes, in the most modern ones, a phrase such as ''God Bless You'' or ''Forget Me Not'' will be included with the words spelled out in ikat technique. Often the backgrounds of these rumals are shot woven.

Other weaving centers send silk sari borders to Sambalpur to be tied and dyed and then incorporate these into their own saris. Two such centers are Berhampur, in southern Orissa, which is noted for weaving silk saris that include supplementary warp and weft brocading, and Bengal, where natural colored tussah or wild silk saris are popular.

The looms used in Sambalpur are counter-balanced treadle type built over a pit in the floor where the treadles are. The weaver sits on a mat on the edge of this pit with his feet on the treadles. The purpose of these low looms is to conserve both wood, which is scarce, and space in the low-ceilinged houses. Often the reed and heddle mechanism hang from the roof beam, but there may as easily be a wooden frame over the loom to hold these parts as well as a dobby attachment used for the supplementary warp patterning in the borders. The shuttle is usually a fly shuttle, which travels through the open warps from a wooden box on one side of the reed to a box on the other side after the treadles have been pressed to change the opening. This process is controlled by a cord which the weaver jerks with his right hand. This fly shuttle mechanism is much faster than a shuttle which is thrown from one hand to the other through the warps, and allows the weaver to produce two saris per day of the simplest design type. It requires great coordination by the weaver to manipulate simultaneously the treadles with his feet, the shuttle release cord which hangs in the center of the loom over the reed with the right hand, and the reed with the left hand. Between transits of the shuttle, the beater containing the reed is pulled forward hard against the woven area to beat in the previous yarn, and then pushed back so that the shuttle will have room to fly across. Faulty coordination will mean either that the treadling sequence will be missed, or that the reed will not be in the right place for the box to catch the shuttle, and instead the shuttle will go flying off across the room, carrying the weft yarn with it.

The more complicated and expensive saris are woven much more slowly, so that each weft yarn can be adjusted as it is woven to better line up with its neighbor. This adjustment produces a loop of yarn on the back of the fabric in areas where there is weft ikat because the fabrics are woven face down and the weaver pulls out a little loop of extra weft as he pulls each weft into line. The weft as it is measured and dyed is therefore a little wider than the finished sari will be, to allow for this adjustment as well as for any shrinkage which might occur during the dyeing. These little loops of yarn on the back are peculiar to Orissa ikat, and are not considered to be unsightly. A local woman wearing a *domuha* sari, which has two pallus and is entirely symmetrical in its design, is just as likely to have the side with the little loops showing as not, since it is not considered important to hide them.

The bedcovers are woven of much heavier cotton than the other fabrics (Pl. 1.29) and must be woven on a two-man loom to obtain a fabric that is up to six or eight feet wide, i.e. much wider than one man could conveniently reach.

As is true throughout most of India, the entire family participates in the work of producing fabric, but only the men do the actual weaving. The women and children do most of the spinning, winding, warp and weft measuring, pattern tying, and sometimes the dyeing. The children start doing simple jobs when quite young, but begin to receive active training at about the age of ten. Women do not weave for two reasons: they are considered to be polluted and might bring bad luck to the tools or the cloth being woven; and they are solely responsible for the household chores and raising of small children. Warp measuring is something which can be done with little concentration or with a baby on one's lap, but weaving involves much more attention and physical involvement.

Usually the parts of a sari are measured separately in four sections: borders to be warp ikat dyed, the non-ikat warp for the center section, weft for the pallu which will be ikat dyed, and the weft for the body of the sari. As in Gujarat, often the yarns for several borders or pallus are measured together to economize on the time spent in tying and dyeing.

In the town of Nuapatna, in Cuttack district, near the coast, ikat weaving is done within a slightly different tradition, although with the growth of a government training center in the state capital of Bhubaneshwar, the traditions are becoming more similar. The saris woven in the Cuttack district until about thirty years ago were always produced in tussah and mulberry silk. Since then, cotton saris have also been produced. Besides the obvious difference of cotton versus silk, there are also some stylistic differences which make the Nuapatna saris distinct.

The traditional garment made in Nuapatna is a silk wedding veil called a *khandua* (Pl. 1.28/Color Pl. 1.3), usually in a shade of red or orange, as Indian brides wear red. The design motifs include the auspicious elephant, a trailing vine with peacocks in it, stars, an eight inch or larger many-petaled flower, a distinctly Orissi creature called a *nabagunjara*, and the *kumbha* or temple motif, which looks like a jagged row of mountains or temple roofs, along the borders. The kumbha is found all over India, not only in ikat but also tapestry weave, brocading and printing. It is also popular in Indonesia under the name of *tumphal*. In Nuapatna saris it often alternates with a motif like a bud on a curving stem. The elephant in Nuapatna ikat usually differs from elephant motives in western Orissa as well as other parts of India in that it has a disproportionately long trunk and carries no rider.

The nabagunjara is a creature composed of parts of nine animals. It appeared in the forest before the hero Arjuna in the Oriya version of the epic *Mahabharata*. The nabagunjara was really Lord Krishna, testing whether Arjuna would recognize him. Arjuna was not taken in by this improbable animal, and recognized it as Lord Krishna. This is a popular scene in Orissi mythology and the nabagunjara often appears painted on temple walls or in other decorative settings.

Besides the khandua, and similarly patterned saris, the most interesting and unusual fabric produced in Nuapatna is the *Gita Govinda* cloth of Jagannatha, an Orissi form of the Hindu god Vishnu.

1.26

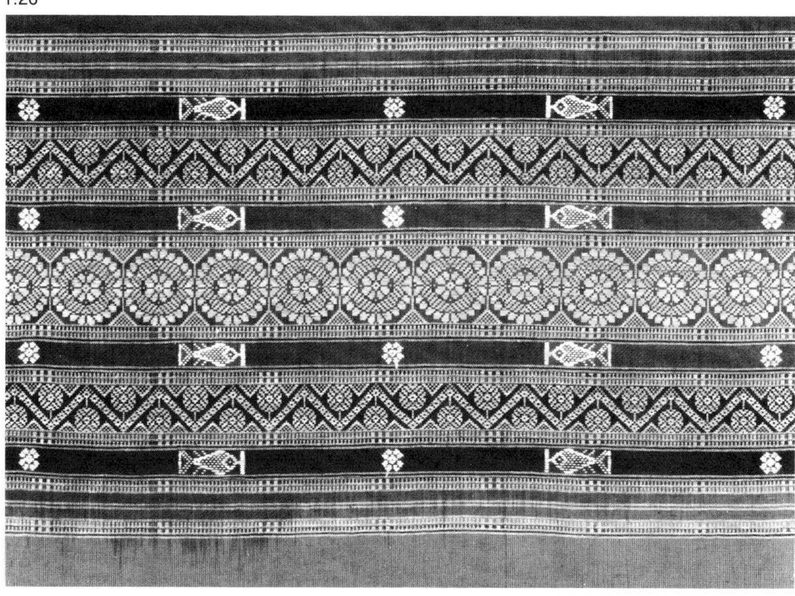

1.27

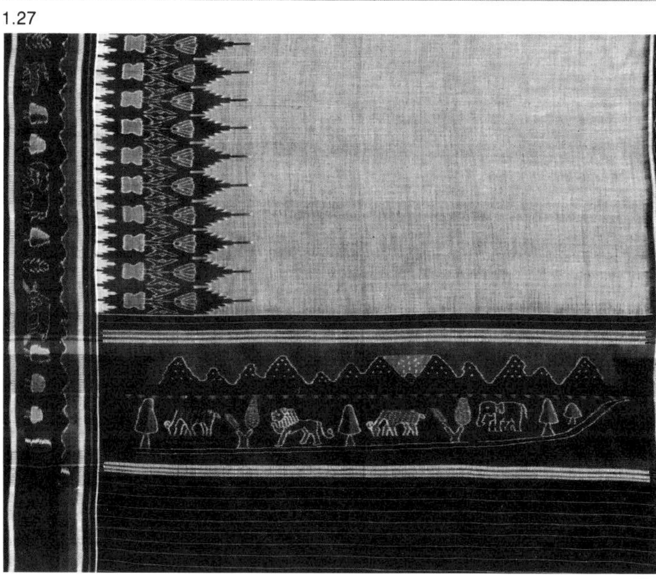

1.29

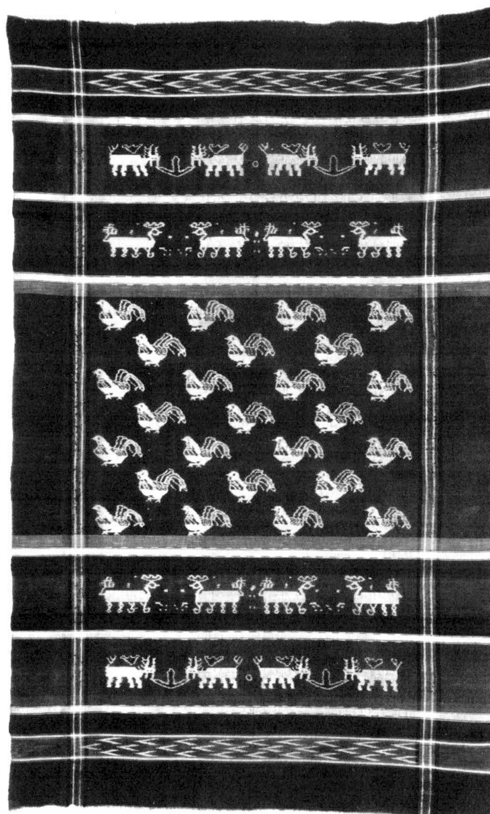

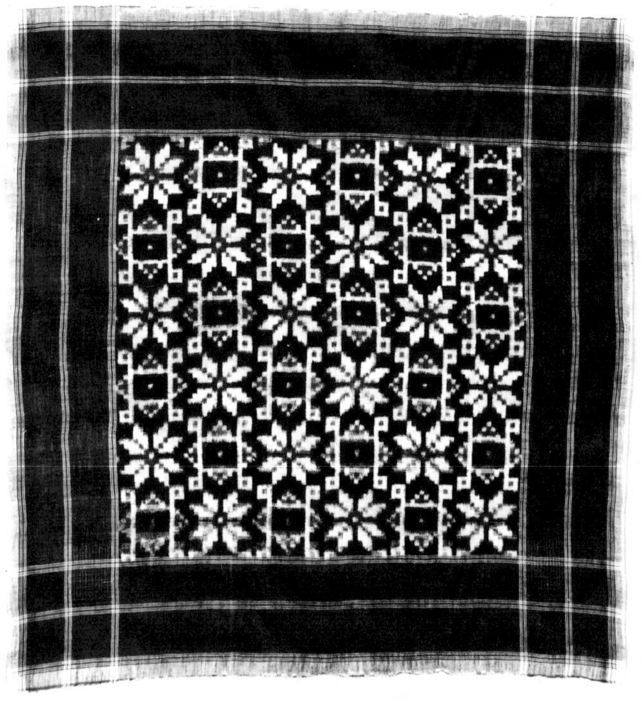

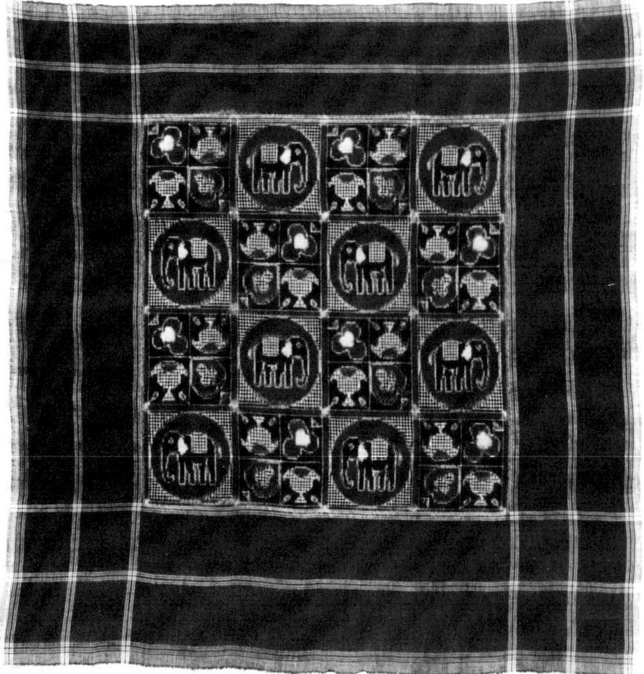

1.30 Handkerchief *(telia rumal)*
Chirala, Andhra Pradesh, before 1959
42¹⁄₈ x 41 in.

Double ikat, plain weave
Cotton; maroon, black, white

1976.9.94/WRel 2832

1.31 Handkerchief *(telia rumal)*
Chirala, Andhra Pradesh, before 1957
42³⁄₄ x 42 in.

Double ikat, plain weave
Cotton; shades of red, white

1976.9.76/WRel 2820

1.32 Handkerchief *(telia rumal)*
Detail of one quarter of field
Chirala, Andhra Pradesh, before 1959
41¹⁄₈ x 44¹⁄₂ in.

Double ikat, plain weave
Cotton; shades of red, white

1976.9.62/WRel 2821

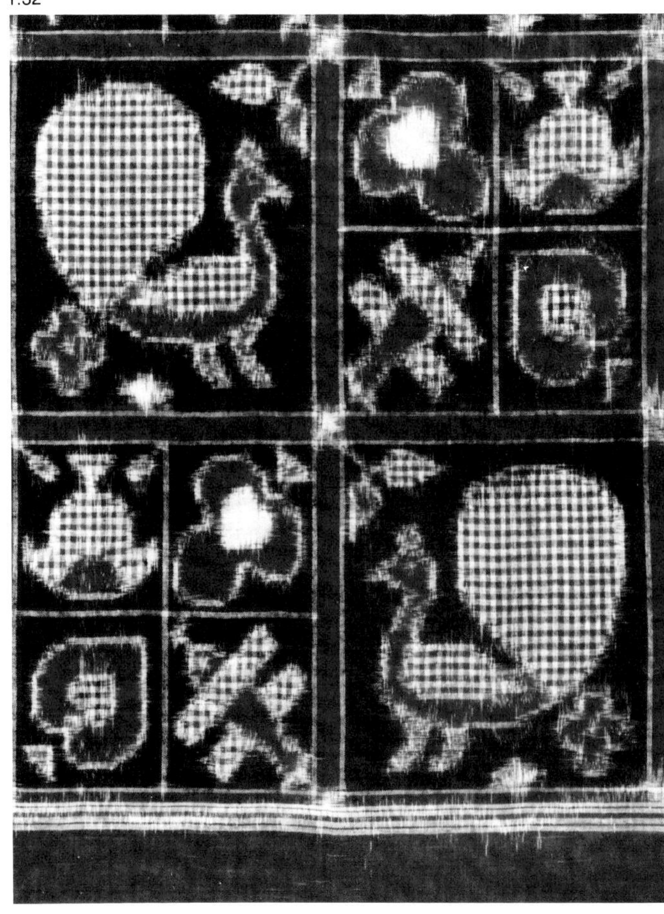

The Jagannatha temple in the coastal city of Puri has been the most important religious, social, and economic institution in Orissa for a thousand years. A red silk ritual cloth made in Nuapatna has ikat-woven Sanskrit words in Oriya script. This is a verse of the *Gita Govinda*, the famous twelfth century devotional poem to Vishnu. According to legend, it was the poet Jayadeva himself who first thought of weaving a verse of it and presenting it to the Lord.

Andhra Pradesh

Two locations in the state of Andhra Pradesh, Pochampalli and Chirala, produce ikat woven textiles.

The textiles of Pochampalli draw their traditions from the *telia rumals* of Chirala (Pls. 1.30-1.32). The telia rumals (literally "oil dyed handkerchief") are about forty inches square, and are deep red and salmon in color with weft ikat motives in squares in the central area bordered in red. The oily smell which is characteristic of the older pieces, and which gives them their name, is a by-product of the alizarine dyes used. Synthetic colors currently in use give the textiles a slightly different color and do not have the oily smell.

Telia rumals, although called handkerchiefs, are actually used as lower garments by men of the lower castes in the area, and as shoulder cloths or head wraps for protection from the hot sun.

Designs in the center of each rumal are either geometric combinations of pink, red, brown, black and white squares (Pl. 1.30), or animals and plants (Pl. 1.31). More recently, machines such as clocks and airplanes have been used within squares (Pl. 1.32). The outlines of the geometric shapes are squared off or stepped, while those of animals and flowers have more natural curves.

The tradition of weaving telia rumals is not very old in comparison to other Indian textile traditions. It started in the late nineteenth century according to Mohanty and Krishna, who suggest (1974:97) that patola weavers from Gujarat were responsible for importing the technique to Andhra Pradesh.

Over the last fifty years, the popularity of the telia rumal has been superceded by that of ikat fabrics woven in Pochampalli (Pl. 1.33), a hundred miles or so northwest of Chirala. At present only a few families of weavers work in Chirala, while there are about four hundred houses of active weavers in Pochampalli, with three to four looms per household.

The weavers have branched out from the traditional rumal to saris, shawls, men's *lungis* (a lower wrapped garment), household textiles including placemats and bedcovers, and yardage. The color scheme has also broadened to include blues, greens, purple and yellow. In the latest stage of growth away from the geometric and animal motives available in the rumal, the weavers are making silk double ikat saris (Pl. 1.34) in blatant imitation of patola saris from Gujarat. These patola (as they are called in stores) take about two weeks to produce, have somewhat simplified designs, and use more colors in a single piece than the Gujarati originals. They cost about one tenth as much as a Gujarati patolu. They are made using essentially the same process but without the care and precision incorporated into an authentic patolu.

1.33 Sari
Detail of pallu, border, and body
Pochampalli, Andhra Pradesh,
before 1959
210½ x 47¾ in.

Warp and weft ikat, plain, supplementary warp and weft weave
Cotton; blue, white, red, green

1976.9.247/WRel 2835

1.34 Sari
Detail of pallu, border and body, 1979
Pochampalli, Andhra Pradesh
201 x 48 in.

Double ikat in imitation of patola, plain weave
Silk; orange, yellow, multicolor

Collection of Cynthia Cunningham Cort

1.33

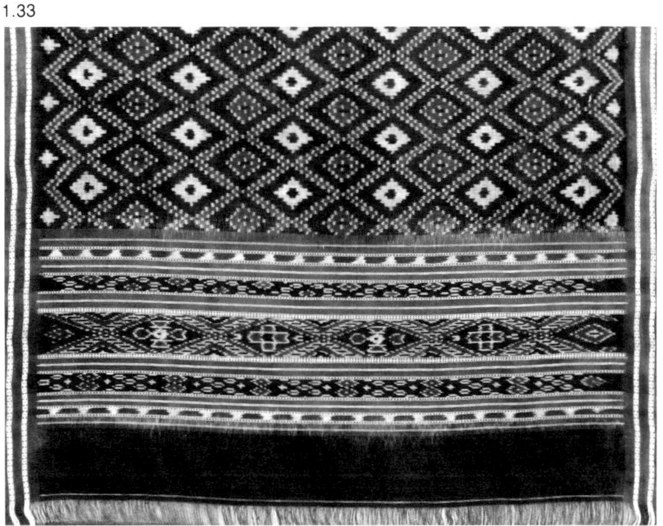

1.34

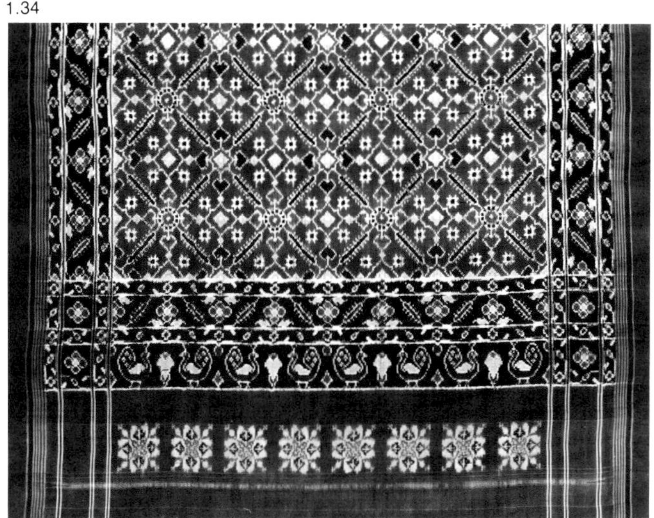

Embroidery, Mirrors and Beads: Elements of Rural Gujarati Textiles

Intricate embroidery embellished with mirrors is a hallmark of rural Gujarat, in northwest India, as well as the neighboring state of Rajasthan and certain areas of Pakistan. Gujarat is one of the primary textile-producing states of India; its capital, Ahmedabad, is the national center of industrial textile production for internal needs and foreign markets. In rural villages, however, much textile work is done in the home. Mill and hand loomed cloth are often combined in a single outfit or garment of a village woman, who assembles the fabric into any one of a variety of garments or textiles, and turns each into a unique creation reflecting her religion, tribal group, social standing and personal taste. She achieves this through use of traditional needlewoman's skills learned from her older female relatives, combining silk and cotton thread, glass mirrors (called *abhla*), shells, beads, metal objects, buttons, and even seeds, assembled to create a dynamic visual and cultural statement in cloth.

Western Gujarat is primarily desert terrain, and the multicolor embroidery and shining mirrors of clothing and household textiles must create a luminous contrast to the barren surroundings in the tiny rural villages (called *gams*). Few of these rural clans have any chance of ever achieving great wealth in their lifetime. Most earn their livings as farmers or herders; others as small scale merchants or craftsmen. Cultural ties within regional caste subgroups, called *jatis*, are strong, and marriages usually take place between members of the same subgroups of a jati, called a *nat* (Elson 1979: 14). Because the herders are largely nomadic, it is somewhat difficult to pinpoint their exact home territory; for centuries subgroups have splintered off and migrated with their herds of sheep, goats or cattle, so it is not uncommon to find Muslim Bannis, for example, in several regions within or even outside of Gujarat.

Because of this ancient tradition of migration, we find that skills, designs and forms employed in textile arts have their origin for the most part outside of Gujarat. For example, the Rabari, a Hindu herding group, probably migrated to their present area of Kutch in the sixteenth century from Marwad in Rajasthan. Their needlework skills are attributed to association with the Mughal courts prior to that time. The mosaic stone inlay of Mughal architecture is likewise seen as the inspiration for Rabari designs. Today, mirrors are pressed into mud walls to decorate house interiors. The Rabari shepherds adapted the designs and techniques of courtly embroidery to fit their materials, "by adapting new stitches and modes of design, and abstracting the older motifs as they drifted further into the past," the Rabari gradually made mirrorwork "an integral part of being Rabari" (Frater 1975: 47). These courtly origins can be traced by frequent use of motives no longer common to Rabari life, such as great flowering trees, parrots, and peacocks, none of which thrive in the desert of Kutch. Certain textile forms, such as the *toran*, also have an ancient origin, which is discussed further below.

The mirrored and beaded objects in the Allen Collection are primarily from the Kutch, Surindernagar, and Saurashtra or Kathiawar regions of Gujarat; a few are from Sindh in Pakistan or were produced by Sindhi refugees living in India. Some of the main *jatis* in the Kutch region that create mirrorwork are the Hindu groups Ahir, Bansali, Kanebi, Rajput, Rabari, Bhardwad, Harijan; the Muslim Banni, who are eighteen groups including the Haliputra, Raisiputra, Mutva, Sumarah, Jehjah, Pathan, Samejah, Hingorah, and Node, as well as the Gracia and Dhanetah Jats, and the Baluch. Some of these jatis live in nearby Kathiawar or Saurashtra, but the primary groups in that area are the Kathi, the Mahajan (including Lohana), and the Rajput. In all areas professional embroiderers, or Mochi, also work but they use mirrors infrequently.

Recently mirrorwork has achieved popularity as a commercial and export item, with an unfortunate corresponding decline in quality. Unfortunate because for the rural tribes who create mirrored and beaded textiles, the objects have traditionally held significance beyond the decorative enlivenment of their surroundings. Certain specific items must be ornamented with mirrors and exchanged between individuals and families in connection with life passages, most specifically, marriage. The objects are customarily created by females as an important and irreplaceable component of the dowry. Although other elements of the dowry are given by the bride's family, such as jewelry, brass vessels or furniture, the dowry textiles must be created by the bride, with the training and assistance of her mother. For the wife will continue to be responsible for domestic textile production throughout her marriage; not the least of these responsibilities is teaching the traditional skills to her daughters (Elson 1979: 11-13; Frater 1975: 48).

In the past, child marriage was the rule rather than the exception, the wedding couple often being as young as ten. Although the bride and groom are now commonly about sixteen, child marriages do still take place. Therefore the embroiderer's craft must be learned by girls from a very early age, in order to be able to create sufficient textiles for the dowry by the time of marriage. Among some groups, such as the Rabari, the groom wears embroidered garments during the wedding, which are made by his female relatives. Among the Ahir, the groom's family gives mirror-embroidered clothing to the bride's family to seal the engagement, and a second set at the time of marriage. The bride and her family also contribute clothing and other goods (Elson 1979: 26). In addition to garments, certain household textiles are mandatory among many Kutch and Saurashtra clans. For Hindu groups such as the Ahir and the Rabari, among others, seven is the number of textiles commonly created: four types of wall hangings, two types of bags, and a quilt cover.

Perhaps the most distinctive object prepared for the dowry is a hanging textile called a *toran*. These objects are made in several different sizes and techniques. They are hung over or to the side of the doorway of a house (see Pl. 1.35). The customary form for the toran is a rectangle about four or five times wider than it is long, to which are appended seven or more pointed tabs a little shorter

1.35

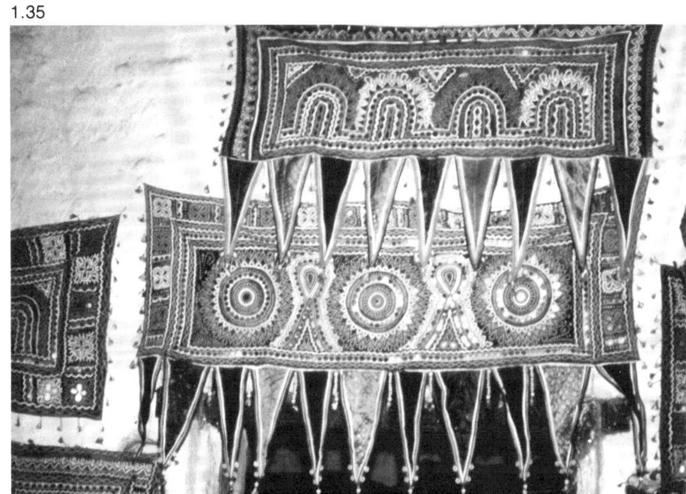

1.35 Interior of Rabari home with torans hung over doorway

1.36 Doorway hanging *(toran)*
Detail of left side of band
Rabari people, Kutch region, Gujarat, mid-late twentieth century
18½ x 34½ in.

Plain, twill, and satin weave; embroidered, with mirrors and metal discs
Cotton and silk; multicolor

EAI 1460

1.36

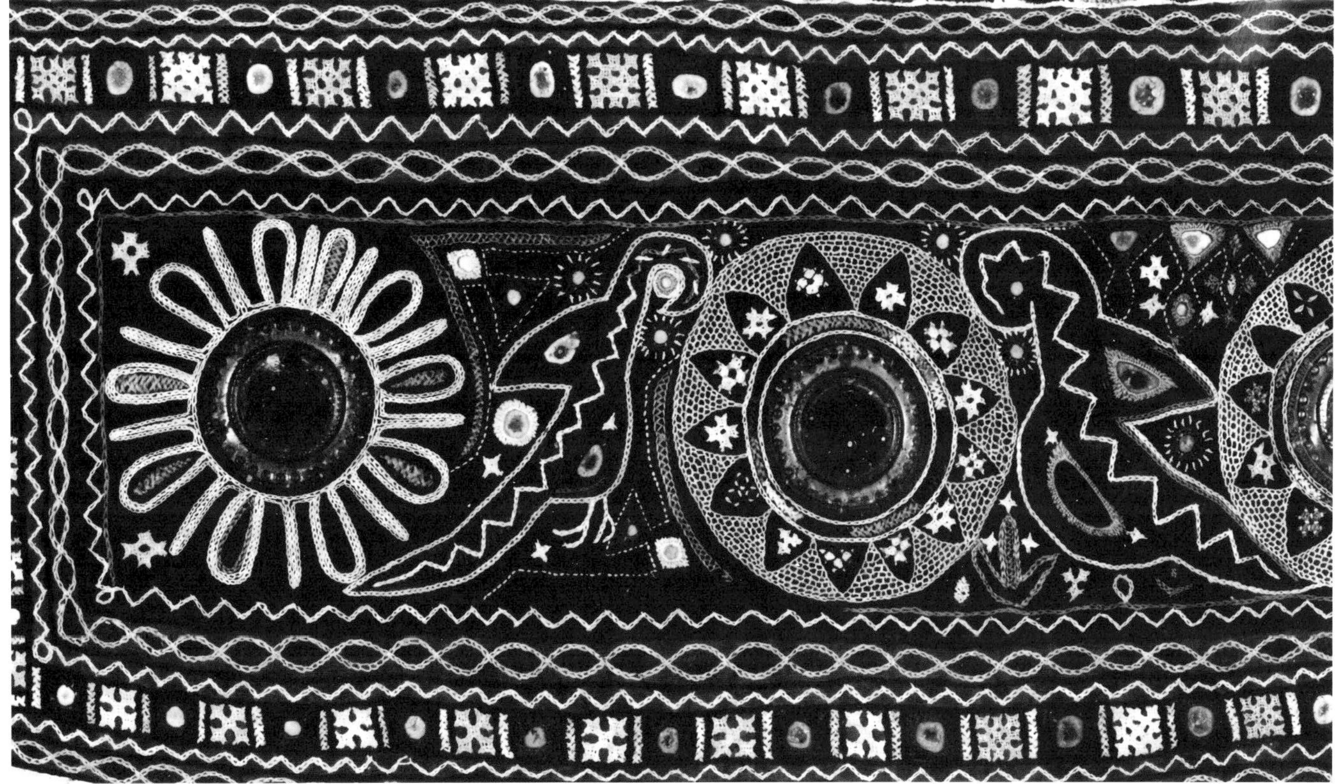

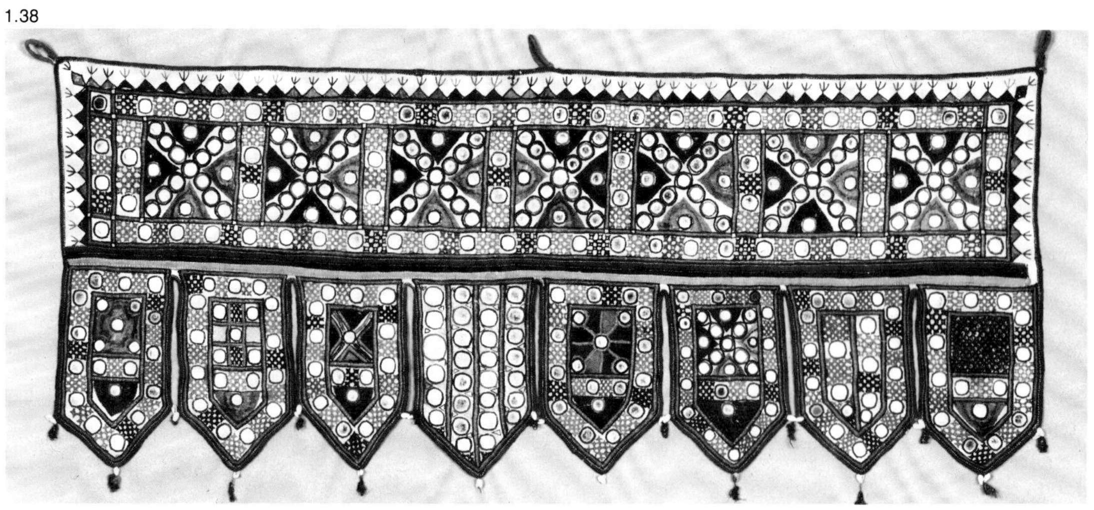

1.37 Doorway hanging *(toran)*
Rabari people, Kutch region, Gujarat,
mid-late twentieth century
23½ x 44 in.

Color illustration

Plain, twill and satin weave;
embroidered, with mirrors; tie dye,
warp ikat *(mushru)*
Cotton and silk; multicolor

EAI 1459

1.38 Doorway hanging *(toran)*
Banni style, Kutch region, Gujarat, late
twentieth century

17 x 42 in.
Plain weave; embroidered, with mirrors
and shells
Cotton and silk; undyed, orange,
multicolor

1976.9.21/EAI 1380

than the rectangle. The tabs may be done in the same technique or a different one from the rectangle. The shape of the toran itself is a link with the courtly roots of mirrored embroidery. An eighteenth century miniature painting in the Watson Collection (No. 2.98, not illustrated; Chandra 1968: no. 114) has a probable Bundi provenance, in present day Rajasthan state. The elegant scene shows a woman reclining on a patio, from the roof of which are suspended multicolor tabs. These tabs strongly resemble those seen on the toran, which suggests that this common household textile has its origins in Rajasthani architectural practices. This suspected cultural link is further borne out by the tie-dyed patterning on the woman's shawl or blanket, a technique commonly used on Rabari shawls, among others. Indeed the Rabari maintain their origins are in Marwad, in Rajasthan (J. Jain 1980: 47).

The Allen Collection includes a number of torans; most are primarily mirrorwork, while one is beaded. Of the four torans illustrated (Pls. 1.36, 1.37/Col. Pl. 1.4, 1.38 and 1.39), two are Rabari (Pls. 1.36 and 1.37/Col. Pl. 1.4). The smaller of the two (Pl. 1.36) features typical Rabari designs of parrots, several types of flowers, and trees, all within a border of lines of zigzags, lozenges, interlaced crosses and mirrors, with a more elaborate zigzag outermost, as shown in the detail. All these are executed in mirrorwork with a variety of stitches used. The tabs, however, are in plain or tie-dyed fabric.

The common parrot design shows a bird present only in the memory of the Rabari, for it dwells in the jungle and not the desert. Here it appears in a clearly delineated form. Its head, wing and belly are filled in with appropriately shaped mirrors. The beak, body and tail are decorated with an embroidered zigzag pattern and its feet are clearly depicted in embroidery. On many Rabari textiles, however, only a very abstracted parrotlike form can be made out, presented as a simple outline (see Pl. 1.40, near top center). This tendency toward extreme stylization in Rabari drawing is seen as reflecting their "close and prolonged contact with Muslim peoples" (Frater 1975: 53-55).

Two main types of large flowers are depicted on this toran. Each has a large round central mirror held in place with a blue or pink metal circle, which is stitched down around the edge. The more common technique is to secure the mirrors with a tightly executed buttonhole stitch. It is probable that the unusually large size of these mirrors dictated the use of the metal circles, which were also desirable for their decorative qualities. In the large daisylike flower on the left end of the toran rounded and straight petals alternate. The other three are more circular in form, with a netlike stitch used to outline the pointed shape of the petals, each of which is decorated with an interlacing stitch. (For further information on stitch terminology, see Irwin and Hall 1973: 201-08.) Small scattered blossoms or stars also appear, and in the upper right, a flowering tree.

Two types of zigzag designs are also featured, a simple embroidered one and a more complex one with mirror infill, each point topped with a smaller diamond. The zigzag design is known as *kungri*, and is meant to symbolize the top of the fortress wall, or by extension, protection of any sort (Frater 1975: 51-53, fig. 8). This protective association of the toran relates to its place above or beside the doorway. Its presence there is seen as auspicious for guests and inhabitants alike; as an alternative to or in combination with the use of textiles, wooden posts and lintels may be carved, or mud walls or furniture may be embossed with similar designs (Dhamija in *Marg* 1965: 48b; J. Jain 1980: 53-54, figs. 72-75).

On the larger toran (Pl. 1.37/Col. Pl. 1.4), although the use of machine stitching to assemble the components is prominently visible, the quality of the piece is nonetheless high, which is seldom the case. It features the same layout of embroidered band above tabs of other types of fabric. In this case, the tabs are made of silk using various techniques for patterning. One fabric is *mushru*, a warp-faced satin featuring a striped pattern. Small amounts of ikat patterning (see Chapter 3) are incorporated, creating subtle color changes within these stripes. This is particularly obvious in the second tab from the left and right. Rabari women use mushru fabric in their skirts and blouses as well (see Pl. 1.43). Another type of patterning used is tie-dye, in the two tabs on either side of the center tab. The green spots at the intersections of the diamond shapes are probably overpainted.

Flowers dominate the design field in the rectangular band here as in the smaller toran discussed above. Only one type of round blossom is seen, which features many small mirrors in concentric circles, alternating with embroidery, rather than the one large mirror used in the smaller toran. Between these larger blossoms are complex designs which could be a form of flowering tree, but more likely represent the village temple (Frater 1975: 52, figs. 11-13). Each small Rabari village has a temple to the Mother Goddess, particularly in the form of Momai Mata, riding a camel. (For further discussion of the Mata, see Chapter 1.) The rounded form seen here which resembles a flower is probably meant to indicate the domed top of the temple. This central band of patterning is enclosed in border similar to that on the smaller toran, but the outermost row is of flowers rather than kungri. Similar border patterns are used on Rabari skirts (Pl. 1.43). In the upper left corner is a small trident, also associated with the temple of the Mother Goddess. The small tassels of narrow strips of cloth bound with metallic or silk thread are commonly found on torans and sometimes on blouses or hats. This toran is lined in loosely handwoven fabric; the smaller Rabari toran is unlined.

The third toran illustrated here (Pl. 1.38) is quite different in motives but similar in format to the first two discussed. It is also from rural Gujarat, but probably was produced by one of the numerous Muslim groups living mostly in the Banni area of Kutch. It shows no recognizable figurative forms, relying exclusively on geometric patterning. The main color used for the designs and for outlining is orange, on a white background, together with numerous other strong bright colors of silk embroidery floss. The main design element in the large rectangular band is a diagonally quartered square, the crossed arms being composed entirely of mirrors. The border designs are less involved than on the Rabari pieces. The appended tabs are all decorated with mirrorwork also, in a number of geometric patterns all outlined in orange. Tiny shells and tassels are appended to the corners of the tabs.

Elson says that of the Banni Muslim clans, only the Jehjah and Kaskalee make torans as part of the dowry. Numerous other items are apparent more important, with the preferable or auspicious number of objects for the marriage being twenty-one (Elson 1979: 69-70). No published illustrations of torans like the one in Plate 1.38 have been located; however the designs and techniques correspond to those on Jat skirts (*Marg* 1965: 46) and a *bokani* or turban band worn by a Meghval Banni man (J. Jain 1980: 103, fig. 167).

Many of the Muslims of Banni region are known as *maldhari*, meaning cattle owners. They raise cattle for milk but also for meat, which is not permissible for Hindus. In addition, many of them, particularly the Meghval, are leather crafters. Some Jat groups are maldhari, while others are engaged in farming for their livelihood (J. Jain 1980: 87).

The fourth toran illustrated here (Pl. 1.39) differs from the other three in that it is not embroidered at all, but is executed in beadwork technique. Beadwork is apparent a more recently developed craft than embroidery, to which it is closely related. It owes its origins at least in part to the availability of Italian beads, which were traded into India through Africa not before the early nineteenth century. The earliest bead artisans were probably the professional Mochi embroiderers (discussed below under Costumes) working in the Kathiawar or Saurashtra area. The figurative element in Kathi beadwork has continued to predominate, mixed in recent years with bolder geometric patterns, such as the swastika motif used as a frieze here. Opaque beads (*chidiya moti*) in white, blue, yellow and light green are combined with translucent ones (*sakaria moti*) in red, green, dark blue, and pearly white to provide visual variety. The entire piece is backed in pink cotton. Each pendant of the toran features a different design, and backed with sheets of red or gold metal foil for added luster.

The techniques of beadwork, referred to by Dhaky as knitting, is more accurately termed netting. The beads are strung onto cotton thread and worked in sequences of three or more creating the pattern in small diamonds. The edges of the designs are therefore always angular. (This discussion is indebted to the work of M.K. Dhaky, in Nanavati's *The Embroidery and Beadwork of Kutch and Saurashtra*, 1966: 61ff.).

In addition to the torans shown here, another type is made by the Kanebi. Rather than a band with dependent tabs, it is an inverted V-shape made in one piece (see Elson 1979: fig. 17).

Several other types of wall hangings are important in rural Gujarat and are commonly used for major dowry textiles. One such hanging is called a *sankia*. This is one of a pair of textiles placed on either side of a doorway. The "L" shaped projection at the bottom points away from the door. Sankia are usually used in combination with a separate toran above the door, or made in one piece with it (*sakh-toran*), especially when made in beadwork (Nanavati 1966: Pls. 93-95). A pair of sankia in the Museum of Cultural History–UCLA (not illustrated here; see Elson 1979: fig. 14) features designs of women, elephants, flowers and birds. It was made by the Ahir, a Hindu farming group living in Kutch, whose designs and techniques are extremely similar to those of the herding Rabari groups; the Ahir were reportedly cattle herders in the past and trace their origins to "the cowherd god Krishna" (J. Jain 1980: 72-74). Similar-shaped textiles are made by a subgroup living in Saurashtra, the Boricha, which lack the appended tabs, as do those made by the Kanebi of Saurashtra (J. Jain 1980: fig. 110; Nanavati 1966: pl. 58).

1.39a

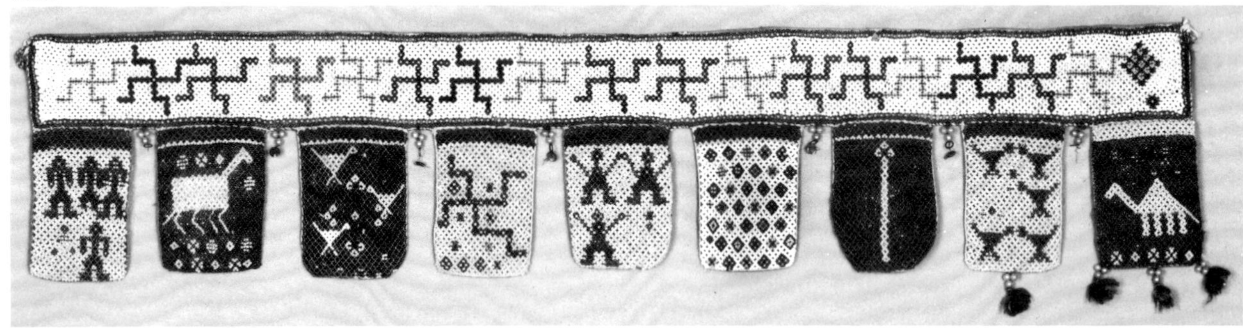

1.39b

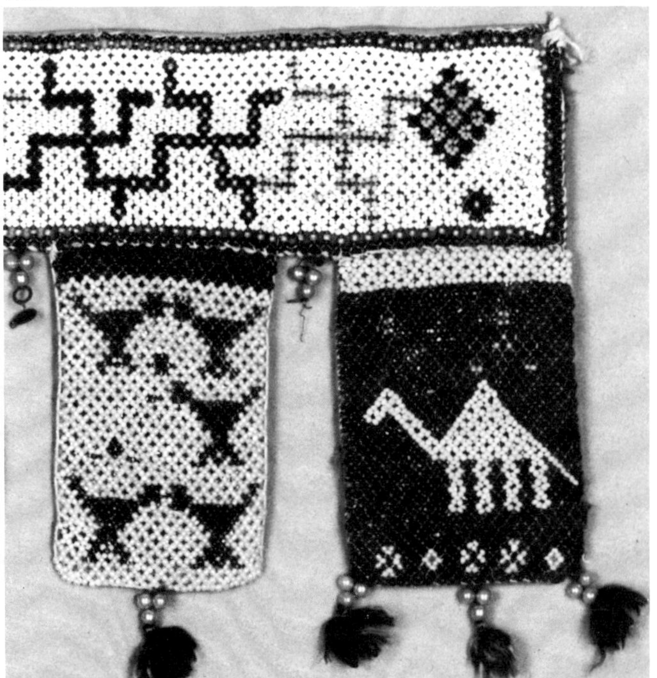

1.39 Doorway hanging *(toran)*
a, overview; b, detail of right two tabs
Kathi people, Kathiawar region,
Gujarat, mid twentieth century
7½ x 37 in.

Netted with beads
White, multicolor

1983.6.2

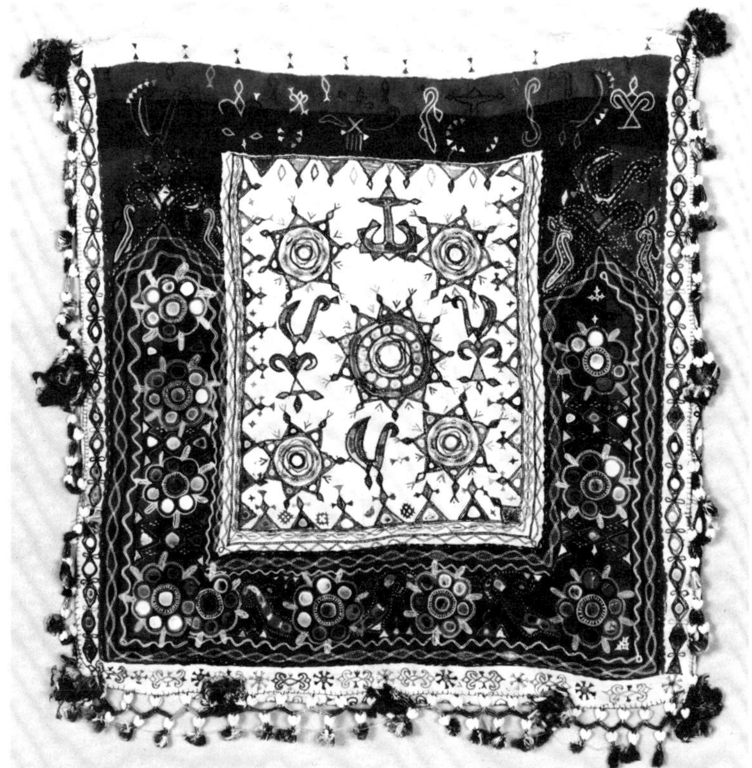
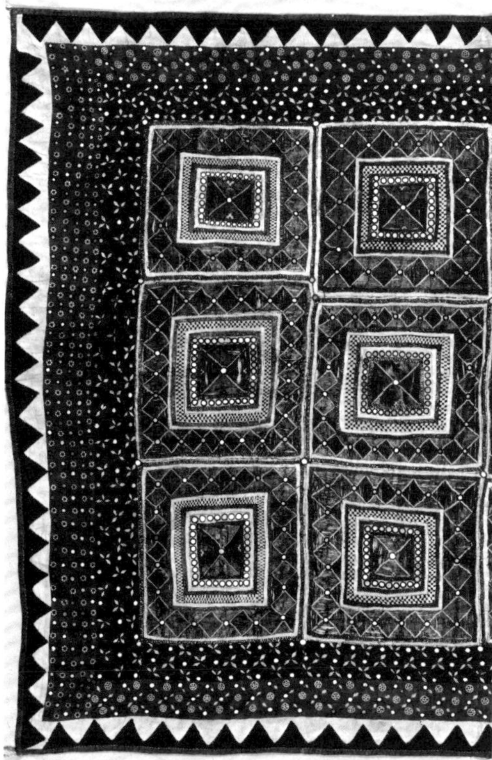

1.40   1.41

Another textile hung in the home is the *tarpudio*, which is hung over windows. A tarpudio in the Museum of Cultural History–UCLA (not illustrated here; see Elson 1979: fig. 16) was made by the Kutch branch of the Kanebi, another Hindu farming group; it is one textile contributed by the bride and her family toward the wedding. Among the Ahir, like the Kanebi, the groom's family also must contribute embroidered clothing and other items to the dowry. The designs used by the Kanebi are also similar to those of the Ahir; this tarpudio features flowers, parrots and peacocks. Although mirrors are not used here, they are featured in many Kanebi textiles.

Besides textiles in unusual shapes like those pictured here, perhaps the most common shape is the simple square, which is called *chakla*. Bags in square shapes are also common, such as the bag called *kothali*, illustrated in Plate 1.40. It was made and used by a Rabari bride, who used it as a container in which to transport her other dowry textiles to her new home with her husband. The kothali is heavily ornamented with embroidery and mirrors, and trimmed with shells, beads and tassels. Another notable feature is its pieced construction; in some Gujarati *jatis*, patchwork textiles are more important than mirrorwork. Sometimes kothali are quilted as well as embroidered (J. Jain 1980: 56, fig. 82). The traditional Rabari designs of flowers, parrot, peacock, temple, and tree are all seen here; a trident represents the local goddess (Frater 1975: 51-53, fig. 8). In addition, the design of a woman carrying a pot on her head appears, a common sight in Indian villages and depicted in many art forms (cf. Pl. 1.6a, upper register just below top border), but among the Rabari its use is restricted to the kothali; living beings are sometimes depicted on household textiles but rarely on clothing. The layout of the designs is the same on both sides of this bag, but the actual motives used vary somewhat.

Closets for storage are largely unknown in Indian homes; chests or wardrobes are commonly used for such purposes. In Kutch and Saurashtra, quilts, cloth mattresses and other textiles not currently in use are often piled on open shelves of stone or wood against one wall. This pile is usually covered with a large quilt cover, which is either embroidered or quilted or some combination of the two depending on the group. Among the Kathi of Saurashtra, this cover is called an *ulech* (Nanavati 1966: 53, Pl. 53). A Mahajan style Kathi ulech is illustrated in Plate 1.41. An almost identical piece illustrated in *Indian Embroideries* (Irwin and Hall 1973: 115, no. 161, Pl. 68B) is described as a

1.40 Dowry bag *(kothali)*
Rabari people, Kutch region, Gujarat, mid-late twentieth century
28 x 28½ in.
Plain weave; embroidered, with mirrors, beads and shells
Cotton; white, black, red, multicolor

EAI 1461

1.41 Quilt or canopy *(ulech* or *chandarvo)*
Mahajan people, Kathiawar region, Gujarat, c. 1900
70 x 54 in.

Plain weave; embroidered, with mirrors, and appliquéd
Cotton and silk; dark red-violet, yellow, dark blue, red

EAI 871

canopy (*chandarvo*). Another very similar piece is shown as part of a Kathi interior recreated in the Shreyas Folk Museum (J. Jain 1980: col. pl. facing 6) but used as a bedcover. Jain states that the Kathi women made ulech, but translates this as ceiling cloth (*ibid.*).

Kathi embroidery, whatever its ultimate use, is readily discernible from that of other nearby groups. First, the mirrors used tend to be much smaller than those used by most other mirror-workers, and are generally incorporated into simpler designs, such as diagonal lines or squares. Although many stitches are used, satin stitch tends to predominate, and is used here for the large, quartered squares, which are embroidered with deep red silk floss. As Irwin and Hall have pointed out (1973: 115), although only one shade of red is used, "the play of light over the sheen of the silk gives the effect of more than one tone of red." The central design of squares is surrounded by several rows of patchwork and applique, in dark blue, red, and a white and blue zigzag outer border. The entire textile is lined with hand block printed fabric.

Costumes

In addition to household textiles, women in rural Gujarat produce and, for the most part, continue to wear mirror-embroidered clothing. For men, the wearing of mirrorwork is largely confined to weddings and other ceremonial occasions. With the exception of a few hats, the Allen Collection contains almost exclusively women's clothing. Also, besides garments for humans, elaborate animal trappings are produced for horses, bullocks, and camels, such as the small band shown in Plate 1.42. This may have been used as a knee band by a camel, possibly during a wedding procession (J. Jain 1980: col. pl. facing 88).

Throughout much of Gujarat, distinctive garments are worn that are seldom seen elsewhere in India. Few women wear the sari except in the larger towns and cities. A blouse and skirt combination with a large shawl is more typical among most Hindu groups and some Muslims (see Pl. 1.43); other Muslim women wear dresses or tunics with trousers. Among those garments that are embroidered, the designs usually correspond to those on the household textiles, specific designs being associated with specific groups.

A gathered skirt called *ghaghro* is probably the most common item of dress for women. A ghaghro worn by Banni women is shown in Plate 1.44. It features borders of geometric designs executed with a number of different embroidery stitches, including chain, buttonhole, and a variant of feather stitch often called long-armed or Cretan (Thomas 1935: 56, 58). Mirrors are incorporated into these designs of circles, squares and diamonds worked in many colors of silk, among which orange

1.42

1.43

1.42 Band or animal trapping
Rabari style, Kutch region, Gujarat, mid twentieth century
4 x 8½ in.

Satin weave; embroidered, with mirrors, balls, seeds, and fringe
Silk; red, multicolor

1976.9.24/EAI 1394

1.43 Rabari girls

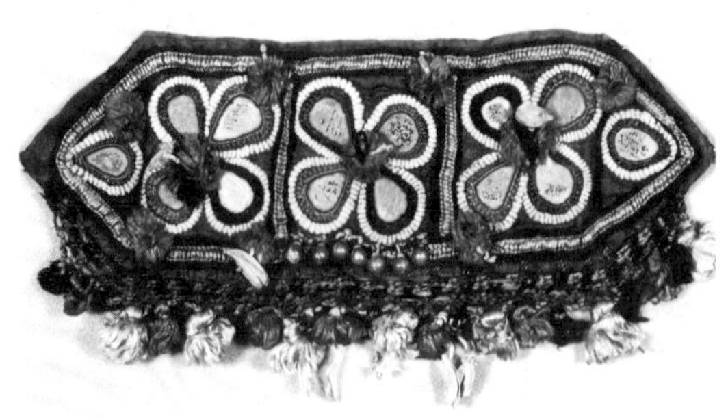

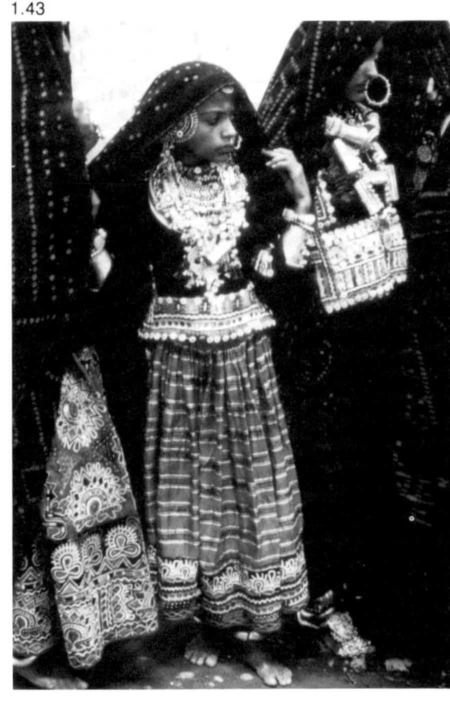

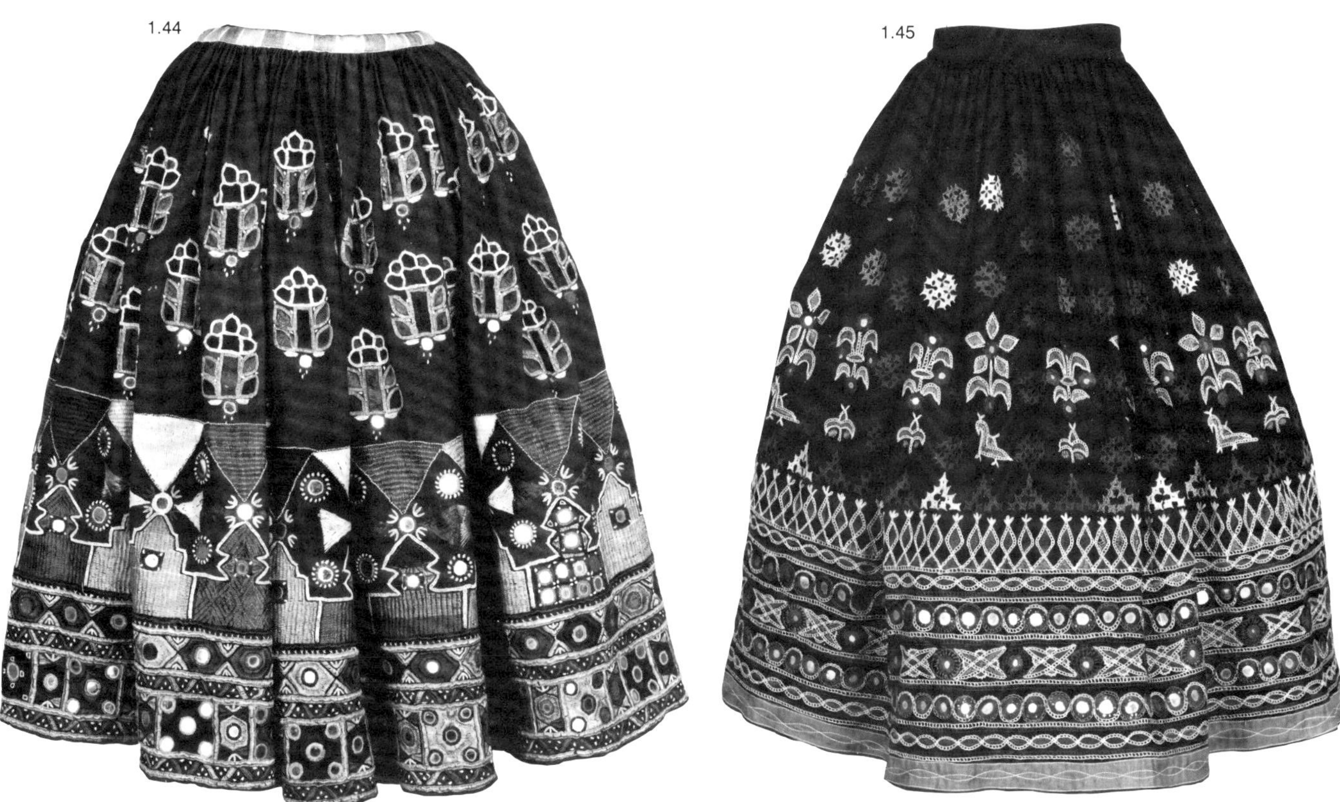

predominates, on a dark red heavy cotton ground. Some of the larger areas, such as a row apparent meant to represent buildings, are filled in with a couching stitch. Flowering trees repeat across the upper area. It is constructed of two pieces sewn together horizontally, gathered into a waistband, through which a drawstring is inserted and tied to secure the skirt. The Allen Collection contains three other textiles with almost identical embroidery; they were made into wall hangings by assembling parts of skirts.

Similar skirts are made and worn by Ahir women. The Ahir skirt illustrated here is hand embroidered but finished on the machine (Pl. 1.45). The lower half features designs of parrots, two kinds of flowers, trees, temples, an elaborate kungri, stylized butterflies, vines, and an ogee border, all embroidered in silk with mirrors inset, on a dark purple cotton ground. These motives are all outlined in orange with open chain stitch; the other embroidery colors are burgundy, green, and blue. The top half has repeated crosses done in interlacing stitch.

Skirts worn by Bhardwad women are very different in form, design and construction (Pl. 1.46). They are commonly made of black handspun wool woven in plain weave with red stripes in supplementary weft. Two long strips are sewn together along the selvages; no other construction is required for the skirt is simply wrapped around the waist. Top and bottom are interchangeable for both are decorated with pointilist patterns of trees, birds, houses and so forth, created by wrapping cotton threads around the warps. This is done primarily in white with accents of pink and turquoise. The remainder of the costume is composed of a mirrorwork blouse and a tie-dyed odhani with a deep mirrorwork border.

Not all embroidery is produced within the home. An important group of professional embroiderers earn their livelihood in Gujarat, primarily in cities, such as Bhuj in Kutch. These artisans are called *Mochi*, which also means cobbler. Plate 1.47 shows the design on a skirt made by Mochi embroiderers. It is worked in chain stitch on a dark blue satin ground. This type of work, often called *Bharat*, chain stitch is used to the exclusion of other stitches because a small hook, the *arhi*, often referred to as a tambour, is used to create the stitches. This allows for faster and much more regular production of stitches, but only chain stitch can be created. Its origin may be in leather workers' awls, for these fine embroiderers also worked on leather objects (Dhamija in *Marg* 1965: 48; Irwin and Hanish

1.44 Skirt *(ghaghro)*
Banni style, Kutch region (?), Gujarat, mid twentieth century
Waist 28, hem 148, waist-hem 29 in.

Plain weave; embroidered, with mirrors
Cotton and silk; dark red, orange, multicolor

1976.9.68/EAI 1386

1.45 Skirt *(ghaghro)*
Ahir style, Kutch region (?) Gujarat, mid-late twentieth century
Waist 28, hem 95, waist-hem 29½ in.

Plain weave; embroidered, with mirrors
Cotton and silk; dark purple, multicolor

1976.9.66/EAI 1384

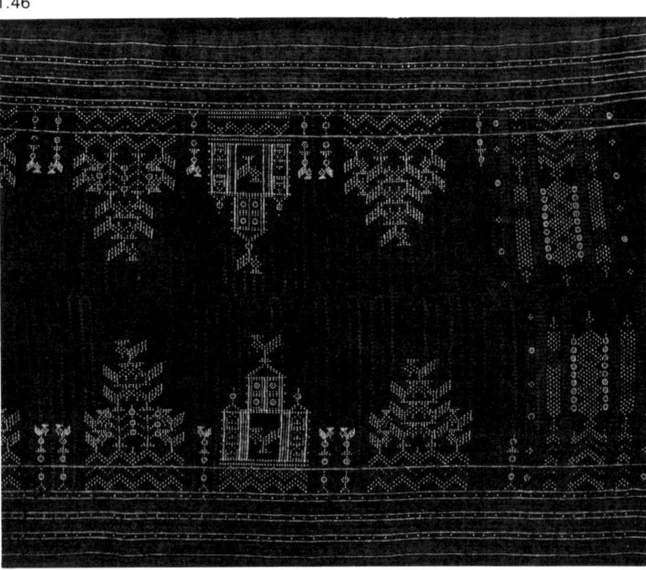

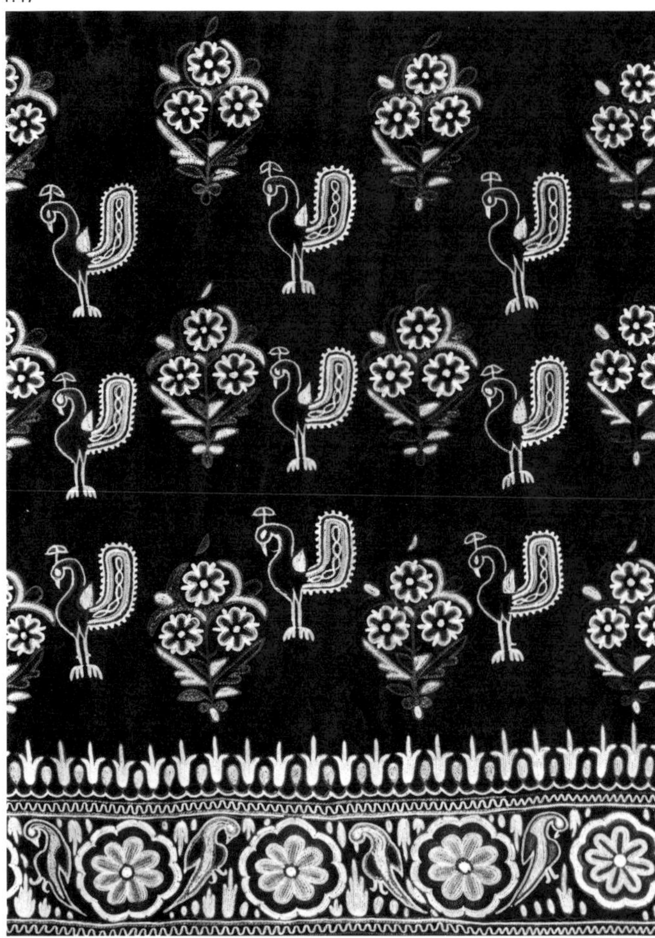

1.47

1970). Irwin and Hall cite (1973: 197) a nineteenth century account which states that Mochi embroiderers learned their trade from Muslim craftsmen: "About 250 years ago a Mussalman beggar, *fakir*, skilled in embroidery, is said to have come from Sind, and taught his art to some families of the shoe maker, *mochi*, caste who both in Bhuj and in Mandvi are famous for their skill" (*Gazeteer of the Bombay Presidency*, 1880: v. 5, 125-26).

Several types of blouses are also worn. Blouses may be densely embroidered and covered with mirrors, or may be made of the striped mushru fabric seen in the Rabari torans. The two blouses illustrated here are both from the Banni Muslim area, similar blouses are also worn by Harijan women (Elson 1979: 69-87). These blouses, called *coralo* among the Banni, are generally constructed from a number of rectangular pieces, are basically backless, and have little or no sleeves.

An exquisite coralo made by a Meghval Banni woman is shown in Plate 1.48. It is so densely embroidered that almost none of the purple or green silk ground fabric is visible. (The cotton lining of the blouse is also purple; in some places the silk is abraded and this lining appears to be the ground fabric.) The back of the blouse, however, which covers only the shoulders, is not embroidered, and is made of tie-dyed rust-colored cotton. The primary colors used for embroidery are orange and white, with black and many other colors used in varying, lesser amounts. The white flowers on the lower half are surrounded by orange; the tightly packed open chain stitches which create the flowers give them a third dimension by forcing the mirror centers to stand up from the cloth. Orange or black silk tassels are attached to the centers of the pinwheel forms in the central section, and along center front and at the lower back corners tiny white cowrie shells are attached along with the tassels. This type of flowers, pinwheels, and leaf or wing forms in alternation with single mirrors for the borders is particularly characteristic of Meghval work (J. Jain 1980: pl. 128), although used to some extent by other Banni groups as well.

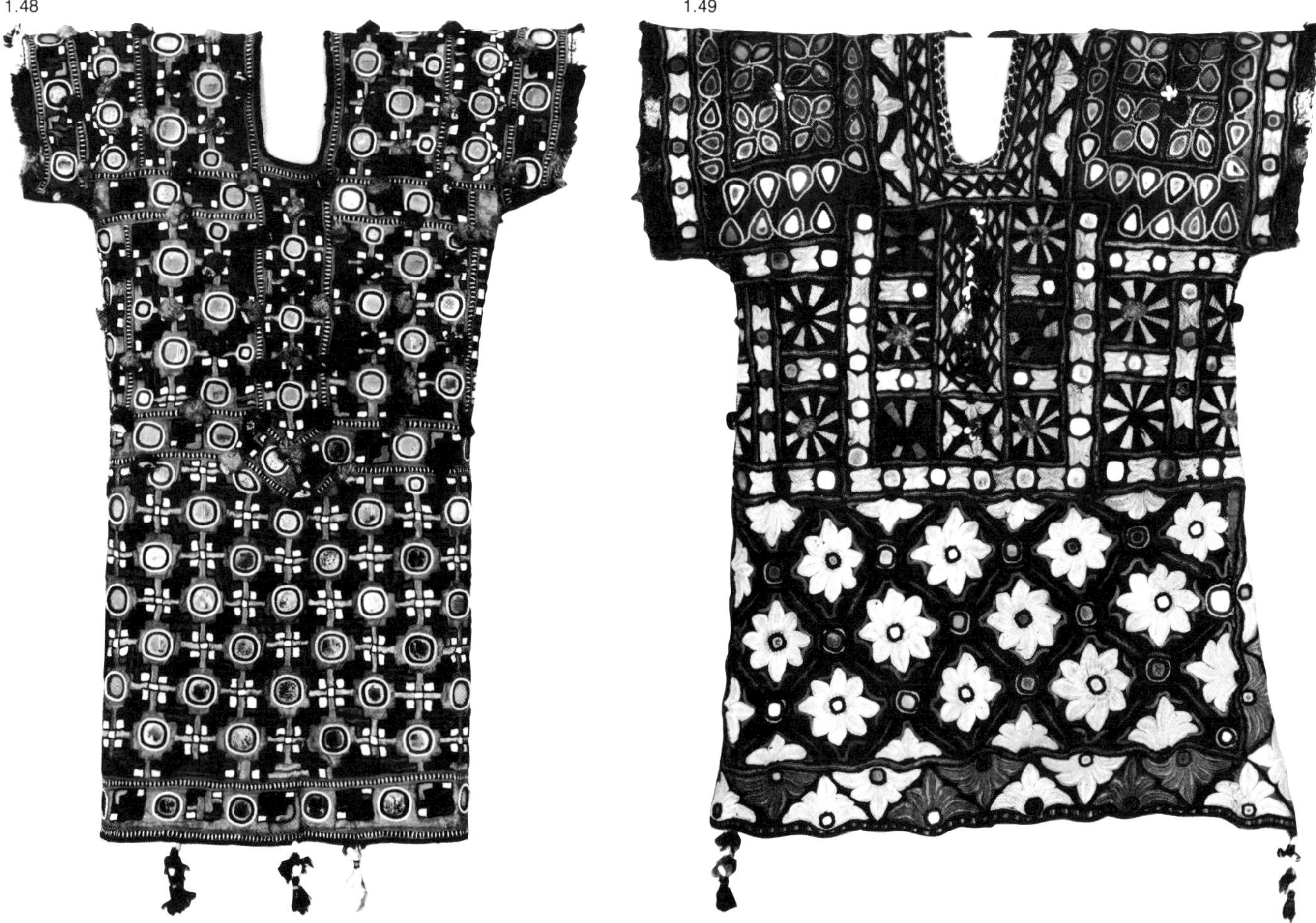

A blouse with similar construction and design layout is detailed in Plate 1.49. Jain illustrates a turban band with almost identical designs which he identifies as Meghval (1980: 221, pl. 167). Elson illustrates a Harijan woman wearing a very similar blouse, noting that although the Harijans are Hindus, they have long been closely associated with Muslim neighbors, from whom they "often borrow embroidery patterns and techniques. . ., and Muslim women have also adapted a number of Harijan designs and techniques for their own use" (1979: 84, fig. 85). The blouse in the Allen Collection has a green silk ground, which is visible in square areas surrounding the mirrors, and the interstices are filled with a very regular interlacement of purple, red and orange lines executed in satin stitch. Running, buttonhole, chain, and couching stitches are also used. In addition to mirrors, tassels and shells, tiny flower-shaped sequins and cardamom seed pods are also attached. The back shoulder area is made of tie-dyed cotton.

Among Jat and Baluch groups dresses take the place of blouse and skirt combinations. The dress illustrated in Plate 1.50 is from the Gracia Jat group; it is called a *churi* (Elson 1979: 41); Jain, however, calls the dress a *ghagho*, and classes all the jat groups as a subgroup of the Bannis (1980: 87-88). The red color of the dress and the minute precision of the embroidery stitches on the bodice identify it as Gracia; a woman embroidering a similar dress is shown in Plate 1.51. Among the Dhanetah Jats, black is much more common than red, and the embroidery uses larger, bolder designs similar to those of the Gracia. The Gracia women treat their garments with extreme reverence. "No man is ever supposed to touch it, and each Friday night at sunset women are expected to fold their unworn churis, pray, and wave a stick of burning incense over the garments" (Elson 1979: 54). In contrast to the tightly fitted shape of the Banni blouse, the churi is cut extremely full, with the extra fullness gathered into the bodice. It may be worn belted or loose.

1.48 Blouse *(coralo)*
Meghval Banni people, Kutch region, Gujarat, late nineteenth-early twentieth century
Neck-hem 24, bust 34, hem 21

Plain weave; embroidered, with mirrors, shells; tie dyed
Silk and cotton; purple, with orange, white, multicolor embroidery

1976.9.176/EAI 1392

1.49 Blouse *(coralo)*
Banni style, possibly Harijan, Kutch or Surindernagar region, Gujarat, mid twentieth century
Neck-hem 27, bust 28, hem 21 in.

Satin and plain weave; embroidered, with mirrors, seeds, spangles and shells; tie dyed
Silk and cotton; green with orange, multicolor embroidery

1976.9.23/EAI 1397

Numerous types of headgear are worn by the various groups inhabiting Kutch and Saurashtra. For men these include turbans, sometimes with embroidered bands tied in, or a square cloth or rumal tied in the back. Two types of hats are common for children, the *natiyo* and the *topi*. Women usually wear a very large shawl, which may cover them from head to foot, called *odhani*, *ludi*, or *chandhanni*.

An Ahir girl's hat, called a natiyo, is illustrated in Plate 1.52. Constructed of a square top piece attached to a long, rectangular back and short strip that goes across the forehead, it features typical Ahir designs of flowers, trees, and parrots. Narrow strips of contrasting silk cloth are worked into the borders, and shells, beads and white buttons are attached to each corner of the top.

The topi is another form of child's hat, usually worn by boys. The topi shown in Plate 1.53 features designs and colors almost identical to those of the blouse in Plate 1.49, so is most likely Meghval Banni as well.

A long, wide shawl is commonly worn over the head and shoulders by women in Kutch and Saurashtra. These may be made of wool or cotton depending on the group; some feature embroidery along the borders or as isolated motives, while others depend only on the printed or dyed designs of the cloth for their patterning. A number of groups wear printed odhanis which are made in imitation of tie-dye technique, or sometimes with floral prints. This type of printing has been in use since the fifteenth century (Gittinger 1982: fig. 14, 29). The genuine or imitation tie-dye patterns are common among the Ahirs, Rajputs, Jats, Banni and Khatrie (Elson 1979: Col. Pls. IV and VIII, figs. 22, 45, 48 and 119). A woolen shawl worn by Daysee Rabari women is detailed in Plate 1.54. Elson

1.50 Dress *(churi* or *ghagho)*
Gracia Jat people, Kutch region, Gujarat, mid-late twentieth century
Neck-hem 50, waist 40, hem 183½ in.

Plain weave; embroidered, with mirrors
Cotton; red with white, multicolor embroidery

1983.10.1

1.51 Gracia Jat woman embroidering dress

1.50

1.51

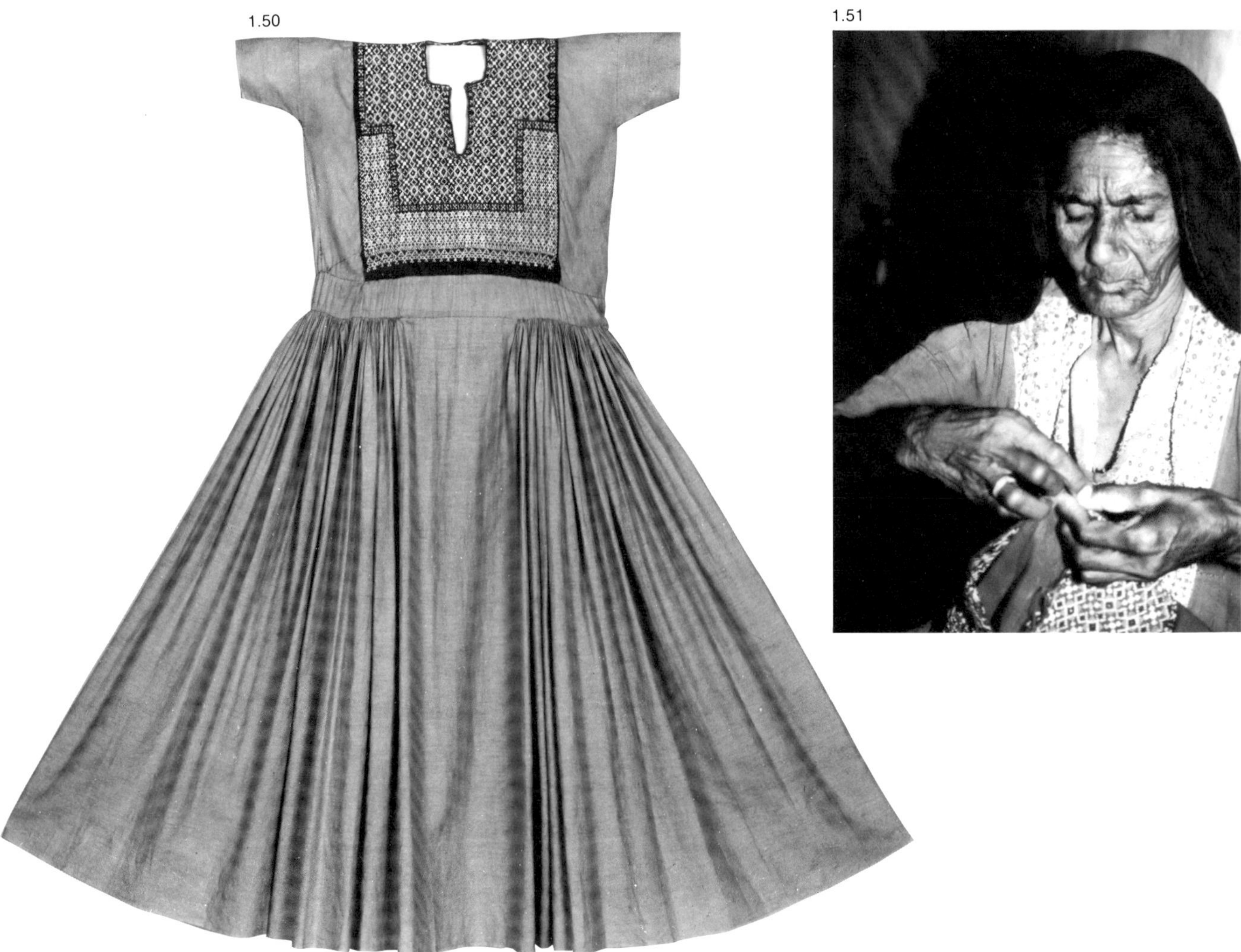

1.52

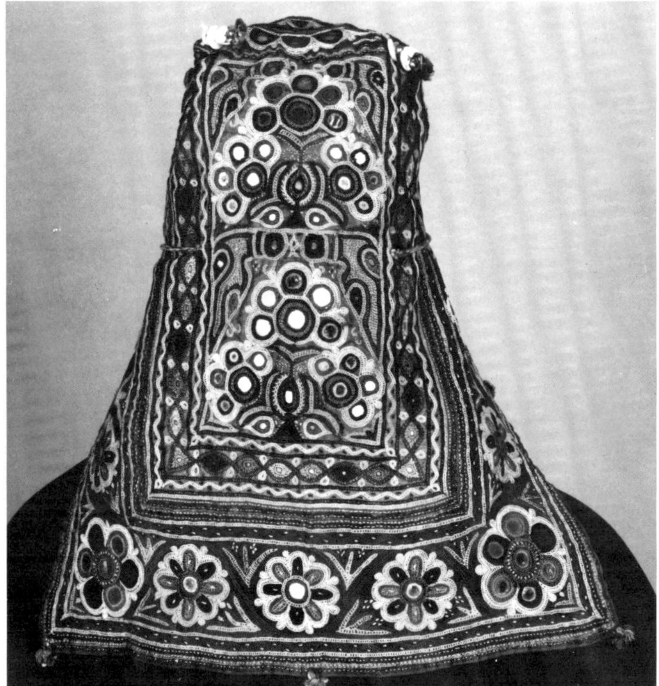

1.53

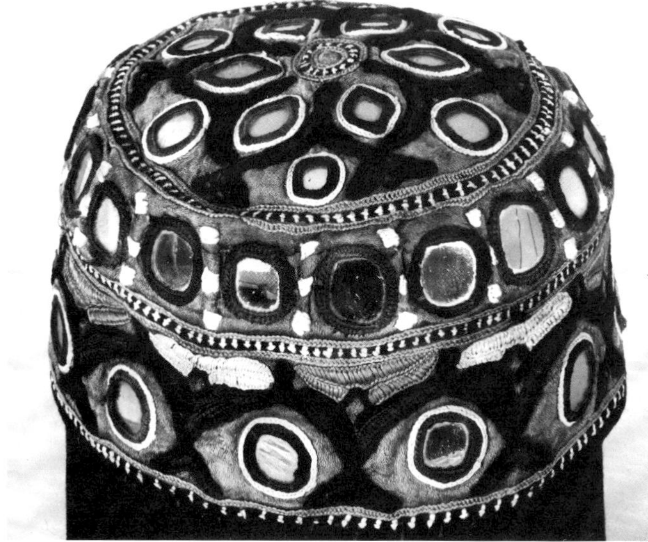

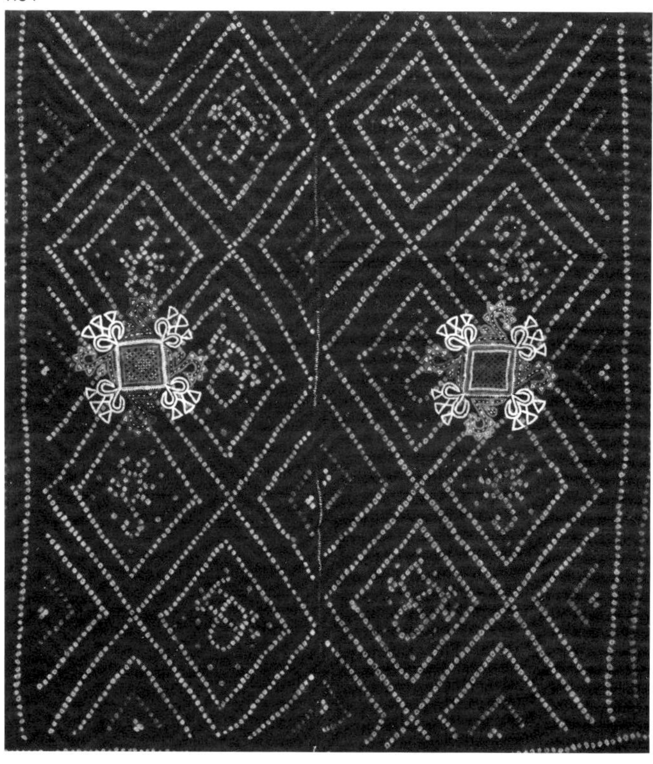

1.52 Girl's hat *(natiyo)*
Rabari people, Kutch region, Gujarat,
mid-late twentieth century
Length 14, diameter 5 in.

Satin and plain weave; embroidered,
with mirrors, buttons, shells, beads
Silk; blue, with multicolor embroidery

EAI 1458

1.53 Boy's hat *(topi)*
Banni style, Gujarat, mid twentieth
century
Satin weave; embroidered, with mirrors
Silk; green, with black, multicolor
embroidery

1976.9.9/EAI 1382

1.54 Woman's shawl *(odhani* or *ludi)*
Detail of center
Daysee Rabari people, Kutch region,
Gujarat, mid twentieth century
111 x 48 in.

Plain and supplementary weft weave;
tie dyed; embroidered
Wool and cotton; dark brown and
orange, with multicolor embroidery

PRel 1491

(1979: 98-99, fig. 101) terms this an "*odhni*," while Jain (1980: 49-50) terms it a "*ludi*," using "*odhani*" for shawls made of fibers other than wool. The Daysee herd sheep, among other animals, as well as growing crops, and spin the woolen yarn for the odhani or ludi. However, other groups are responsible for the weaving and dyeing. The cloth is woven by Harijans, and the customary diamond grid pattern is tie-dyed in orange on a dark brown or black ground by Khatrie dyers (Elson *op cit*.); this shawl also features scorpion and bird designs. The resulting garment, made of two lengths seamed together along the selvedges, is then embroidered with isolated floral motives near the ends and center; the central motives are seen on the back of the woman's head when the shawl is worn (Jain 1980: 58, fig. 63). The brightly colored embroidery is done here in cotton floss, although silk is sometimes used; the loosely woven wool is backed with a piece of cotton fabric to give support to the embroidered area.

47

The North East Frontier Area

1.55 Bag
Gauhati, Assam, before 1959
28 x 14½ x 3½ in.

Warp faced plain and supplementary
weft weave
Cotton; white with multicolor

1976.9.218/WLI 2784

1.56 Bag
Detail of body
Khampti people, Lohit District,
Arunachal Pradesh, before 1959
29½ x 12¼ x 6½ in.

Warp faced plain and supplementary
weft weave
Cotton, black with purple and
multicolor

1976.9.216/WLFI 2775

1.57 Bag
Detail of center design
Lushai people, Assam, before 1956
33 x 15½ x 3½ in.

Warp faced plain and supplementary
weft weave
Cotton; red with bluish purple and
multicolor

1976.9.103/EAI 1406

The people of the North East Frontier area differ in many respects from most of the rest of India. The North East Frontier is that jut of land separated almost completely from the Subcontinent proper by Bangladesh. The area is also bounded by Burma, China, Tibet, and Bhutan. The people are usually termed Indo-Mongoloid racially; their languages are considered subgroups of the Tibeto-Burman family, and there is considerable variation of dialect from tribe to tribe. These people have lived in the mountains and intermontane valleys for thousands of years; in ancient Indian literature such as the *Vedas* and the *Mahabharata* they are called the "Kirata" or hill people. The recent recorded history of the peoples is scanty, and very little predates the British presence in India. This area has at times been under control of other countries than India, especially the near neighbor Burma.

The seven states that now comprise the North East Frontier area of India are relatively new as political entities, but the people who inhabit them are heir to an ancient tradition. The many small cultural groups that live in the hills and valleys of this rugged terrain are generally referred to as tribes. The modern units are the states Assam, Manipur, Nagaland, Tripura, Meghalaya, and the territories Arunachal Pradesh and Mizoram. Each state is home to a number of tribes, and some tribes inhabit more than one state. Political boundaries have shifted over the centuries and even during this century one finds reference to the same tribe as living in different states. The Naga tribes are a good example: they may be located in Nagaland as one might expect, or in Manipur, Assam or Arunachal Pradesh. However, before 1963 Nagaland did not exist as a political entity, part of what is now Nagaland was formerly part of the North East Frontier Agency which in 1972 became the modern territory of Arunchal Pradesh, and in nineteenth-century sources the entire North East Frontier area may be referred to as Assam.

There is diversity in terms of religious beliefs as well, including Hindus, Christians and Muslims; Buddhism apparent made inroads here only in the very far north near Tibet. The indigenous Naga religion is animistic. Christianity was introduced by missionaries attracted by the reputation of Naga tribes as fierce headhunters in need of being converted to peace-loving ways. This reputation earned the Nagas a great deal of autonomy under both British and Indian rule.

1.55

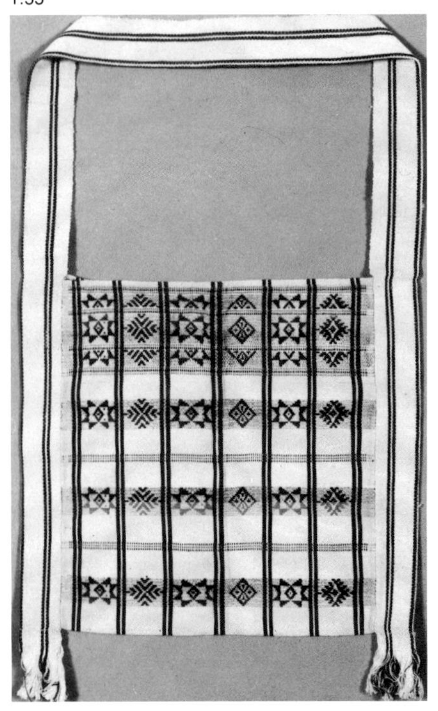

1.56

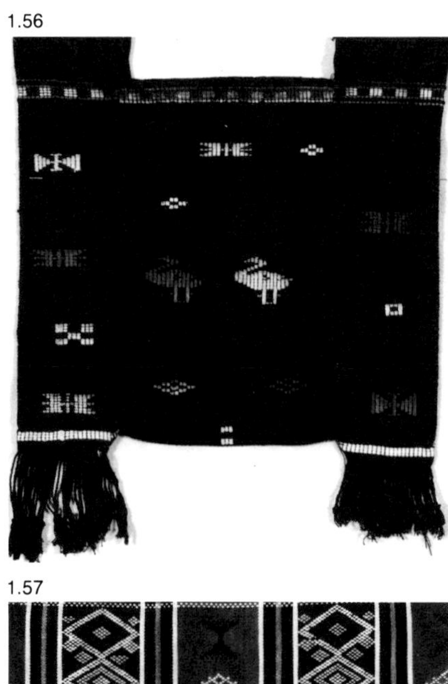

1.57

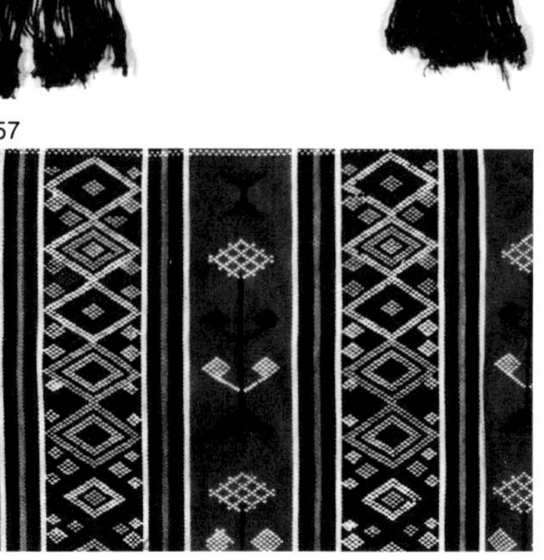

1.58

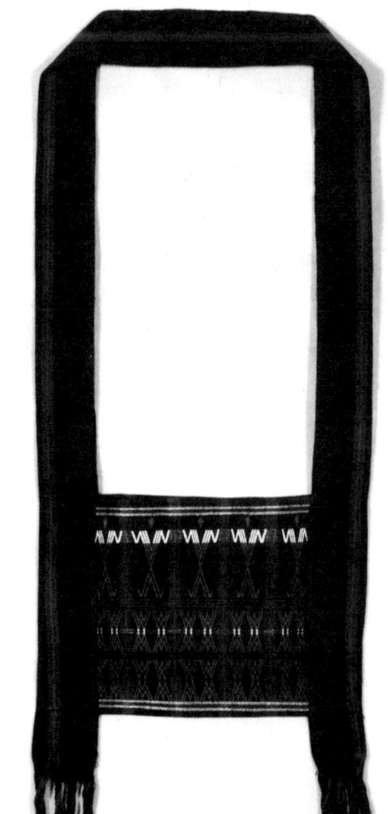

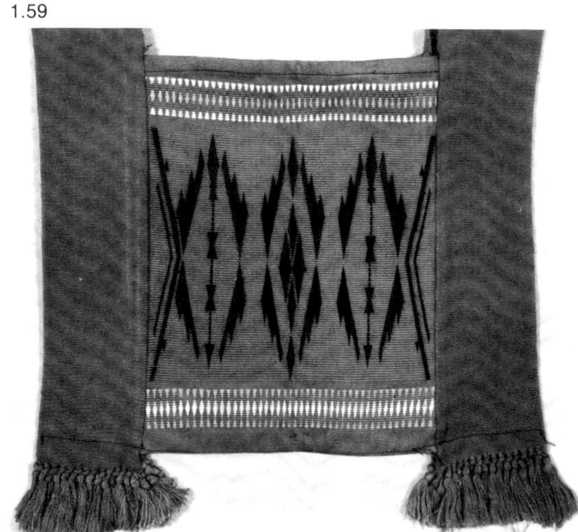

1.59

1.58 Bag
Ao Naga style, Nagaland, before 1959
37 x 12 x 4 in.

Warp faced plain and supplementary
weft weave
Cotton; blue with green, red, and
yellow

1976.9.219/WLI 2767

1.59 Bag
Detail
Angami Naga style, Nagaland, before
1960
25½ x 12 x 5½ in.

Warp faced plain and supplementary
weft weave
Cotton; red, multicolor

WLI 956

Early information about costume and textile arts comes from British travelers and administrators in the nineteenth century who were fascinated by the rugged quality of the mountainous terrain and its inhabitants. The standard ethnologies on the Naga were mostly written early in this century. The works of J.H. Hutton on the Sema and the Angami (1921a, 1921b), with J.P. Mills on the Ao (1926), and C. von Fürer-Haimendorf (1933) are particularly useful for descriptions or photographs of garments and textiles and their manufacture by Naga women. They comment on skill at weaving, basketry, and sometimes wood carving, largely to the exclusion of all other arts. These popular arts have continued to develop, and recently with boosts from the Indian government agencies, some North Eastern tribal textiles are being produced commercially rather than domestically. Until that intervention, almost all textile production was largely a domestic activity. In this part of India, weaving and embroidery are exclusively the work of women; basketry on the other hand is done by men.

The costumes and textiles of the North East do not for the most part resemble those of the rest of India either in form or in design. Women do not wear the sari nor men the dhoti. Women's costume for most tribes consists of skirt, a shawl, an apron, and sometimes a bodice. Men wear either a loincloth or a larger kilt, in some areas a jacket, a shawl, a sash or belt, often a helmet, and sometimes leggings. Helmets, belts, and leggings are in many cases made in basketry techniques of cane. Most weaving is done on the backstrap loom, commonly featuring supplementary-weft patterning on a warp-faced plain weave ground; in Assam a frame loom with fixed heddles is used. Embroidery is sometimes applied after weaving is completed. Cotton is the most common fiber, wool is occasionally used today and was more so in the past, while silk is largely confined to Assam. As is true in many parts of the world, commercial yarns have largely supplanted handspun, and when yarn is hand dyed, the dyes are almost always synthetic rather than natural.

The designs of North East tribal textiles are distinctive as well, being largely composed of angular geometric shapes and patterns. Diamonds, triangles, zigzags, squares and rhomboids are combined in a great variety of ways. Colors are often strong and bright, the most common being black, red, and blue, woven in stripes with white, yellow or green accents. Tribal identity could formerly be determined by these patterns as could status within the tribe, but these distinctions no longer hold up well as tribal weavings are often produced commercially for sale to other tribes or foreign markets. Bags are a popular commercial item for almost all tribes (Pls. 1.55-1.59).

Nagaland

Naga is a general term applied to fourteen tribes in Nagaland and two tribes now part of Manipur. It is probably derived from the Sanskrit *nag*, "mountain" and was given to the mountain dwellers by plains people. However, within this large group most tribes do not call themselves Naga but use the name of their individual tribe or a regional name for a group of tribes (P. Singh 1977: 8-9). The Naga tribes of Nagaland are: Angami, Ao, Chakhesang, Chang, Khemungan, Konyak, Phom, Pochurg, Rengma, Sangtam, Sema, Yimchunger and Zeliang; in Manipur, Naga tribes are Kabui and Tangkhul.

Textiles play an important role in Naga society and differences in clothing are important markers of life's passages. As Verrier Elwin, a leading authority on North Eastern tribal art and culture, explained: "The importance of weaving to the tribal mind is illustrated by the numbers of words there are for every thing to do with it, even when the general vocabulary is small" (Elwin 1959: 35). There are a number of beliefs associated with cloth. Among most Naga groups, only women are allowed to weave, but they may not weave during that time when their husbands have gone off to fight. "If this prohibition is not observed, the husband will get his legs caught in a tangle of creepers when going through the jungle, and thus meet with an accident" (Hutton 1921a: 51); nor should a woman weave when she is pregnant (*Census of India 1961* v. III pt. VII-A:6). Hutton further observed that among the Sema a woman's garment, once worn, must not come in contact with a man's weapon, lest the weapon lose its effectiveness (*ibid.*: 18).

There is apparent little variation in design based on garment use; that is, a wrap-skirt or shawl would have the same designs although in general the skirt is several inches smaller than the shawl in both length and width and the woman's garments tend to be smaller than the man's (*Census of India 1961* v. XXXIII pt. VII: 21).

The absolute simplicity of construction of North East tribal garments makes them extremely versatile in application. This is especially true for the shawl, a large rectangle that can be worn in a number of ways. Mills and Hutton (1926) called this garment a "bodycloth" and give a number of names of types of the cloth based on its design but do not provide a basic name for the garment. In Assamese it is termed "chaddar."

The simplest way of wearing the cloth, and probably the most useful for warmth, is to drape it around the shoulders, leaving one end longer; this end is then thrown back over one shoulder. If the cloth is sufficiently long and drapes well, the weight is probably enough to hold there for moderate activities. However, there are a number of other more ingenious ways to wrap and tie the cloth for additional security, style, or display of the pattern. Women sometimes wrap the shawl around their body, bring one end from back to front under one arm and up over the other shoulder. The opposite end is brought to the front under the other arm, and two corners are tied over the opposite shoulder (see Barkataki 1969: pl. 7). The man's shawl may be folded in half across the width, wrapped from side to side under one arm with the fringed ends at the top, and all four corners tied over the opposite shoulder. The shawl is then secured at the waist by a belt (see Ripley 1955). A third method is to fold the shawl lengthwise two or three times until it is a narrow band about eight inches wide. It is then wrapped back to front at the waist, crossed over in front, brought to the back over the shoulders and crossed over again, brought to the front around the waist and tied. Hutton describes another method used by the eastern Sema Nagas, known as *aghaopucho*, "'bird garb,'. . .because used when going into the jungle to snare birds. . .", It is a complicated arrangement in which the shawl is wound around the body, folded and crossed in the back, with two corners knotted at the waist in front, the third corner coming over the right shoulder and the fourth under the left arm, and these two corners knotted over the chest; over this is worn a belt (Hutton 1921a: 15, pl. facing 37). Plate 1.60 and other published illustrations reveal that there are almost as many ways to wrap and tie this all important garment as there are pattern variations in the design.

Certainly the oldest and possibly the most complex Naga piece in the Allen Collection is a man's shawl or loin cloth/kilt, which dates to the late nineteenth or early twentieth century. Woven as are most Naga textiles on the backstrap loom, it is attributable to the Kalyo Kengyu, Konyak or closely related Chang people who live in the Tuensang district of Nagaland (Pl. 1.61/Col. Pl. 1.5). The cloth is very dark blue, with red squares woven in the central area and light blue stripes alternating with the dark blue in the warp direction along the borders parallel to the selvedges. Two large concentric circles evenly arranged all over the field, and a human figure within a double V with curved ends are formed of small cowrie shells sewn to the cloth. This cloth is undoubtedly connected with headhunting raids for which the Konyak and Chang were well known. The circles may symbolize the moon or human heads, for the raids on neighboring villages were made under light of full moon (Hutton 1927: 377f., cited in Elwin 1959: 48). Mills and Hutton found that the Ao used similar cloths, called *Zuporisu* or *Zubasu*, and that this type "can only be worn by a man who has burnt the whole or part of an enemy's village, and, unlike most insignia of valour, the right to wear it cannot be bought from the village elders. The daughter of such a man may wear circles of cowries on her cloth on dance days" (Mills and Hutton 1926: 38).

Although all weaving was done by women, only the man who actually used the cloth could sew on the cowries. Other designs are also done in cowries, most commonly three straight lines at the lower edge. Should a fourth row be added, among the Angami and Chakhesang it could symbolize extramarital liaisons (Hutton 1921a, cited in P. Singh 1977: 49, 57, Pl. 17). Dancers wearing garments with cowrie shell designs are shown in Plate 1.60 (also Elwin 1959: facing 40; and Elwin 1961: facing 81). The sex-linked suitability of particular items of decoration, especially cowrie shells, varies from one Naga group to the next. In most cases, Hutton found, cowries were appropriate only for men because of their association with combat and headhunting, but among a few groups, wives of men entitled to wear cowrie-embroidered cloths were likewise so privileged (*ibid*.: 19; 1921b: 27).

The red squares on this cloth are probably executed in dog hair or goat hair, the red perhaps symbolizing fire or blood. Two very similar cloths are in the Musée Barbier-Müller, Geneva, one with green and yellow border stripes rather than light blue which Barbier explains as signifying the social status of the wearer (Barbier 1982: Pls. 32, 33).

The most interesting part of the design, and that which links it closely with major ceremonies of Konyak and Chang life, is the human figure within the curved V shape. The human figure may appear alone (as it does on the Barbier-Müller cloths) or within the curved V in other Naga art forms, or the V may appear alone or with another design such as a lizard or an elephant. Besides textiles, carved shell jewelry and painted wood pillars supporting *morungs* (lodges) or tombs may bear these designs (Barbier 1982: pl. 24; Elwin 1959: 149, 174; *Census of India 1961,* v. XXIII pt. VII: 38 ff). Beyond these applications, the curved V and human figure was tattooed on the chest of a warrior who had completed a headhunting raid (Pl. 1.62; see also Barbier 1982: 17, fig. 9). The curved V is

1.60 Konyak Naga dancers

1.61 **Wrapped man's garment**
Chang, Kalyo Kengyu or Konyak Naga, Nagaland, early twentieth century
62 x 40 in.

Color illustration

Plain and supplementary weft weave; with cowries applied
Cotton and hair; dark blue, light blue and red

1976.9.203/EAI 1401

1.62 Chang Naga man with tattooed design of horns

1.60

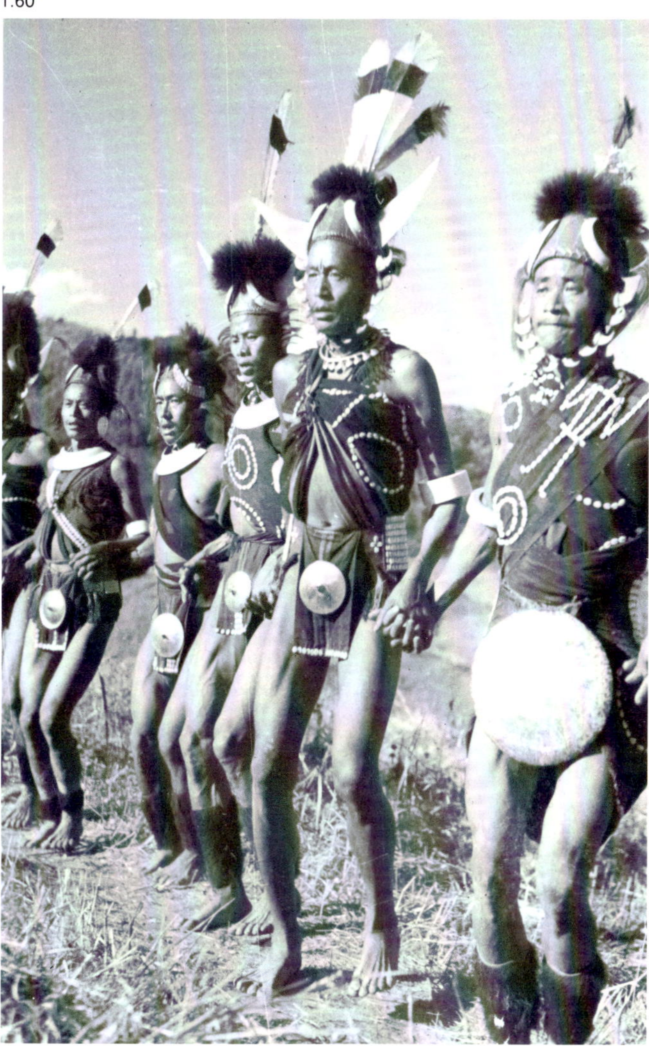

1.62

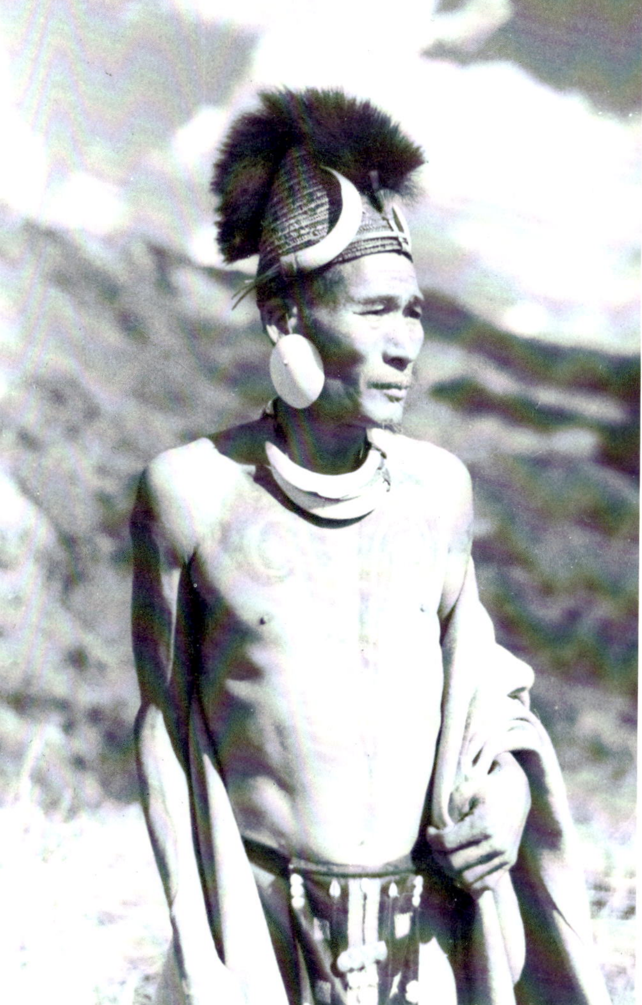

frequently described as symbolizing the horns of the *mithun* bison *(boas frontalis)*, an extremely important animal in Naga society. For a young Konyak Naga man, headhunting is only one of a progression of ritualized events including giving of feasts of merit and sacrificing of a mithun as necessary steps to attaining proper stature within his village and tribe. The mithun is so valued that it is even considered the alter-ego of a human in the underworld and, increasingly as headhunting has faded out, mithun sacrifices have become more important.

Another man's cloth associated with headhunting and related rituals is the warrior's shawl called *tsungkotepsu*, detailed in Plate 1.63. It is made by the Ao Naga for their own use and also for sale to the Sangtam Naga. The two tsungkotepsu in the Allen Collection are black, but dark blue is also used, with red stripes woven in the warp direction. It may be cotton or wool or both. In the center is a plain white cotton band which is then painted in black with specific designs, which represent important objects or images including human heads and mithuns, also roosters, tigers, and *dao* (axe or sword like weapons or tools). The black paint is made by mixing the sap of the *Tangko* tree, rice beer, and ash (*Census of India 1961,* v. XXIII pt. VII: 18). To the Ao themselves, this type of cloth was reserved for exclusive use of warriors who had taken a head and given a feast of merit (Mills and Hutton 1926: 37). To the Sangtams who purchased it from them, it symbolized the completion of an important cycle of giving three feasts of merit, after each of which another special textile could be worn, the highest honor being the right to wear the Ao tsungkotepsu (Elwin 1959: 50; P. Singh 1977).

Because the range of designs is limited, Naga textiles rely for impact on their combinations of designs in different colors and sequences. Recent breakdowns in social structures governing use of designs and establishment of government-operated centers where weavers produce many designs mean that it is not always possible to identify more modern textiles with a specific Naga tribe. Also, in the past it has been true that the same design would be used by several tribes, each of whom would assign it a different meaning. Recent interviews with weavers by various authors have revealed that even very old women from the same village cannot always agree on the meaning of a design. One Naga saying goes "a good weaver copies the pattern of the clouds" (Elwin 1959: 47) or other celestial phenomena, such as the moon symbolism of cowrie circles. Common natural features of the landscape frequently serve as design inspiration.

The other Naga textiles in the Allen Collection, mostly shawls or wrap around skirts, are more recent than those discussed above. Some were probably produced in a weaving center. These cloths show traditional Naga designs of various tribes but perhaps not always combined in orthodox ways. It is very unusual still to find representational or even curvilinear designs in most Naga cloths with the exception of those described on the cowrie embroidered cloth and the *tsungkotepsu* discussed above, and the *chaddar* (shawl) which will be described later.

All have basically the same method of achieving patterning: a striped warp, usually red, black and blue, is woven in warpfaced plain weave, almost always with a black weft. Two or three loom widths are sewn together along the selvedges; the outside strips are usually the same and differ from the center strip. Individual motives or bands of motives, typically squares, diamonds or zigzags, are created by using supplementary wefts. In almost all cases, pattern wefts are interworked with the ground weave ('laid-in') rather than floating on the back. Mills and Hutton in their description of Ao weaving (1926), although providing a valuable record, nevertheless erred in their judgment of this patterning process. They term it embroidery because a needle is used and attribute the use of this technique to the weaver's inability to embroider coarse cloth once it has left the loom. In her definition of supplementary weft patterning Irene Emery pointed out (1966: 140) that this technique "provides the simplest and least restricted means of adding supplementary pattern to ground weave, since wefts can be added at will as the weaving progresses." Although many colors are used, again red, blue and black are favored. This color choice was probably influenced by traditional natural dyes readily available (Mills and Hutton *op. cit.:* 92); on newer textiles, the supplementary-weft patterning is frequently done with commercial embroidery floss, and a wider range of colors is found.

The garments in the Allen Collection fall roughly into three design types, based on the arrangement of the stripes and the type and arrangement of the supplementary-weft patterning. Many varied interpretations are put on Naga symbolism as expressed in textiles, depending on the village or even individual opinion. Mills and Hutton (*ibid.:* 34-41) discuss the design of Ao Naga garments in some

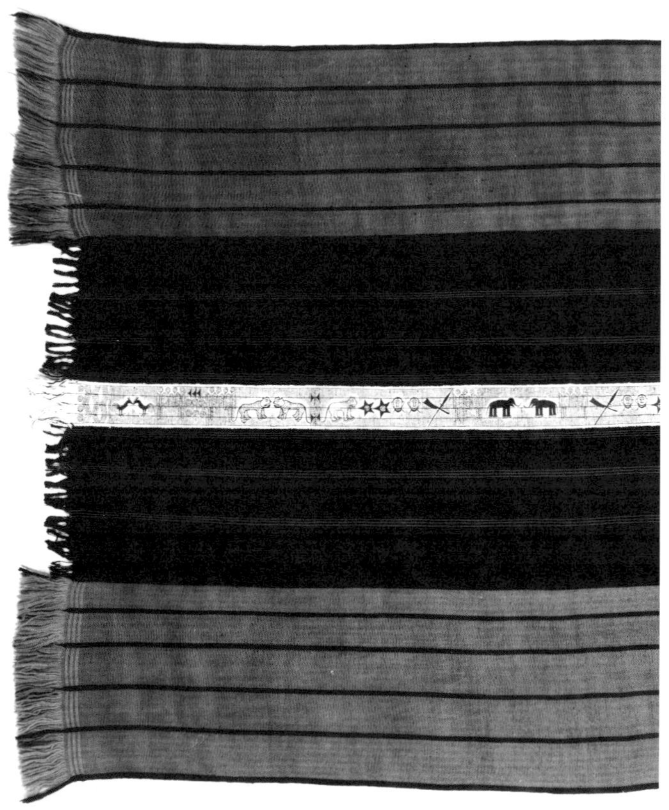

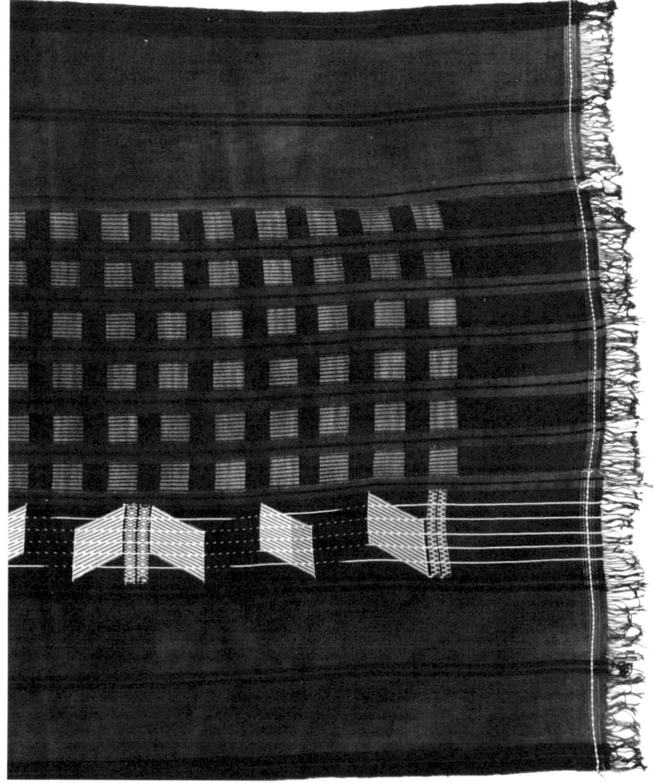

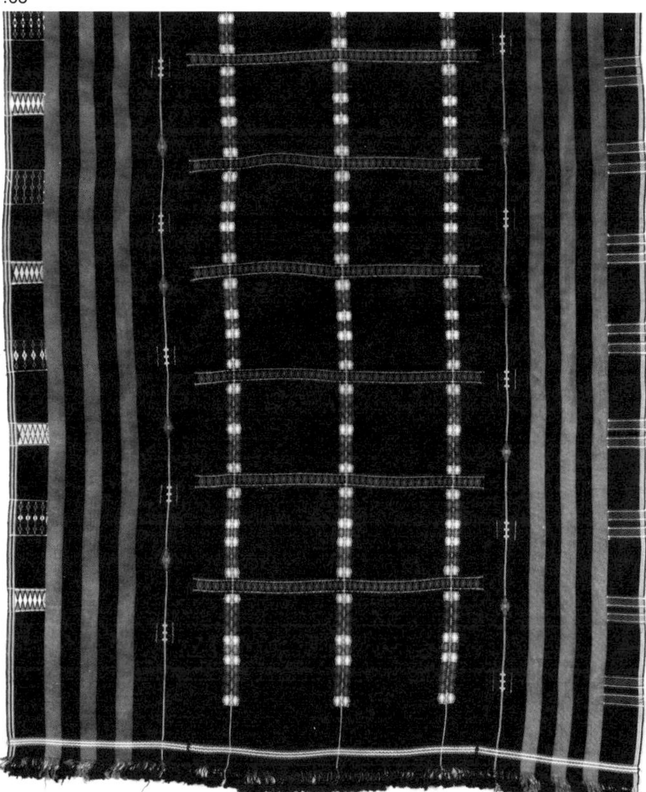

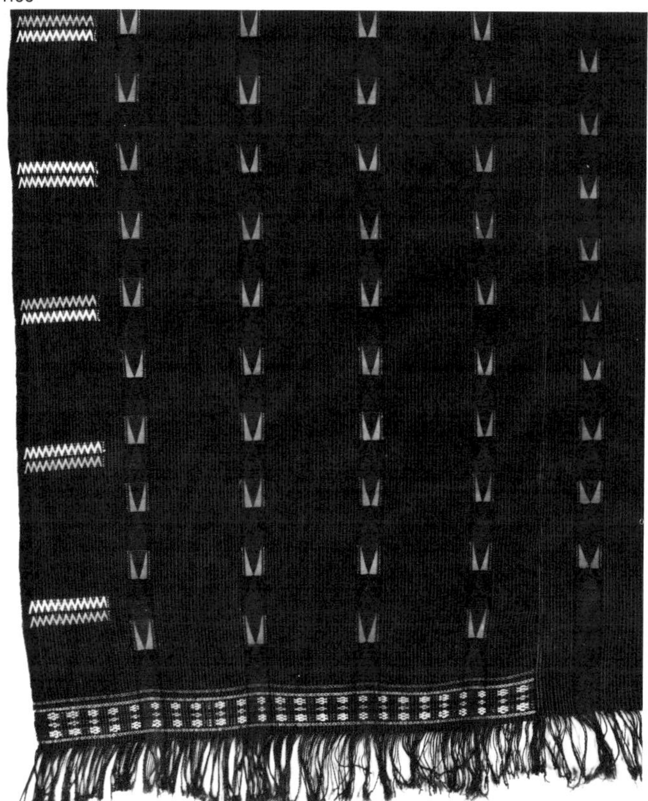

detail, pointing out that different stripe patterns correlate to different stages of man's achievement, earned by giving feasts. Among the Ao, woman's rank is connected to that of her father, not of her husband. They apparent found the whole matter of textile design and rank a confusing one; even among the Ao, they name fifteen "common cloths," noting that: "The variations in pattern from village to village increase the intricacy of the matter, and the fact that the same name is often used for different cloths, and the same cloth often called by different names in different villages, makes confusion worse confounded" (*ibid*.: 35).

In the first type, red wool squares are featured, clearly linking this type to the Konyak shawl discussed above (Pl. 1.61/Col. Pl. 1.5). The squares appear evenly spaced on dark blue stripes in the center panel. In the example illustrated here (Pl. 1.64), each blue stripe alternates with narrow dark red and black stripes. The outside panels have wide dark red bands which alternate with narrow blue, red and black stripes. The overall harmony of this composition is jarringly interrupted by the wide zigzag of alternating bright red and black rhomboids that parades along a blue and white striped band adjoining the center panel, executed in embroidery floss. The very common zigzag is variously explained by different tribes as representing a river, a flight of cranes, an agricultural tool, or "the winding path by which a headhunter went to attack an enemy village" (Elwin 1959: 39, 47-48, 51); this design is used by the Konyak, and is apparent typical of those emphasized at production centers such as the Tuensang Cottage Industries Center.

The second type uses a different placement of stripes to achieve its effect, almost the reverse of the first type. Here, as detailed in Plate 1.65, the center panel is composed of broad bands and narrow stripes, while the outside panels feature narrow stripes. This skirt cloth is a delicately executed example of a backstrap weaver's achievement. The warp striping in the central panel is confined to three extremely thin yellow and green stripes, each 1/16'' wide, which are all but hidden by the supplementary-weft patterning that surrounds them. The rows of concentric diamonds progress in a regular arrangement of light blue, red, yellow, and green. This pattern is bisected at intervals by bands of red diamonds running perpendicular in the weft direction, creating six-inch squares across

1.67 Shawl or cover *(chaddar)*
Detail of center
Meitei people for Naga use, Imphal,
Manipur, before 1965
74½ x 51¾ in.

Plain, complementary warp, and
supplementary weft weave;
embroidered
Cotton; black with red, white,
yellow, green

1976.9.233/EAI 1405

1.67

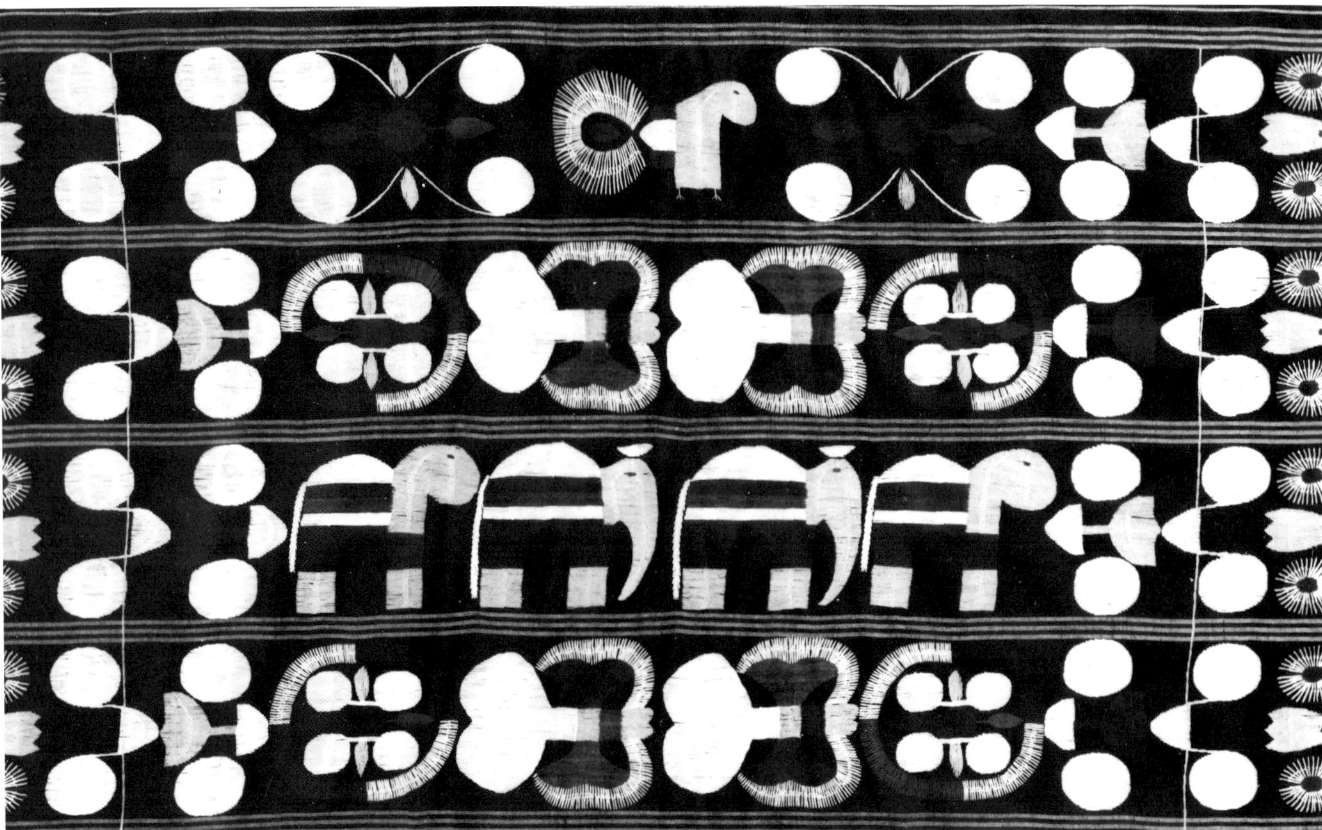

the central field. The strident combination of red and black in the side panels is cooled considerably by the introduction of a tiny green stripe just two warps wide. This softens the eye's transition and subtly unifies the design. In the black areas, on one side are blocks of two different diamond patterns in various colors, and on the other are bars of yellow, green and red flecks. On the inner edge of the side panels red diamonds alternate with tiny yellow and orange blossoms.

In the third type, consisting of two panels rather than three, regularly spaced very narrow red and black stripes are used rather than the broad black or red bands seen in the first two types. Bright blue stripes appear every four to five inches, and on these red and black diamonds or triangles are woven (Pl. 1.66). This design is termed *tenik*, or eyes, while a very similar one of bright pink triangles is referred to among the Ao as *yongzujang*, meaning cucumber seeds which they are thought to resemble (*Census of India 1961* v. XXIII pt. VII: 20-21, pls. 3-5).

In addition to these wrapped garments, small shoulder bags (*eptechai*) are woven. Formerly, the bags were plain dark blue or with very simple patterns, used for carrying betel leaves (*pan*), rice, or tobacco into the field or jungle, but recently made bags feature ornate decoration similar to that seen on the garments (*ibid.*: 21). The bag shown in Plate 1.58 has Ao designs, while that in Plate 1.59 is Angami (*ibid.*: pls. 7ff). They are made of handwoven fabric but assembled by sewing machine; two-part construction, with strap and sides formed of one piece and stitched to a second piece folded forming the bag body, is characteristic.

Manipur

To the south of Nagaland is Manipur, which shares its eastern boundary with Burma. Manipur is the home of numerous tribal groups, among them Naga, Kuki (Kuki-chin), Mizo, and Lushai, who live primarily in the hills. The people usually called ''Manipuri'' are the Meitei people of the plains. Historically, Burma has had as much influence as the Indian subcontinent, and Shan Burmese tribes inhabit Manipur as well. About seventy percent of the population lives in the Manipur Valley plain, which represents only ten percent of the country's area (R.K.J. Singh 1975: 1, 14). Its warm climate is suitable for cultivation of pineapples and orchids as well as the staple rice. Weaving is an important activity, and in 1975 the tiny state contained the sixth largest number of looms of any state in India (*ibid.*: 45).

Naga groups living in the state of Manipur can be distinguished by their textile design. Two garments in the Allen Collection are ascribed to the Tangkhul Naga (not illustrated). The first is made of four loom widths. Again red and black are commonly used for warp stripes and bands varying in width; fine yellow and white stripes provide a bright contrast. One difference from other Naga textiles is the use of supplementary warps to provide a dotted pattern, either black floats on a white stripe or vice versa, in the side panels. Supplementary weft patterning frequently creates a pattern in the end borders of elongated zigzags said to represent spears (Roy 1979: 49). Small crosses may also be scattered throughout the body of the cloth with two colors and running up the center. Tangkhul textiles are further distinguished by thin fringes that emerge from the face of the cloth at intervals.

An interesting object said to be Angami Naga in origin, which has become quite popular recently as a tourist item, is usually referred to as *Naga chaddar*, meaning shawl (Pl. 1.67). It is made, however, by the Meiteis, another cultural group that inhabits much of Manipur. The designs of this cloth are large embroidered elephants, horses, flowers, butterflies, peacocks and other creatures, embroidered in a type of couching known as Roumanian stitch, here on a black background, although red is also common. The design is known as *shamilami*, or among the Tangkhul, *leivat* (Roy 1979: 39). These cloths are now being made in other sizes and shapes. Four other textiles in the Allen Collection (not illustrated) feature this same design all on red ground; one is a chaddar, one a small table cover, the third a drawstring bag, and the fourth a pillow cover.

Another tribal group whose home is Manipur is the Mizo. The distinctive Mizo textile designs are easily recognizable. Although similar in construction to Naga textiles, the Mizo shawl in the Allen Collection (Pl. 1.68) does not resemble them in its uninhibited approach to design. Clearly the weaver's greatest devotion here was to color. Black and white cotton warp stripes alternate with narrower stripes of dazzling spectral variety, with the outside edges being hot pink wool and the center strip red wool. The tightly warp faced structure all but obscures the ground weft, which is white in the outside panels and red in the center panel. However, every two inches one-quarter inch black weft stripes are introduced, creating a light gray shadow effect. Not only supplementary weft patterning is used, for rows of multicolor diamonds at either end, but weft faced plain weave bands, primarily in

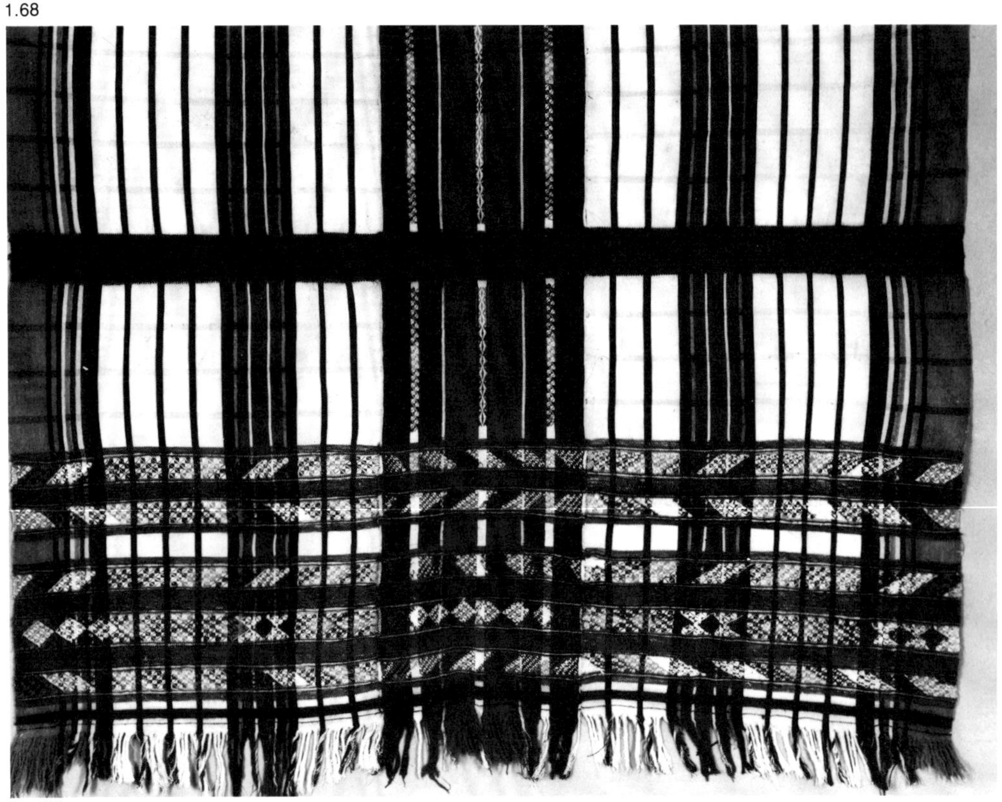

1.68 Shawl
Detail of lower third
68 x 48 in.

Mizo people, Manipur, before 1962
Plain (warp faced and weft faced) and
supplementary weft weave
Cotton and wool; white and black with
multicolor

1976.9.328/WLI 2779

red wool, are inserted between them, a single weft interlacing with six warps; the same structure is used to create two-inch wide black bands at two intervals nearer the shawl's center. The total effect is one of chromatic excess; nevertheless careful planning by the weaver went into this extravagant creation.

A great contrast is presented by the approach to color used in Meitei wrap-skirts (*phanek*). Although the regular repetition of very narrow red, white, and black stripes causes the surface to undulate and shimmer violently, and leads the eye to the tranquility refuge of the silk embroidered borders. A typical design is *Akoybi mayek*, consisting of lotuses within circles, worked in two shades of dark red with blue, black and white accents on a black ground. Similar skirts are illustrated in Nilima Roy's *Art of Manipur* (1979: pls. 9, 16, col. pls. 3 and 11). The design is an ancient one, and another interpretation tells us that it is based on a snakeskin pattern used by a god who had manifested himself in serpent form (Roy 1979: 36).

Assam

The largest state of the seven North East provinces, Assam was formerly an even larger area encompassing Nagaland and the other smaller states. The whole North Eastern area is often referred to as Assam in the older sources such as W. Robinson's *Descriptive Account of Assam* (1841) and Major John Butler's *Travels and Adventures in the Province of Assam* (1855), both of which include material oh Naga tribes. Generally speaking, as for Manipur, the people of the Assamese plains are somewhat distinct from the hill people who belong to Naga and other tribes.

Historically, Assam was for a long time part of the Ahom kingdom which originated in Burma. As early as the tenth century A.D. Assamese weaving is mentioned in literature; the name of the country is given as Kamarupa, famed for its professional artisans (*tantuvayas*) as well as domestic craftspeople. The early sources mention both cotton (*karpasa*) and silk (*kosaja*) garments, in addition to hemp and bark cloth. Assamese weavers apparent supplied cotton cloth to the Ahom kings (Choudhury 1959: 363) and cotton is still one of the major fibers used. Sericulture and silk weaving have likewise been a continuing tradition for many centuries. Assam is given as one possible conduit for silk from China into India, whence it spread to the Middle East and Europe.

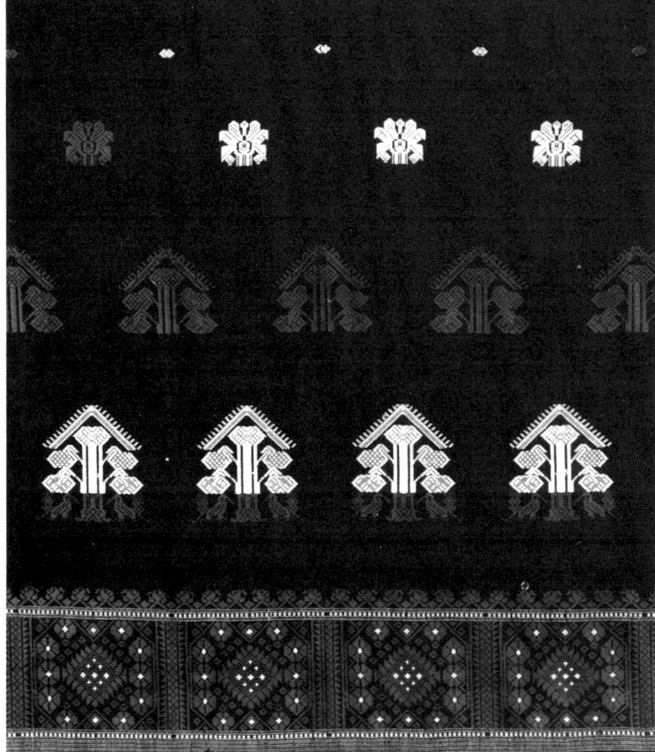

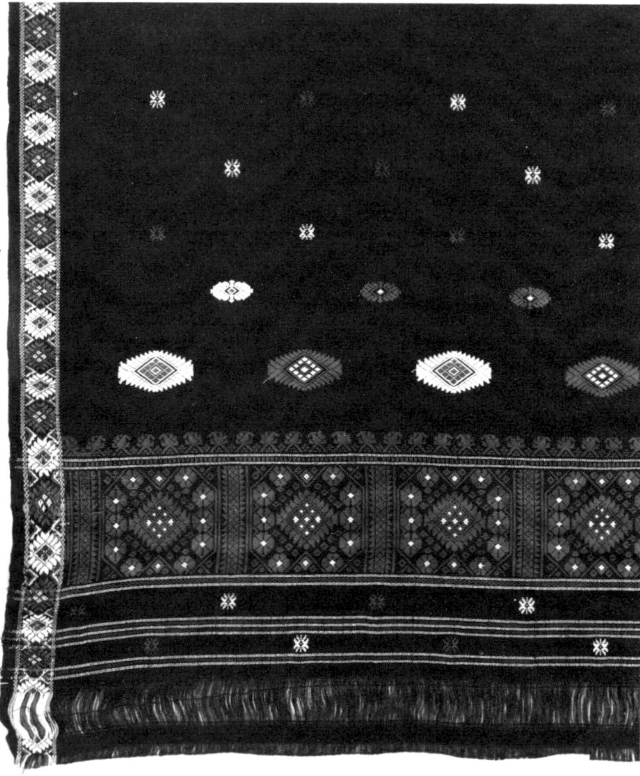

In Assam the same designs are used on both cotton and silk textiles, with supplementary weft patterning the most common means of achieving the angular, stylized designs of flowers together with birds, animals or houses. Assamese weavers use a type of frame loom usually referred to as the throw shuttle loom. This differs from the tribal backstrap (loin) loom which uses body tension to control the warp, and where the weft is held on small stick shuttles. The Assamese loom uses a foot-operated heddle system of strings within a bamboo frame rather than the hand-operated string heddle system required by the backstrap loom. On this type of loom, a weaver can produce a wider fabric than on the backstrap loom. In the last few decades, the fly-shuttle mechanism has been adopted by many Assamese weavers to speed up production. Government centers encourage the use of such technological improvements. Power looms have also been introduced but few individual weavers can afford to purchase this type of equipment. Even a fly-shuttle loom could cost a full-time weaver six weeks wages (150 Rs in 1961), approximately fifteen times the cost of a frame loom, and he or she would need to sell perhaps fifty garments to recoup this expense (*Census of India 1961* v. III pt. VII-A: 6, 16, 20). Nor are many Assamese women full-time weavers. Most professional weavers have been men, immigrants from neighboring Bangladesh.

Most of the Assamese fabrics in the Allen Collection are *mekhla*, a woman's wrapped lower body garment that may be translated as loin cloth. They are of one loom width which varies from thirty-one to thirty-six inches. The ends are always decorated with individual motives floating above a band of joined motives; sometimes the sides are decorated as well. Of the mekhla in the Allen Collection, seven are made of cotton, three of which are illustrated here (Pls. 1.69-1.71), and five are silk, one of which is illustrated (Pl. 1.72).

Of the cotton pieces, the mekhla in Plate 1.69 has no side borders; its end borders feature a band of angular floral forms, above which are rows of tree and house motives, some with birds, and butterflies, executed in red, white, yellow, and aqua on a black background. The fineness of the cotton ground and evenness of the patterning indicates it may well have been woven with the aid of a fly shuttle.

The other cotton mekhla is deep purple (Plate 1.70); it features very similar red end borders with isolated red and yellow lozenges and stars above. However, of all the Assamese textiles in the Allen

1.69 Loin cloth *(mekhla)*
Detail of border
Gauhati, Assam, before 1958
108 x 33¾ in.

Plain and supplementary weft weave
Cotton; black with white, red, yellow, turquoise

1976.9.136/WLFI 2786

1.70 Loin cloth *(mekhla)*
Detail of border
Gauhati, Assam, before 1958
74 x 35½ in.

Plain, supplementary warp and weft weave
Cotton; violet with red, yellow, light blue

1976.9.143/WLFI 2798

1.71 Shawl or cover
Detail of two thirds
Assam, mid twentieth century
68 x 33¼ in.

Plain and supplementary weft weave
Cotton; black with white, yellow, green, orange

1976.9.263/WLFI 2790

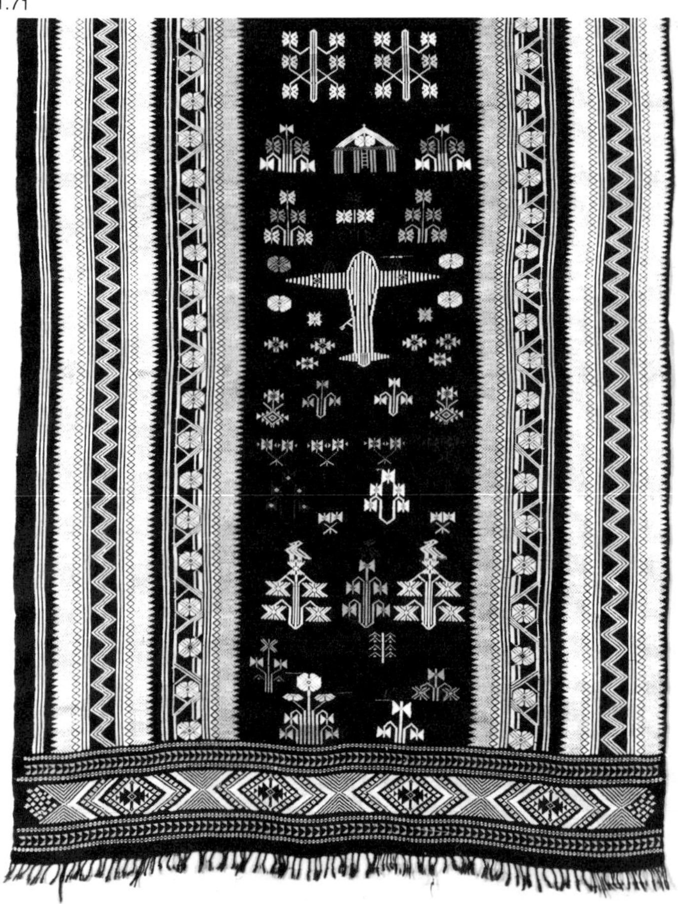

Collection, it is unique in having side borders which are executed in supplementary warp rather than supplementary weft patterning, possibly with the use of a dobby attachment. It too may have been woven on a fly shuttle loom.

The third cotton garment illustrated here (Pl. 1.71) also has side borders, but they are extremely wide, each border covering about a third of the cloth. The outer border is white and the inner border dark yellow, as are the end borders with their typical bands of stylized angular flowers. However, this cloth shows important differences from the two discussed above in addition to the wide borders. First, the overall layout of the design is vertically asymmetrical—the border at one end is almost twice as deep as that at the opposite end, though the design is the same. Also, the entire field is filled with motives, not just a small space at the ends. These are mostly flowers, houses and trees similar to those in Plate 1.69 done in a wide variety of colors. However, in the center of the cloth, a large white airplane appears. The apparent modernness of this design does not necessarily mean that this cloth is newer than the others; it may be older, and is certainly well used. The black background and multicolored pattern yarns have all faded as the result of wear and washing; the fabric, although thicker, is much softer than the other two pieces discussed above. It seems likely that an innovative Assamese weaver created this piece for herself with special care and attention.

It is also likely that Assamese pieces formerly used more patterning all over than in recent years, and had side borders. A case in point is a silk mekhla in the Allen Collection (not illustrated). The designs are much the same as those shown in Plates 1.69 and 1.71 above, but recognizable objects are utterly lacking—only lozenges, diamonds, and stars are used, repeated in dark pink and green, now badly faded, along the length of this cloth, which is nearly twice as long as any of the others, though among the narrowest in the group. At intervals from six inches to two feet the design changes, either in motif, frequency of repetition, or scale. A subtle enhancement of the pattern colors in the border is created by the addition of gold color silk in the ground weft.

1.72

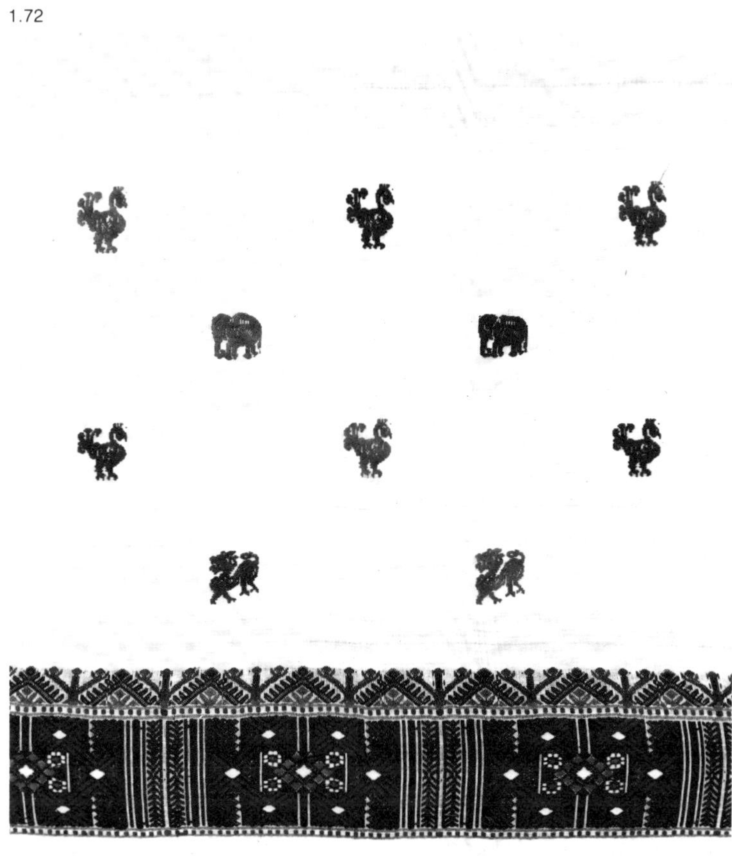

1.72 Loin cloth *(mekhla)* or shawl
Detail of border
Gauhati, Assam, before 1958
93 x 32½ in.

Plain and supplementary weft weave
Silk and cotton; undyed with black,
red, yellow, blue, green

1976.9.142/WLFI 2789

Assamese silks are the products of three types of silk worm. *Edi* (or *endi*, sometimes called *erandi*) is from *attacus ricini* which feeds on castor plants. *Muga* is from *antheroea Assamoea* feeding on three plants called *campa*, *mejankari* and *adakari*. They yield a thicker yarn than the third variety, *pat* (or *patta*), produced by *bombyx textor* or *bombyx croesi* worms fed on mulberry trees. *Pat* is the finest of the Assamese silks and the smoothest in texture. In the ancient manuscript the *Harsacarita*, Assamese silk "white as Autumn's moonlight," is mentioned as an appropriate gift for a king (Choudhury 1959: 365). In modern Assam, silk garments are suitable wedding gifts from the bride's mother to both bride and groom (*Census of India 1961* v. III pt. VII-A: 45). Both silk pieces discussed here are muga silk.

The silk mekhla illustrated here (Pl. 1.72) has much less patterning than the one discussed above; the border is quite narrow and the style is even more angular, the floral patterns appearing rather boxed in. This band is unusual in the great number of colors used although bright blue and black predominate. Above are individual animal motives: lion, rooster, elephant, and another rooster. The more common lozenge forms are completely absent. This is probably one of the newest Assamese pieces in the Allen Collection. It was collected in 1958.

Arunachal Pradesh

Formerly known as the North East Frontier Agency, Arunachal Pradesh is the northernmost of the seven provinces. The people are mostly Buddhist, especially in the western areas. In addition to the weaving, basketry, and metalwork arts common to the other provinces, mask making plays a prominent role.

Only five textiles from Arunachal Pradesh are in the Allen Collection; four are jackets, the other a bag. Small, simply constructed jackets are worn by both men and women in certain tribes of the

North East. Often these are quite plain but those of the Mishmi of the Lohit District and the Apa Tani of the Subansiri District usually have decorative weft patterning and embroidery.

The Idu Mishmi customarily favor black jackets. Often these are made of a single loom width with a center front opening and neckline woven in (Pl. 1.73). Occasionally sleeves are added. Bands of diamonds and crosses in white, yellow and red run along the lower hem and around the waistline. Up the center back the same patterns or more complex variants appear. Elwin documented some two dozen geometric patterns commonly found on Idu Mishmi jackets, and illustrates two young Mishmi men, each of whom wears two jackets (Elwin 1959: 58-61, 129, 130). He quotes Dalton's statement (1872) that the Idu were formerly famed for wearing jackets of nettle fibers, "so strong and stiff that, made into jackets, it is used by themselves and by the Abors as a sort of armour" (*ibid.*: 131). The jacket illustrated in Plate 1.73 is made of cotton and hair.

The Apa Tani of the Subansiri area favor a light color background for their jackets, usually white. The cotton for these garments is grown by the neighboring Daflas Tribe, for whom the Apa Tanis in turn weave clothing. A cotton jacket in the Allen Collection (Pl. 1.74) is white with a broad blue and black band running up center back. Fürer-Haimendorf's description of Apa Tani cloth is apt for this particular jacket: "Their clear strong dyes and their use of bright borders on white cloths, and their clever multicoloured embroideries produce beautiful effects. The restraint in the choice of ornaments . . .seems also expressive of a developed aesthetic tradition. . ." (1955: 168). Elwin states (1959) that the wool used for the decoration was in the past gotten from Bhutanese blankets, which were unravelled and overdyed to suit the Apa Tani taste.

It should be noted in closing that the above observations cannot be taken as an assessment of the present state of the textile arts in the North Eastern Frontier Area. Political conflicts and conflagrations have proved a stumbling block that few if any researchers have been able to detour for two decades. One can only speculate on the changes that may have taken place since Ruth Reeves assembled her collection in the 1950s. The appearance of Naga-style cloths made up as skirts for Western markets has been noticeable recently, and it is hoped that political and economic troubles have not forced the North Eastern tribes to abandon their traditional artisanry.

1.73 Jacket

Idu Mishmi, Lohit District, Arunachal Pradesh, before 1964
Neck-hem 31½, hem 43, shoulders 22 in.

Plain and supplementary weft weave; embroidered
Cotton and hair; black with white, yellow, red, purple

1976.9.294/EAI 1454

1.74 Jacket

Apa Tani, Subansiri District, Arunachal Pradesh, before 1963
Neck-hem 23, hem 24, shoulders 32 in.

Plain and supplementary weft weave; embroidered
Cotton and wool; undyed, blue, black, multicolored

1976.9.304/EAI 1453

1.73

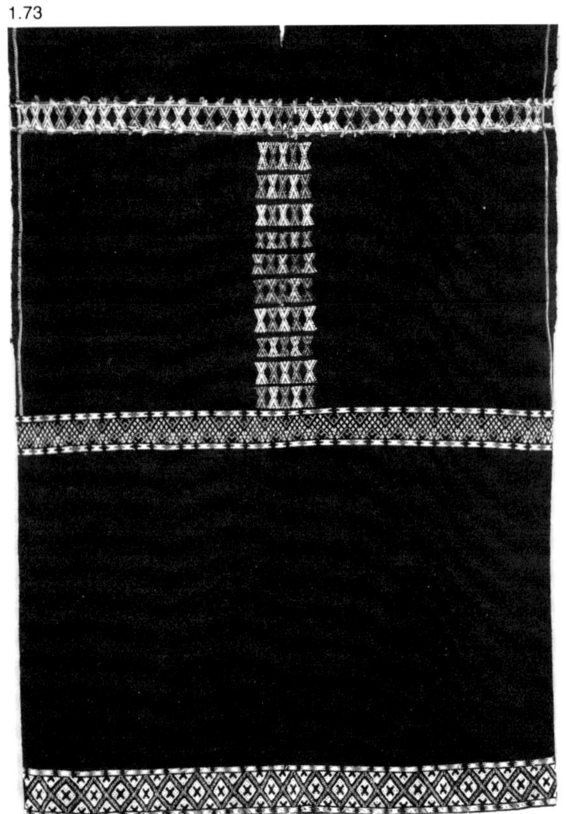

1.74

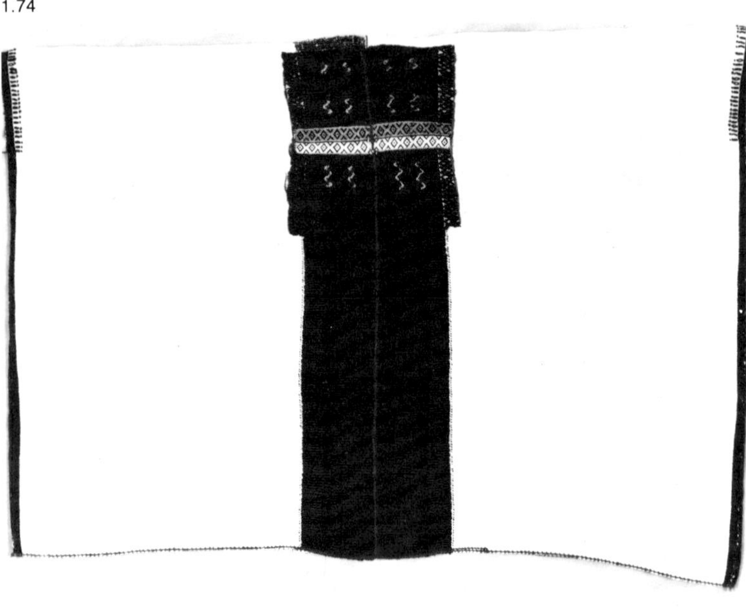

Part II: Paintings of South Asia

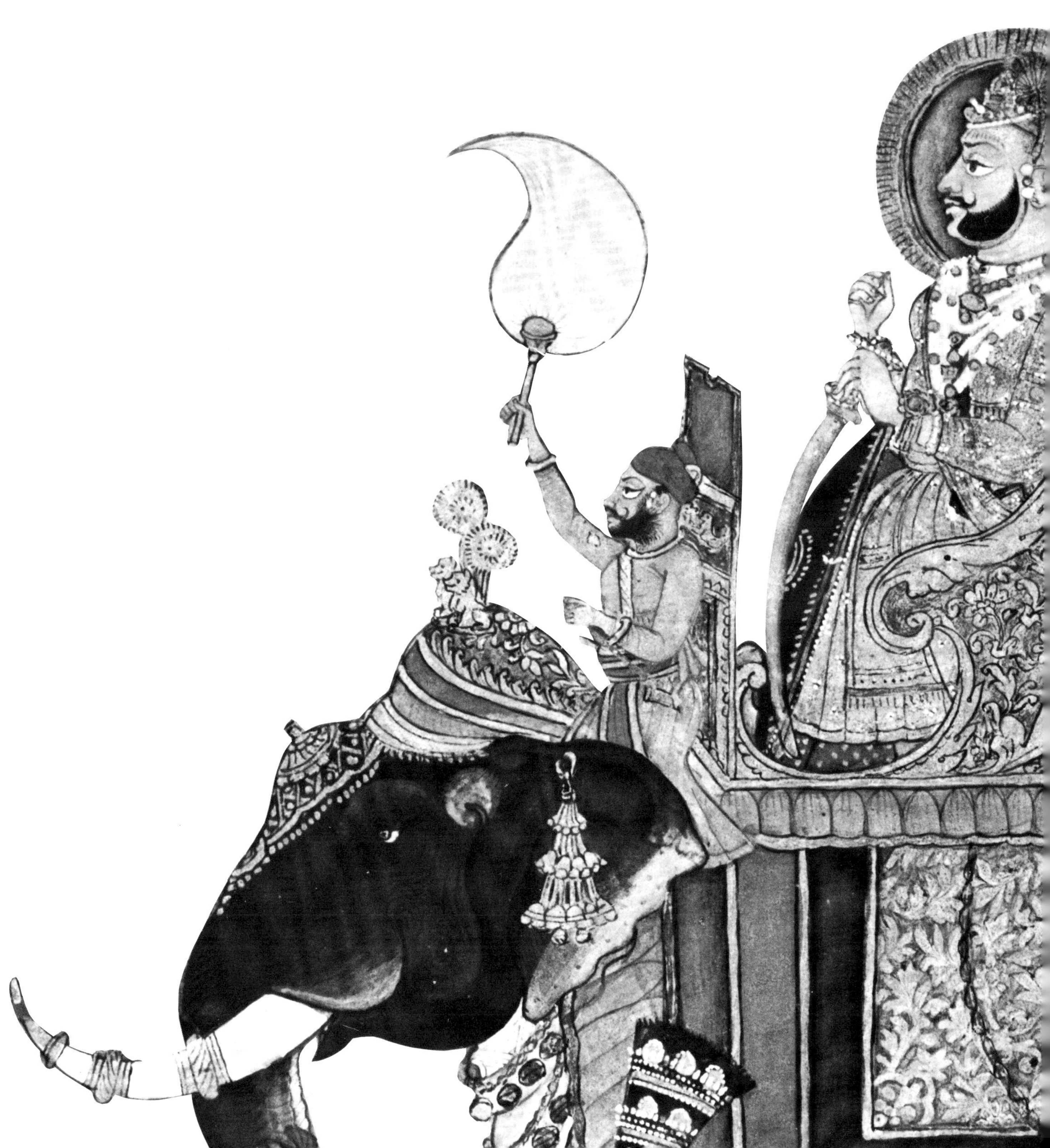

A World of Gods and Humans: South Asian Miniature Paintings

South Asian miniature paintings portray a world of gods and humans. Each painting was part of a cohesive group of paintings which were meant to be viewed as a book. Unsewn leaves were kept between wooden covers or wrapped in cloth. The wealthy patrons who commissioned the paintings enjoyed them in the leisure of their own quarters. The emphasis throughout is on characters as expressions of the theme or narrative that is the subject of the painting. Landscape elements are visualized to substantiate and echo the theme. The painter was entrusted with the task of instilling meaning in a variety of conventional topics. Creativity rested in the degree to which new meaning could be brought to established compositions and themes. Repetition had a positive connotation if sufficient force of character could be brought forth.

The world of gods which we see in the paintings in this exhibition reflects sectarian traditions that changed with the generations. The world of gods in South Asia is one of multiplicity. Many gods, with many forms, express an awareness of the complex nature of the universe. This complexity is comfortably handled in visual form. Iconographic conventions such as multiple arms or deities that are part-human and part-animal are firmly based in the visual vocabulary of South Asian religious traditions. They are solutions to the time-honored mysteries regarding the nature of the divine. The painter was able to explore not only hieratic images but scenes of devotion, and scenes from the legendary lives of the gods (nos. 2.1-2.56).

The world of humans is recreated by individual portraiture as well as by scenes of courtly and private life. Men are shown in stylized postures with attributes particular to nobility, such as the sword and flower, indicating that war and peace were under their control. Hunting and courtly scenes create a vision of the noble life. Women are shown in the privacy of inner quarters or having embarked upon a religious path. The emotions associated with longing and pining are favoured in many paintings. Interactions between men and women are a popular theme in Indian poetics and paintings. The stages of love, from separation to union, found favor among the courtly patrons (nos. 2.51-2.102).

The themes of miniature paintings developed within several cultural settings. The four major threads in the history of South Asian miniature painting are represented in this exhibition. These four are: palm-leaf-manuscript illustrations from Eastern India, palm- and paper-manuscript illustrations from Western India, paintings in the Mughal style and Rajput paintings.

The development of a tradition of miniature painting was intricately connected to the illustration of religious texts. The earliest extant manuscripts with painted illustrations are from the eleventh century in Eastern India. The subject matter of these texts and of the paintings was primarily Buddhist. In the midst of lines of verse, small rectangular areas were devoted to the depiction of images and of scenes from the life of the Buddha. These early manuscripts were made from palm leaves, the long narrow shape of which influenced the size and shape of manuscripts even after the introduction of paper in the fourteenth century. The subjects of the paintings on these manuscripts were not always direct illustrations of the verses. Oftentimes, auspicious divinities or events connected in an edifying way with the tradition from which the texts arose were represented. This tradition carried on until the end of the twelfth or beginning of the thirteenth centuries.

Meanwhile, in Western India another tradition of manuscript painting arose and reached a high degree of excellence. The eleventh century saw the production of many Jain manuscripts on palm leaves. The depiction of highly angular, boldly colored figures is typical of these manuscripts. The style reached its stride after the fourteenth century when paper became widely available in South Asia. Jain and Hindu subjects were subsequently depicted on various manuscript leaves. Women exhibiting dancing poses, groups of horsemen, and episodes from secular life, joined the strictly religious themes to highlight and decorate the text.

The remaining history of South Asian miniature painting can be broadly divided into two groups: Mughal and Rajput. This classification is tied to patron groups. There are numerous stylistic, regional and period distinctions within both of these classes. Mutual influence permeated the relationships of local schools as well as that of the two broad classifications. The identification of style is a complex study which has undergone many revisions over the past centuries. *

* The reader is encouraged to consult the first catalogue of the Watson Collection written by Pramod Chandra, an expert in the field of miniature painting, or any other source in the bibliography for a discussion of the various styles. Dr. Linda Leach's glossary of painting styles, *In the Image of Man,* New York, 1982, pp. 40-48, is a clear, handy reference for introducing one to or refreshing one's memory of the individual schools of painting. Differentiation of workshops and stylistic divisions has progressed over the last century but a definitive structure, agreed upon by all scholars, is yet to come. See for example, the views of W.G. Archer and B.N. Goswamy on the classifications of Punjab Hill paintings.

The Mughal Style developed various aspects under a succession of Mughal emperors who ruled the Northern region of South Asia from the sixteenth to the eighteenth centuries. This style, concerned with realism and a natural appearance, represents a major stream of artistic influence. Mughal paintings use soft colors and shading, and reflect a strong interest in decorative elements. Intricate floral and geometric patterns decorating major edifices and objects of daily use appear in the backgrounds of paintings. Subjects were given different emphasis according to the predilections of particular rulers. The end of the Mughal style (late eighteenth century) was marked by provincial variants which rapidly integrated elements of local styles.

Rajput paintings from the sixteenth to the nineteenth centuries came from two geographical regions: Rajasthan/Central India and the Punjab Hills. There were schools within each of these areas which had distinctive characteristics. The historical circumstances surrounding the schools have been the object of considerable research. The patron-painter relationship as well as the movements of artists who rarely signed their names to paintings explain the overlapping and borrowing we see among the paintings and the difficulty in definitely attributing certain paintings to a particular time or place. The Rajasthan and Central Indian schools produced the earliest miniature paintings of the Rajput class, beginning in the early sixteenth century. Extensive use is made of patches of flat, vibrant color to create the mood of particular paintings. Figures are treated in an abstract fashion. The Punjab Hill schools began in the seventeenth century and produced a variety of styles. Some, such as the Basohli school, are markedly folkish while others, such as the Kangra school, produced works both refined and elegant.

Mughal paintings favored dynastic chronicles, nature studies and portraiture; Rajput paintings excelled in representing religious and poetic ideas. However, all types of miniature painting explored themes which include worship scenes, epic events, portraits and selected scenes from daily life. Many paintings were strongly associated with the medieval devotional movements that produced a profusion of literature expressing love of God and the importance of unifying one's soul with God. The relationships of lover and beloved, God and soul, are explored at different levels, in a variety of forms, although the nominal title of a painting might specify a *raga* (musical mode) or a specific event. The use of complex analogy and metaphor was as central to the success of individual paintings as was the use of color and figural interpretations. Considered thematically, the paintings offer an opportunity to explore a world of gods and humans, while viewing a highly developed form of art.

Texts Illustrated in this Catalogue

Alamgir Nama—A history of the reign of Aurangzeb, one of the Mughal Emperors, written by Mirza Muhammad Kazim. The word *alamgir* means world conqueror, a title claimed by Aurangzeb.

Bhagavata Dashamskanda—Several medieval poet-saints who were devoted to Krishna translated and commented upon the tenth chapter of the *Bhagavata Purana*, thus making the text available to a wider audience.

Bhagavata Purana—A Sanskrit text dedicated to Vishnu. The tenth chapter focuses on Krishna's earthly career as a child, a cowherd and a lover.

Gita Govinda—A Sanskrit poem written by Jayadeva in the late twelfth century. It describes the love of Krishna and Radha including moments of separation and union.

Hamir Hath—A saga describing the downfall of Raja Hamir Dev. The extreme pride of the king is an important component of his downfall.

Kalpasutra—A Jain text written by Bhadrabahu. The text is devoted to the miraculous life of Mahavira, the historical leader of the Jain sect, and includes brief descriptions of other Jain leaders, as well as rules for monks and nuns to follow.

Kavipriya—A poem written by Keshavadasa in the sixteenth century. It illustrates the intricacies of Hindi poetics by describing a woman longing for her lover during each of the twelve months of the year.

Martiram's Work—A seventeenth-century poet who wrote verses focused on *shringara-rasa* (erotic sentiment), verbally exploring the beauty and behavior of various types of women.

Nemipurana—A text describing the life and deeds of Neminatha, the twenty-second of twenty-four Tirthankaras (Jain leaders), who sought and achieved spiritual knowledge and then taught mankind.

Ragamala—A series of verses describing the various musical modes, *ragas,* which are personified as men and women. The imagery of Radha and Krishna is often employed in transferring the verbal image into a visual form.

Ramayana—An epic recounting the life of Rama, the seventh incarnation of the Hindu God Vishnu. Much of the plot revolves around the abduction of Rama's wife, Sita. Rama, his brother Lakshmana, and an army of bears and monkeys recover Sita from the evil demon, Ravana.

Rasikapriya—Written in the late sixteenth-century by Keshavadasa, this poem analyzes classes of heroines as well as their beauty and behavior as examples of aspects of Hindi poetics. Krishna and Radha often assume the roles of hero and heroine in illustrations of the ideals.

Sangrahani Sutra—A portion of the Jain canon in which the stages of spiritual progress are described.

Satsai—A collection of approximately seven-hundred verses written by Bihari in the early seventeenth-century. The emotions and interactions of lovers are described in brief, pointed couplets. Krishna and Radha, the ideal lovers, are the implicit representatives of these emotions.

Yusuf-Zulaykha—A Persian poem written by Hakim Nuruddin Abdurrahman Jani in the late fifteenth century. Based on the Biblical story of Zulayka's obsessive love for Yusuf, it symbolizes the intense relationship between God and humanity.

Themes From Ascetic Traditions:
Buddhism and Jainism

Fifteen-hundred years after the inception of Buddhism, palm-leaf manuscripts were illustrated with small paintings depicting Buddhist deities, scenes from the life of Buddha, and episodes from edifying tales. The subjects of the paintings played a magico-religious role by conferring a tone of auspiciousness on the manuscript, but did not necessarily directly illustrate the content of the script on a particular leaf. These manuscripts were produced in the great monasteries of Eastern India during the Pala period. The style of painting was remarkably conservative for almost three hundred years. Figures were outlined and then painted. The compositions were limited by the small rectangular space available on a narrow palm leaf. The folio in this exhibition is typical of the early Eastern manuscript style (no. 2.1).

Jainism, another ascetic tradition, was the subject of many medieval manuscripts in the early Western Indian tradition as well as of paintings in various Rajput styles. Jainism grew in North India during the sixth and fifth centuries, B.C. The historical founder of this religion was Mahavira (c. 540-468, B.C.) who was born as a noble but abandoned wealth and secular power for the religious life. According to Jain texts such as the *Kalpasutra,* his major life events, including his birth and his renunciation of the world were foretold and accompanied by miraculous events (nos. 2.2, 2.3, 2.7, 2.9). Jainism focuses on the doctrine of *ahimsa,* harmlessness to all creatures. One actualization of this doctrine is that all Jain monks carry brooms to sweep away insects before they sit to meditate (no. 2.8). A strong belief in transmigration, which entails the consequences of one's act following one's essence to subsequent lifetimes, permeates the religion (no. 2.5). Mahavira is one in a long line of Tirthankaras, world saviors (no. 2.10). The antiquity of lineage gives credence to Mahavira's teaching. Each Tirthankara is attached to a resting place which is in fact a cosmic diagram (no. 2.4). Decorative patterns with auspicious values are a common element in Jain paintings (no. 2.2 obverse and reverse).

It is a common phenomenon for a new religion to establish its superiority by utilizing deities from established religious traditions as attendants. In early Jain art and texts, Krishna and Balarama, two Hindu deities, serve as attendants to the Jina. The continuity of this pattern is established in an eighteenth-century painting which shows blue Krishna and fair-complexioned Balarama as attendants of Neminatha (no. 2.6). It is noteworthy that this painting is from Mewar, the home of the Vallabhacarya cult, which is dedicated to Krishna as Shri Nathaji.

2.1a

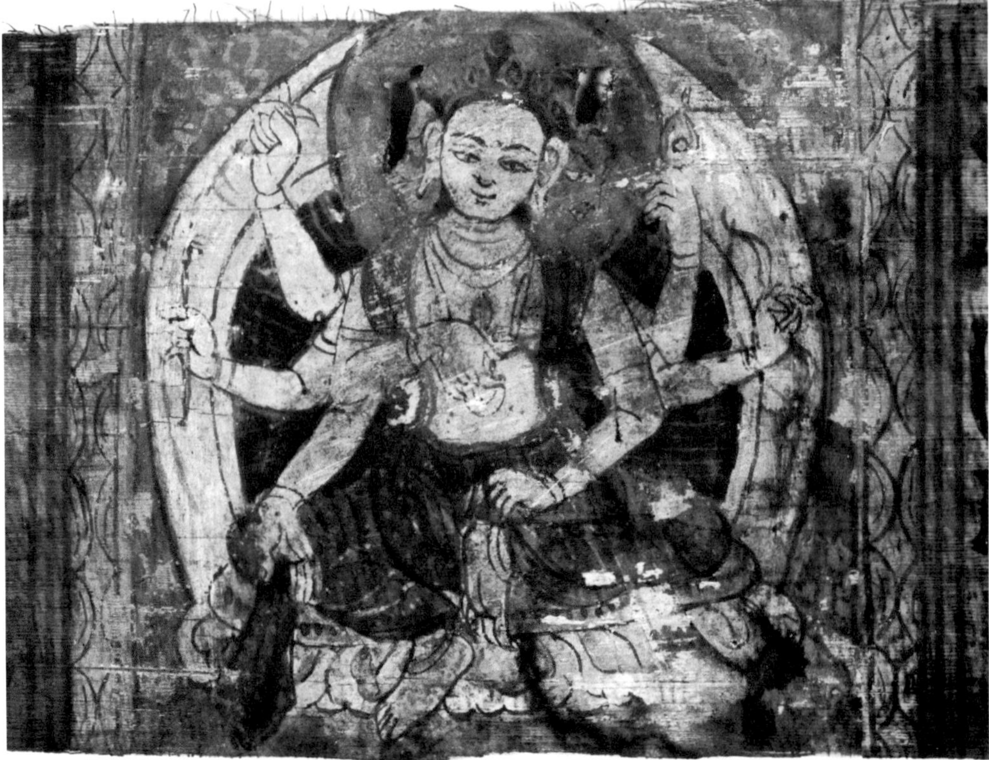

2.1 Folio from an Unidentified Buddhist Ms.
Eastern Indian Style,
thirteenth century A.D.
1⅝ x 16⅝ in.

This manuscript leaf contains two miniature paintings. To the left a three-headed, seven-armed deity sits on a lotus seat. The central face is white, the secondary ones are yellow and red. In three of his four right hands, he holds a noose, an arrow, and a thunderbolt, while the last hand extends downward, in the gift-giving gesture. Of his three left hands, one holds a discus or conch shell, another holds and a bow while the third hand rests clinched in his lap. The deity wears a red loincloth and a green, spotted shawl. A green halo surrounds his crowned head. In the background a larger pink nimbus rests against a red background. While multiple limbs and heads are a feature of Indian iconographical vocabulary, it is very unusual for the number of arms to be uneven. The group of attributes and the white body color are usually associated with forms of Avalokiteshvara.

The second painting shows the Buddha reclining on a cot, recalling the Death of the Buddha *(mahaparinirvana)*. The unaccompanied Buddha lies on his right side with head resting on his hand. His skin is yellow, his robe orange. He is depicted according to the norms established for a great man, i.e. topknot, tuft of hair on his forehead, elongated ears, arms that extend to his knees. It is the pose alone that suggests the identification of this painting. The background (which has been damaged) is green. The juxtaposition of a hieratic Tantric deity and the figure of the historical Buddha is common in the Buddhist art of Eastern India.

Pramod Chandra, *Indian Miniature Painting*, Madison, WI, 1971, no. 1

1.2

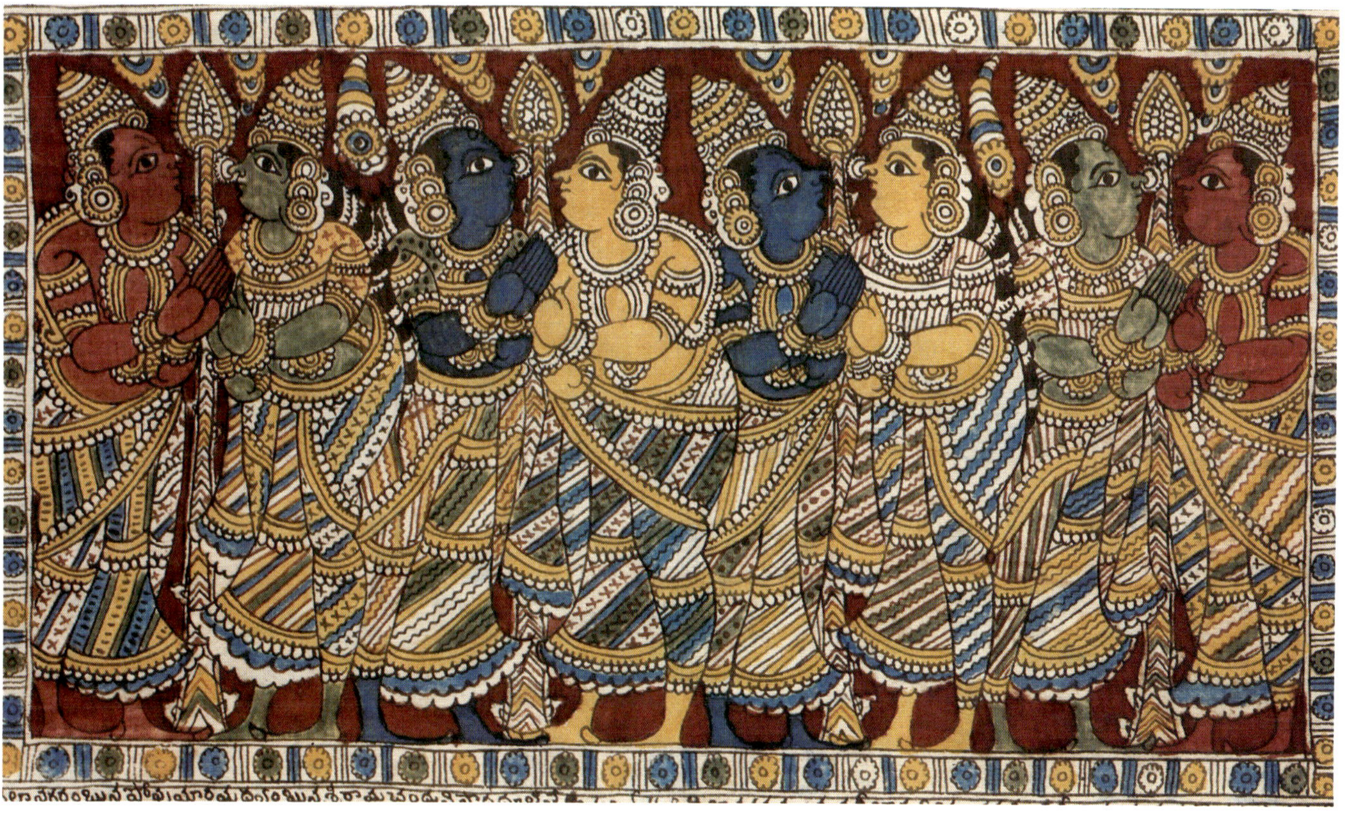

2.1b

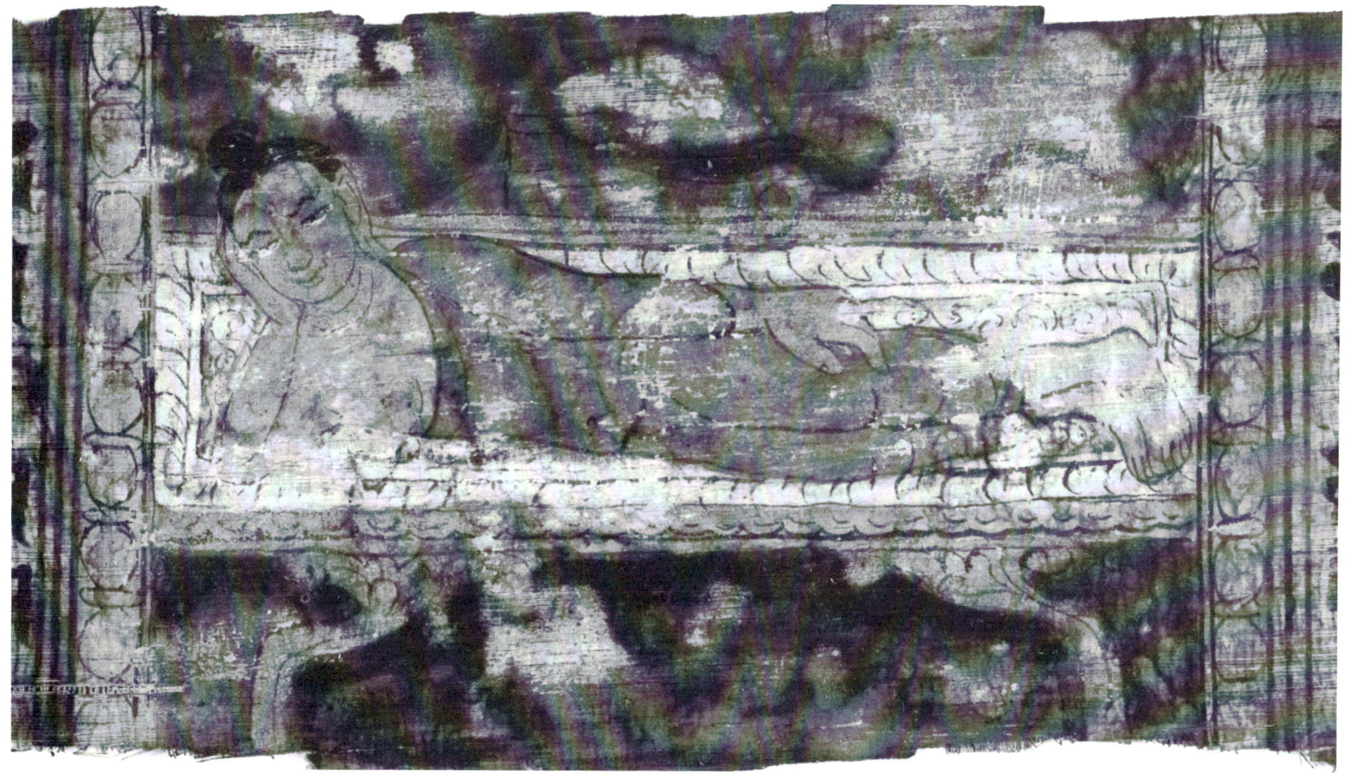

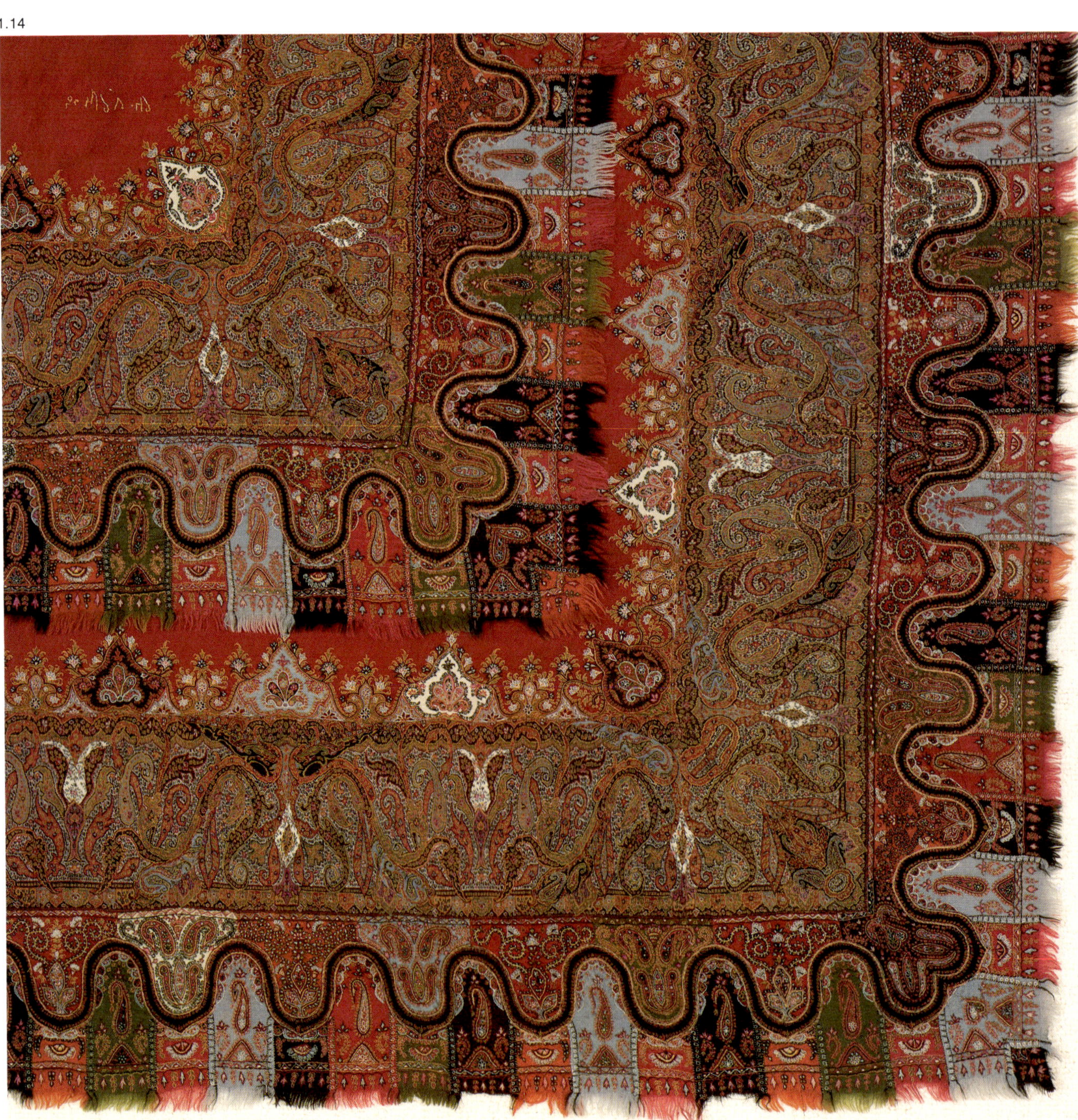

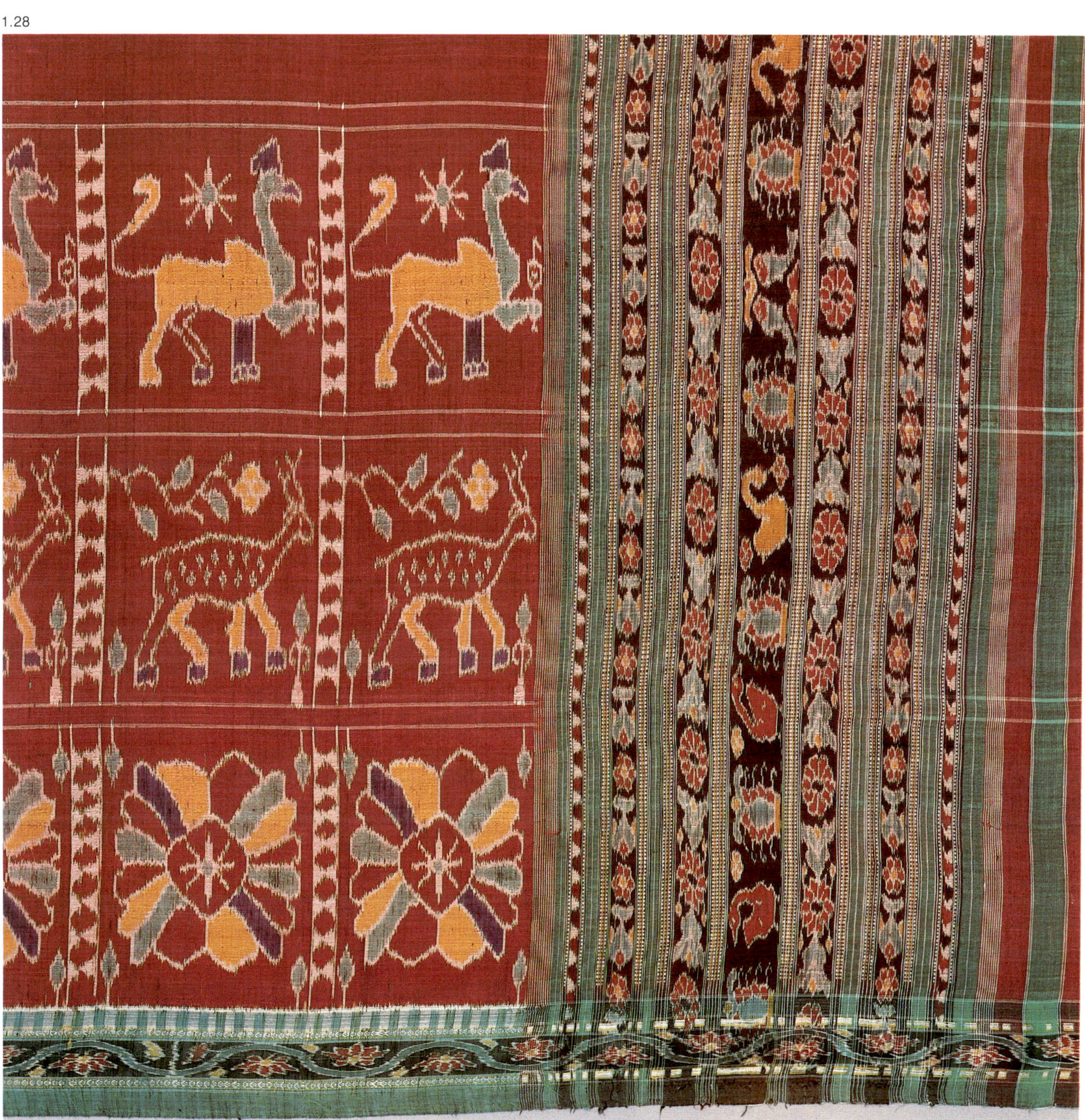

1.37

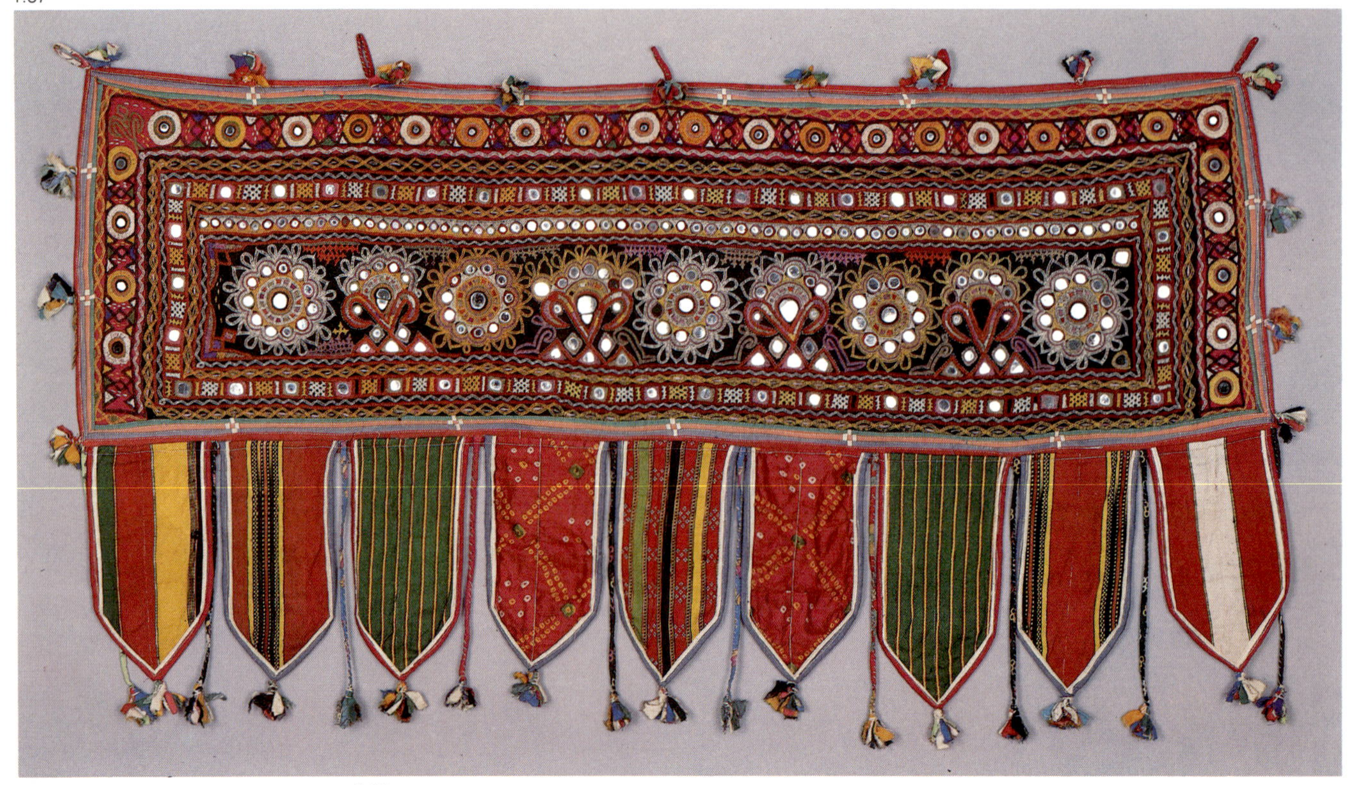

1.61

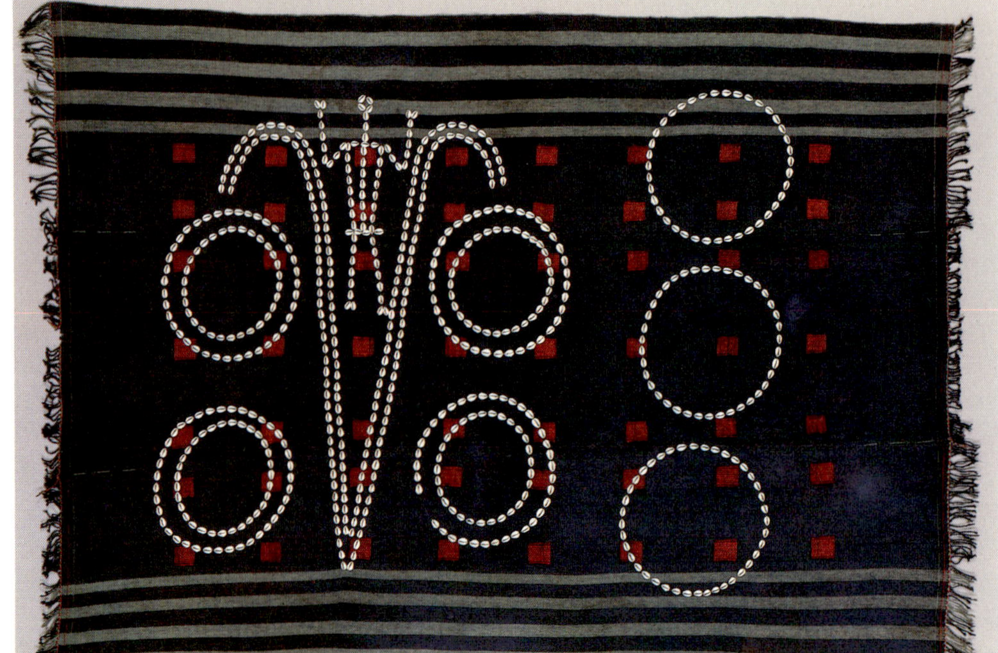

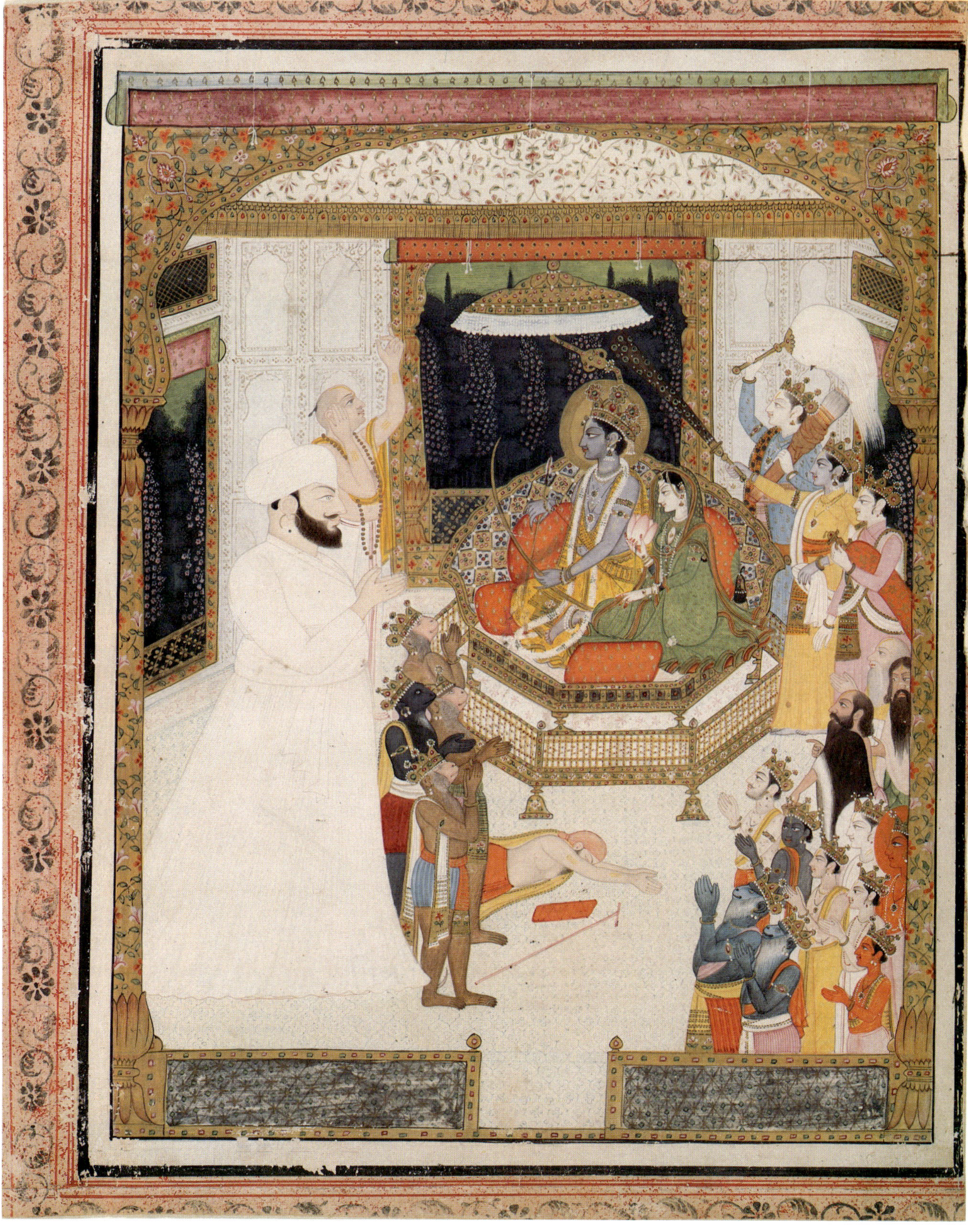

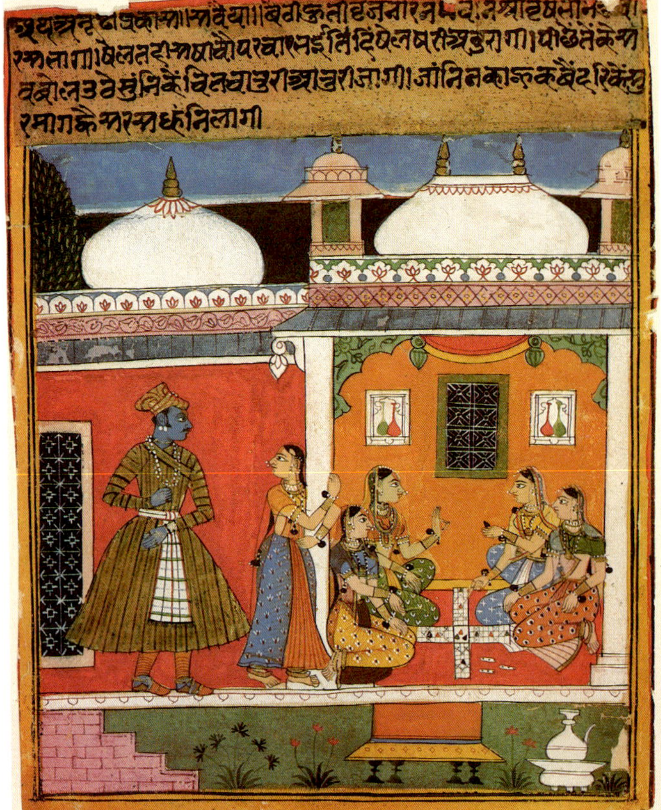

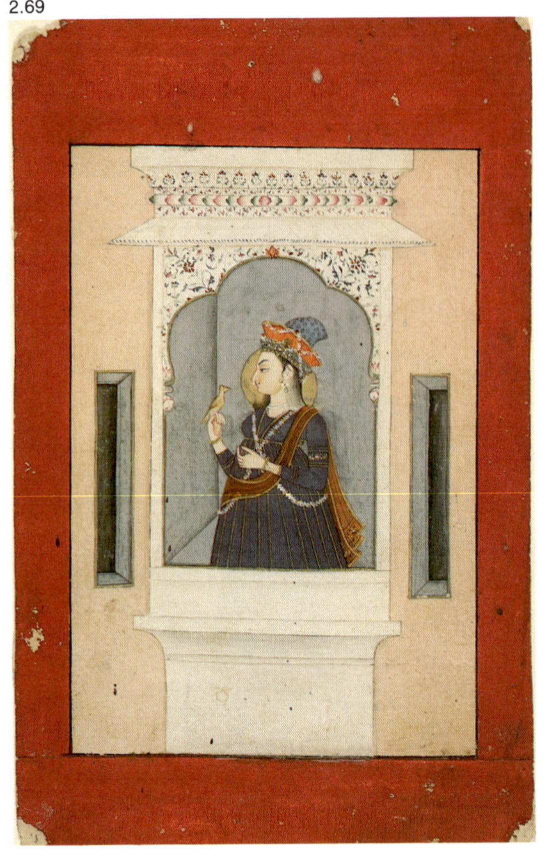

2.75

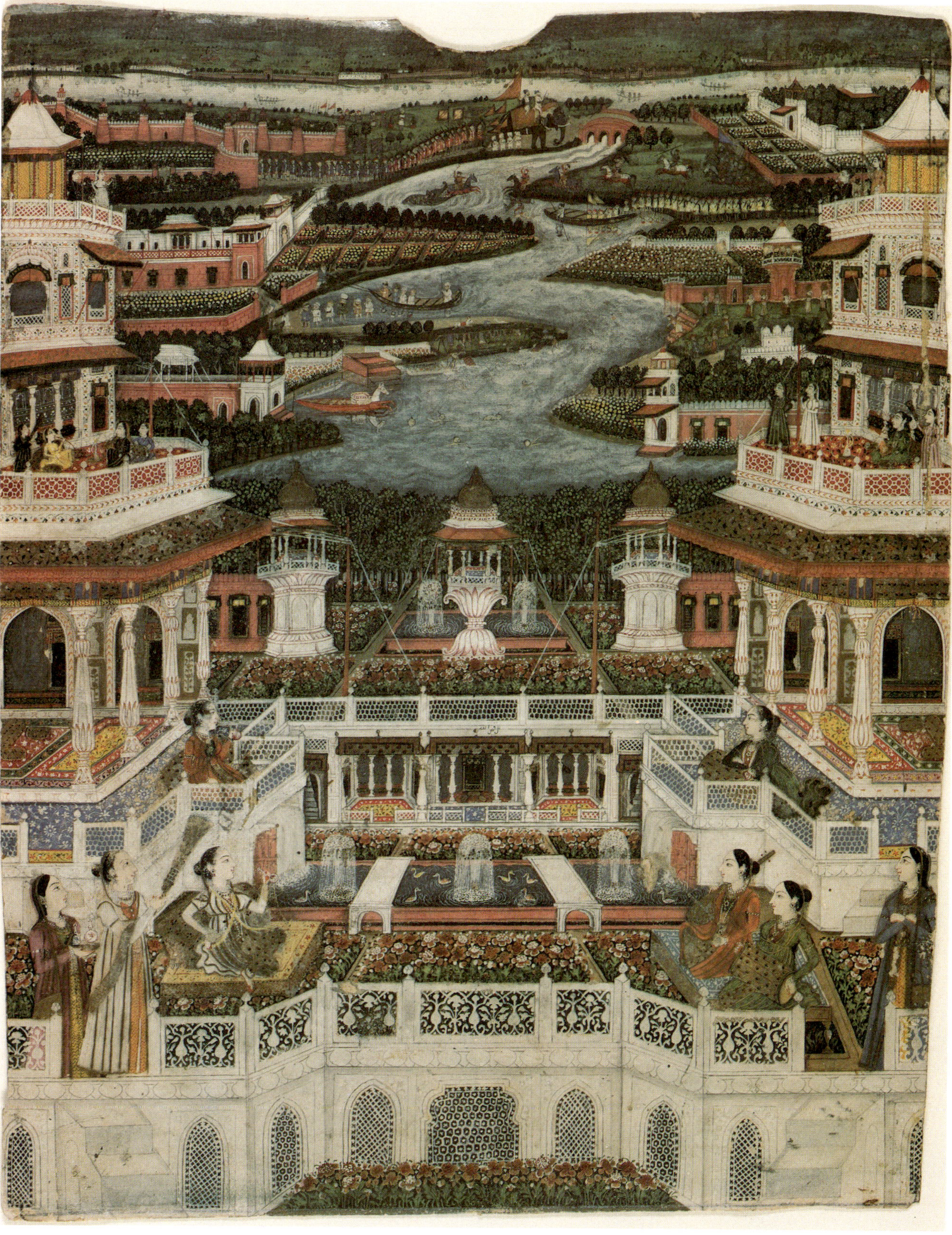

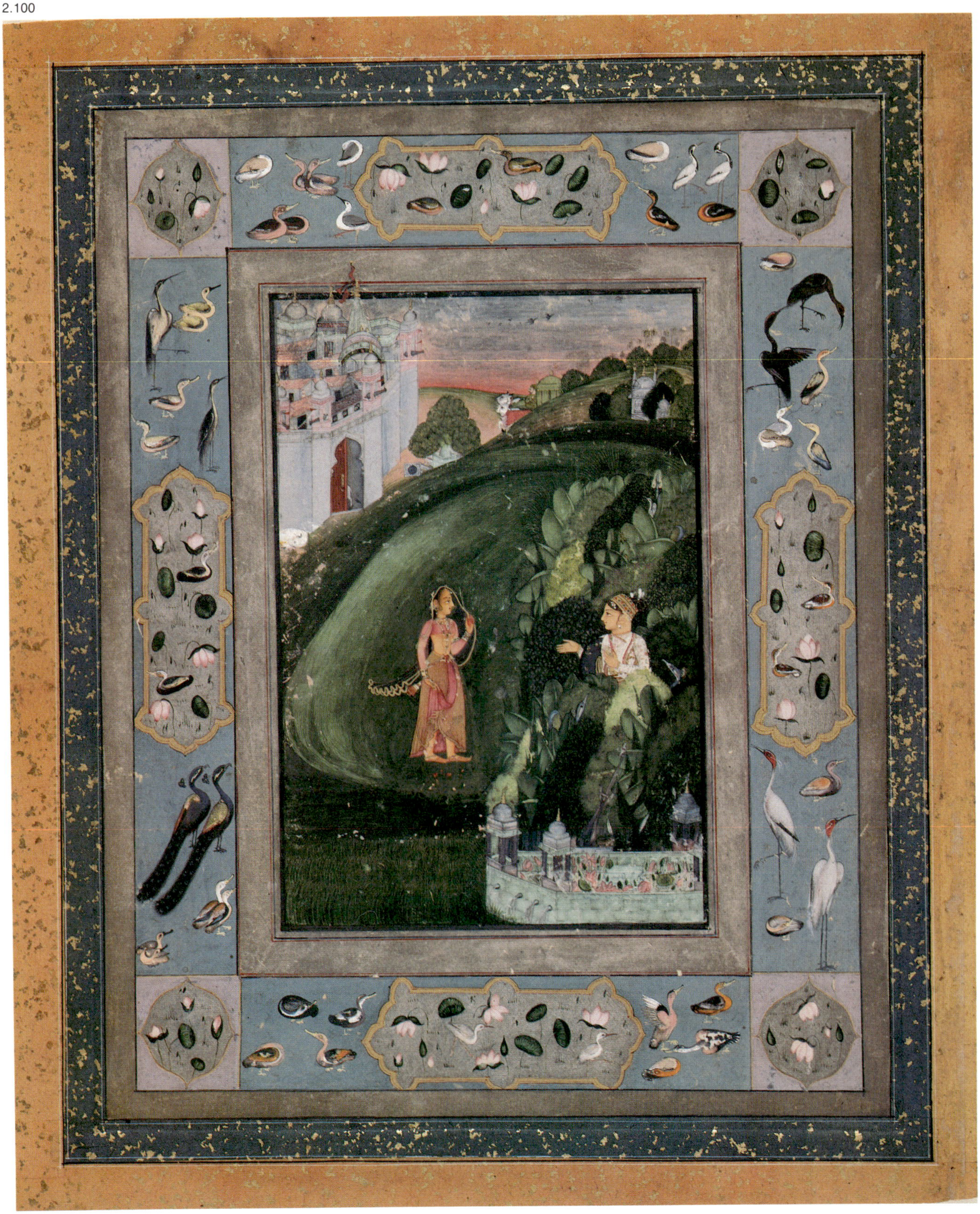

2.2a

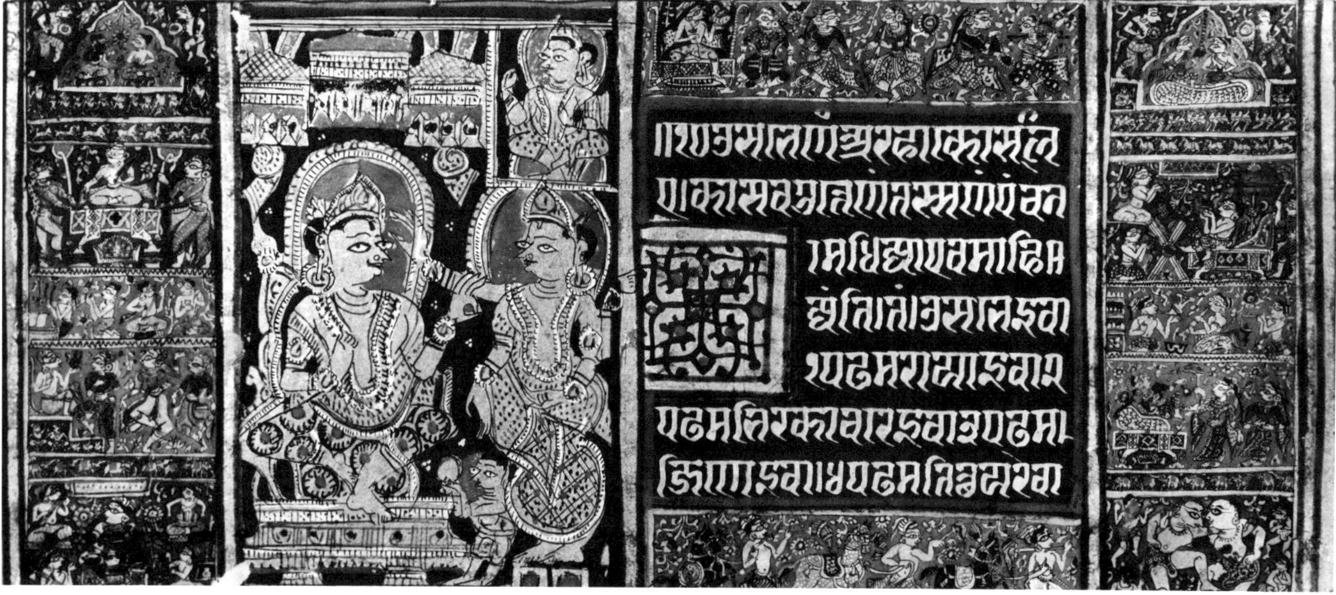

2.2b

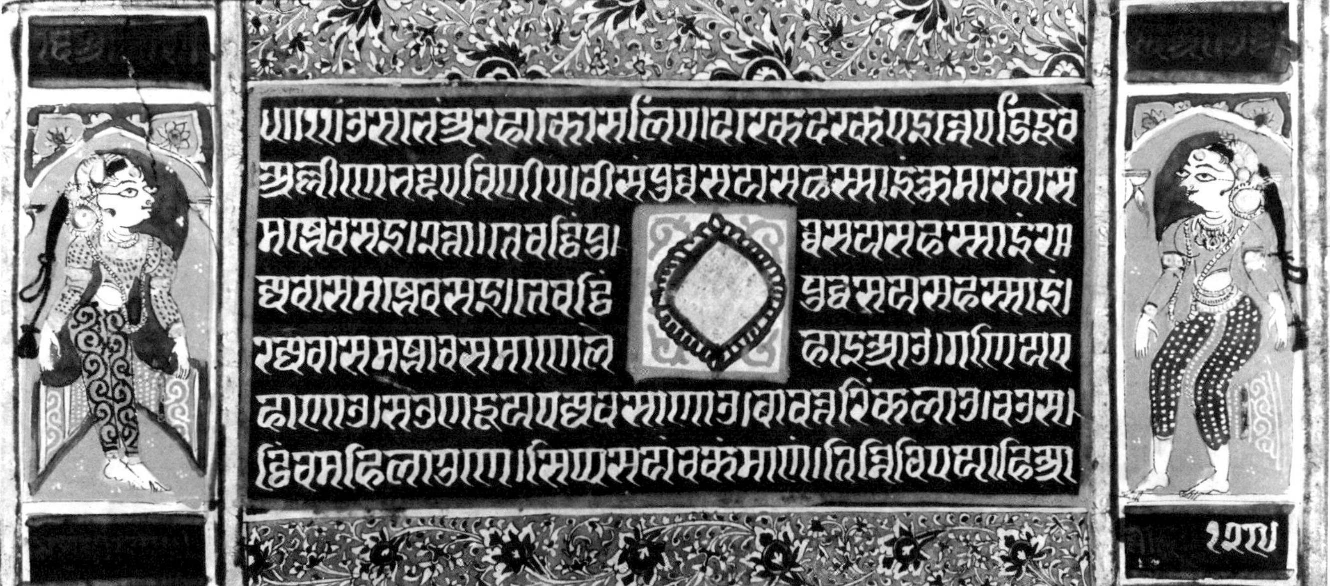

2.2 Four-Armed Deity Applies *Tilaka* to Enthroned Male: Folio from a *Suvarnaksari Kalpasutra* Ms.
Western Indian Style, c. 1475
4¹/₄ x 9⁷/₈ in.

In this folio, the large central painting depicts a four-armed deity applying an auspicious red mark to the forehead of an enthroned male figure. A small male figure at the base of the throne holds a mirror. Above the four-armed deity is another male figure, seated. The composition suggests a ceremonial context. The lavish use of gold in this cen-

tral portion emphasizes the scene's importance. Within the border areas, a deep yellow paint is used rather than gold. Pink, blue, red, brown, white, and black pigments color the small detailed compositions.

On the left of the folio, there are five registers with small bands of animals or a simple wavy line separating each scene. From top to bottom: two men sit within an arch with a warrior at either side and a row of marching figures flanked by two four-armed figures beneath; a male figure sits on a swing with two females in attendance; a

group of musicians play their instruments; three women dance before an enthroned male; and a male figure sits on a platform surrounded by musicians. The right margin is similarly divided. From top to bottom: two men sit inside an arch with two warriors flanking; an enthroned male figure holds a manuscript, two facing figures sit with cupped hands, a gesture of respect, and a fly-whisk waving attendant stands behind the throne; three musicians; a reclining woman with two female attendants; and two large wrestlers with four excited observers.

Above the text, a group of females dance and play musical instruments for the pleasure of an enthroned male figure. The male holds a bird in one hand, a lotus in the other. Below the text, three attendants holding fly-whisks lead horses.

The border decorations record incidents from every-day life. There is no apparent, specific narrative which they illustrate. The use of figural compositions for decorative panels is a small but significant aspect of ornamentation.

On the reverse, two women in dancing poses flank the text portion of the folio. Illustrations of classical dance poses on manuscripts of the *Kalpasutra* are typically Western Indian.

P. Chandra, *Indian Miniature Painting*, no. 3, color illustration of the obverse.

2.3 The Transfer of the Embryo: Folio from a Ms. of the *Kalpasutra*
Western Indian Style,
late fifteenth century
4⅝ x 11¾ in.

Trishala, the mother of the Jina, reclines on her bed. Harinegameshin, a goat-headed deity, stands behind holding a small gold object which is in fact the embryo of the Jina, Mahavira. The god Indra has commissioned Harinegameshin to transfer the embryo from the womb of a brahmin woman to that of the *kshatriya* queen. She lies under a canopy decorated with peacocks. Gold, green, white and black paint complement the color scheme which is dominated by red and blue. The reverse of the folio has several lines of text in black ink interspersed by three large red dots.

P. Chandra, *Indian Miniature Painting*, no. 4.

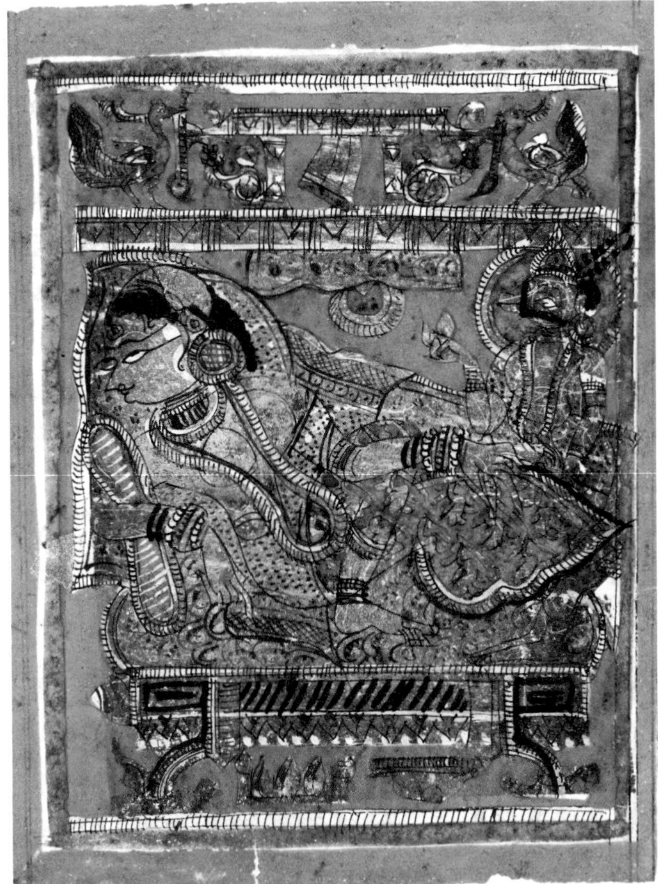
2.3

2.4 *Samvasarana* of a Tirthankara: Folio from a Ms. of the Kalpasutra
Western Indian Style,
late fifteenth century
4⅝ x 3¾ in.

The *samvasarana* is the resting place of the Jina after attaining knowledge. The gods, led by Indra, create the place so that the Jina can provide an edifying discourse. The enclosure is circular in plan, has twenty-thousand steps on four sides, as well as doors, roads and ponds before each set of steps. The theme of the painting emphasizes the cosmic nature of the Jina's experience.

P. Chandra, *Indian Miniature Painting*, no. 6.

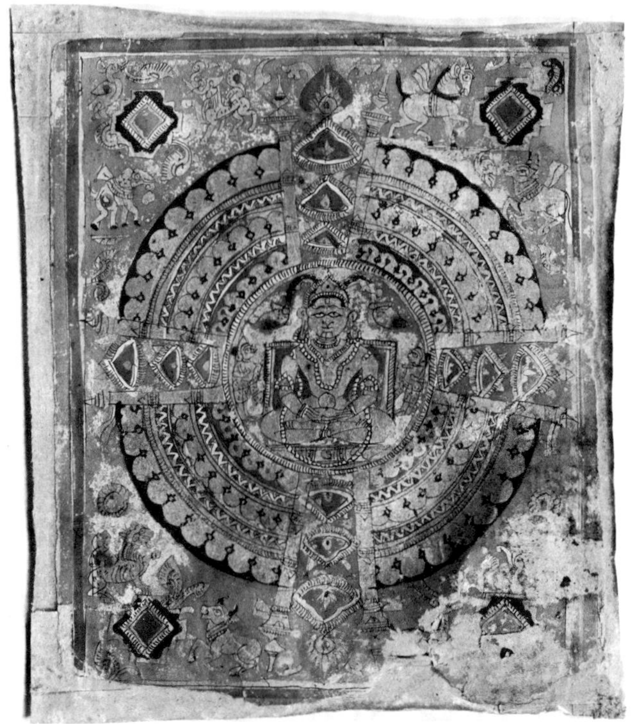
2.4

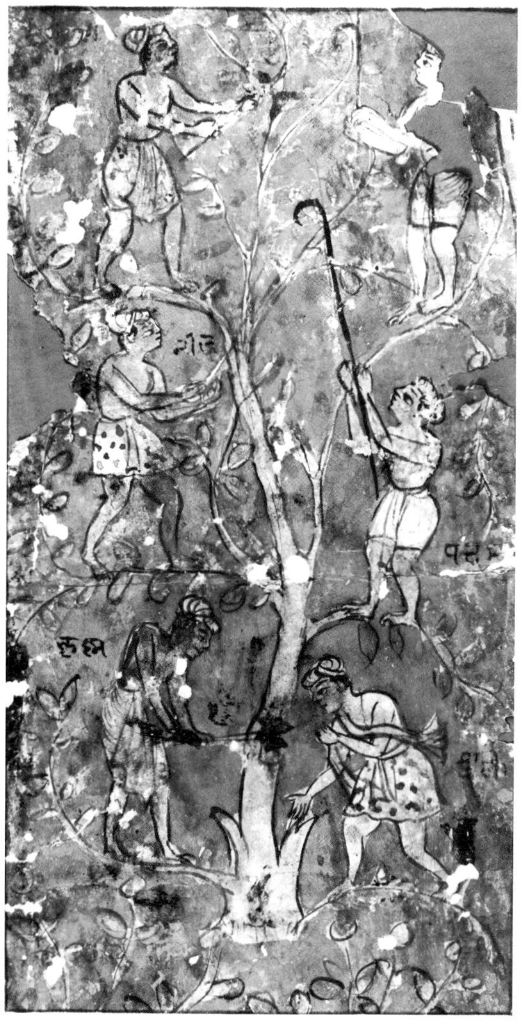

2.5 Doctrine of the Six *Lesyas:*
Folio from a Ms. of the
Sangrahani Sutra
Gujarat, c. 1625
7¼ x 3¾ in.

This painting illustrates the story of
different states of existence. The men,
whose body color reflects their spiritual
status, relate by their actions to the
central Tree of Life. The dark figure at
the bottom attempts to chop at the
roots thereby indicating a very base
nature. The white figure opposite uses
only the fruits and flowers that have fal-
len to the ground, indicating a higher
stage of religious progress. The yellow
tree is set against a flat red background.

P. Chandra, *Indian Miniature Painting,*
no. 84.

2.6 Neminatha and Worshippers:
Folio from a Ms. of the *Nemipurana*
Probably Mewar,
early eighteenth century
4⅝ x 4⅛ in.

The blue figure of the Tirthankara
Neminatha is described in the brief inscription above the painting. The cross-
legged figure has three heads. The
shrivatsa symbol on his chest is between two pronounced breasts. A
conch shell, his identifying attribute,
lies on his seat before him. Neminatha
sits beneath a stylized tree and gold
umbrella.
    A naked ascetic and a royal figure sit
to one side while Krishna, recognizable
by his blue color and peacock crown,
and Balarama sit to the other side.
From the Kushan period onward,
Krishna and Balarama are employed
in Jain art as attendants of the
Tirthankaras, attesting to the superiority
and religious powers which the Jinas
possess. Neminatha's legendary kin-
ship is tied to Krishna in certain Jain
traditions. A group of nine women sit
along the lower edge of the painting.
They are richly attired in cloth with a
variety of fabric designs, all of which
are highlighted in gold.

P. Chandra, *Indian Miniature Painting,*
no. 92.

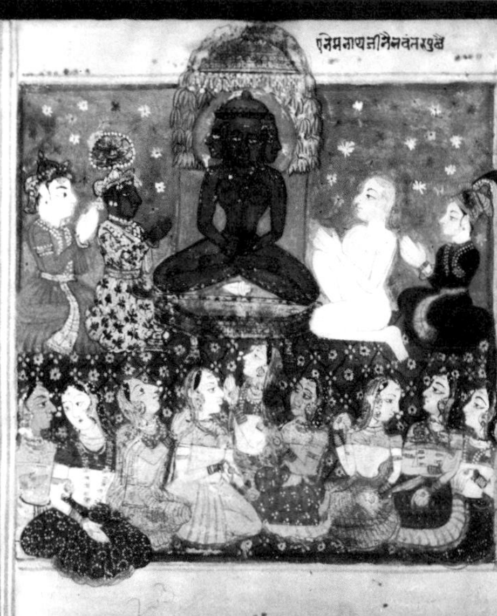

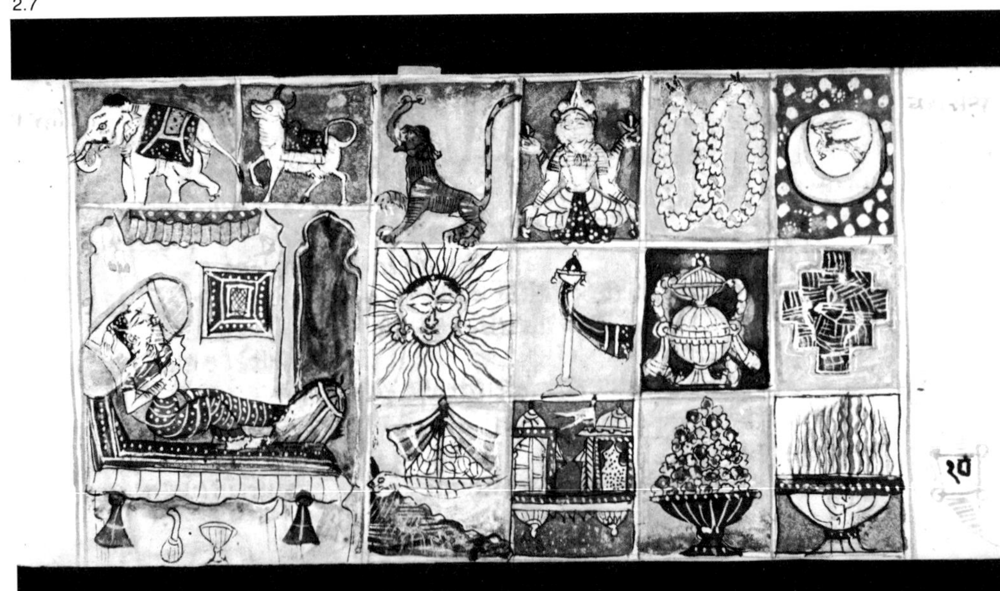

2.7 The Mother of a Tirthankara Dreams of Auspicious Symbols: Folio from a *Kalpasutra* Ms.
Probably Marwar, c. 1650-1675
4¹/₂ x 7⁷/₈ in.

Fourteen auspicious symbols appear in compartments before the reclining figure of the mother-to-be. These symbols are: an elephant, a bull, an elephant-headed tiger, the Goddess Shri, two garlands, the moon, the sun, a banner, a vase, a lotus lake, a ship, a mansion, a pile of jewels and a smokeless fire. Such auspicious symbols appear in the dreams of each Tirthankara's mother presaging the birth of a Jina. Twelve lines of text on the reverse side are composed in black and red ink.

P. Chandra, *Indian Miniature Painting*, no. 141.

2.8 Jaina Monks Addressing the Laity: Fragment of a *Vijnaptipatra*
Nagaur, mid-eighteenth century
20³/₄ x 7⁷/₈ in.

Not illustrated

This large painting was part of a *vijnaptipatra*, a letter inviting a monk to visit a Jain community. Three monks addressing their respective congregations hold manuscripts in a prominent position. Each monk has a small broom, an important Jain monastic accutrement. The monks, aware of the value of every aspect of life, use the broom to remove insects from the ground, lest they be inadvertently injured when the monk sits to preach, meditate, etc. The monks must be members of the Shvetambara sect since they appear clothed. Their congregations include lay men and women as well as one nun, who is dressed in white.

P. Chandra, *Indian Miniature Painting*, no. 148, black-and-white illustration.

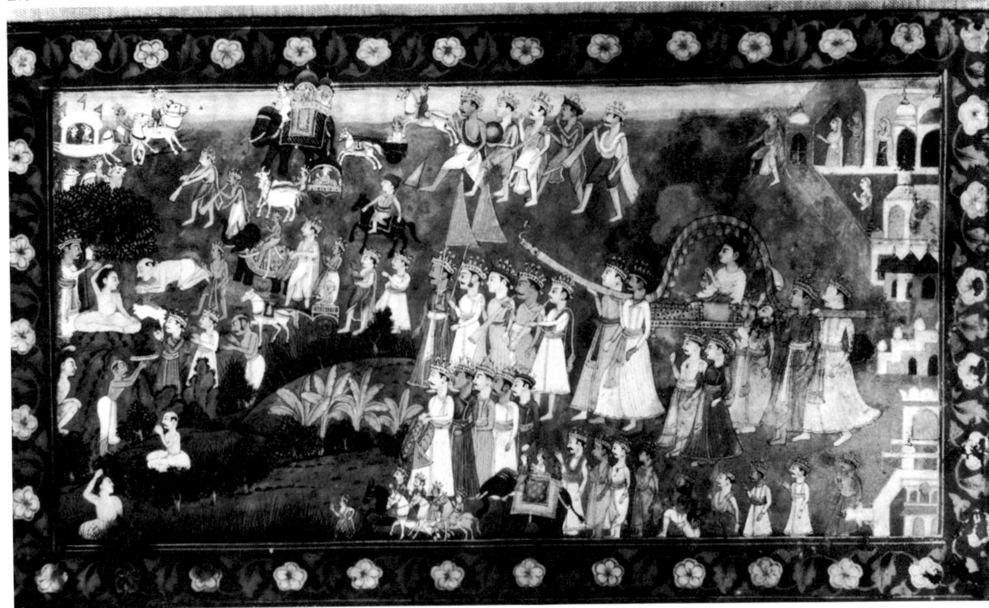

2.9

2.9 A Tirthankara Renouncing the World
Rajasthani Style,
late eighteenth century
3³/₄ x 7¹/₂ in.

The transition from a secular to a religious life is a focal moment in time. In this painting, a Jain Tirthankara leaves the palace on a palanquin. A procession of musicians, flagbearers and various deities accompany him. Surya driving his horse chariot and Indra riding on an elephant move toward the left. In a second appearance, the Tirthankara now seated under a tree, has discarded his princely raiments and is shearing his locks, which an attendant gathers on a tray. According to a widespread tradition, sages embarking upon serious meditation seat themselves under a tree and rid themselves of worldly attachments. Against the green background, a hilly, lightly forested terrain is depicted. The costumes in yellow, orange, white and pink are highlighted in gold.

P. Chandra, *Indian Miniature Painting*, no. 215.

2.10a

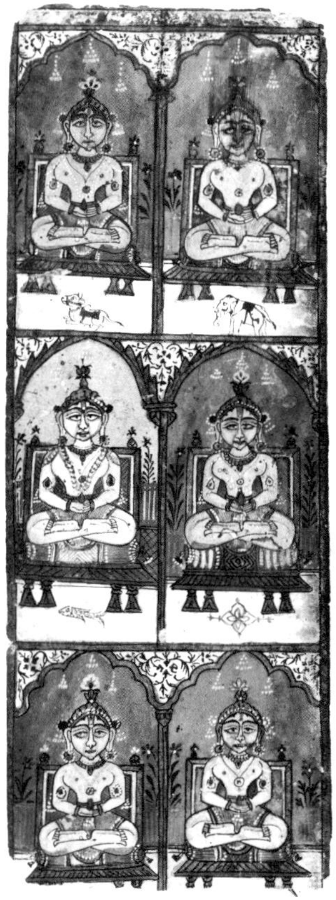

2.10b

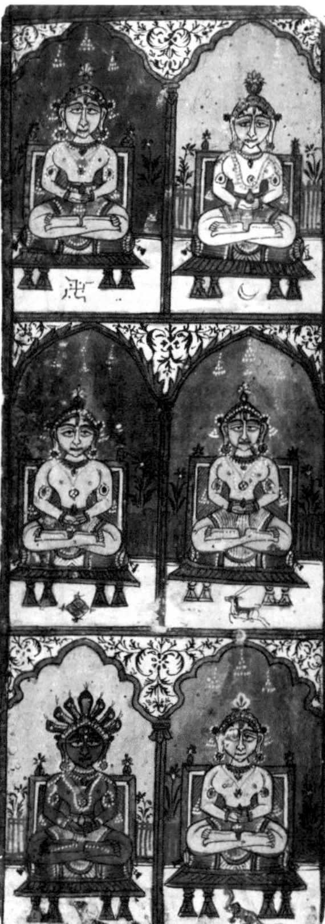

2.10c

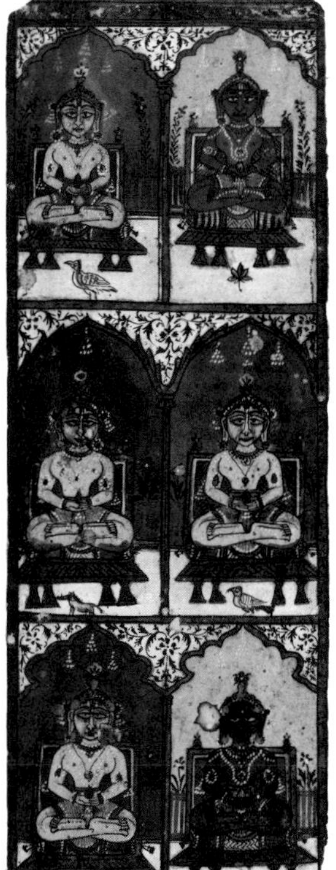

2.10d

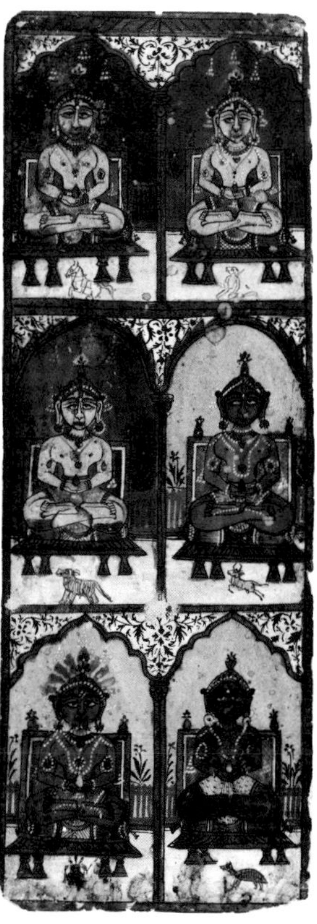

2.10 Jain Tirthankaras: Four Folios
Rajasthani Style,
late eighteenth century
8¾ x 3 in.

Each of the four folios of this set is divided into six panels. A cross-legged, enthroned Jina with hands in the meditating gesture occupies each panel. Each of the twenty-four figures holds a small, flame-shaped jewel in his hands. Beneath each throne, an animal or auspicious symbol is depicted. The identity of individual Tirthankaras is not always clear. Sixteen of the figures are yellow, and two each are white, blue and orange. The remaining two figures are green and have crowns with serpent hoods. The serpent hood is an attribute of Parshvanatha, one of the Tirthankaras. Yellow is the background color for all but the yellow figures. Eleven of the yellow figures sit against a green background, three against blue and two against orange. The objects under the thrones include: a bull, an elephant, a fish, a floral design, two undecipherable objects, a swastika, a crescent moon, a geometric symbol, an antelope, a fantastic lizard-like creature, another elephant, a bird, a lotus, a horse, another bird, another lotus, a conch shell, another horse, a kneeling Naigemesha who is the goat-headed deity of Jainism, a broad-nozzled animal, a bull, a small water vase with vegetation and a brown animal of an indeterminate species. The range of colors and symbols are representative of Jain iconography although specific patterns are not evident.

P. Chandra, *Indian Miniature Painting,* no. 221.

Themes from Shaivite Traditions

2.11 **Shiva and Parvati**
Bundi, end of the seventeenth century
4³/₈ x 4¹/₄ in.

Not illustrated

Shiva, with a snake emerging from his topknot, turns toward Parvati. In addition to a third eye, the moon crescent is placed on his forehead. A snake and a garland of skulls lie on his shoulders. His right hand holds a rosary while the left rests on the tiger skin upon which he sits. Nandi, Shiva's bull mount, rests nearby. A few clumps of green growth and a narrow stream complete this fragment which has an unpainted background.

P. Chandra, *Indian Miniature Painting,* no. 112.

Shiva is a great Hindu God. His consort is Parvati, with whom he shares two sons, the elephant-headed Ganesha and the warrior Skanda. Nandi, a bull, is Shiva's mount. Some of Shiva's typical attributes include a drum, a rosary, a trident and a flame. His hair, which is usually depicted as the matted locks of an ascetic, is ornamented with a skull and crescent moon. Shiva's fierce aspect is emphasized by a skull necklace and the animal skins which he wears and upon which he sits. There is a vertical third eye on his forehead. Snakes comprise his ornaments as well as his sacred thread which all twice-born male Hindus wear across their chest (nos. 2.11, 2.15-2.17). The supramundane aspects which overlay a basic anthropomorphic form have roots in the elaborate mythology which surrounds Shiva. His power is exemplified by a blue throat, the repository of a poisonous draught which would have killed a lesser being (no. 2.17). His benevolence is captured in the painting illustrating the story of the descent of the Ganges River from heaven. Shiva, seated with Parvati, allows the river to break her fall upon his head because a direct passage from heaven to earth would have rent apart the earth (no. 2.16).

Shiva is also worshipped in the form of a phallus, *(linga),* an indication of unreleased power. The theme of a woman or group of women worshipping the Shiva *linga* is portrayed in three paintings in this exhibition. The Bikaner painting is a delicate portrayal. Attention is focused on the woman making the offerings to the *linga* by the concentration of the pictoral elements in one corner under a tall tree. The broad expanse of muted color behind her, further highlights the devotee and her object of devotion (no. 2.12). The Mughal painting of the same theme evokes a mystical feeling, located in a natural setting within which trees bear fruit and nighttime travelers light fires for warmth and comfort (no. 2.13). The Basohli painting has an intense religiosity owing to the simplified naturalism of the figures and the strong, mood-evoking expanse of background color (no. 2.14). These three paintings offer an excellent basis for comparing the way in which different schools handle a single theme.

The Goddess is another source of adulation in Hinduism. There are many forms of the Goddess, both benign and terrible. Ferocious forms of the Goddess are considered particularly powerful. The four-armed Goddess seated upon the recumbent corpse of Shiva, her consort, suggests the power of time, of the stage in the universal order where abandon replaces attachments (no. 2.18). Another popular form of the Goddess is Durga killing the Buffalo-Demon. Mahisa, a demon, was troubling the gods. They all concentrated their powers and created the Goddess upon whom they bestowed all of their best weapons. The Goddess, riding her lion mount, battled the demon, who had assumed the form of a buffalo. She vanquished him, thus returning the heavens to the god. This active posture of the Goddess was the source for many paintings, including the Orissan example in this exhibition (no. 2.19).

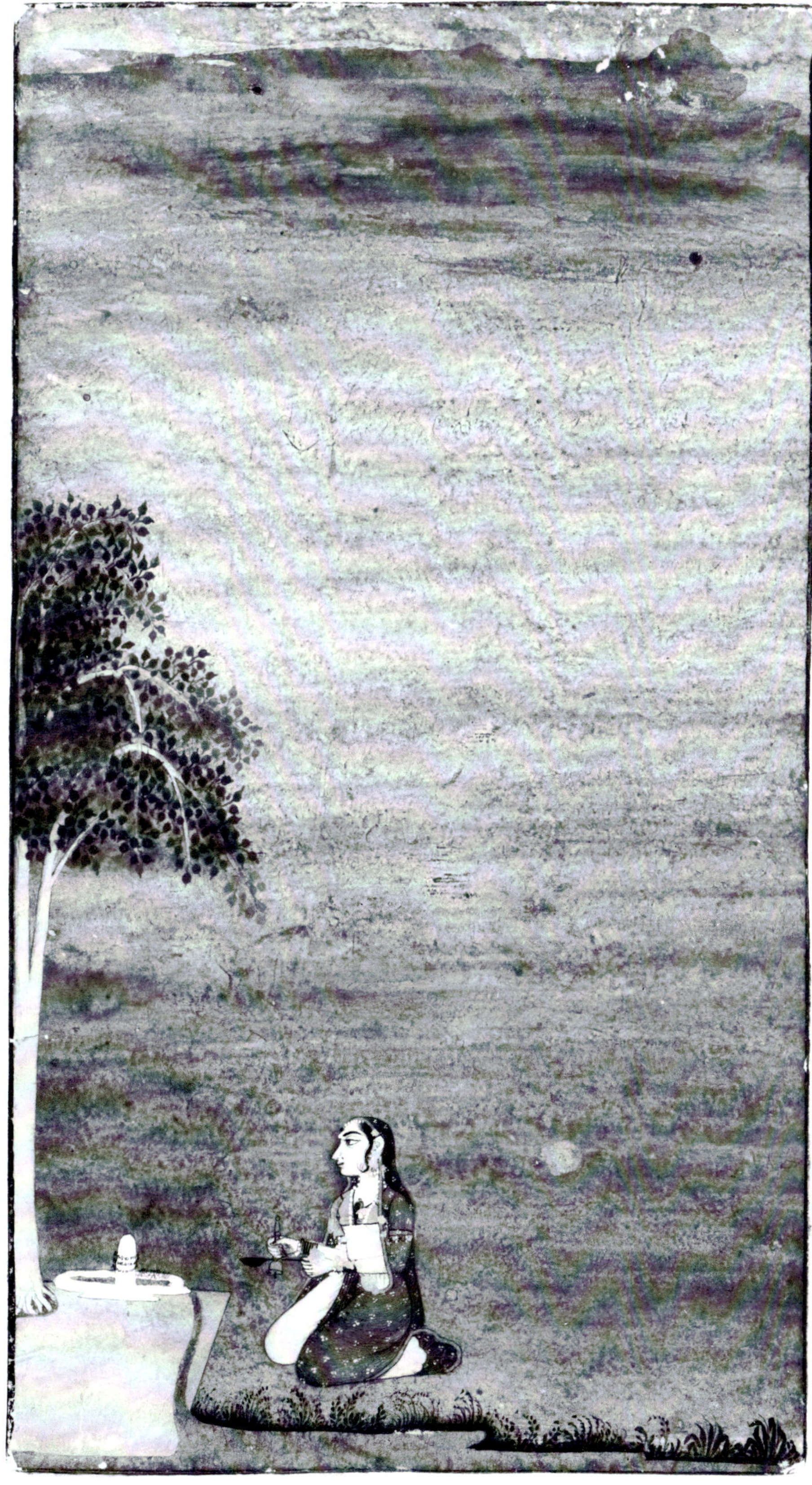

2.12 Lady Worshipping a
Shiva *Linga*
Bikaner, c. 1690
5⅝ x 3⅛ in.

A garlanded white *linga* is on a pink
platform at the base of a tree that fades
into the border of the painting. A kneeling woman rings a gold bell and offers
clarified butter from a spoon. Her
brightly colored dress, maroon scarf,
orange blouse and yellow skirt stand
out in high contrast to the muted green,
gray and blue background.

P. Chandra, *Indian Miniature Painting*,
no. 173.

2.13 Women Worshipping Shiva *Linga*

Mughal Style, period of Muhammad Shah (1719-1748)
5½ x 4⅛ in.

In this painting, the *linga* is placed within a shrine located at the base of a group of pear trees. A small lamp inside the niche provides abundant light. Three women are on the ground in front of the shrine. The foremost makes an offering to the *linga* while her companions wait. The women wear simple clothing. Their long hair has a golden sheen which complements their sparse jewelry. In the foreground, various floral and vegetative patterns are spread across the ground. Against the deep brown hillock in the background the shadow of a tree surrounds three seated figures before a fire. A pair of white birds can be seen in the dark night sky. The aura of mystic devotion is enchanced by predominantly dark colors with sparse, pointed use of lighted areas.

P. Chandra, *Indian Miniature Painting*, no. 33.

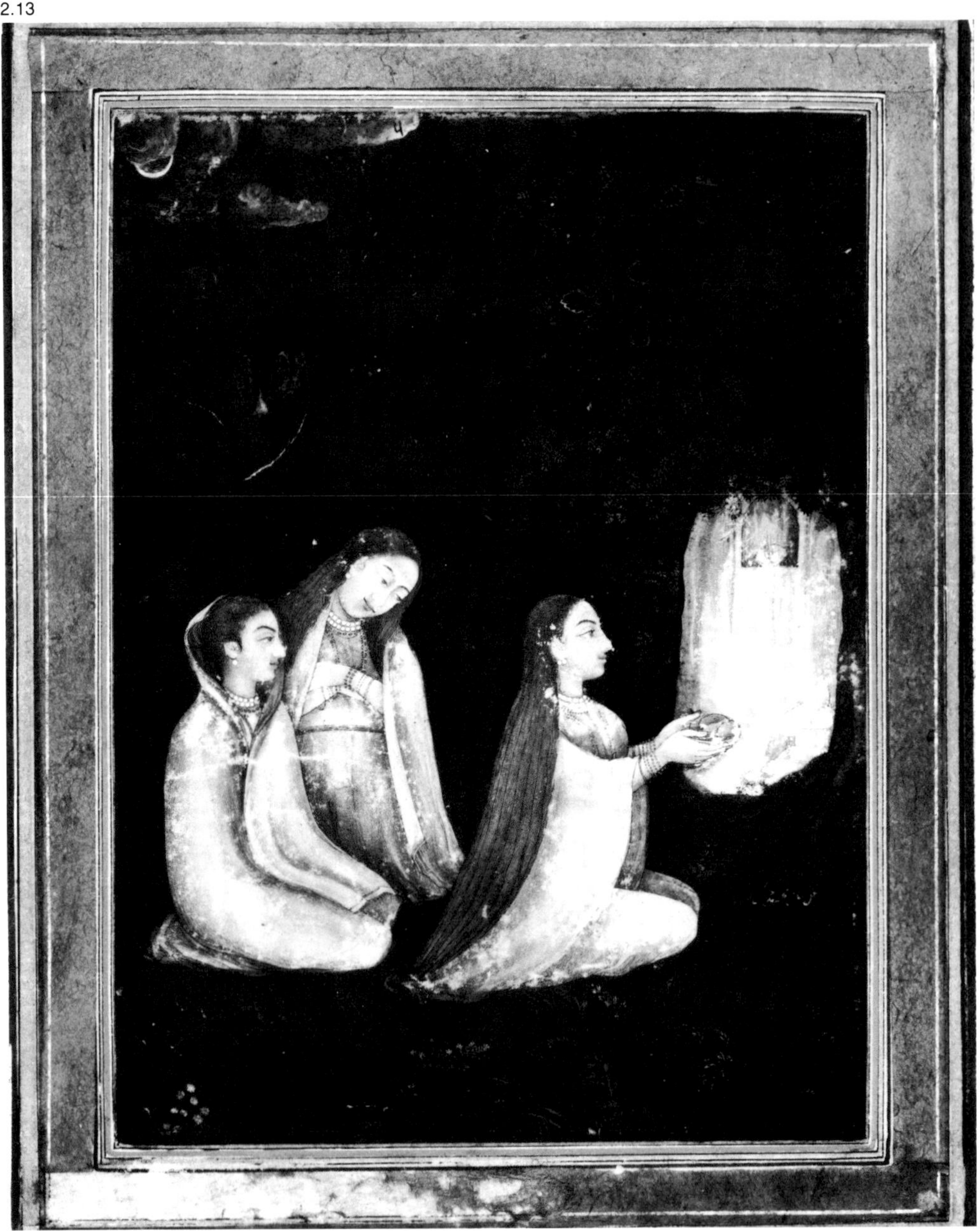

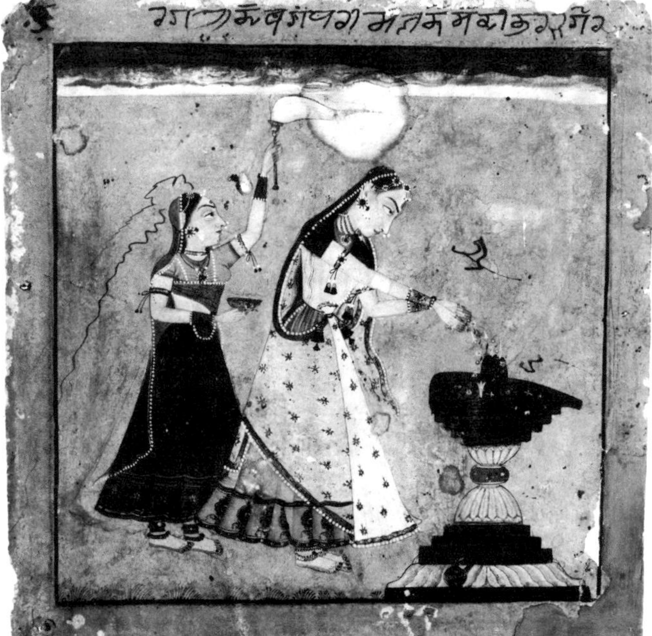

2.14

2.14 Ragini Devagandhari
Basohli Style, c. 1730
6⅞ x 6⅞ in.

The theme of a musical mode is identified in an inscription on the upper border of the painting. A women offers worship to the Shiva *linga* by scattering flowers upon it. Her attendant, who is depicted on a smaller scale, stands behind the queen holding a fly-whisk and a small bowl which contained the offered flowers. The different scales of major and minor figures is a common technique of religious art, employed to emphasize status.

P. Chandra, *Indian Miniature Painting*, no. 230.

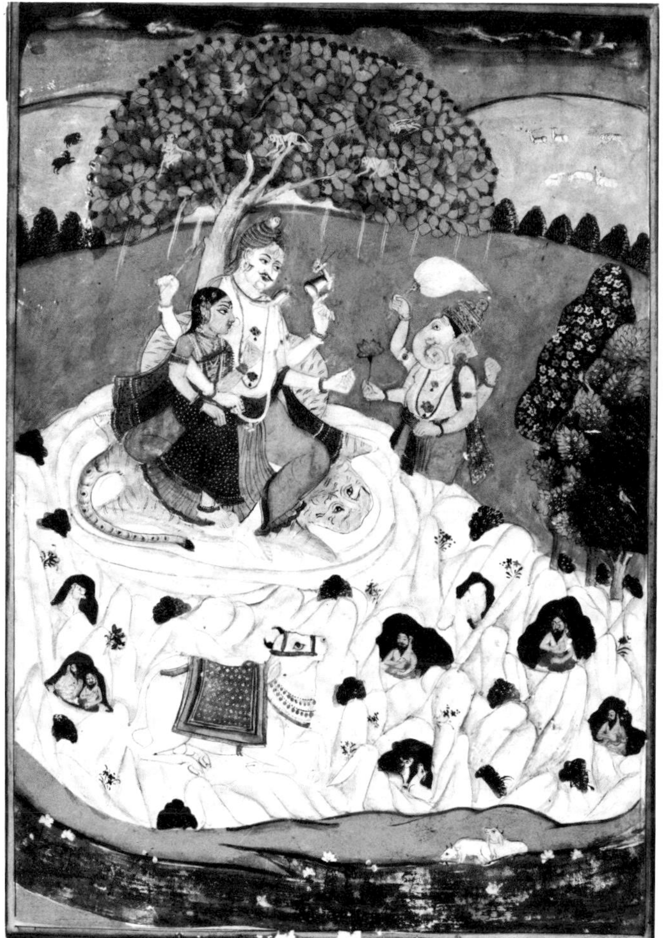

2.15

**2.15 Shiva and Parvati
on Mount Kailasha**
Deccani Style, early nineteenth century
9⅝ x 6¾ in.

The iconography of Shiva is unmistakable, including his matted locks, vertical third eye and the snake around his neck. The four-armed deity sits on a tiger skin. His upper hands hold a black antelope and a trident; one of his lower arms embraces Parvati while the other extends toward his elephant-headed son, Ganesha. Ganesha also has four-arms. Two of the elephant-headed deity's hands are empty while the other two hold a fly-whisk and a lotus. Parvati sits on Shiva's lap. The bull Nandi lies on the mountain below the divine pair. Small caves filled with ascetics and various animals dot the mountain.

P. Chandra, *Indian Miniature Painting*, no. 72.

2.16 The Descent of the Ganges
Kangra Style, early nineteenth century
9 x 6 in.

In the midst of a pink mountain range,
Shiva and Parvati sit in a cave on Mt.
Kailasha. The bull Nandi is in attendance. From the topknot of Shiva's
matted locks, the River Ganges
springs. A male ascetic, standing in a
yogic posture, receives the river in his
cupped hands. The Kangra artist
echoed the loving relationship of Shiva
and Parvati by wrapping creepers
around each of the three background
trees and placing the pairs of birds on
either side of the deities. The austerity
of Shiva which is implied by the iconographic conception of this figure is
tempered by the mood of love and
union.

P. Chandra, *Indian Miniature Painting*,
no. 253, black-and-white illustration.

2.17 Shiva Seated on an Elephant Skin
Jaipur, early twentieth century
3¹⁄₈ x 8¹⁄₈ in.

Not illustrated

The six-armed Shiva holds a trident,
discus, rosary, drum, conch shell and
water pot. He wears snakes as armlets.
From his snake-encoiled topknot, the
River Ganges emerges as a thin
stream of water. His blue throat
signifies the strength of his austerity,
because the poisonous solution he
swallowed did no more harm than to
color his throat. The snake and skull
garland further emphasize the power
derived from his austerities. The third
eye on his forehead is capped by a
crescent moon. Shiva sits upon an elephant hide, the skin of a defeated
enemy. The setting is Mount Kailasha,
with a river and a city in the distant
background. The precision and attention to detail seen in this painting reflect
the influence of photography.

P. Chandra, *Indian Miniature Painting*,
no. 201.

2.16

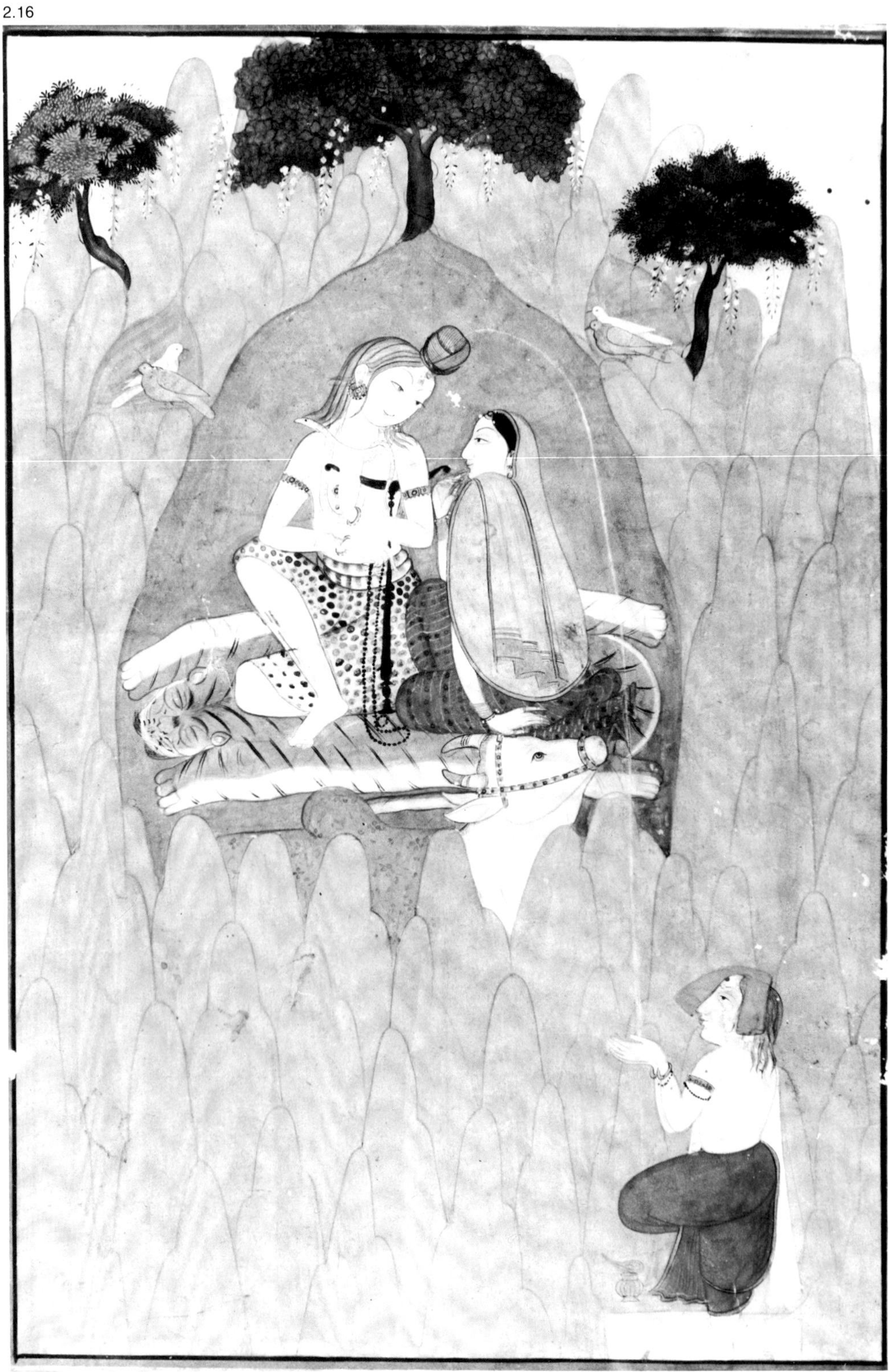

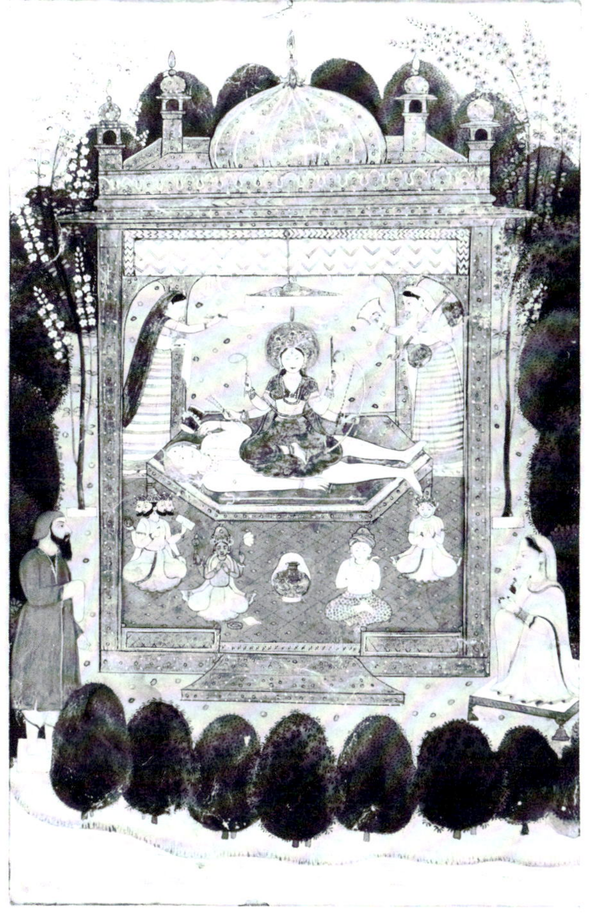

2.18 A Hill Chief and his Consort Adoring the Goddess

Kangra Style, late eighteenth century
7⅝ x 4⅞ in.

Surrounded by an arbor of green and flowering trees, an open-sided, golden pavilion houses the Goddess and her retinue. The four-armed Goddess sits under a golden umbrella. The attributes she holds include the moon, an elephant goad, a bow and five arrows of different colors. She sits upon a recumbent Shiva, recognizable because of his third eye, drum and trident. Four gods sit on the rug before the Goddess. Four-headed, four-armed Brahma holds a water pot, a manuscript and a rosary, while his fourth hand rests on his knee. Vishnu, also four-armed, holds the club and a lotus bud. His front hands are folded while the discus and conch shell lie on the ground before him. Shiva, with his two hands folded, wears an animal-skin *dhoti* and has a snake around his head. His hair is wrapped in the matted locks typical of ascetics. The fourth deity, whose hands are joined before his chest, is probably Indra. Two women attend the Goddess, one waving a fly-whisk and holding a white cloth, the other waving a fan and holding a stringed musical instrument. Outside the pavilion, the hill chief and his consort prepare to offer obeisance to the Goddess.

The love and reverence due to the Goddess is emphasized by the range of attendant figures as well as by the golden pavilion. The encirclement of the pavilion by lush vegetation emphasizes the cosmic recognisance of the Goddess' power. The river in the foreground and the suggestion of hills in the background reflect the actual environment of hill shrines.

P. Chandra, *Indian Miniature Painting*, no. 238, black-and-white illustration.

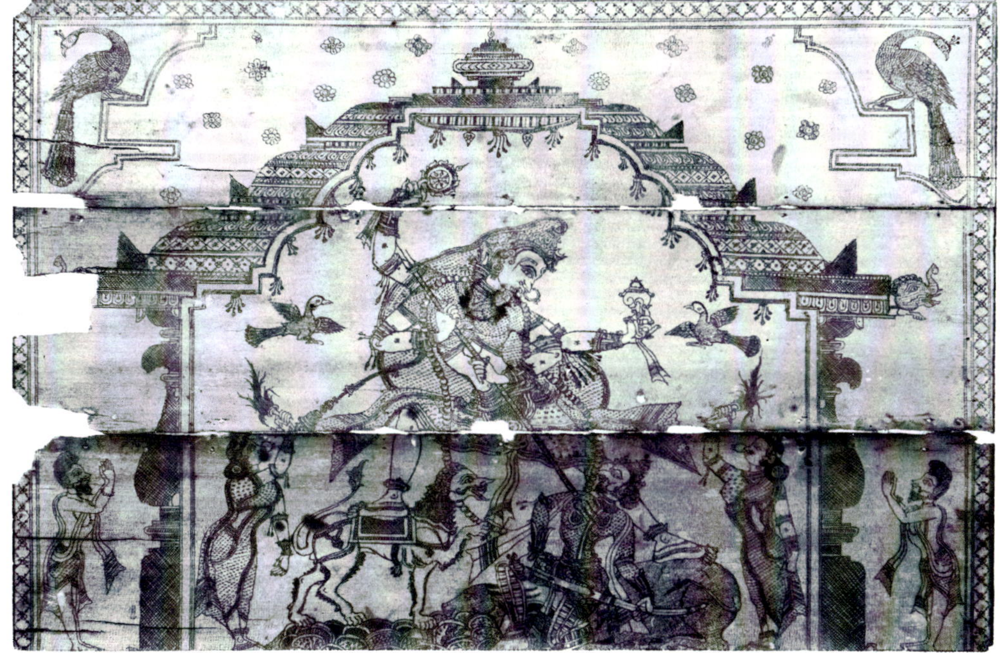

2.19 Devi Slaying the Buffalo-Demon

Orissa, eighteenth or nineteenth century
4⅞ x 7½ in.

The four-armed Goddess slays the buffalo in which a demon resides. The powerful aspect of the Goddess has a long antiquity in India and finds numerous depictions in stone reliefs beginning in the early centuries of the Christian era. This painting is executed on three attached palm-leaf strips. The dark brown surface of the palm leaves are painted in black giving the appearance of fine etching. The architecture is similar to that in other Orissan paintings from the eighteenth century.

P. Chandra, *Indian Miniature Painting*, no. 8.

Themes from Vaishnavite Traditions

The Hindu God Vishnu is the preserver of the world. His mount is Garuda, a bird. There are many hieratic forms of the God, some of which place him in the company of his consort, the Goddess Lakshmi (no. 2.20). One of the most popular aspects of Vishnu is the ten incarnations he undertakes to preserve order in the world. Depending on the nature of the threat, Vishnu assumes an appropriate form. The incarnations include: the fish, the tortoise, the boar, the man-lion, the dwarf, Parasurama, Rama, Krishna and the Buddha. An incarnation yet to come is Kalki, a white horse (no. 2.21). Of these incarnations, Rama and Krishna are the most popular as subjects for miniature paintings.

Rama is known from the great Sanskrit epic the *Ramayana* of Valmiki which was translated into Hindi and other vernacular languages in the sixteenth century. The epic revolves around the abduction of Sita, Rama's wife, by a demon king named Ravana. Rama, accompanied by his brother Lakshmana, attempts to rescue Sita from the walled city of Lanka. An army of bears and monkeys, gathered during a self-imposed forest exile, follow Rama in his journey and into battle. The monkey Hanuman assumes a prominent place as devout attendant of Rama and Sita in religious practice and in art (no. 2.23).

The Ramayana was a subject of many manuscript illustrations. In some folios, the epic is recorded as a series of distinct episodic moments (no. 2.22). This method of narration precluded the need for textual accompaniment and echoes the style of narrative portrayal used on temple walls where long horizontal registers contained depictions of episodes from various tales. The artist made selected use of background features, such as a consistent background tree, to bring attention to the central figure, in this case Rama, in each frame. The master served by unflinching followers (nos. 2.24, 2.26), and the just and virtuous hero (no. 2.27) are among the themes extrapolated from the narrative flow. A compositional technique which integrated the divine and human worlds shows an historical figure approaching a deity. The God Rama, a just and virtuous king, is thus worshipped by gods and man alike (no. 2.25).

Paintings which illustrate aspects of Krishna are a testament to the virtuosity of the South Asian artist. Topics include Krishna as an object of devotion (nos. 2.28-2.34); episodes from the mythological life of Krishna as child, cowherd, and lover (nos. 2.35-2.37, 2.42, 2.43, 2.47-2.52, 2.55, 2.56); and illustrations of romantic poetry and musical modes which draw on the well-known qualities of Krishna to metaphorically express tone, mood or circumstances even though Krishna is not named in the written verses (nos. 2.38-2.41, 2.44, 2.46, 2.53, 2.54).

Krishna is the object of fervent devotion in many shrines and temples throughout the subcontinent. His color is blue or black, which reflects his connection to Vishnu. Cults devoted to Krishna, which emphasized various aspects of his character, grew during the Medieval period. In Nathadwara, in the Mewar region of Rajasthan, a cult arose which focused on Krishna as Shri Nathaji. Vallabhacharya (1479-1531, A.D.), a poet-saint, encouraged a complete surrender of one's self to God. The images associated with his cult emphasized the protective as well as the playful aspects of Krishna (nos. 2.29, 2.30, 2.32, 2.33). The pose of these Krishna images, in which one hand is held up above the head, suggests the story of Krishna lifting Mt. Govardhan to protect his companions from the wrath of Indra, a great Vedic deity, who sent torrential rains upon the Brindavan area. Enshrined figures of the flute-player Krishna (nos. 2.28-2.31) are shown in similar compositions. Many scenes from the childhood of Krishna are illustrated in paintings. In this exhibition, the birth of Krishna and a moment in his childhood are represented. The birth of Krishna was entangled in a switching of babes, from a regal to humble setting (nos. 2.51, 2.56). The purpose of the change was to avoid the evil designs of King Kamsa; the result of the change was to create a God who led the simple life of a cowherd, a familiar occupation to rural India. As a child, he was the delight of his parents and everyone whom he met. The ambivalence between his birth status and circumstances of his childhood is expressed in a painting that enriches the environment of a typical cowherd with palace walls (no. 2.42).

A large number of paintings focus on the relationship of Krishna and Radha, the divine lovers. The loneliness of separation (no. 2.47) as well as the bliss of union (no. 2.40), with the nuances of the lovers' relationship in between (nos. 2.37, 2.49) created narrative depictions as well as symbolic representations of the union of the soul and God. The cow-maids, of whom Radha is one, are all entranced by Krishna. The way in which he fills the needs of all is expressed in paintings of the *Rasa Mandala* which show Krishna in the company of many women, each of whom feels he is immediately beside her (no. 2.43).

Romantic poems and musical modes are depicted in paintings by figural compositions that evoke the appropriate tone and mood. Although not the exclusive source, Krishna and Radha provide the basis for many such paintings. The *Raga Dipak* (musical mode of light) shows Krishna and Radha with candles burning before them (no. 2.53). The *Raga Hindola* (musical mode of the swing) is visualized as figures in a mood of passion being swung to and fro (no. 2.49). The wealth of symbolism which permeates the paintings of all styles and regions enriches many of the depictions of Krishna and Radha. The excitement of union is enhanced by lightning surrounding dark clouds as Krishna and Radha embrace (no. 2.40). The loneliness of separation is evoked by the anguished figure of Radha searching for Krishna in a stark wooded area (no. 2.47).

2.20

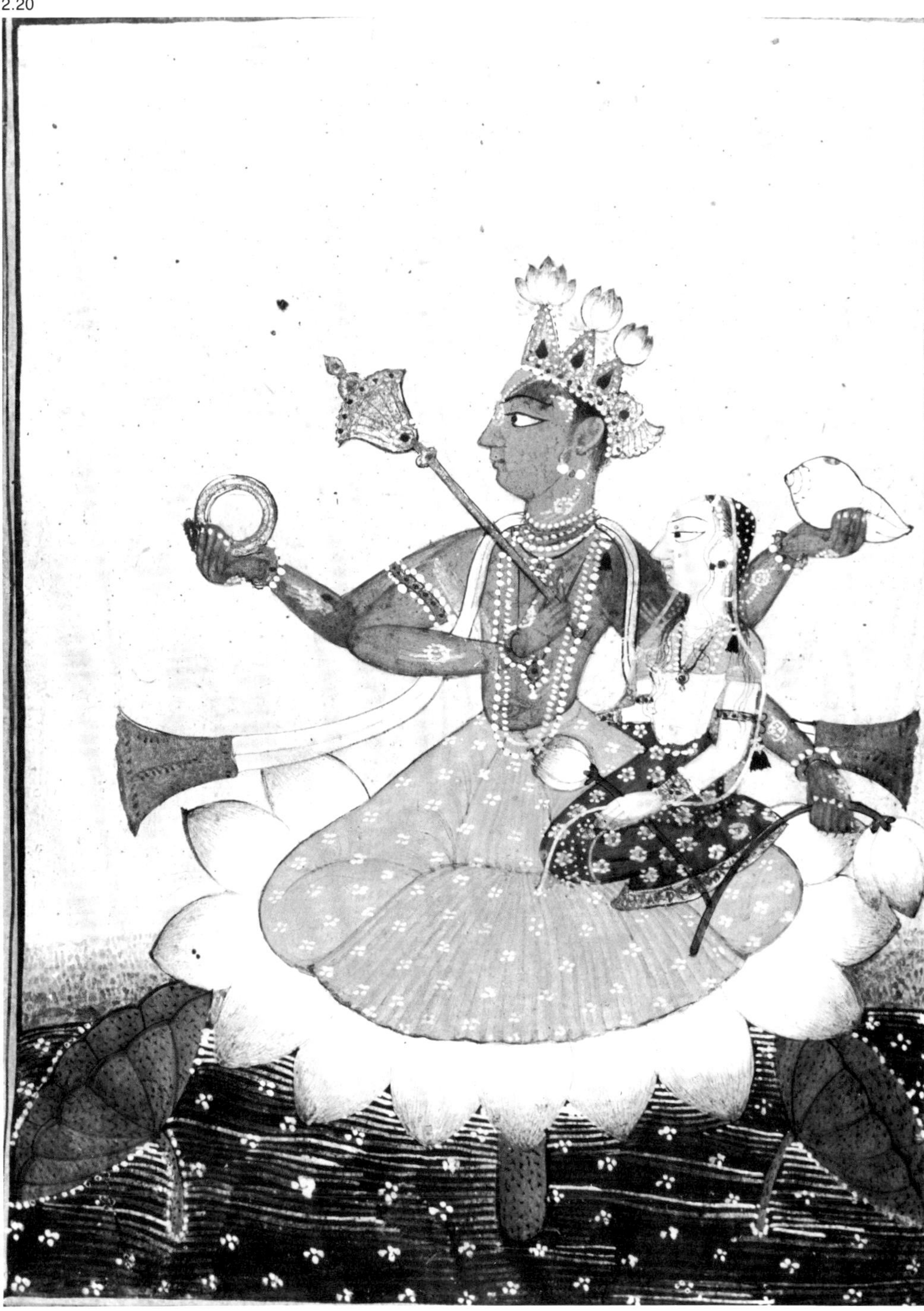

2.20 Lakshmi-Narayana
Basohli Style, c. 1730
7 x 4⁷/₈ in.

The four-armed male deity is Narayana, a form of Vishnu. His body is blue-gray in color. In his hands he holds a lotus, a conch shell, a club and a discus. His crown is surmounted by three lotus buds, a typical form of head dress for various deities depicted in the Basholi and other Punjab-Hill schools. Narayana's fair-complexioned consort, Lakshmi, is seated on his lap and holds a closed lotus bud. The hieratic scaling is typical of South Asian religious iconography. Attention is focused on the large figure of Narayana as the dominant character. The pair sits atop a lotus arising from the cosmic waters. The strong yellow background is topped by a narrow black band, indicating the sky.

P. Chandra, *Indian Miniature Painting*, no. 229.

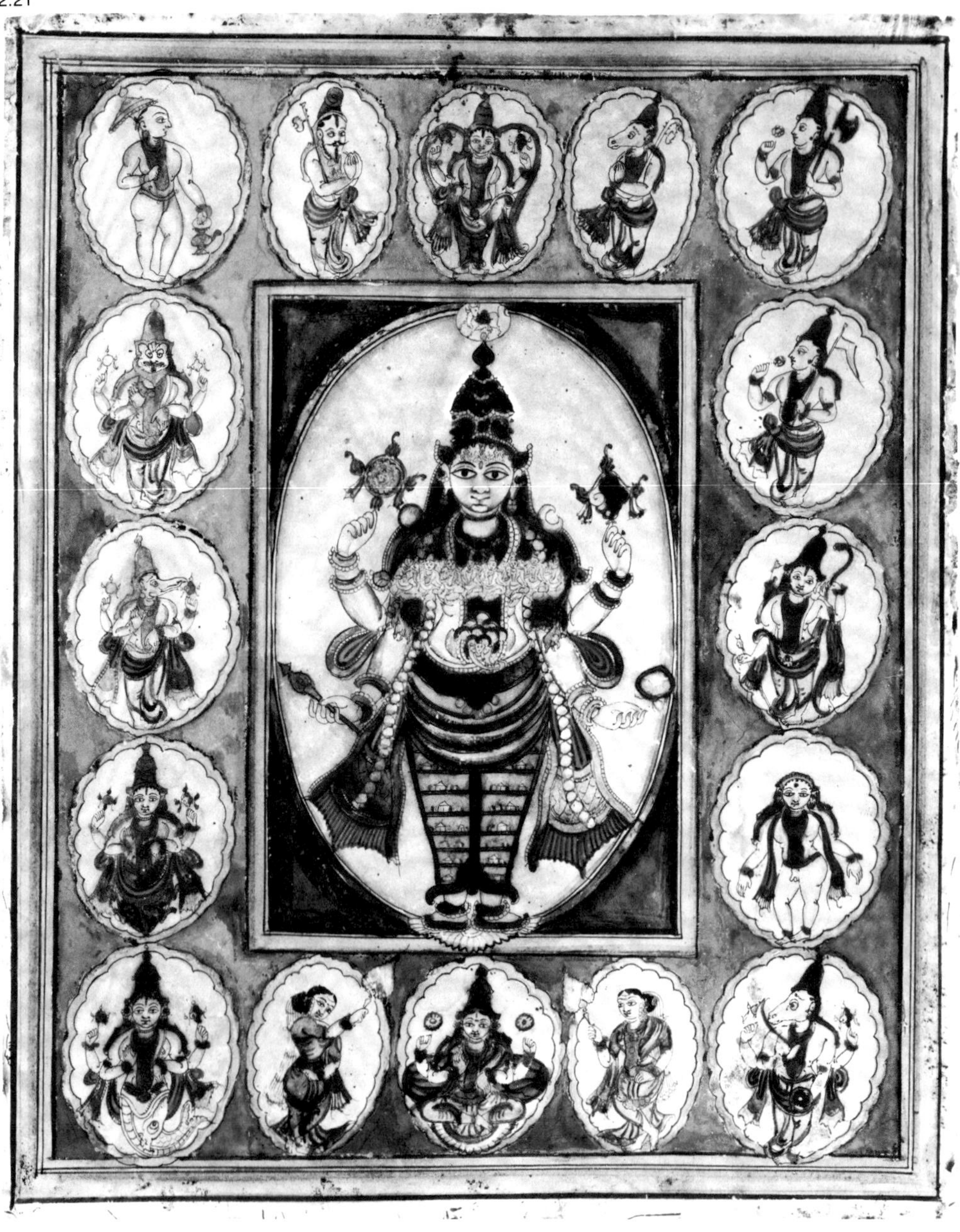

2.21

2.21 Vishnu and his Incarnations
South India, twentieth century
10¼ x 8¼ in.

The iconography of this painting reflects an interest in the cosmic aspect of Vishnu. In the center, within an oval panel nestled in a rectangular frame, stands a four-armed Vishnu. He holds the wheel, conch shell, club and lotus bud that make up his typical attributes. Above his tall crown is a small, encircled bull. Since the bull is usually associated with Shiva, it is difficult to explain the presence of this animal in a predominantly Vaishnavite context. Across the forehead and chest of Vishnu are a group of human figures, all male. These may be Vaishnavite saints from the area in which this painting was made.

The ten incarnations of Vishnu decorate the left and right borders of the painting. On the left, from the bottom, are the fish, tortoise, boar, manlion, and dwarf. On the right from the top are Parasurama, Balarama, Rama, Krishna, and Kalki. In the central top position stands Garuda, identifiable by the broad, stylized wings behind him. As the bird mount of Vishnu, his presence is appropriate. Narada and Tumburu flank Garuda. At the bottom, we see a four-armed female figure seated against a bolster. She holds two lotus buds and is probably Lakshmi, the consort of the God. The Goddess is flanked by two fly-whisk-waving attendants. The style of the Goddess' skirt, as well as the fact that she wears a blouse and has a braid which can be seen behind her left shoulder, distinguish the feminine character of this figure.

P. Chandra, *Indian Miniature Painting*, no. 271; he had identified the central figures in the top and bottom borders as figures of Vishnu.

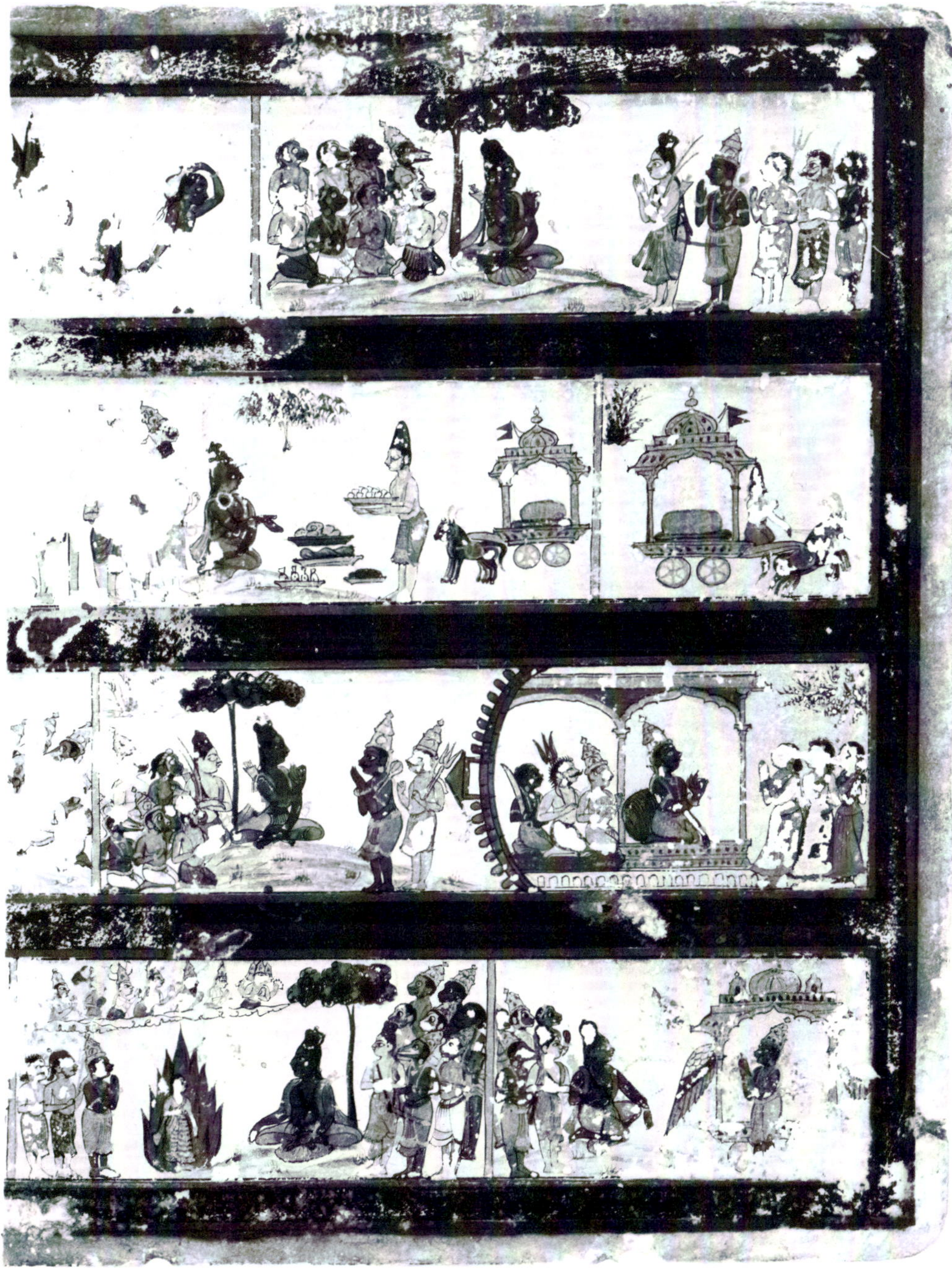

2.22 Scenes from the *Ramayana*
South India (probably Tanjore),
eighteenth century
6 x 4⅝ in.

This fragment contains four registers with scenes from the great epic, the *Ramayana*. In the top register, on the left, we see an ogress falling. In the course of his wanderings, Rama and his companions were often challenged by evil beings such as this female ogress. On the right, Rama sits under a tree with some of his troops as Lakshmana reports on current efforts being made to discover the whereabouts of Sita. At the left of the second register, Rama receives trays and baskets of gifts. To the right, the driver who has delivered the gifts leaves with his empty chariot. Reading from the left of the third register, Rama is seated under a tree receiving a report from his generals while Ravana, the evil abductor of Sita, sits in his walled city of Lanka. The bottom register shows Sita undergoing the test of fire, which will prove that she remained chaste during her long captivity, while an aerial chariot appears on the right.

Rama is depicted in a green color while his monkey and bear troops are represented in yellow, orange, blue, pink, brown, and green. This fragment suggests the typical compositional format of temple cloths as well as of temple plinth decoration, where rows of long rectangular panels are decorated with a narrative cycle. The empty chariot at the end of the second register suggests that the registers should be read from left to right.

P. Chandra, *Indian Miniature Painting,* no. 268, black-and-white illustration.

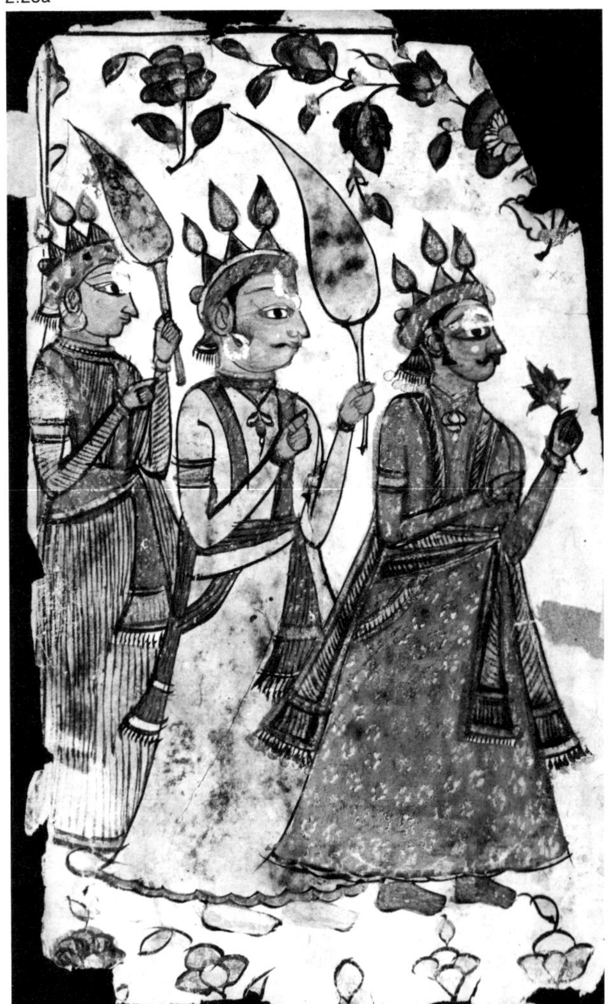

2.23a

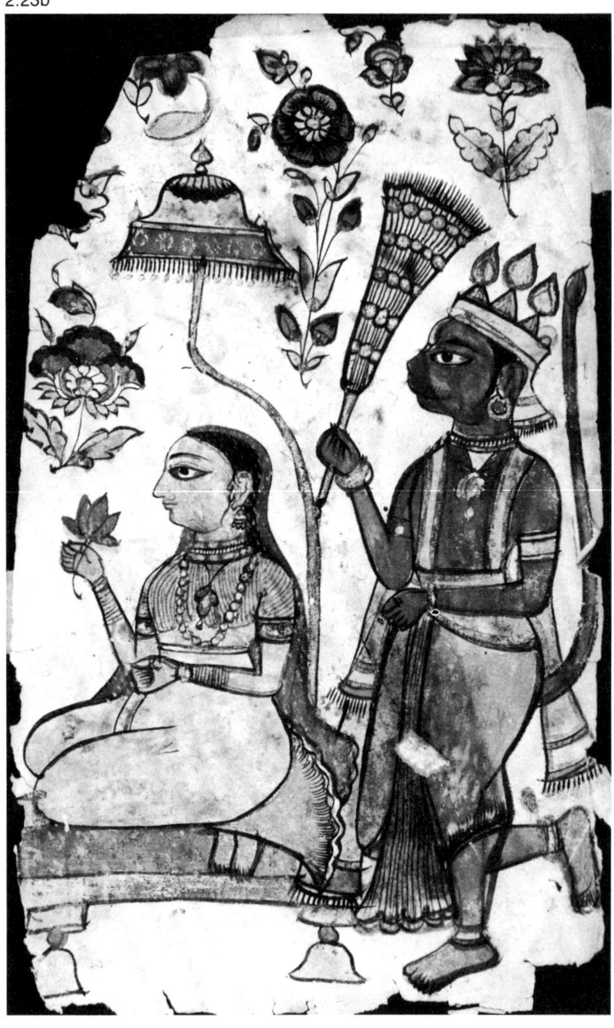

2.23b

**2.23 Folio from a Series
Illustrating the *Ramayana***
Gujarat, late eighteenth century
10 x 6 in.

The obverse of this fragment depicts
two fly-whisk bearers walking behind a
male figure who holds a flower. The
reverse shows Hanuman, the monkey
god, standing behind Sita who sits on a
low pedestal. Hanuman aided Rama in
the search for and recovery of Sita. He
is known for his great strength, exemplified by such feats as the carrying of
a mountain top with a life-saving herb
when Rama was injured. Hanuman
never becomes proud and willingly
acts as the attendant of Rama and his
queen, Sita. The floral pattern in the
background is reminiscent of the painting style of a century earlier (cf. no.
2.37).

P. Chandra, *Indian Miniature Painting*,
no. 86.

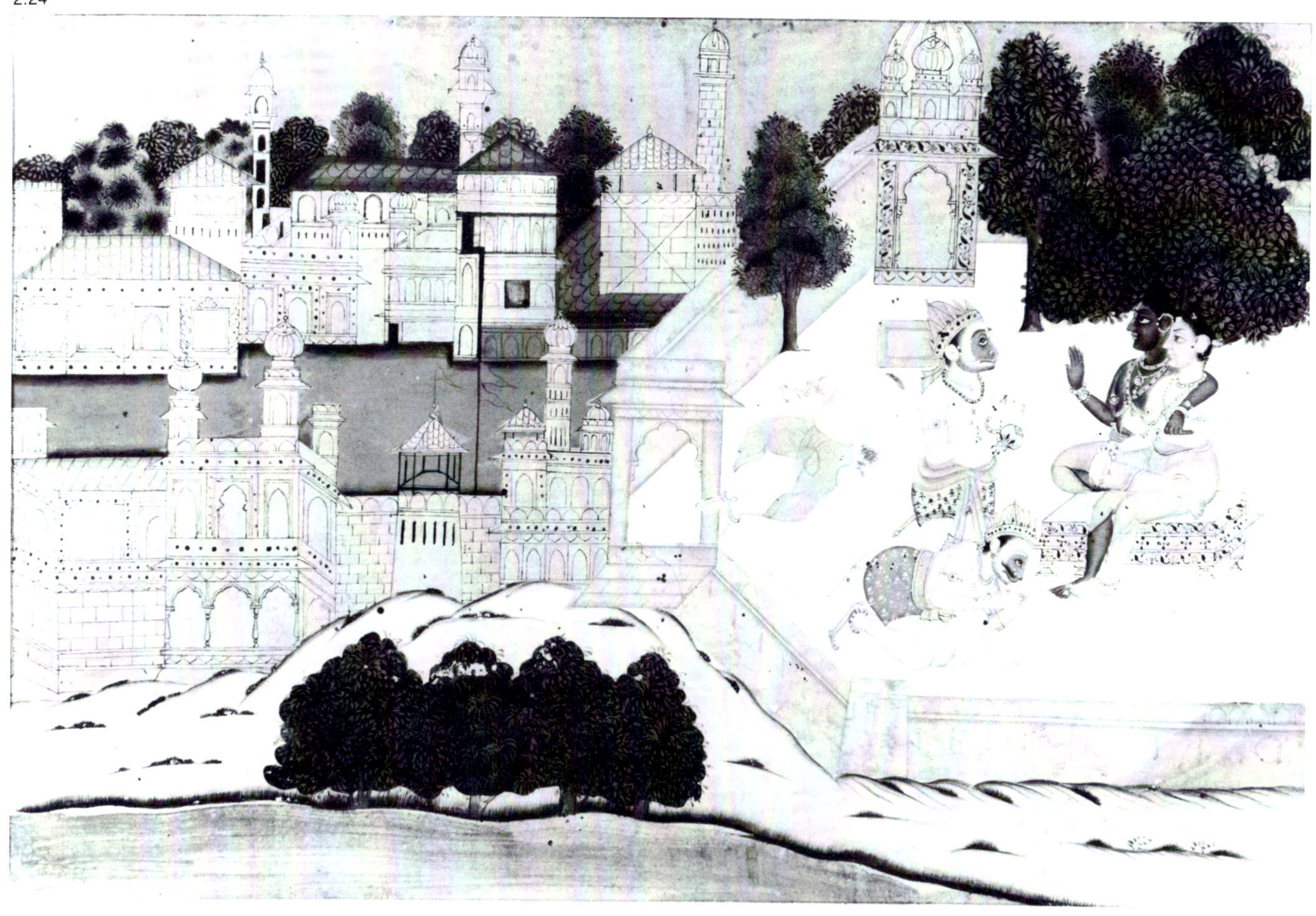

2.24 Rama and Lakshmana Receive the Monkey Chiefs: An Episode from the *Ramayana*

Bundelkhand, late eighteenth century
6¾ x 10¼ in.

The blue-colored Rama, seated with his free arm around his brother Lakshmana's shoulders, greets two crowned monkey chiefs, each possessing a club. The city of Lanka is seen in the background, encrusted in gold. Distant trees indicate the forest in which the legendary city was located. This scene may depict the monkeys reporting back to Rama after they had searched the city for Sita. The headless, handless corpse in the center may represent a demon killed in the process of the monkeys' foray into the city. The borders of the painting are partly missing.

P. Chandra, *Indian Miniature Painting,* no. 209.

2.25. Raja Jagat Prakash (c. 1770-1789) of Sirmur

Kangra Style, late eighteenth century
9⅞ x 7⅞ in.

Color illustration

Rama, holding a bow and arrow, and Sita, grasping a lotus, are enthroned to receive the homage of the Raja, along with an assortment of ascetics, characters from the *Ramayana* epic, and other divine beings. The wide audience of devotees emphasizes the supremacy of Rama's divine character. The three males behind the throne, in blue, yellow and pink tunics, are the three brothers of Rama. They act as attendants, waving fly-whisks and holding Rama's arrows and other accoutrements. In front of them are a group of bears, gods (including Indra) and three long-bearded ascetics who fold their hands in praise. To the left, a group of three monkeys and one bear flank a prostrate ascetic who adores the divine couple. The large figure of the Raja, dressed in white, and that of a priest behind him complete the audience.

On the reverse are several lines from the *Padma Purana* which describe the attributes of Vishnu as Narayana, and name his ten incarnations.

P. Chandra, *Indian Miniature Painting,* no. 239, black-and-white illustration.

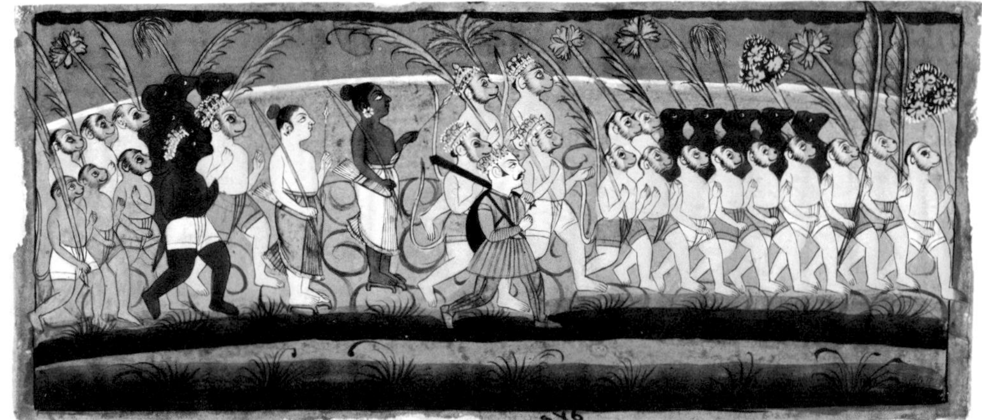

2.26 Rama's Army:
Folio from a Ms. of the *Ramayana*
Probably Marwar,
early nineteenth century
3⅛ x 7⅝ in.

Blue-skinned Rama and his fair-skinned brother Lakshmana carry a bow and arrow each. Troops made up of beige monkeys and grey bears accompany their own crowned leaders. Several animals carry uprooted trees and branches as weapons. The background is made up of bands of color: dark and olive green as the ground, pink with red swirls in the middle, silver and blue at the top.

P. Chandra, *Indian Miniature Painting*, no. 153.

2.27 Battle Between Rama and Ravana
Pahari Style, late nineteenth century
8¼ x 9¼ in.

The quintessential battle of might, in its good and evil forms, is represented in this painting. The ten-headed Ravana wears silver armour over a pink costume. His red leggings and yellow cummerbund are decorated with gold bands. The elongated crown on his ten heads is inset with jewels. His nature as warrior and king, albeit evil in nature, is quite clear. The weapons with which he wages battle with Rama include the axe, sword, spear and noose, among others. The ability to rejuvenate severed limbs was a divine gift and emphasizes the underlying Indian thought according to which good and evil both have access to divine patronage. By contrast, the blue-skinned Rama and his white-skinned brother Lakshmana are quite simply attired in yellow *dhotis* and a few bejewelled ornaments. Both brothers carry bows and arrows. The simplicity of clothing and weapons does not deter Rama, the righteous one, from victory. The colors are strong and vibrant. The green ground is set against a broad red background with a curved strip of blue at the top. Efforts to depict vegetation are limited to a schematic series of black tufts of grass highlighted in red and white.

P. Chandra, *Indian Miniature Painting*, no. 265.

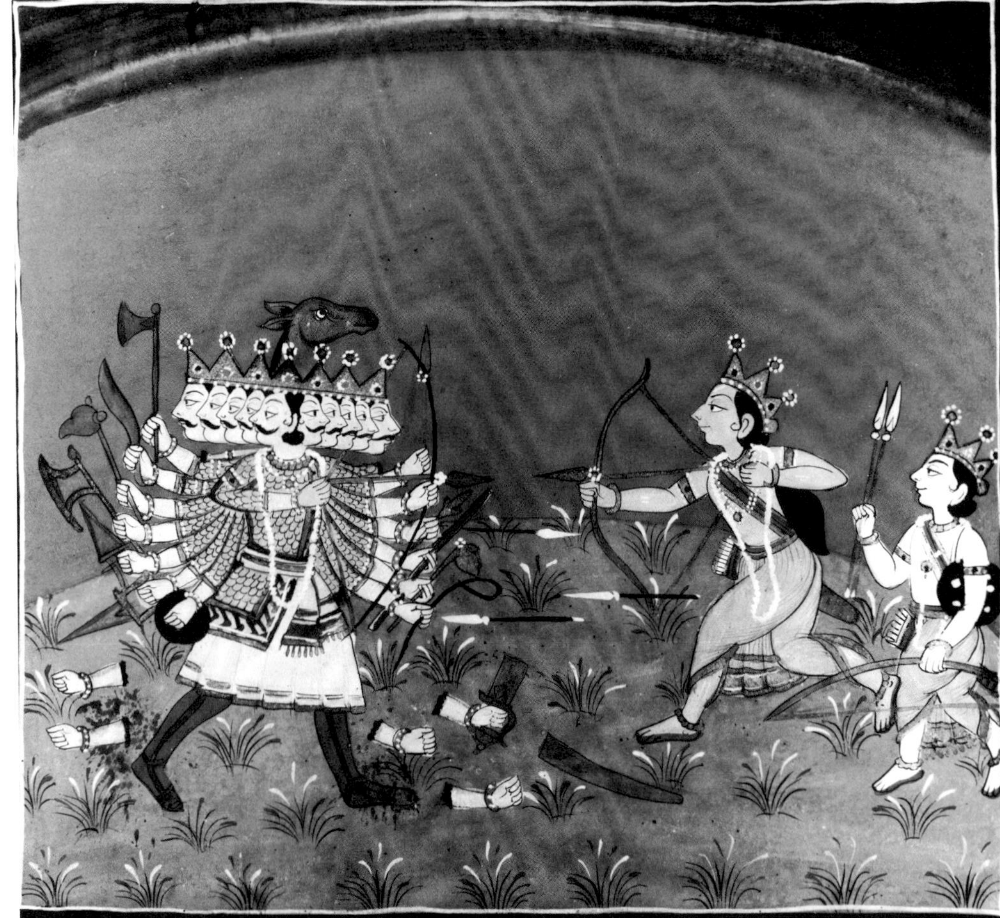

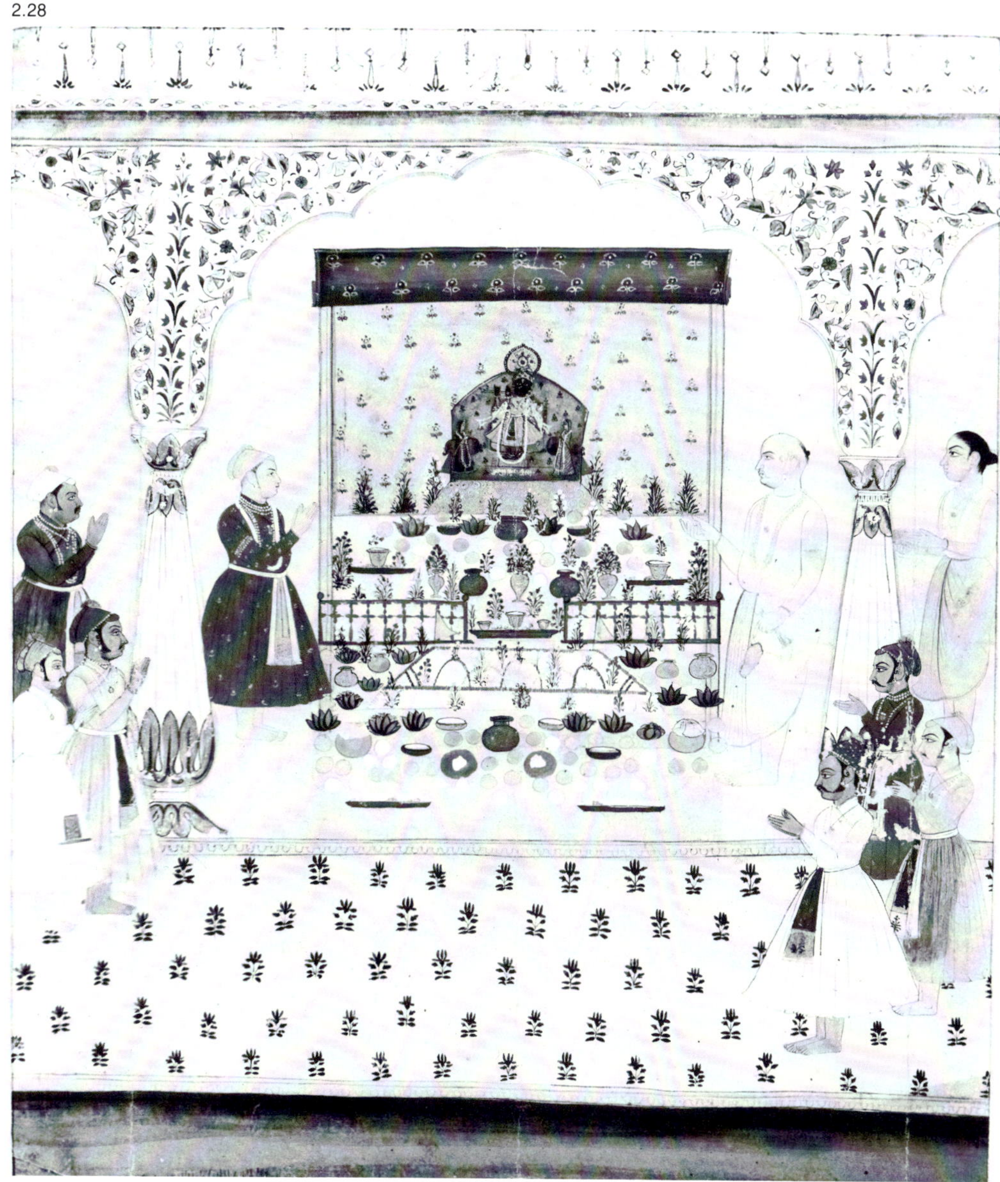

2.28 Worship at a Krishna Temple
Rajasthani Style,
early eighteenth century
14 x 11 7/8 in.

The central image is of Krishna playing
on the flute. On the altar beside him
are two small female figures. A large
group of offerings, some on the inside,
others on the outside of a small red
fence, are placed before the deity. The
devotees include the priest and an
acolyte on the right, as well as two
groups of laymen. Delicate floral
designs which suggest cloth patterns
are used in several areas of the
painting.

P. Chandra, *Indian Miniature Painting*,
no. 211, black and white illustration.

2.29 The Image of Shri Nathaji
Kishangarh, mid-eighteenth century
6¹/₂ x 4³/₄ in.

The blue figure of Krishna wears a
white tunic encrusted in a gold floral
pattern. His left hand is raised in the
gesture suggesting the lifting of Mt.
Govardhana. This iconographic form of
Krishna was popular among followers
of the Vallabha sect which was located
in Rajasthan, not far from the area
where this painting was made. A red
background is inside a yellow arch and
pink frame. The yellow is decorated
with a deep blue creeper, the pink with
a golden floral creeper. In the foreground, golden bolsters, footstool and
ritual implements stand on a blue and
gold rug. There is a chartreuse area
which meets a low white retaining wall
near the upper edge of the painting. A
small strip of blue at the top symbolizes
the sky.

P. Chandra, *Indian Miniature Painting*,
no. 161, black-and-white illustration.

**2.30 The Festival of Holi in the
Shrinathadwara Temple**
Mewar (Nathdwara), c. 1830
8³/₈ x 6 in.

The bright and vivid colors which are a
hallmark of the Mewar school serve the
narrative theme of this painting. The
spring festival of Holi, in which colored
powder is thrown by hand and by specially made syringes, is connected to
Krishna. In this painting, there are three
images of Krishna. The central figure in
the upper register is the classic blue
figure of Shrinathadwara, i.e. Krishna
holding Mt. Govardhana. At the base
of the shrine which surrounds the large
image is a small golden figure of
Krishna as flute player. On the opposite
side stands a priest who is showering
red powder onto the image. In the
lower register, on a small throne in the
midst of an arbor of trees, is the bust of
the child Krishna. Musicians with
drums and cymbals play the music to
which chants are sung in honor of the
deity. A priest is about to place colored
powder on the image.

P. Chandra, *Indian Miniature Painting*,
no. 103.

2.29

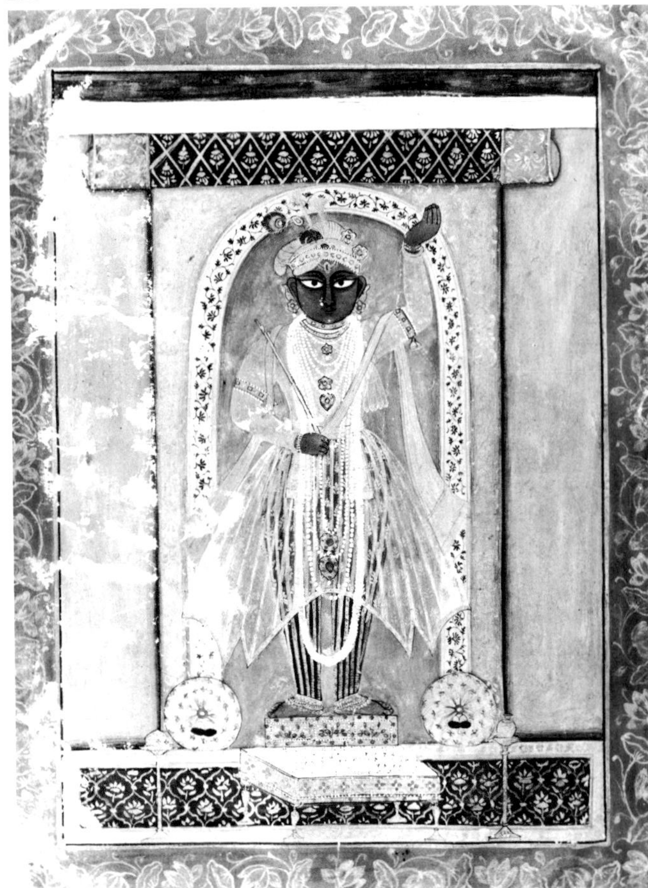

2.30

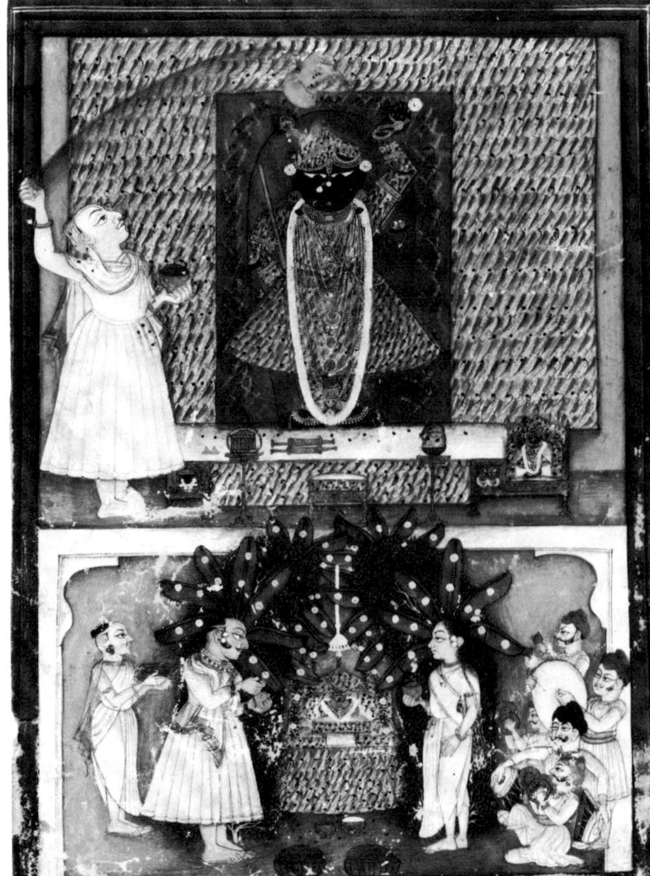

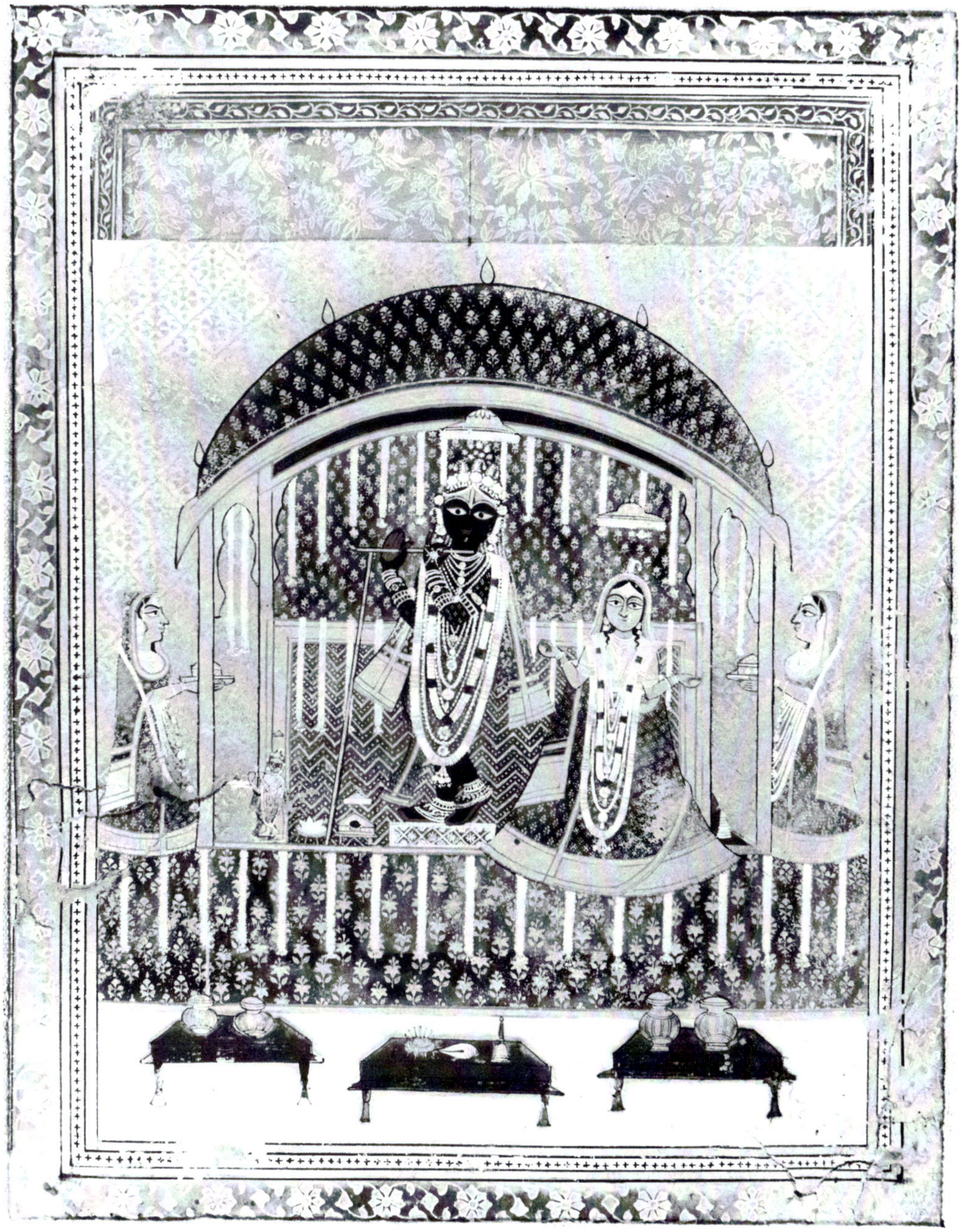

2.31 The Image of the Flute-Playing Krishna
Jaipur, mid-nineteenth century
6¼ x 5 in.

Inside a garlanded pavilion, the richly ornamented image of a black Krishna plays the flute while standing on a low white platform. His headdress has floral motifs rather than the usual, stylized peacock form. Above his head is a golden umbrella. Golden-skinned Radha stands on one side under an honorific umbrella. There is a small golden image of Krishna the flute player opposite Radha. Two female devotees carry trays with offerings. In the foreground, on three stools, are a bell, a conch, an incense holder and four water pots representing an array of ritual implements. Every surface area of this delicate painting is high-lighted in gold. The scene is one which suggests an actual image-shrine. The devotional nature of Krishna-worship lent itself to such depictions.

P. Chandra, *Indian Miniature Painting*, no. 198.

2.32 The Temple at Shrinathadwara
Mewar (Nathdwara),
mid-nineteenth century
5⅞ x 3⅞ in.

Not illustrated

This diagram of the temple is filled with images of Shrinathadwara and various devotees. Two figures of Ganesa appear on the outside of the inner compound wall. The elephant-headed deity grants auspiciousness to certain ventures and is often placed above doorframes and entryways. All figures are very small, exhibiting a sketch-like character. The background colors include pink, beige, and olive green, with red, yellow, blue and white used as highlights. This is a fragment of a larger composition.

P. Chandra, *Indian Miniature Painting*, no. 104.

2.33 Shri Nathaji in Goloka

Mewar (Nathdwara),
mid-nineteenth century
Painting on cloth
52 x 40½ in.

This type of painted cloth called a
(picchavai) hangs behind images of
Krishna in shrines of the Vallabha sect.
The central figure of this cloth is Shri
Nathaji, a form of Krishna. His left hand
is raised to support Mt. Govardhana,
which shields his companions from the
torrential rain which Indra sends down.
His right hand is behind his back and
supports two lotus stalks. He wears an
elaborate peacock crown; garlands of
flowers and jewels cover his elaborate
cloth dress. *Gopis* (female milkmaids)
are in attendance on either side, with
banana and mango trees behind. In
the sky above, gods, including Shiva,
Indra and their consorts, hover in sky
chariots. The pedestal of Sri Nathaji
holds a jug of Jumna River water and a
container of betel-nut leaves. Groups of
cows flank the pedestal. Immediately
below are incidents from Mt. Govardhana. To the left, four-armed, black
Krishna receives offerings of food. To
the right, cowherds are ready to extract
a portion of the *gopis'* market earnings
as Krishna and his brother Balarama
look on from pavilions. A register with a
row of cows and cowherds is followed
by the River Jumna and its bathing
ghat at the bottom. Cows and floral
designs border the perimeter of the
cloth. The iconography of this temple
cloth suggests the theme of the autumn
full moon.

P. Chandra, *Indian Miniature Painting,*
no. 109, black-and-white illustration.

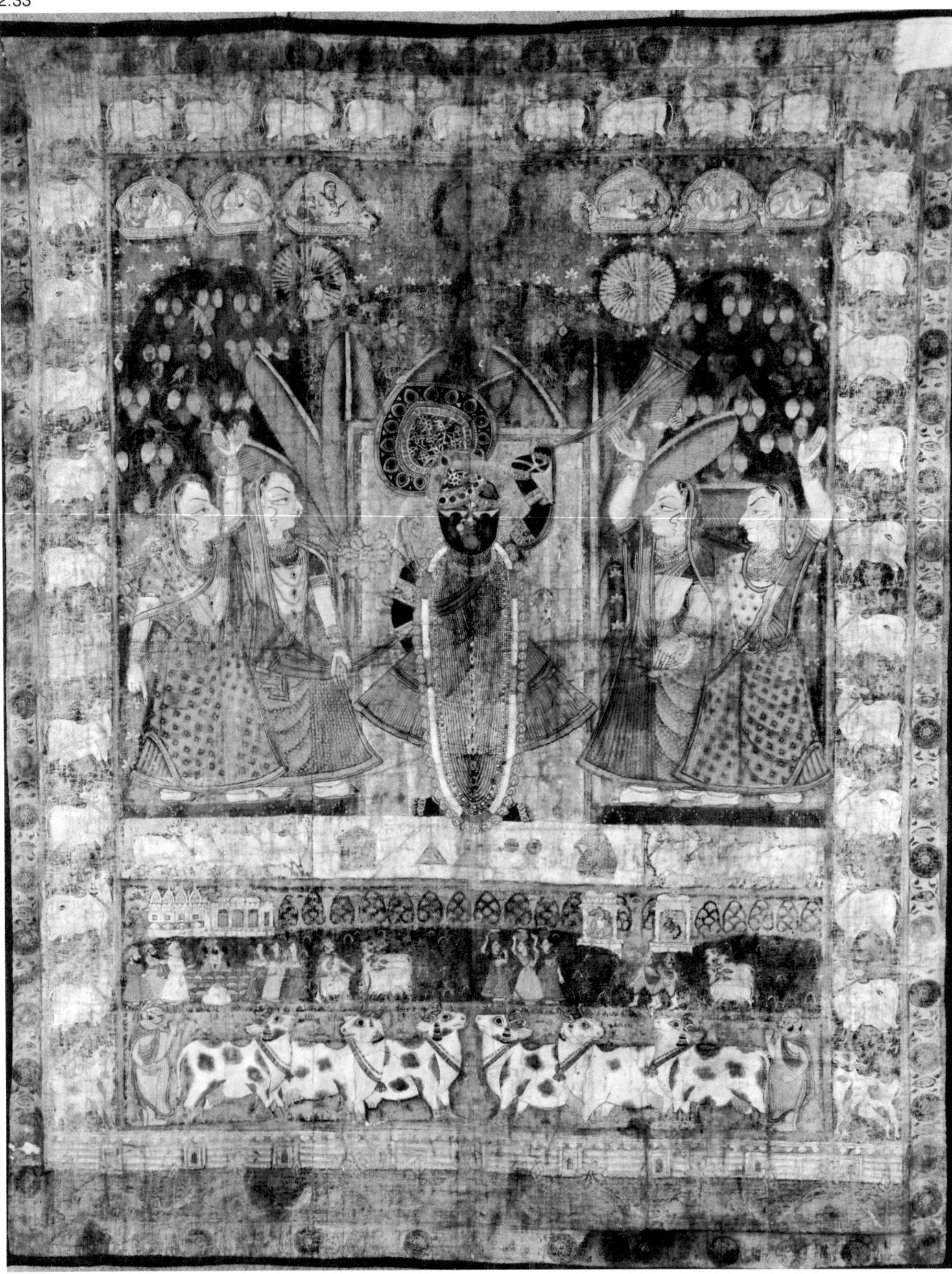

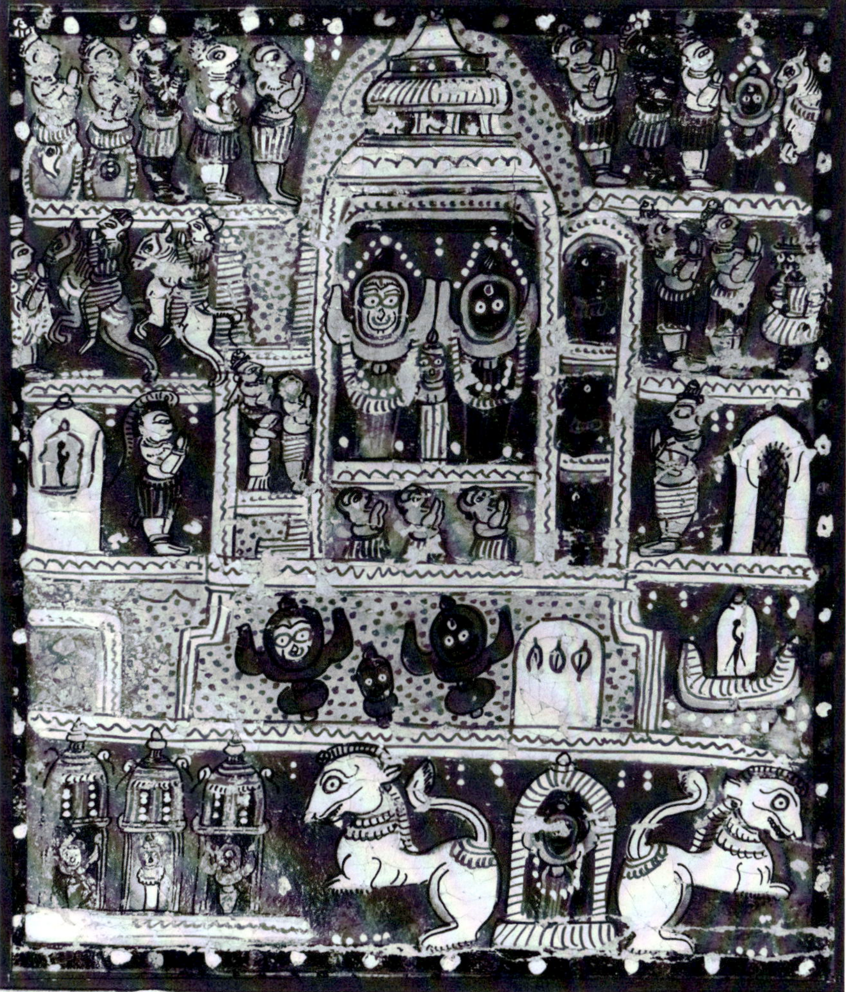

2.34 **A Jagannatha Pat**
Orissa, twentieth century
7 1/8 x 6 1/2 in.

The center of this painting is the shrine
in which the black Jagannatha Krishna,
the lord of the universe, is shown next
to his fair brother Balarama. Their small
sister Subhadra stands between the
two. The iconography of this type of
painting is quite standardized, yet several of the narrative features have been
significantly reduced or altered. The
pair of figures facing the multi-headed
Ravana in the second register hold
their hands folded in a gesture of greeting and respect, yet they are supposed
to represent Rama and Lakshmana
defeating Ravana. The figure in the
register immediately below has only
one head, though he is meant to represent the multi-headed Brahma. Also,
the angled lines in the second register
from the bottom have only one step,
suggesting an arch, although they are
meant to represent a series of steps
leading to the inner sanctum of the
temple complex. The reductionist manner of representation is a fairly typical
phenomenon in periods wherein
iconographical conventions are frozen.

P. Chandra, *Indian Miniature Painting*,
no. 9

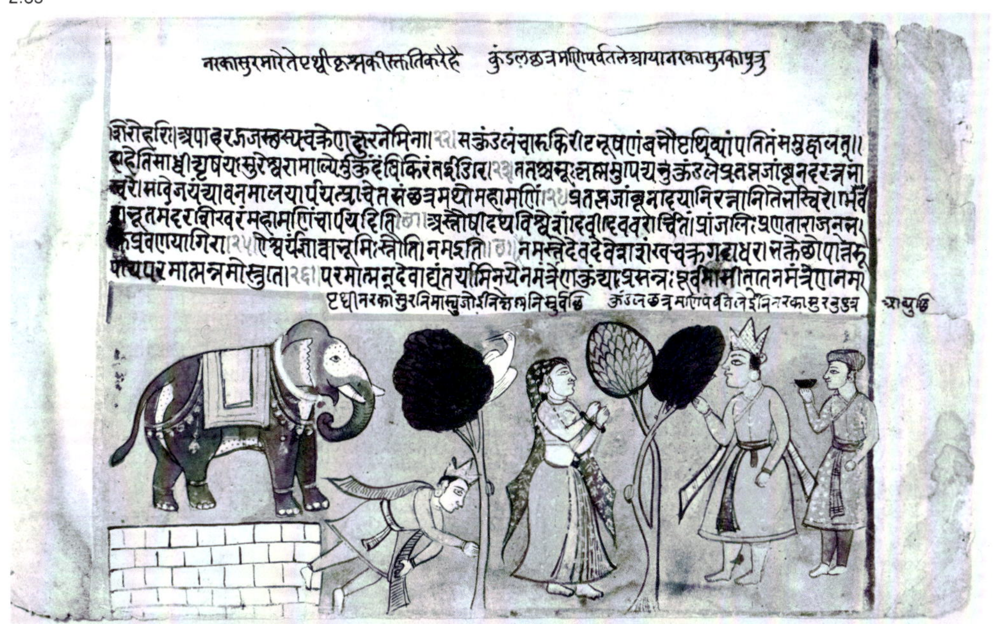

2.35 **The Goddess Prithvi Lauds
Krishna: Folio from a Ms. of the
*Bhagavata Purana***
Gujarat, early seventeenth century
7 3/8 x 12 1/2 in.

According to the identification of the
scene inscribed at the top of the folio,
the Earth Goddess, named Prithvi,
praises Krishna for having killed
Narakasura, a demon. The bold
orange, yellow and pink costumes,
which are outlined in red, stand out
against the pale green background.

P. Chandra, *Indian Miniature Painting*,
no. 83, black-and-white illustration.

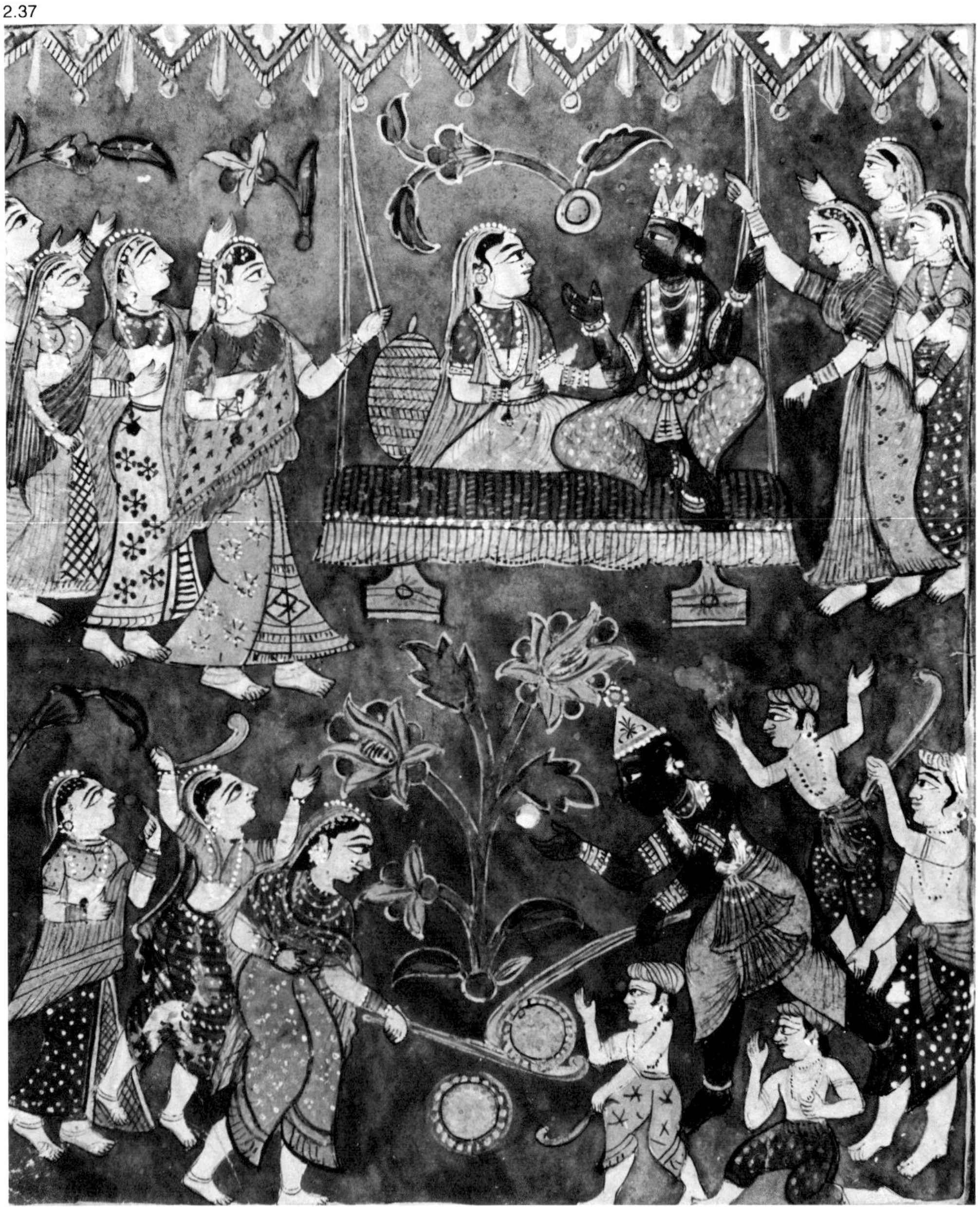

2.36 Radha Conversing with Confidantes
Mewar, c. 1625
8¹/₄ x 6³/₄ in.

Not illustrated

In the lower register, Krishna meets a group of four females in a wood. The deep blue of the stylized central tree is setoff by light blue, white and yellow highlights, and by green trees on either side. In a compartment above, Radha, leaning against a bolster, speaks with two confidantes. Next to this room, a brown hill, hidden amongst a group of vines and trees, completes the composition. The night sky, highlighted by a bright moon, is painted in a glittering mica blue. The activities and emotions of separated lovers were popular themes for painting. Radha and Krishna are the ideal lovers visualized in this painting.

P. Chandra, *Indian Miniature Painting,* no. 87, black-and-white illustration.

2.37 Krishna and Companions Playing: Folio from a Series Illustrating the *Bhagavata Purana*
Gujarat, mid-seventeenth century
8¹/₂ x 7 in.

This folio contains two scenes. In the upper scene, Krishna and Radha sit in a swing while a group of women rock and salute them. In the lower scene, Krishna leads a group of males in a game against Radha and two female companions. There are brightly colored, abstract floral plants scattered across a deep blue background. The patterns on the clothes worn by the women at the upper left are distinctive. Other miniatures from the series to which this folio belongs are dispersed throughout several museums.

P. Chandra, *Indian Miniature Painting,* no. 85, black-and-white illustration.

2.38 Krishna Surprises the *Gopis* at a Game of *Chaupar:* Illustration of the *Rasikapriya* of Keshavadasa
Mewar, mid-seventeenth century
7¹/₂ x 7 in.

Color illustration

Krishna, dressed in gold, approaches a pavilion in which four females sit playing a game of *chaupar.* The figure embracing the pole is the first to note his arrival. Krishna stands against a wall, which is bright red, a color associated with passion. The white pavilion has delicate, multicolored decorations on the roof. Pink-domed balconies flank the central white dome. A black background and light blue sky are behind. The use of jugs inset in windows and in the foreground are typical decorative details. The use of pink for

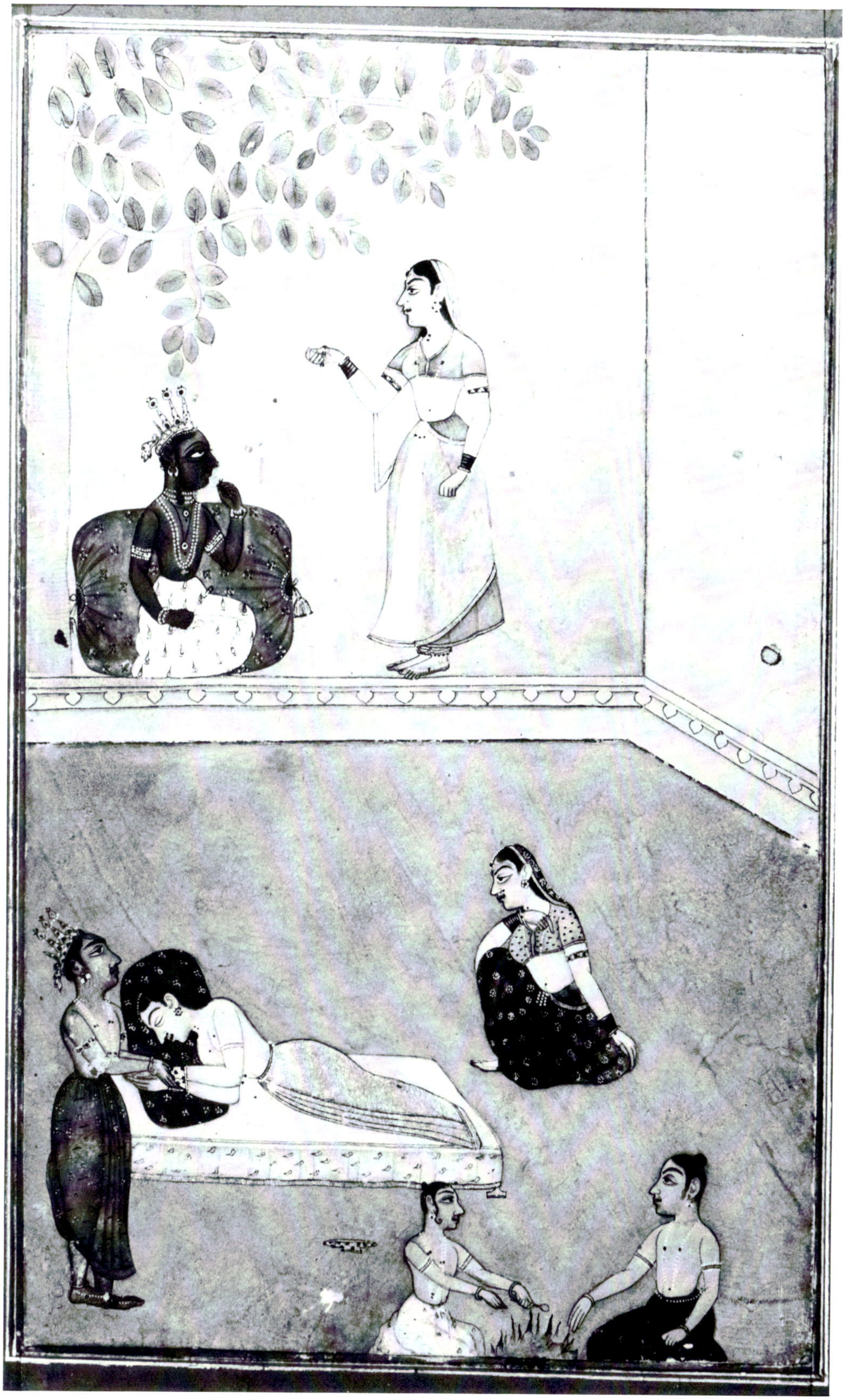

the brick stairs reflects the tone of terra-
cotta bricks. The use of broad areas of
bright colors is typical of the Mewar
style. The mood of the painting is created by the use of color rather than the
facial expressions of the figures. The
lines of text at the top are hastily written
on a separate piece of paper which is
attached to the painting.

P. Chandra, *Indian Miniature Painting*,
no. 88.

2.39 Krishna Waking the Sleeping Radha: Folio from a Series Illustrating the *Rasikapriya* of Keshavadasa
Bikaner, v.s. 1748/ A.D. 1691
7¾ x 5 in.

In the foreground, two male figures
offer oblations to the sacred fire. With
their hair tied in neat topknots, both figures wear jewelry and embroidered
dhotis, one red, the other pale pink.
Thus, they do not truly represent
ascetics but perhaps brahmins, members of the priestly caste. The main
scene on the light green background,
which makes up the lower portion of
the painting, depicts the blue, crowned
Krishna waking the sleeping Radha.
Krishna wears an orange *dhoti* decorated in red and gold. Radha's golden
dress shimmers against the plain
yellow bedcover trimmed in pink and
gold. The attendant sitting nearby
wears pink and orange clothes.

In the upper portion of the painting,
a young maid approaches the seated
flute-holding Krishna. He wears a white
dhoti. The bolster behind him is orange.
The deeper hue of his skin and the
long curly tendrils of his hair and the
jewelry which he wears are markedly
different from their portrayal below. The
yellow background with its architectural
band suggests an interior wall, but a
tree seems to grow out of it. Perhaps
the scene at the top represents
Radha's dream. The red and white
ruled border of the painting, which is
inscribed with four lines of text, is a
separate piece of paper. The delicate
rendering of the figures is typical of the
Bikaner style.

P. Chandra, *Indian Miniature Painting*,
no. 172, black-and-white illustration.

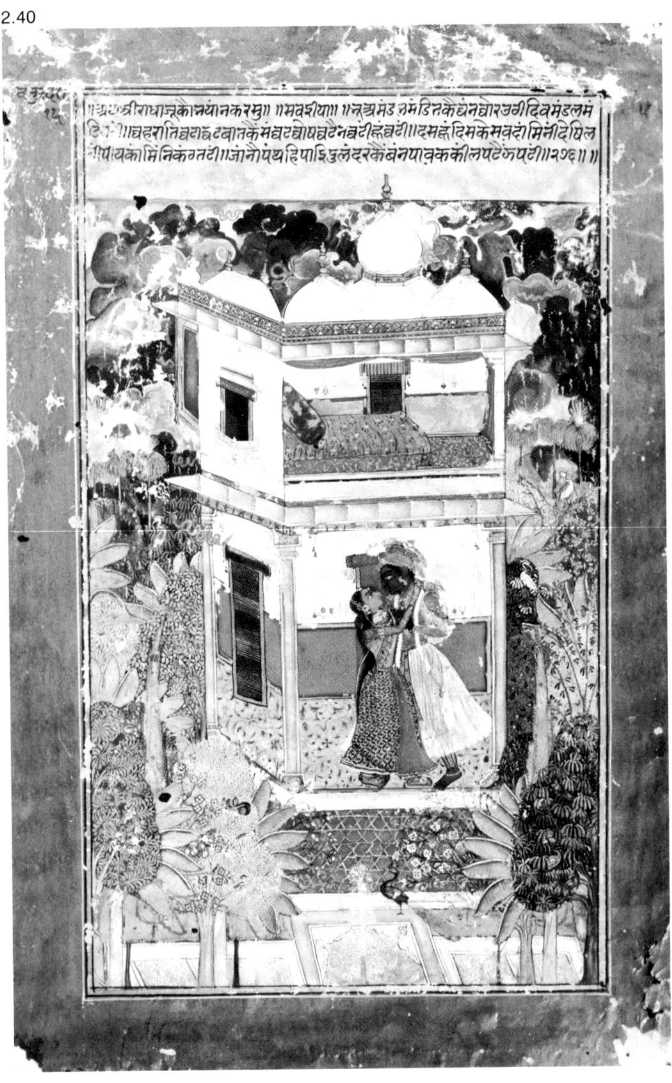

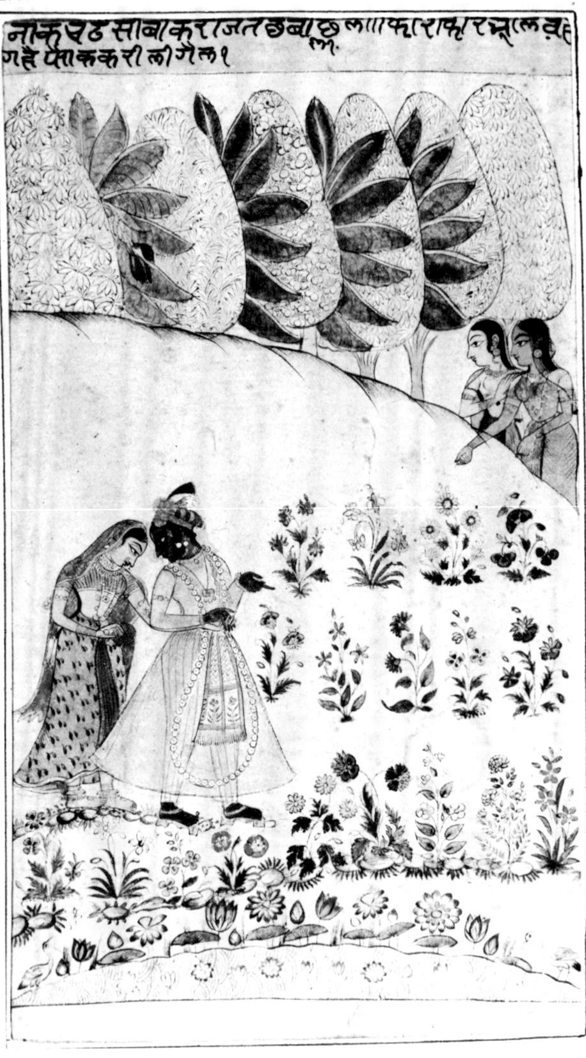

2.40 The Frightened Radha Clings to Krishna: Folio from a Series Illuminating the *Rasikapriya* of Keshavadasa
Bundi, late seventeenth century
10¼ x 6⅞ in.

Radha, the married cowmaid, embraces her lover Krishna. The romance of the moment is suggested by the empty bed in the upper story, Radha's loose free-flowing hair, and the peacocks scattered amongst the trees. Peacocks, half-hidden among the foreground trees, symbolize desire. The stormy gray-blue sky pierced by golden lightning bolts electrifies the moment. Metaphorically, Radha is the bright lightning clinging to the dark cloud who is Krishna. The range and nuance of color employed in the dense vegetation surrounding the lovers is captivating.

P. Chandra, *Indian Miniature Painting*, no. 110, color illustration.

2.41 Krishna Leading Radha through a Garden
Ajmer, early eighteenth century
9⅞ x 5½ in.

Krishna leads the reticent Radha through a garden of stylized flowers. The mood of the scene reflects the aspect of the relationship described in the lines of text, according to which the male lover is flirtatious, and so his lady is walking a stony, or difficult, path. Here, the stony path is literally depicted as a series of small rocks. Krishna's costume is yellow with pink waist scarf, Radha's clothing is primarily pink and orange. Two maids watch the scene from behind a small hillock. The horizontally arranged plants are red, yellow, orange and pink with black-outlined green leaves. The trees in the background include unpainted mango trees interspersed with green banana trees. The lotus pond in the foreground has two cranes, one at either end. The background is unpainted, a common technique of the style.

P. Chandra, *Indian Miniature Painting*, no. 187, color illustration.

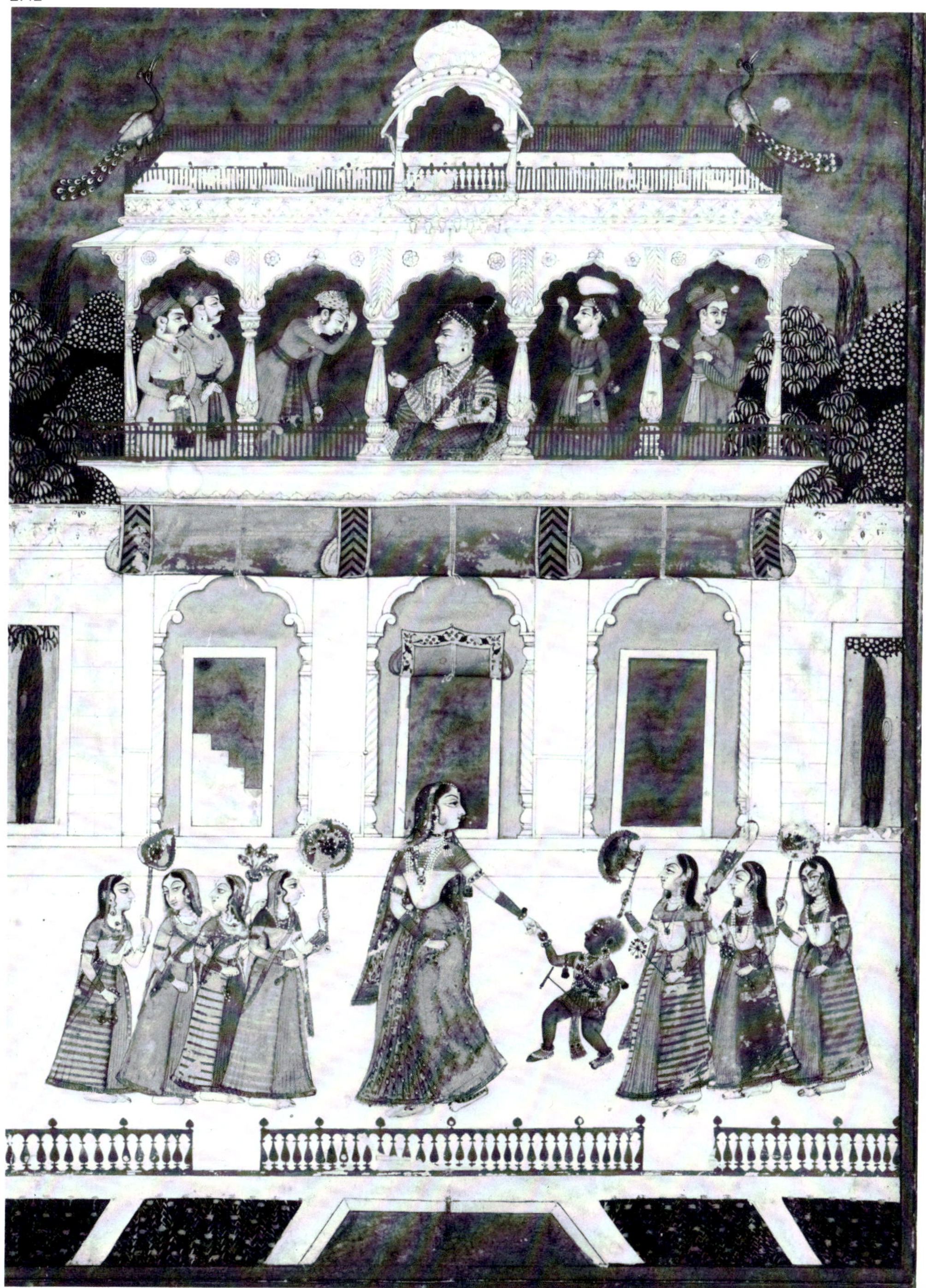

2.42 The Child Krishna Playing with his Mother
Bikaner, early eighteenth century
9³/₄ x 7 in.

The childhood of Krishna is an endearing topic for art and literature. Here Yashoda, the adoptive mother of Krishna, leads the child across a terrace. Both figures are heavily bejewelled. Each carries a toy in their free hand as do the female attendants on either side. Note the use of peacock-feather fans rather than the usual white fly-whisks. The peacock is associated with Krishna and its shape is an integral part of his headdress. A group of men watch the women from a balcony.

The bright orange of the rolled-up curtain is reiterated in the costumes of the figures. Yellow, red, blue and green are complementary colors used in the costumes. The sky and inset doorways are gray-blue. The delicacy that characterizes the Bikaner artists is evident in the carefully drawn faces and the decorated terrace pavilion.

P. Chandra, *Indian Miniature Painting*, no. 180, black-and-white illustration.

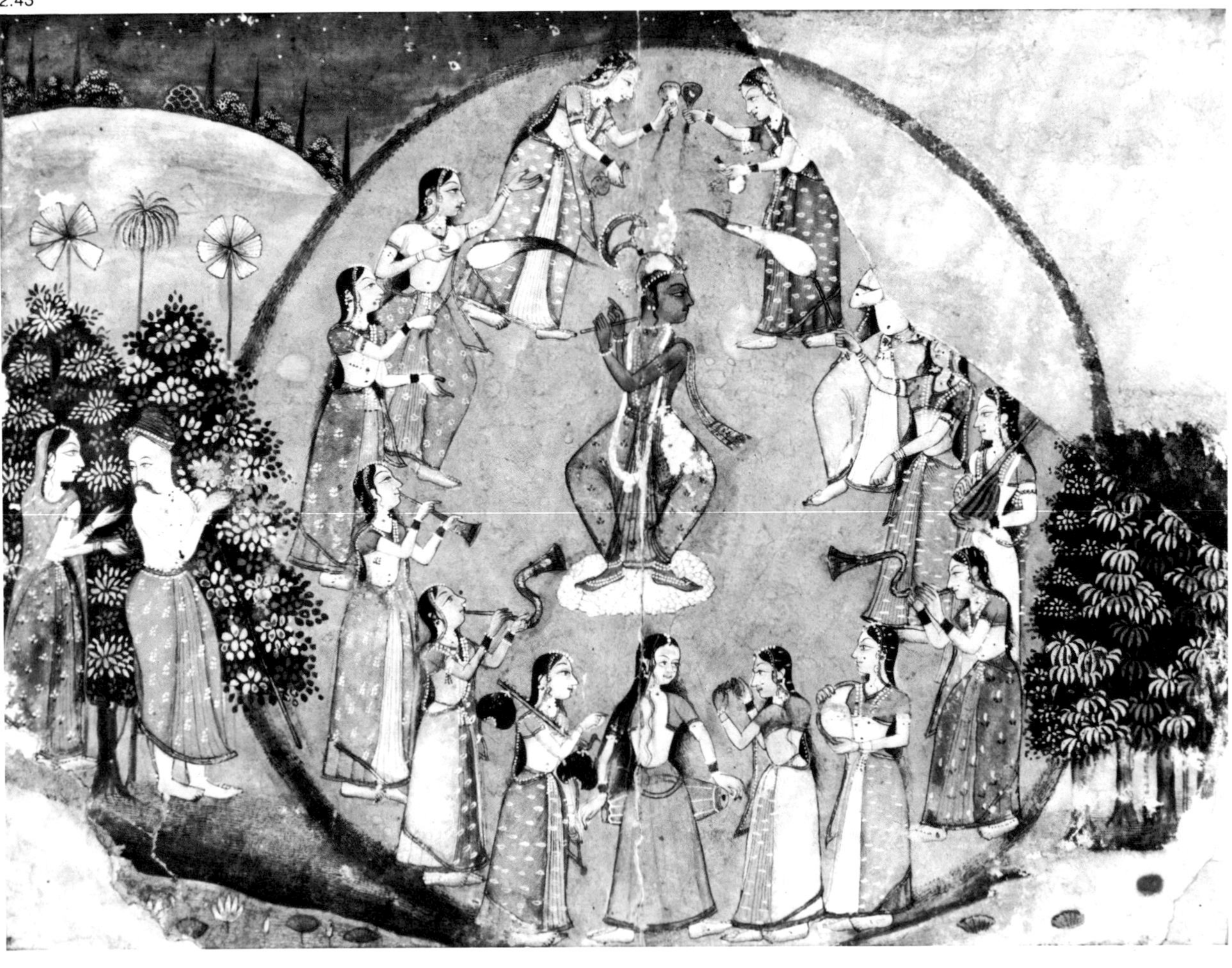

2.43 Rasa-Mandala

Bikaner, early eighteenth century
6⅛ x 8⅜ in.

In this night scene, Krishna the flute
player stands on a lotus set in the middle of a circle of female musicians.
Each maiden imagines Krishna to be
with her alone. His status as a beloved
God is suggested by the two women
who wave fly-whisks and the two who
pour colored powder onto his head.
Yashoda and Nanda, Krishna's adoptive parents, look on from the side.

   Though damaged, the painting pre-
serves both the color and the vitality
which the artist imbued into this classic
theme. The charisma of Krishna,
whose flute playing could draw cow-
maids into the forest in the depths of
the night, is emphasized by his stance,
a classical dance pose, upon lotus
base. The costumes of the maids vary
between orange, yellow, pink, blue,
green and brown. White and gold
highlight the garments.

P. Chandra, *Indian Miniature Painting,*
no. 179, black-and-white illustration.

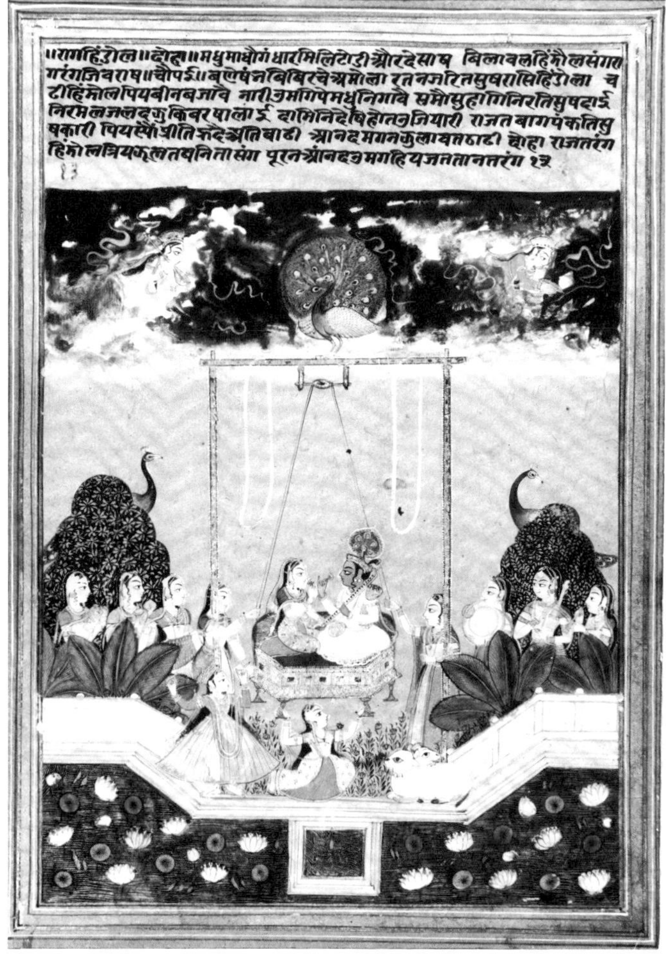

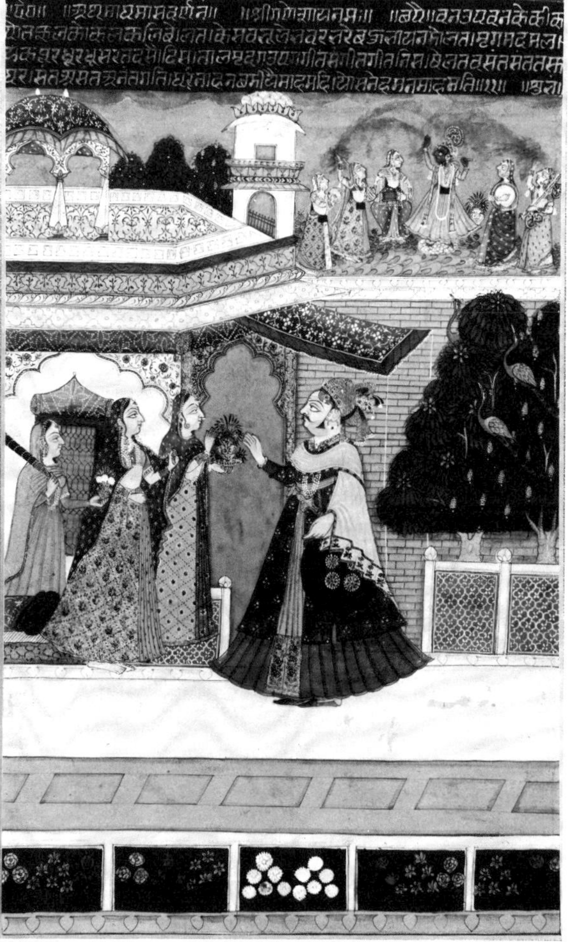

2.44 Raga Hindola:
Folio from a *Ragamala* Series
Probably Jaipur,
first half of the eighteenth century
7¼ x 6 in.

Krishna and Radha sit on a golden
swing with a group of dancing and
music-making cow-maids, one of
whom gently rocks the lovers.
Apsarases, musical demigods, peer
out from lightning-studded clouds. This
iconography is often employed to sig-
nify the *Raga Hindola,* a musical mode
to be sung on spring mornings. The
inscription at the top consists of the
name of the *raga,* the main descriptive
verse and a commentary.

P. Chandra, *Indian Miniature Painting,*
no. 192, black-and-white illustration.

2.45 The Month of Magha:
Illustration to a Verse from the
Kavipriya of Keshavadasa
Marwar, mid-eighteenth century
11½ x 6¾ in.

In the foreground, an elaborately
dressed nobleman, sword and shield
at his side, approaches a pair of well-
dressed women and their companions.
The pavilion is richly decorated in a
variety of colors and floral patterns.
The eclipse of the month of Magha is
implied by the background scene.
Krishna plays his flute, accompanied
by a group of female musicians. Two of
the women throw colored powder at
Krishna, thus suggesting the spring-
time festival of Holi, which occurs in the
month following Magha. The verse at
the top is in silver paint on a deep blue-
black band.

P. Chandra, *Indian Miniature Painting,*
no. 145, color illustration.

2.46 Krishna Converses with a Woman: Folio from a Series Illustrating the *Satsai* of Bihari
Mewar, mid-eighteenth century
7³/₈ x 7¹/₈ in.

Krishna, dressed in bright yellow, speaks to a well-ornamented woman. A golden cup and tray are on the ground before them. A red background and plain white floor color the architectural setting. In the lower pavilion, two women converse, one of whom gestures toward the outdoors. The green wall behind them is pierced by a doorway; the floor is a plain white. Outside, Radha, identifiable by the golden dress she wears, walks beside a pond filled with blossoming lotuses and a trio of ducks. The green grass is set against a brown background and a thin strip of blue sky. The inscription above suggests that the setting for this scene is the dawn. It notes that the woman has decorated her feet and that her eyes flit about like a bird, a description of excitement connected with love.

P. Chandra, *Indian Miniature Painting,* no. 96.

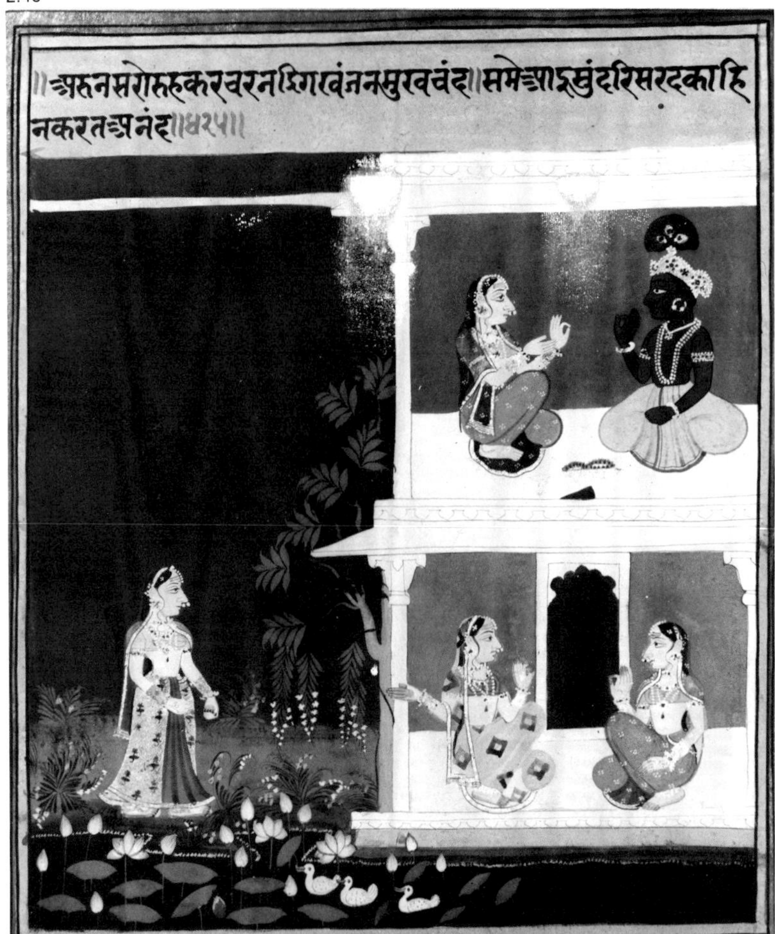

2.46

2.47 An Illustration to the *Gita Govinda*
Kangra Style, late eighteenth century
7 x 10¹/₄ in.

The pining Radha, who leans against the branches of a tree, is being encouraged by her companion to continue the search for Krishna. Within the sparse outlines of this tracing, which is minimally painted, the anguish of Radha is striking. The downward glance, the gesture of reaching with both hands toward the branches of a barren tree in the midst of other leaved trees, and her bent posture create the notion of the sorrow of separation from one's beloved. Intertwined trees in the foreground echo the posture of the central figure. Radha the cow maid is Krishna's beloved. Her romance with Krishna is an elaborate interplay which symbolizes the relationship between humankind and God.

P. Chandra, *Indian Miniature Painting,* no. 237.

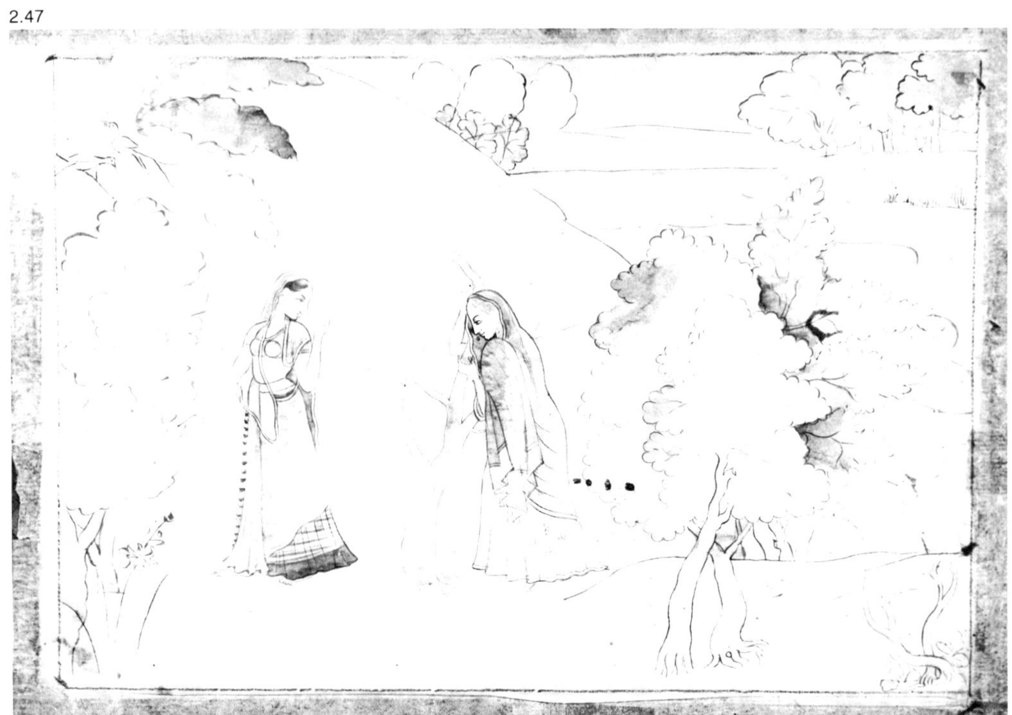

2.47

2.48 Krishna Playing the Flute
Deccani Style (probably Shorapur),
late eighteenth century
9⁷⁄₈ x 7¹⁄₈ in.

Not illustrated

Krishna sits on a rock under a tree, playing a flute. A group of cows, some suckling their young, as well as a cowherd and a milkmaid are mesmerized by the music. A flock of birds surrounds and perches upon the stylized tree. Cranes are scattered in the lotus pond in the foreground. This type of bucolic scene elicits a sympathetic response from those devoted to Krishna because it emphasizes the accessible nature of the God.

P. Chandra, *Indian Miniature Painting*, no. 70, black-and-white illustration.

2.49

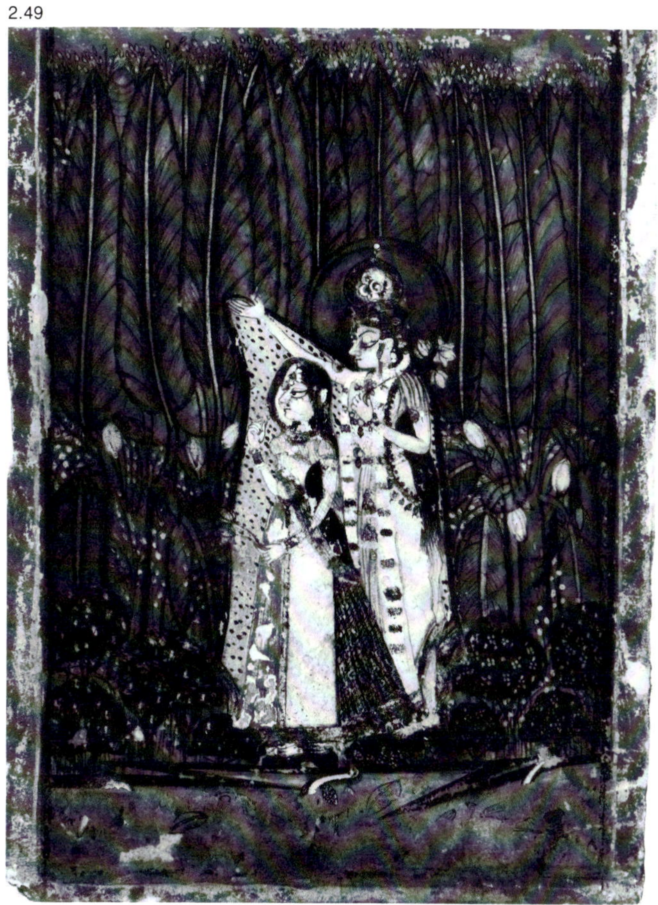

2.49 Krishna Sheltering Radha
Kishangarh,
end of the eighteenth century
4³⁄₄ x 3¹⁄₈ in.

Krishna, depicted in a pale gray-blue color, shelters the delicate figure of Radha, his beloved consort, with a blue spotted cloth. The dense green foliage of banana trees is set off by a number of flowering bushes with pink lotus-like buds. In the foreground, three water cranes cavort in the dark gray lotus pond. The deep orange color of the background at top matches the border. Radha's dress is orange and green, her blouse blue. Krishna wears a yellow *dhoti*. Gold is used at the edges of garments and to accent jewelry. Their brightly colored garments provide a needed contrast to the deep-toned background.

The protective aspect of the relationship between deity and human soul is thus portrayed by the figures of Krishna and Radha. The natural setting, the thick enclosure of trees, reiterates the notion of shelter.

P. Chandra, *Indian Miniature Painting*, no. 166, black-and-white illustration.

2.50

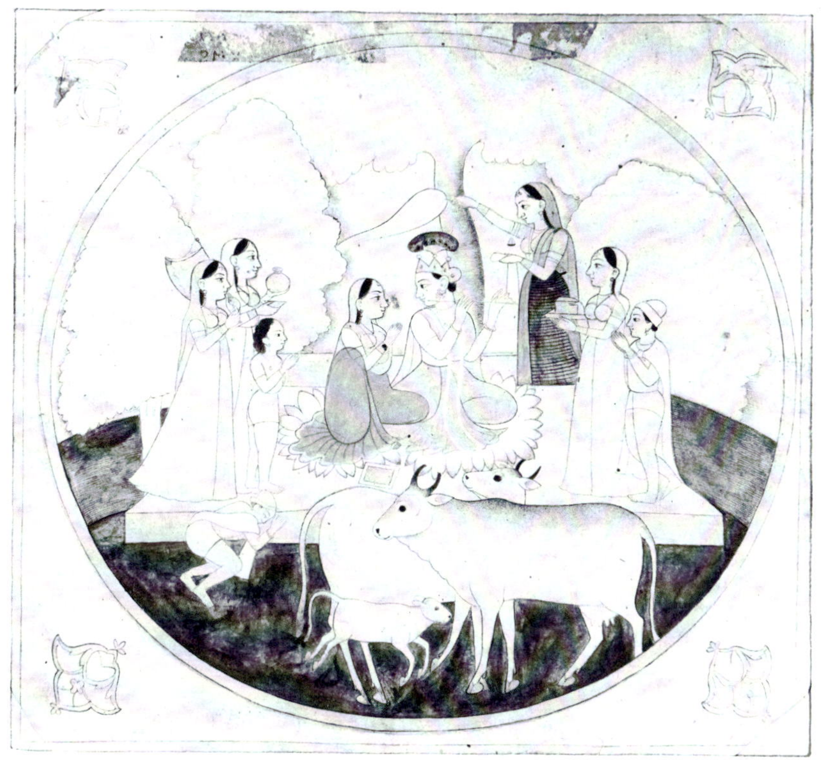

2.50 Adoration of Krishna
Kangra Style, c. 1800
6¹⁄₈ x 7 in.

This carefully balanced composition is focused on the flute-playing Krishna who sits in front of the large tree in the central portion of the oval frame. Next to him is Radha, with folded hands. These two figures are seated on a pair of lotuses. On either side of the platform which underlies the lotus seats are three devotees. The figure immediately next to the tree waves a fly-whisk and holds a white cloth in her other hand. In the foreground, on a green area, are two cows, a frolicking calf and a kneeling cowherd. In the hill schools, the oval frame became an acceptable variation of the standard rectangular shape in the Kangra style. The painting is not finished.

P. Chandra, *Indian Miniature Painting*, no. 246. Other examples of figures holding a white cloth in paintings in this exhibition include nos. 2.18 and 2.25. The use of cloth as an offering to express respect in secular and religious contexts is well attested in many Northern areas of the Subcontinent.

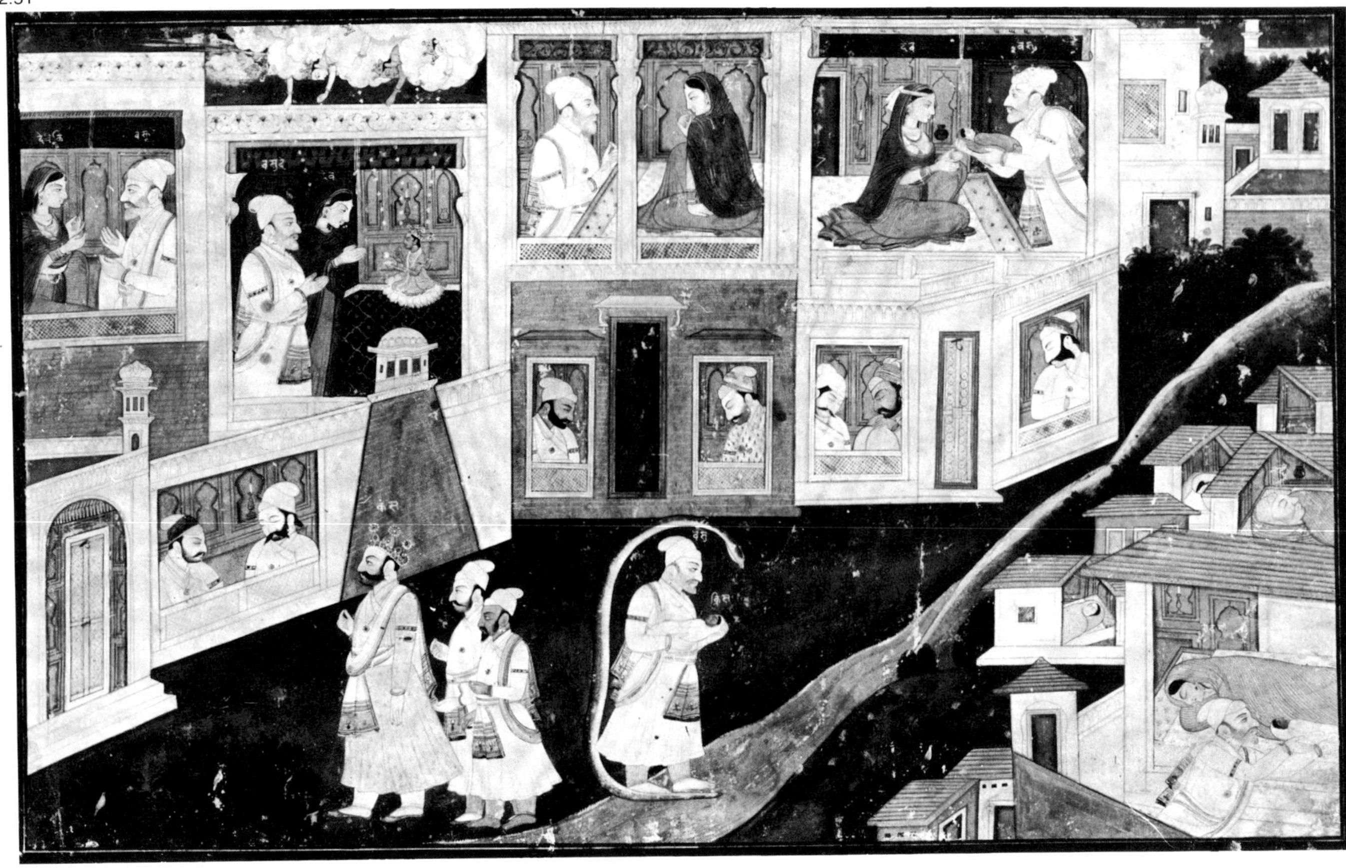

2.51 The Transfer of Babes

Kangra Style, early nineteenth century
11¾ x 18⅞ in.

One of the pivotal moments in
Krishna's life took place immediately
after his birth. Born to the royal family
of Devaki and Vasudeva, Krishna was
a threat to the crown of the evil king
Kamsa. To save his newborn son,
Vasudeva carried Krishna to Yashoda
and Nanda, a family of cowherds.
Vasudeva took their newborn daughter
Rohini back to his palace-prison.
Rohini is the Goddess in disguise.

Aspects of the transfer are depicted
in this large, complex Kangra painting
which can be divided into four main
narrative units. On the left, Devaki and
Vasudeva are depicted in the palace,
first in conversation, then worshipping
the four-armed figure of Vishnu, of
whom Krishna is an incarnation. Gods
in the clouds above shower flowers onto the auspicious scene. In the lower
scene, Kamsa and two attendants
approach the locked gates, the guards
of which are asleep. In the middle of
the painting, Devaki and Vasudeva discuss the imminent arrival of Kamsa and
the need to save their son. Having
passed through open doors which

should have been locked and past
guards who are miraculously asleep,
Vasudeva, protected by a serpent,
fords the river holding his dark-skinned
son. In the corner at the lower right,
Vasudeva places Krishna by Yasoda's
side. At the top right, Vasudeva has
returned to the palace and presents
the fair-skinned babe Rohini to Devaki.
A white fillet is knotted around Devaki's
forehead. This unusual costume detail
appears in other paintings from the
Punjab Hills which narrate the birth episode. The gray walls, deep gray sky
and candles suggest night. Inscriptions
identify several of the characters in this
complex series of scenes.

P. Chandra, *Indian Miniature Painting*,
no. 250.

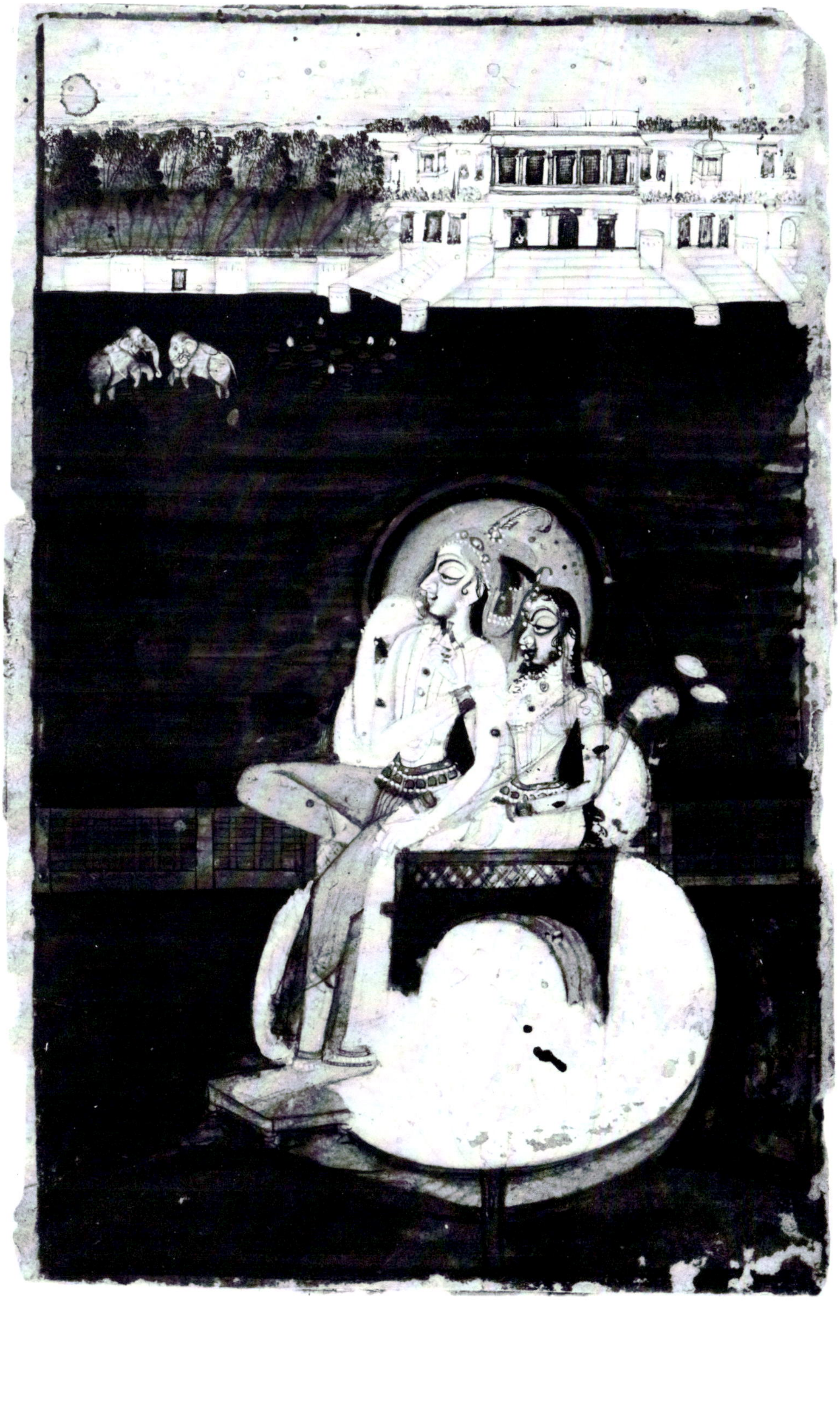

2.52 Radha and Krishna Seated by the River

Kishangarh, early nineteenth century
5½ x 3⅜ in.

The divine natures of Krishna and Radha are emphasized in this portrayal. They share a nimbus and a lotus-based throne. Each has four arms, an anatomical feature reserved for supra-mundane creatures in South Asian iconography. One of Krishna's hands holds a lotus while resting on Radha's shoulder, and another of his hands fondles one of her breasts. His other two hands are unfinished. In two of her hands, Radha holds a lotus bud and a small green bud. Her third hand holds one of Krishna's hands, and her fourth hand hangs at her side. Radha is enticing Krishna, who responds as a lover. The river, with elephants amidst a lotus bed, and a palace in the distance represent the interest in depicting background scenes that was fostered in the later phases of miniature painting. The painting is unfinished.

P. Chandra, *Indian Miniature Painting*, no. 167.

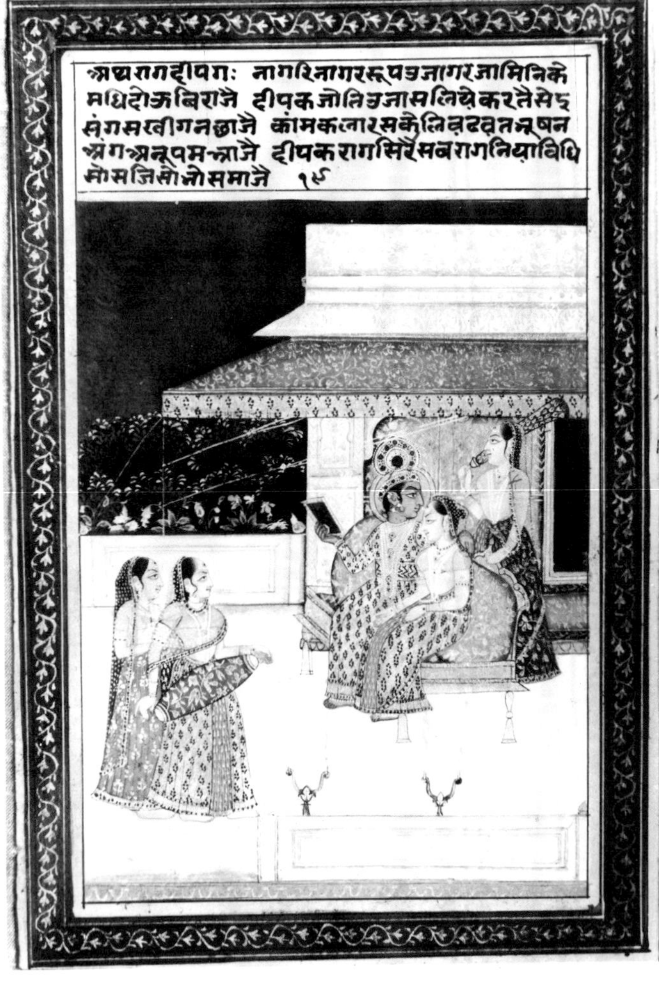

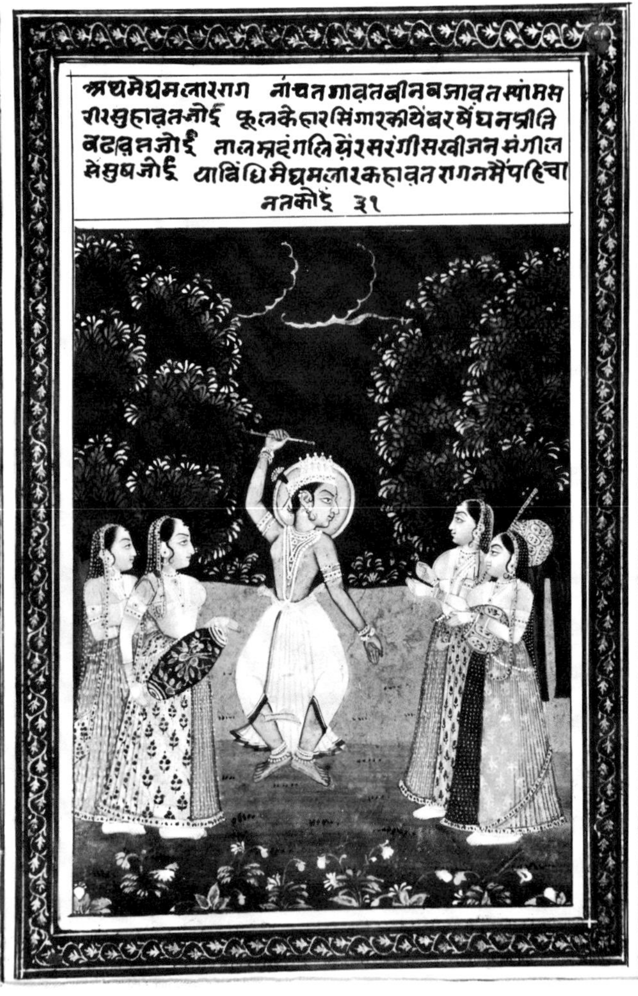

2.53 and 2.54 Two Folios from a *Ragamala* Series

Jaipur, c. 1825

5¹⁄₈ x 3⁷⁄₈ in.

2.53 Raga Dipak

Radha and Krishna with an attendant holding a peacock-fan and two female musicians are used to depict the *Raga Dipak*, the musical mode of lamps. According to literary references this musical mode is meant to be sung at midday, yet it is regularly depicted as a night scene in painting, perhaps because of the inclusion of candles and lamps *(dipaka)* which give the *raga* its name. In this painting, Krishna holds a mirror while Radha sits at his side. All of the costumes are heavily decorated in gold with deep blue, yellow, orange and pink as supporting colors. The canopy, roof and walls of the pavilion are similarly encrusted in gold.

P. Chandra, *Indian Miniature Painting*, no. 195.

2.54 Raga Megha Malhar

Krishna, assuming a dance pose, appears suspended in the air. He holds the flute raised in his right hand. The women play instruments or keep time by clapping their hands. *Megha Malhar* is a *raga*, musical mode, of the rainy season. The dark sky with golden lightning appropriately suggests an imminent storm. The verse at the top names the *raga*.

P. Chandra, *Indian Miniature Painting*, no. 196.

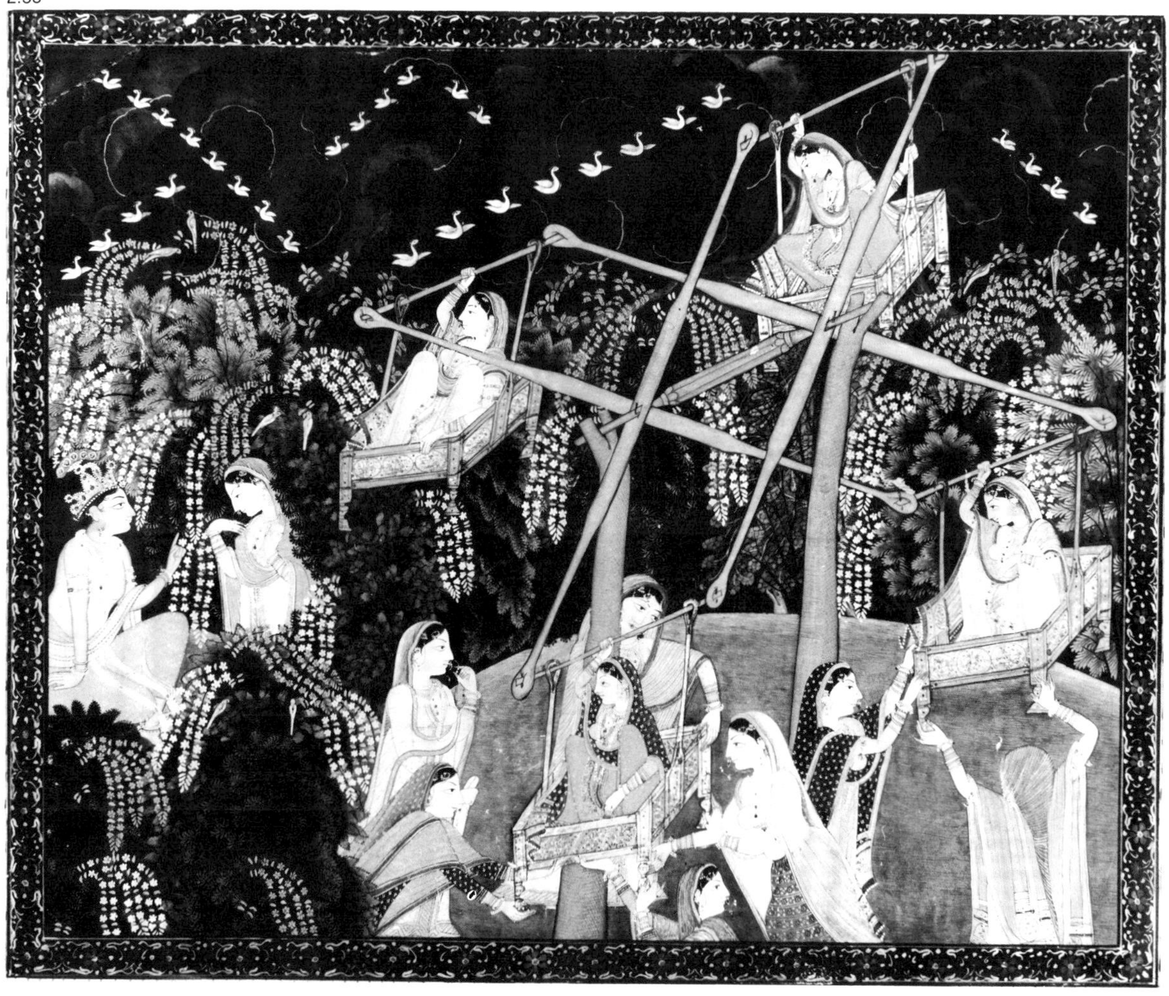

2.55 Entertainment During the Rainy Season
Kangra Style, mid-nineteenth century
7³/₈ x 9¹/₄ in.

Lush vegetation, in a wide range of greens, surrounds the clearing where a hand-turned wooden wheel is ridden by a group of richly clothed women. The gold-trimmed clothes which the women wear add a sharp, precise quality to this painting. Orange, yellow, blue, pink, and red are employed to create their richly patterned fabrics. In a nearby clearing, a shy Radha approaches the richly bejewelled and garlanded Krishna. The pairs of birds in the trees, and the numerous, multi-colored flower garlands celebrate the meeting of the two lovers, while the dark clouds cradled by arches of golden lightning symbolize their union.

The jagged line of cranes in the cloudy sky emphasizes the shape of the wooden wheel. It is interesting to note that the artist cared little for a realistic representation of the wheel, and settled upon depicting it from a multitude of perspectives.

P. Chandra, *Indian Miniature Painting*, no. 259.

2.56 Folio from a Ms. of the *Bhagavata Dashamskandha* by Krishnadasa
Kangra style, late nineteenth century
3¹/₄ x 3¹/₄ in.

Not illustrated

The newborn Krishna is held by his mother before being carried away to the village where he will be raised. His father looks on from an adjacent pavilion. A guard in the foreground suggests the prison in which Krishna's natural parents are being held. The painting is done in a simple manner. The lines of script which surround the illustration alternate between red and black.

P. Chandra, *Indian Miniature Painting*, no. 263.

Portraiture

The idea of painting individuals appealed to Rajput rulers as well as to Mughal Emperors. After the seventeenth century, portraits appear along with manuscript illustrations throughout North and Central India. Under Mughal patronage, many fine, solemn portraits were painted. Numerous Rajput kings had a distinct interest in formal portraits of themselves and their ancestors which reinforced their legitimacy to rule. In fact, in certain schools there was a tradition of depicting son with father as though to emphasize continuity of lineage.

Portraits of male figures can often be associated with historical rulers (nos. 2.61, 2.63-2.65, 2.67-2.68). It is common for a line of script on the border or the reverse to name the particular king. Some portraits were made during the life-time of the ruler, others are posthumous copies (no. 2.65). Postures are remarkably conservative over time and space. Standing figures are distinguished by costumes of different styles as well as by facial features, while attributes, such as the flower or plume and the sword, have a remarkable consistency. The connection of the sword with a ruler, even as a young boy, emphasizes the importance of strength and prowess (no. 2.64).

Portraits of women are character studies as much as portrayals of individuals (nos. 2.57-2.60, 2.62, 2.69-2.70). Standardized formulae were not applied to portraits of women; rather, the ideal woman was interpreted according to regional standards. Certain paintings reflect ancient Indian themes, such as the woman in a tree, which recalls the fertility of womankind (no. 2.60). A young woman is said to be able to ripen the fruits of a tree by a simple touch of her foot. The interpretation of women as delicate and fragile is apparent in three portraits from the Bikaner school (nos. 2.60, 2.62, 2.69): each portrait is set against a different background—a tree, a plain expanse of color, and a palatial setting—and yet the overwhelming statement is similar in the refined handling of figure, costume and setting. Traditional views of women are complemented by paintings which portray European women (nos. 2.57, 2.59).

2.57 A Lady Pouring Wine
Deccani Style,
early seventeenth century
6⁵/₈ x 3 ¹/₂ in.

Not illustrated

With light-colored hair flowing around her face, the woman in this portrait is dressed in European clothes. The peculiar set of her hat and her unnatural grasp of the small wine cup indicate only a budding familiarity with European customs. Her bright pink dress with green, orange and gold accents is set against a dark background with delicate plants sketched around the ground.

P. Chandra, *Indian Miniature Painting*, no. 61, black-and-white illustration.

2.58 A Yogini
Deccani Style,
early seventeenth century
5¹/₄ x 2³/₄ in.

Not illustrated

This *yogini*, a female mystic, dances in an ecstatic moment. The tattered ends of her red robe, the way in which the gold-edged green shawl flows around her shoulders and her topknot testify to her religious character. Her feet rest on wooden sandals which are golden. The religious, mystical life was one of the alternatives offered to women in a traditional society.

P. Chandra, *Indian Miniature Painting*, no. 62, black-and-white illustration.

2.59 A Lady with a Wine Cup
Mughal Style, late seventeenth century
5¹/₈ x 3 in.

In what appears to be a copy of a European work of art, the artist has portrayed a woman holding a wine cup and a basket of brown fruit. Her light brown hair distinguishes her from Indian women, whose hair was always depicted as black. Her costume is pink and blue, with gold and white trim.

P. Chandra, *Indian Miniature Painting*, no. 24.

2.59

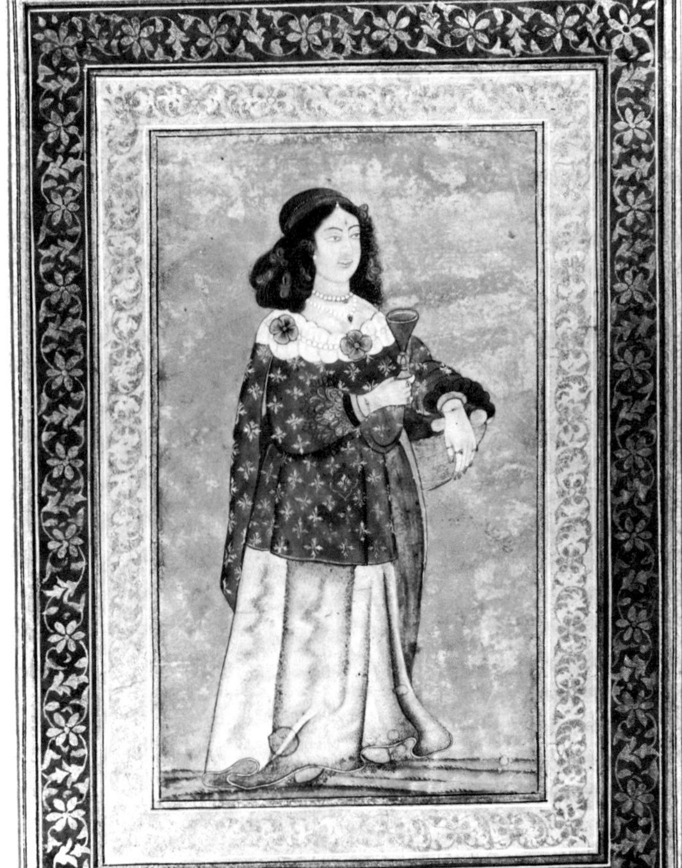

""

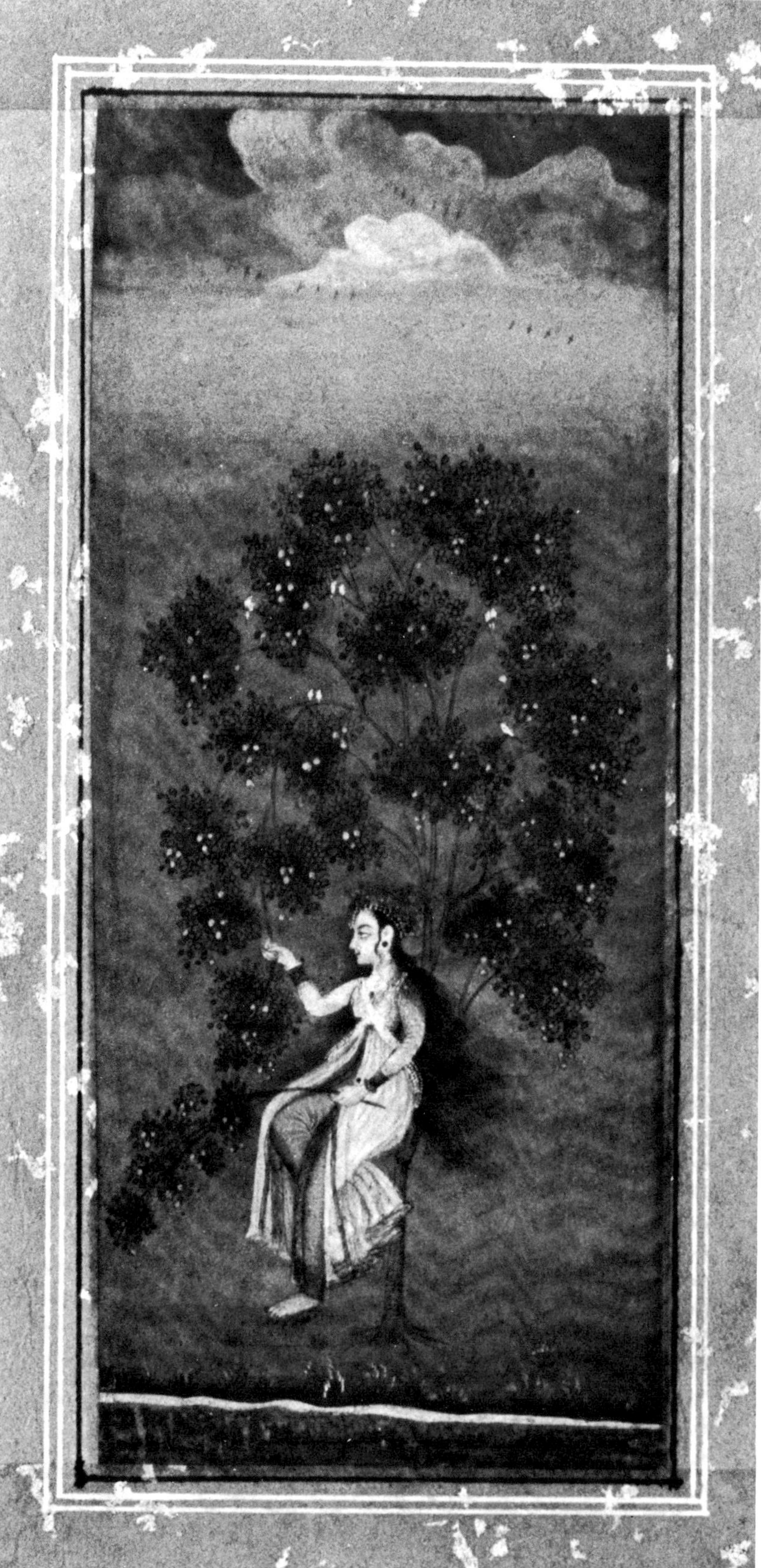

2.60 Lady and Tree
Bikaner, late seventeenth century
4½ x 2 in.

The motif of a lady seated in a tree, grasping a broken twig in one hand and a branch of the tree in another, was popular in the Rajasthani school of Bikaner. It partakes of the ancient Indian theme according to which the touch of a woman's foot could bring a tree into flower and fruit. The figure in this painting wears a gold-trimmed, white gossamer tunic over pink pants. Strings of pearls cross her bodice. Atop her head with its loose flowing hair is a golden crown. Pairs of white birds are perched on branches of the kumquat tree with its orange fruits. Lines of gray birds dot the cloudy sky. A river flows in the foreground.

P. Chandra, *Indian Miniature Painting*, no. 175, black-and-white illustration.

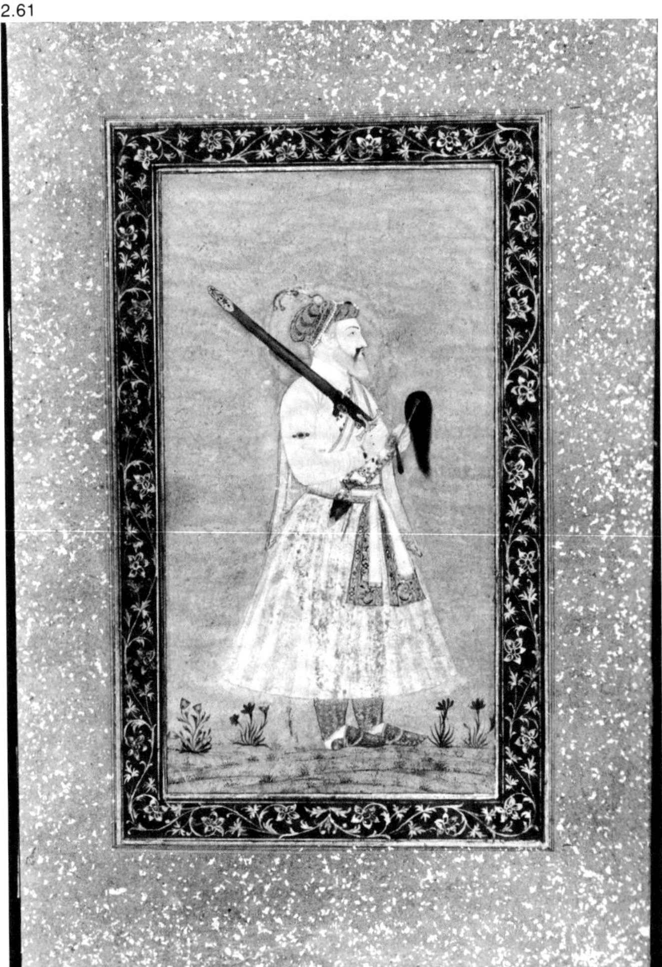

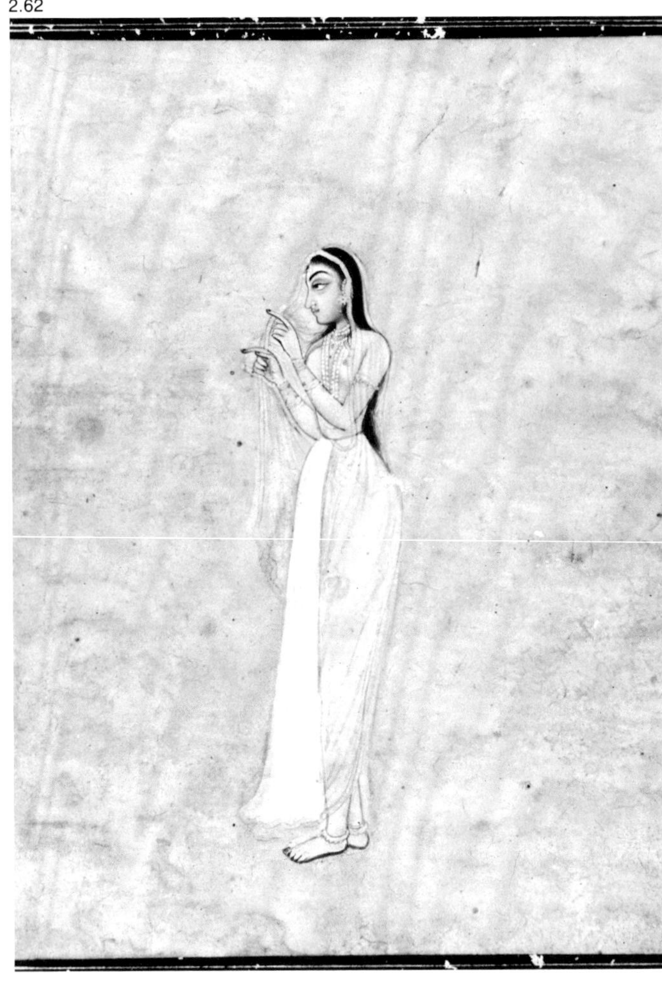

2.61 Portrait of Shah Jahan
Mughal Style, c. 1700 or later
7⁵/₈ x 4¹/₈ in.

Individual portraits of this great
Emperor were popular during his
reign, when the Taj Mahal was built.
The tradition of inlay work and decorative floral patterns that are found on the
great architectural facades of Shah
Jahan's reign are hinted at in the ornamental treatment of the weapons and
the cummerbund he wears. The aged
emperor is nimbate, a common picto-
rial device for enhancing royal stature.
His red-orange turban and shoes as
well as green pants and sheer white
tunic are decorated with gold. He
holds a maroon sword case and a
black fly-whisk.

P. Chandra, *Indian Miniature Painting*,
no. 28.

2.62 A Lady Adjusting her Veil
Bikaner, early eighteenth century
6³/₄ x 5¹/₈ in.

This portrait is from the same school as
no. 2.60, being just a bit later in date.
Here symbolism has been left aside
and the woman is simply adjusting her
veil. Devoid of any background ornamentation, the painting is a character
study. The fabric of her veil and upper
bodice has a gossamer quality. Her
hair hangs loosely, reaching past the
small of her back. Her jewels establish
her courtly roots. The deep pink area
between her hands and arms indicates
a reworking of that portion of the figure.

P. Chandra, *Indian Miniature Painting*,
no. 178.

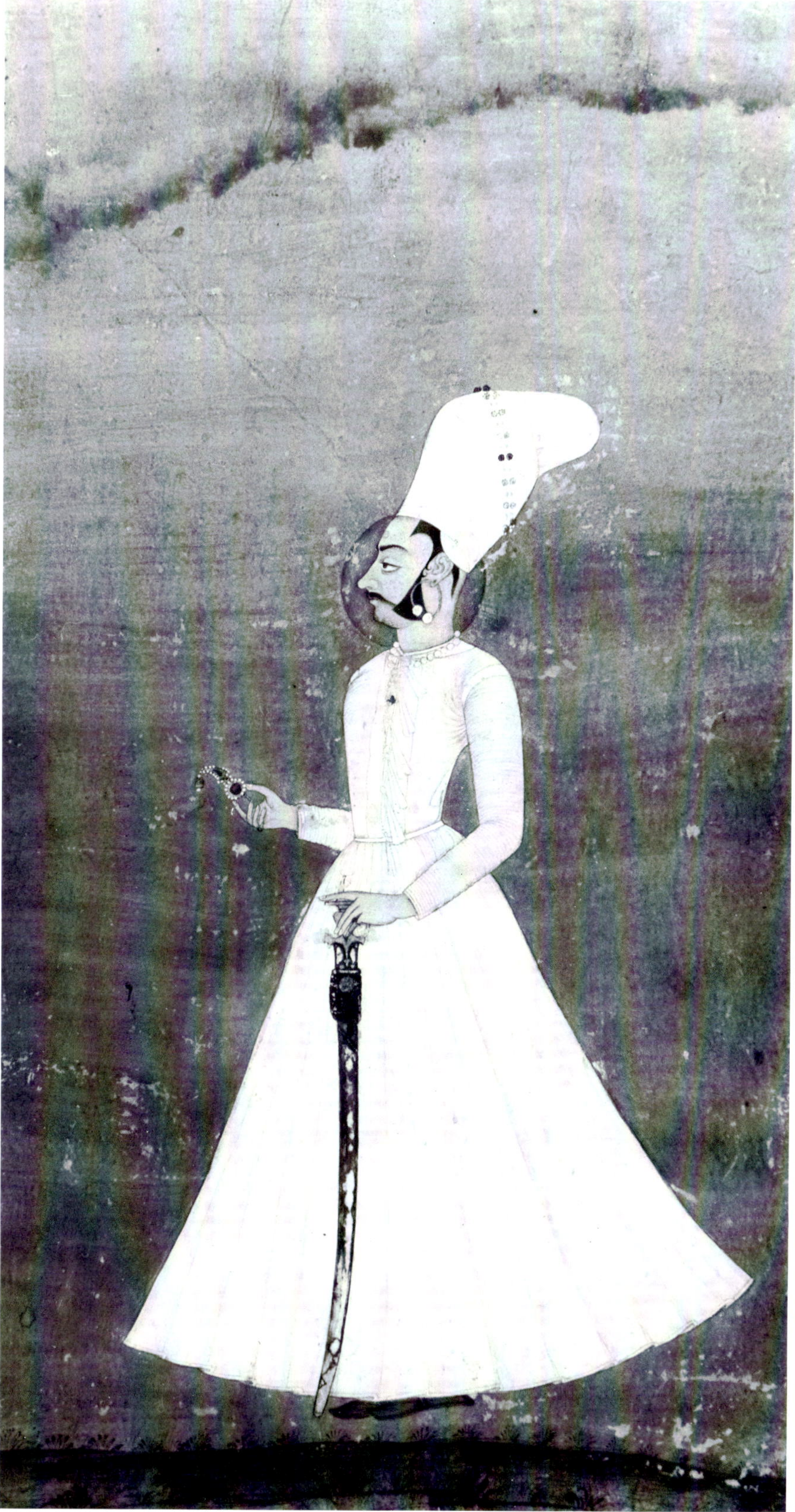

2.63 Portrait of Maharaja Ram Singh of Jodhpur

Marwar, mid-eighteenth century
9³/₄ x 5³/₈ in.

In this youthful portrait, the nimbate Maharaja wears the high turban that was in fashion during his reign. His white tunic is carefully tailored. Note the rows of creases that decorate the sleeves, a feat possible with a thin, well-starched fabric. The geometric pattern of his hair is repeated in other portraits as well. One hand holds an aigrette, while the other rests on his sword. The gray background is broken at the bottom by a small patch of green grass. An inscription on the reverse identifies the figure.

P. Chandra, *Indian Miniature Painting*, no. 147. The figures in nos. 2.64, 2.67 and 2.68 of this exhibition share the same basic pose as the Maharaja in this painting. They are from several different locales. There was a significant amount of interplay between artistic traditions in different areas.

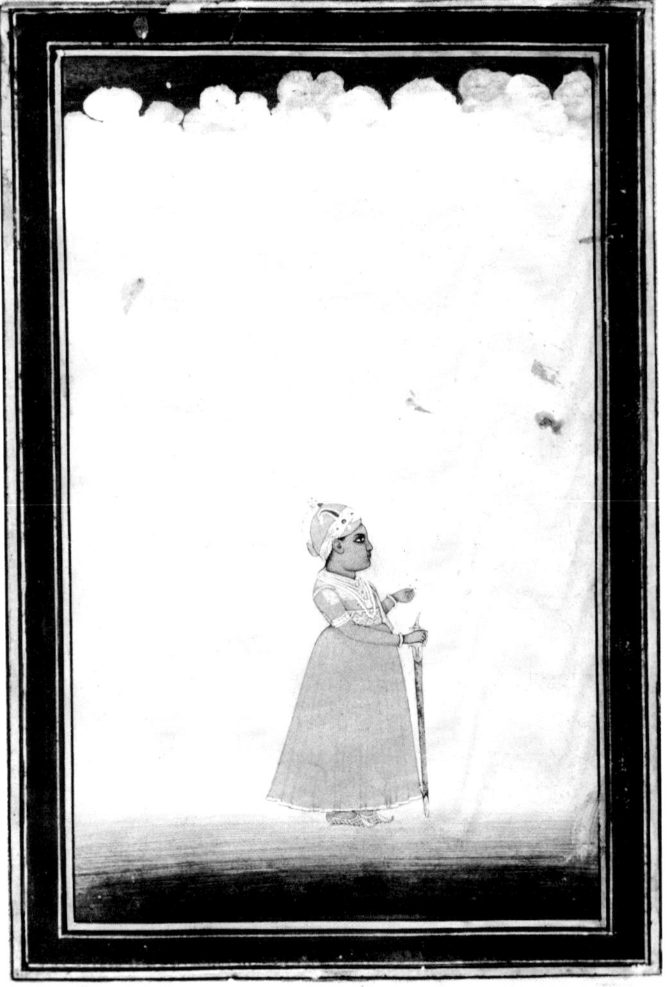

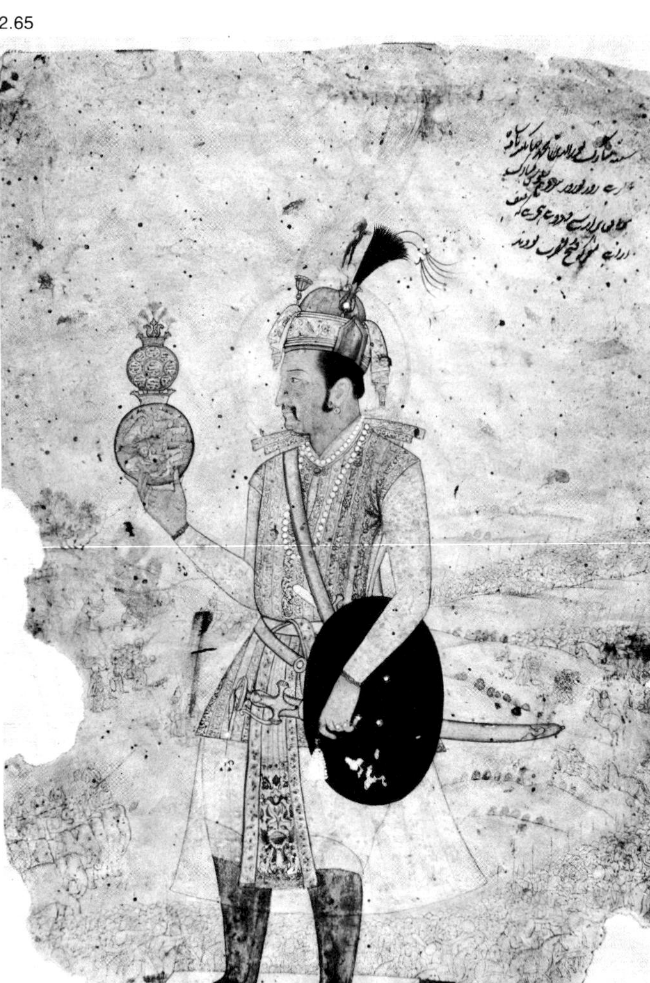

2.64 Maharaja Sawaiprithvi Singh (1768-1778) of Jaipur
Jaipur, c. 1775
6¼ x 3⅞ in.

The young Maharaja is dressed in bright orange. He holds a flower in one hand and a sword in the other. This composition mimics that used in portraits of adult monarchs (cf. nos. 2.63, 2.67 and 2.68), indicating that it was a pose appropriate to royalty. The sky shows thick white clouds against a band of blue. Dark green grass is sketched against a light green background.

P. Chandra, *Indian Miniature Painting*, no. 193.

2.65 The Emperor Jahangir Holding a Globe
Mughal Style, late eighteenth century
8⅞ x 6⅜ in.

This portrait emphasizes the peace and harmony made possible by the imperial victory and command of the great Mughal Emperor Jahangir. The prominent figure stands against a pale green and beige background with a sketch-like rendering of the imperial troops in the background. The globe in his hand relates the names of Jahangir's illustrious ancestors and shows deer and lions in peaceful company. His costume indicates an attempt at portraying a rich pattern of embroidery. Jahangir ruled in the early seventeenth century. This is a copy of a painting done almost two hundred years earlier. The late Mughal school produced many copies of favored paintings from the Imperial library.

P. Chandra, *Indian Miniature Painting*, no. 25, black-and-white illustration.

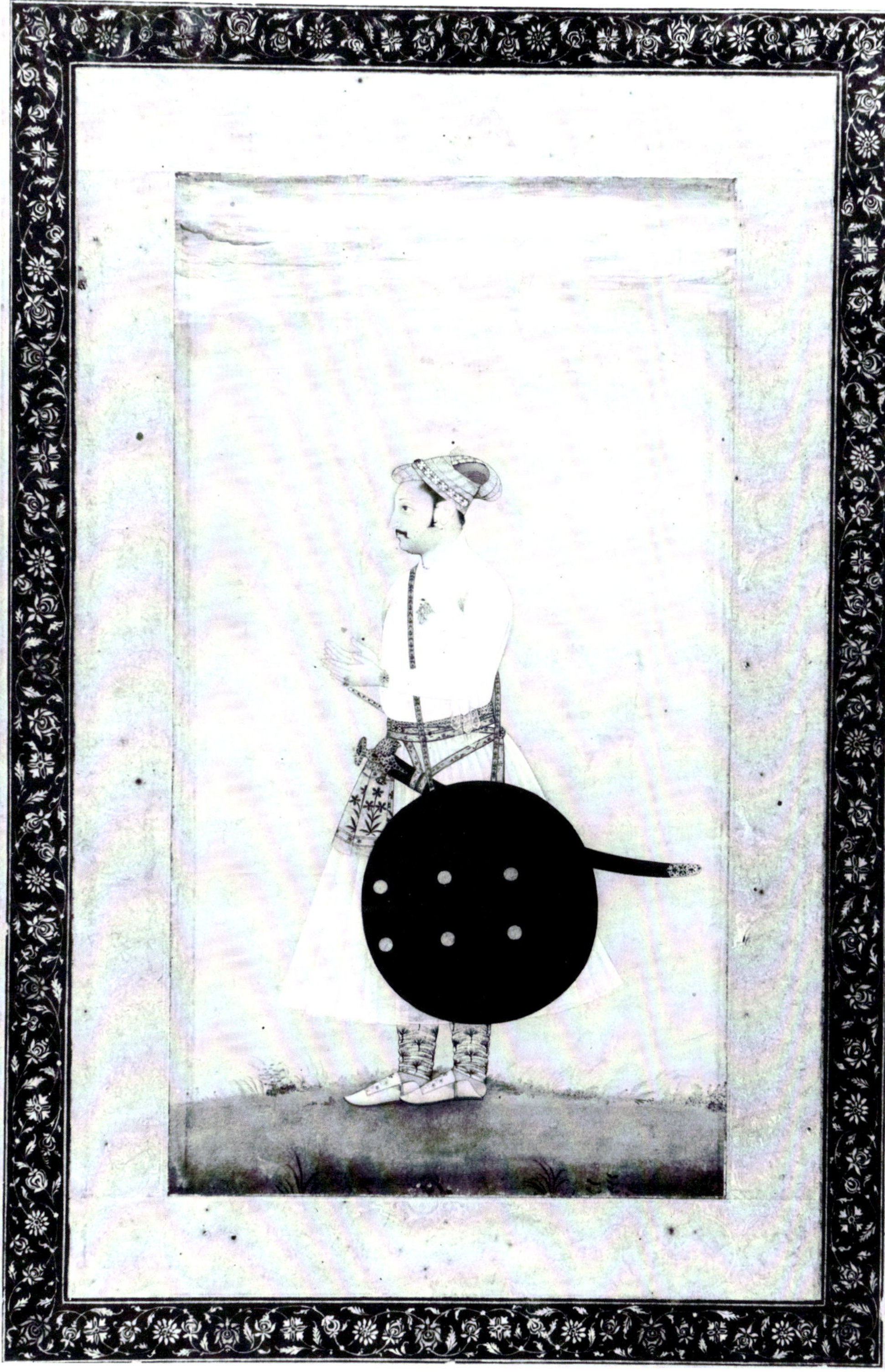

2.66 **Portrait of a Nobleman**
Mughal Style, late eighteenth century
8½ x 4¾ in.

Nobles as well as emperors and kings were the subjects of portraiture. This armed noble holds his hands cupped before his chest in a gesture of respect. He wears golden pants with a pink floral pattern and a white tunic cinched by a golden waist scarf. His jewelry includes a pendant which has the shape of a bird. The ground is a yellow-green which meets an apple-green background. A thin border of blue and white is at the top. This portrait was executed with a finely handled brush.

P. Chandra, *Indian Miniature Painting*, no. 29.

2.67 **Portrait of a Rajput Chief**
Kishangarh, late eighteenth century
7³/₈ x 4 in.

Not illustrated

The halo as well as the traditional attributes of sword and lotus-bud attest to the eminent status of the figure in this portrait. His tunic has a green-yellow hue, with orange printed pants beneath. His slippers, as his sword, are a deep maroon. A homogeneous light blue area comprises the background.

P. Chandra, *Indian Miniature Painting*, no. 165, black-and-white illustration; Chandra suggests that this figure may represent Sawai Pratap Singh of Jaipur (1778-1803).

2.68 Portrait of Rao Shatrujit (1762-1801) of Datia

Bundelkhand, late eighteenth century
7⁵/₈ x 5⁵/₈ in.

Against a broad pink border, the blue
oval frame surrounds the portrait of
the king. He exhibits the familiar
eighteenth-century portrait pose, face
in profile, body at a three-quarter turn,
with one hand holding a flower and the
other resting on a sword. His loosely
wrapped yellow turban matches the
color of the shawl about his waist. The
gossamer white tunic covers black and
gold pants. The halo remains a stock
motif signifying royalty. An inscription
on the reverse identifies the king.

P. Chandra, *Indian Miniature Painting,*
no. 204, black-and-white illustration.

2.69 Princess and Bird

Bikaner, late eighteenth century
6¹/₂ x 4¹/₂ in.

Color illustration

The refined life of the court is exemplified in this portrait. The princess stands
in a tall, white, delicately ornamented
tower. A small bird has perched on her
hand. She wears a gold-streaked blue
dress and a silver, orange and blue
cap. A nimbus indicates her royal stature, as it was employed for royalty as
well as for deities in South Asian paintings. In addition to its role as a courtly
pastime, the offering of succor to birds
as an indication of a benevolent character has a history that reaches back at
least two thousand years before this
painting was made. According to another legend, birds must be placated
so that they will refrain from revealing
the secrets of the inner chambers. The
reinterpretation of classic themes is
seen in many areas of South Asian arts.

P. Chandra, *Indian Miniature Painting,*
no. 184, black-and-white illustration.

2.70 Portrait of a Lady

Company Style, mid-nineteenth century
7 x 4¹/₈ in.

Not illustrated

Wearing a white shawl decorated in
pink and a yellow skirt, the lady walks
towards the left. Movement is suggested by the tilt of her shoulders and
the fall of her drapery. A slight smile is
evident behind the large jeweled ring
which decorates her nose.

P. Chandra, *Indian Miniature Painting,*
no. 79, black-and-white illustration.

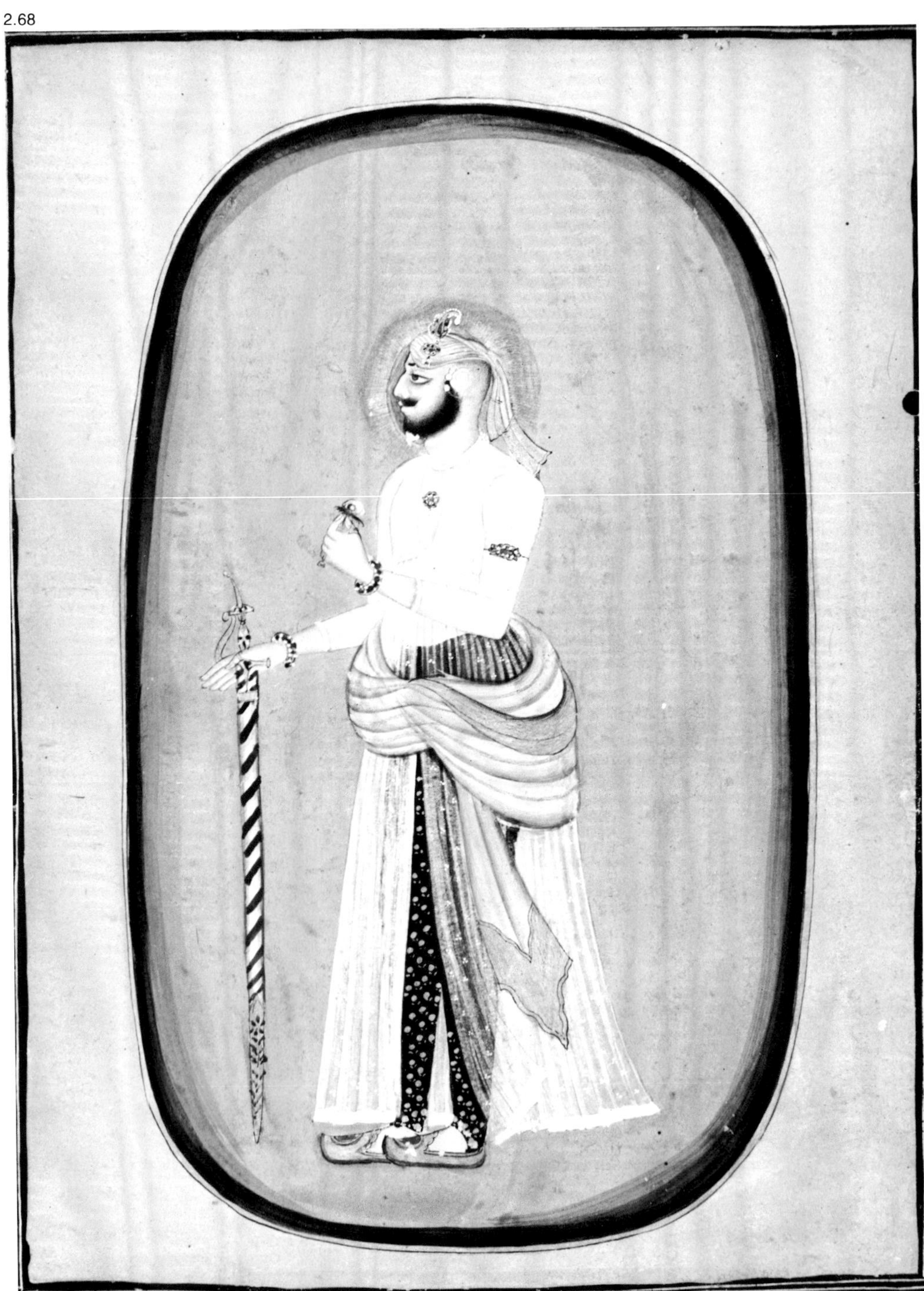

Themes from the World of Humans

Miniature paintings showing human interactions are imbued with a sense of leisure made possible by nobility and wealth. The public and private lives of the ruling class, which possessed the means to commission, enjoy and preserve the albums of miniatures, provided the basis for much of the subject matter. However, many of the themes are more than representations of everyday life. Verses from medieval poetry which explored the depths of aesthetic theory were frequently illustrated by courtly scenes. *Ragamala* paintings are based on verses describing the mood of musical themes. The visual iconography consists of men and women engaging in familiar, often romantic, activities. A woman preparing to meet her lover or a musical entertainment in an inner courtyard might visualize a specific literary reference while resonating with ideals deeply implanted in the cultural history of the subcontinent (nos. 2.91, 2.96, 2.97).

Scenes from the public lives of rulers depict true-to-life episodes which emphasize heroism and grandeur. A favorite activity of the rulers who were the subjects of so many paintings was the hunt. Rulers and nobles, whether astride mounts or observing from the safe vantage-points of rooftops, enjoyed the sport of hunting the many wild beasts which roamed in wooded and hilly areas (nos. 2.71-2.74). Though not the norm, some hunting expeditions included women of the *zenana*. One painting in this exhibition illustrates an episode from a specific story, the *Hamir Hath,* wherein a queen makes love to a guard while her husband is distracted by the hunt (no. 2.72). In addition to hunting scenes, Mughal and Rajput rulers are shown leaving their palaces for the relaxation of a boat ride (no. 2.77), participating in formal processions (nos. 2.75, 2.76), and engaging in battle (no. 2.78).

The more passive activities of the ruling class which were frequently depicted included formal courtly portraits showing specific monarchs receiving large groups of supplicants or sitting amidst a group of courtiers at specified festival times (nos. 2.79-2.81, 2.83). A ruler at leisure would oftentimes smoke a water pipe with a few courtiers nearby, if we are to trust the numerous documentation of the paintings which are devoted to such compositions (nos. 2.86, 2.87).

The interior courtyards, gardens and chambers of the palace are the setting for interactions among groups of women. Living in palace areas protected by male guards, a woman and her companions would enjoy a refined, luxurious existence (no. 2.89). Playful activities such as swimming, idle conversation, and musical entertainment are components of the vision of the wealthy life that we see recorded in miniature paintings (nos. 2.90, 2.92, 2.94). Forays into the surrounding countryside are idealized by the romantic conventions of different times and painting styles (nos. 2.88, 2.93, 2.95). The juxtaposition of the refined, restful activities of women against the vigorous hunts and battles of men defines the traditional view of society (nos. 2.93, 2.94).

The theme of lovers in every moment from separation through union was expertly handled by painters (nos. 2.89, 2.96-2.102). Formal encounters are depicted in court settings (no. 2.83), but the beauty and nuance of a loving relationship are fully explored in the intimacy of individual encounters. A prince crossing the river to meet his beloved, a woman stealing into the forbidding forest at night, and a woman impatiently waiting for her lover evoke different moments in the romantic cycle (nos. 2.99, 2.100, 2.102). The moods of the paintings are echoed in background details such as a vine surrounding a tree to indicate union or an empty bed to suggest separation. Ultimately, many of the paintings of lovers refer to the theme of the relationship between God and human beings.

2.71 A Prince Restraining an Elephant

Mughal Style, c. 1615
7 x 10 in.

The princely class rode caparisoned elephants for various types of excursions. The restraining of these temperamental beasts is a frequent subject of paintings. In this example, possibly the prelude to a hunt, the prince uses an elephant hook to slow the pace of the elephant. A companion horseman holding a spear and whip turns to judge the progress of the situation. Two attendants run alongside, each holding a staff with firewheel and a bit of rope. The foreground is covered in blue-green grass. The yellow background is edged by a white and blue band at the top indicating the sky.

P. Chandra, *Indian Miniature Painting*, no. 15, black-and-white illustration.

2.72 An Episode from the *Hamir Hath*

Kangra Style, early nineteenth century
10³/₈ x 13¹/₂ in.

The combination of a scene from the hunt and of a lovers tryst is especially appropriate to the portrayal of the private life of a monarch. Except for the disloyal guard who is making love to the queen, it is only female companions who accompany the hunting king. The juxtaposition of the king, aiming at his prey which may be the deer or rat before him, against the guard, who aims at a fierce tiger as he makes love to the queen, is a purposeful statement about an ineffective ruler.

This richly colored painting incorporates the technique of continuous narration. The figure of the queen is shown twice in this painting. At one moment she is riding her horse just behind the tent in the central foreground. She glances ahead as though imagining the tryst scene in which she is involved on the right edge of the painting, as her horse stands next to that of her lover in the foreground.

P. Chandra, *Indian Miniature Painting*, no. 251.

2.73 Raja Dhian Singh

Pahari Style, mid-nineteenth century
9¹/₈ x 6¹/₂ in.

Not illustrated

The Raja and two retainers embark on a hunt. All three figures are clothed in white with minimal accents of pale colors. The human figures are painted with a practiced hand. It is likely that the horse is the work of an apprentice. Several artists often worked on a single painting.

P. Chandra, *Indian Miniature Painting*, no. 262.

2.71

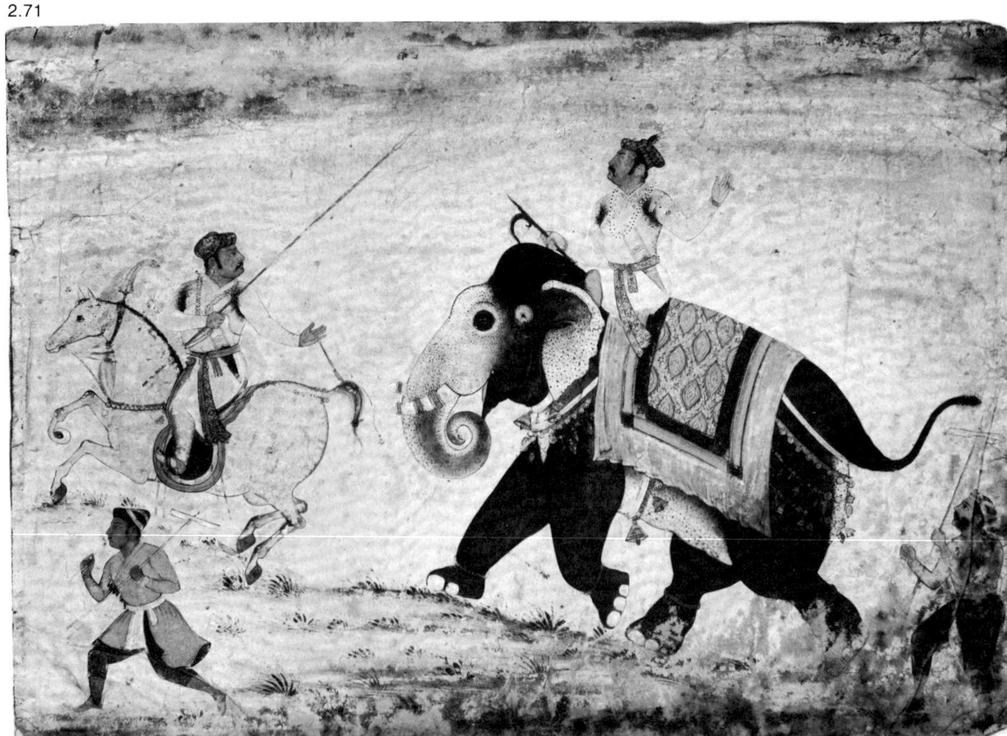

2.72

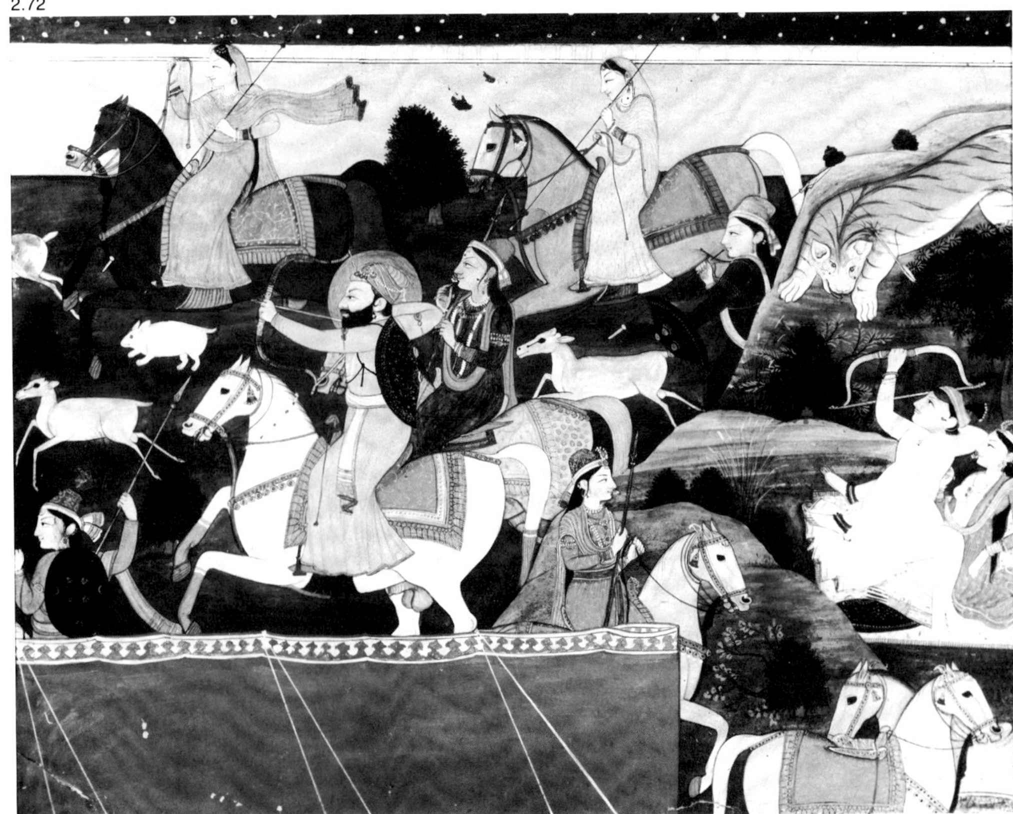

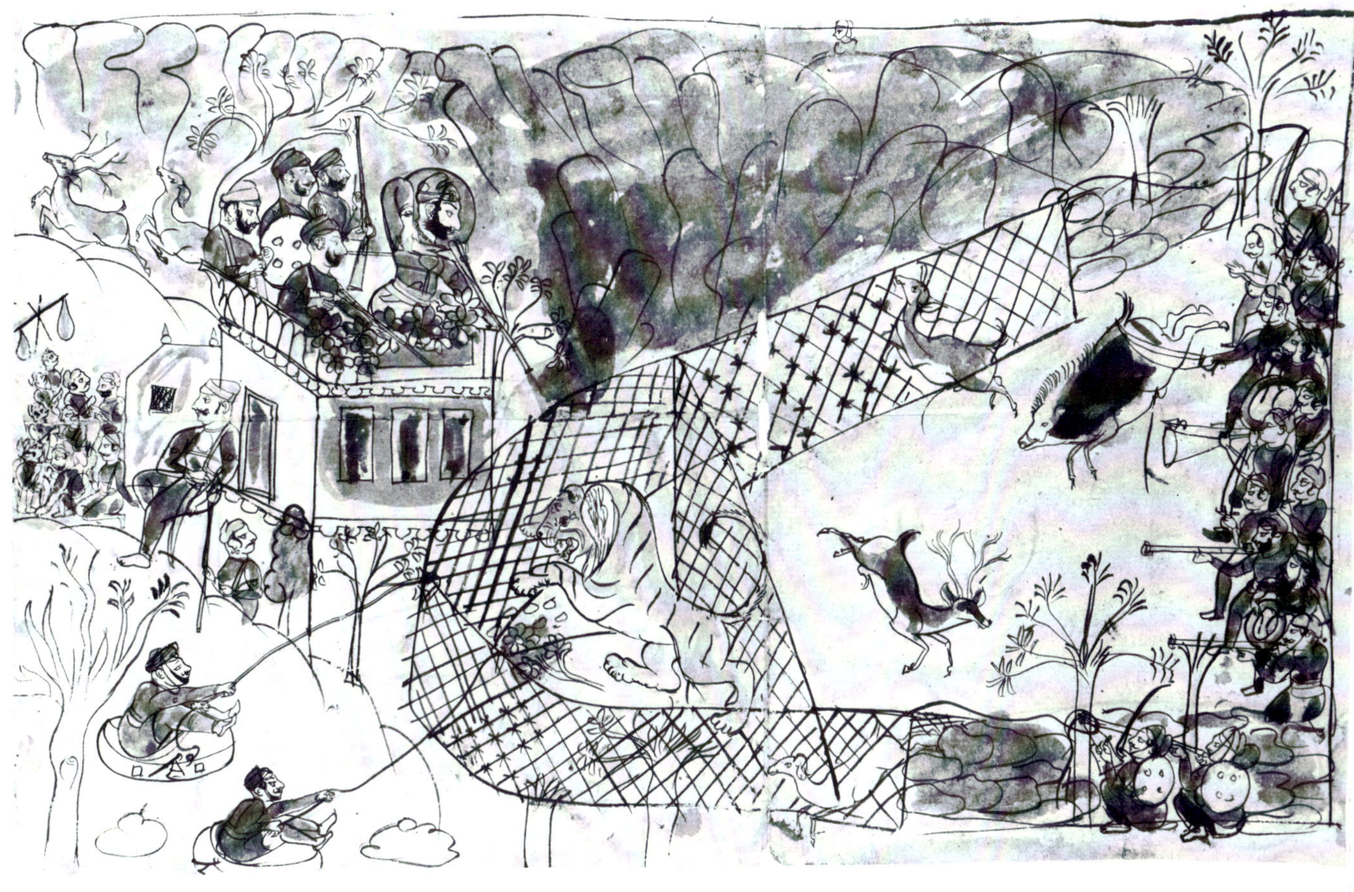

2.74 Shatrusal II (1865-1888)
Shooting a Tiger
Kotah, c. 1875
11½ x 18¾ in.

The royal hunt was a favorite activity of royalty and was a particularly popular subject for Kotah painters. In this sketch-like painting, the king shoots at a trapped tiger from the safety of a rooftop. Beaters hold the net upright in front of the tiger while a vertical row of their fellows chase a boar and two deer into the range of the king. Among the lightly colored features are the green costumes of the figures, the orange-and-black striped tiger, brown deer and gray mountains.

P. Chandra, *Indian Miniature Painting*, no. 128.

2.75 Ram Singh II (1827-1865)
of Kotah in a Procession
Kotah, mid-nineteenth century
12¼ x 19⅛ in.

Color illustration

As the king passes through the cloth market, the worlds of men and women are clearly delineated. In the center of the painting, the nimbate king with an honorific umbrella about his head, sits on a richly caparisoned and heavily chained elephant. His golden garment is speckled with white and green. The driver sits astride the elephant's neck waving a fly-whisk as he controls the animal with an elephant goad. The figure sitting behind the king may be a prince. Following behind the elephant is a small tented palanquin in which the king's favorite wife would travel. Above the tusks of the elephant, a courtesan dances in a small cage. A second female dancer is on the ground below. On the balconies above the cloth-seller shops, a group of young women enjoy the passing procession. Three lively children and an elderly, presumably widowed (if we are to trust her white garments which are the color of mourning), woman complete the balconies' occupants. Light green banana plants and a few darker green trees appear behind the balcony against a royal blue sky. Rows of soldiers wear an array of costumes. Some mimic European-style garments and weapons, while others are in traditional Indian military attire. A row of musicians leads the procession which passes by the cloth merchants.

P. Chandra, *Indian Miniature Paintings*, no. 123, black-and-white illustration.

2.76 Maharana Shambhu Singh
(1861-1874) in Procession
Mewar, c. 1875
10½ x 14½ in.

Not illustrated

The regnal procession underlined the power and authority of local rulers. The young king, according to an inscription on the red border, proclaims himself a king of kings. He sits on an open throne-like seat placed over the back of the elephant. The gold halo as well as the fly-whisks waved by the driver and the king's companion reiterate his authority. The vast retinue includes orange-clad soldiers holding blue scabbards, and retainers with multi-colored turbans carrying flags, fans, banners and tassled spears. Silver as well as gold is used. The green background receds into distant golden-colored mountains and a blue and white sky.

P. Chandra, *Indian Miniature Painting*, no. 106, black-and-white illustration.

2.77 Aurangzeb Crossing
a Lake in a Boat
Mughal Style, c. 1700
7⅛ x 11¾ in.

Not illustrated

Scenes of royal leisure activities are a common Mughal theme. The Emperor Aurangzeb sits under a golden umbrella at the front of his boat. Four courtiers stand behind him, one of whom holds a hawk. The gold-embossed clothes of the courtiers are richer than the simple outfit of the aged Emperor. Boatmen and an armed guard complete the figural group. Outside the pink-walled city in the distance, a group of elephants and standard-bearing troops are setting out toward the countryside.

P. Chandra, *Indian Miniature Painting*, no. 30, black-and-white illustration.

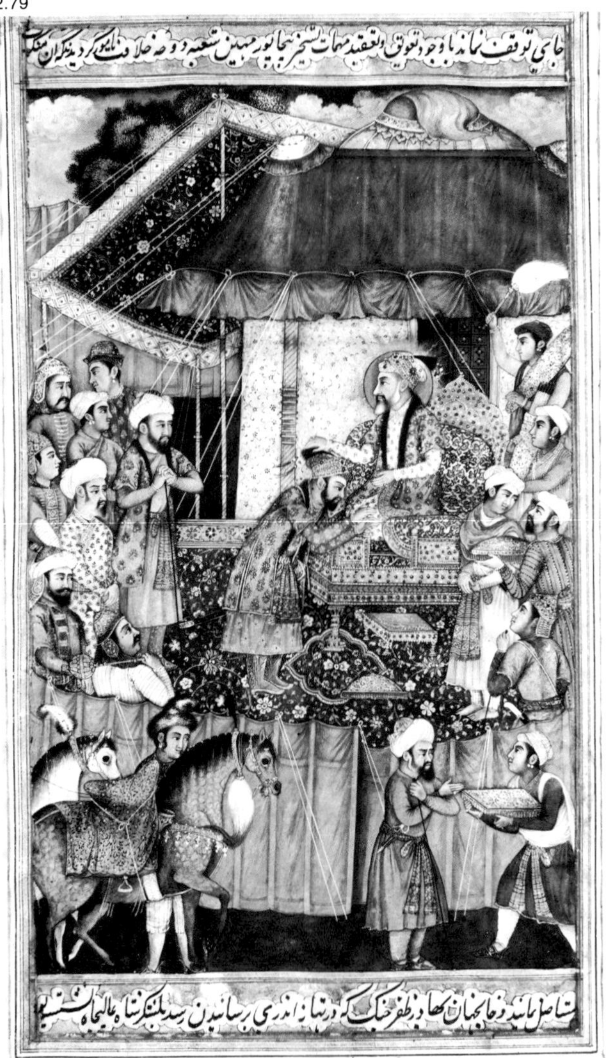

2.78-2.80 Four Folios from a Ms.
Illustrating the *Alamgir Nama*
Mughal Style, late eighteenth century
8⅝ x 5¾ in.

2.78 Aurangzeb at the Siege of
a City: Folio from the *Alamgir Nama*

Not illustrated

The Emperor, enthroned on a palanquin, indicates with a hand gesture acceptance of the respectful greeting of a horseman whose beast is elaborately caparisoned. In the background, a battle is being waged, a city besieged. The vast empire of the Mughals was won and controlled through many battles. Thus their depiction as significant, heroic episodes was remembered in painting long after the actual event.

P. Chandra, *Indian Miniature Painting*, no. 49.

2.79 Aurangzeb Receiving Homage
from a Nobleman

In an elaborate tent, an aged Aurangzeb magnanimously receives a nobleman who reaches for the Emperor's feet, a gesture of respect and homage. The Emperor as well as two of the nobles wear fur-trimmed, golden jackets. All of the costumes are elaborate and richly colored. Orange fabric comprises the wall which delineates the court from the outside where attendants wait for their noble masters. The tradition of illustrating historical manuscripts reached its high point in the early seventeenth century. The courtly life was a fascinating subject for imperial and noble clients.

P. Chandra, *Indian Miniature Painting*, no. 48.

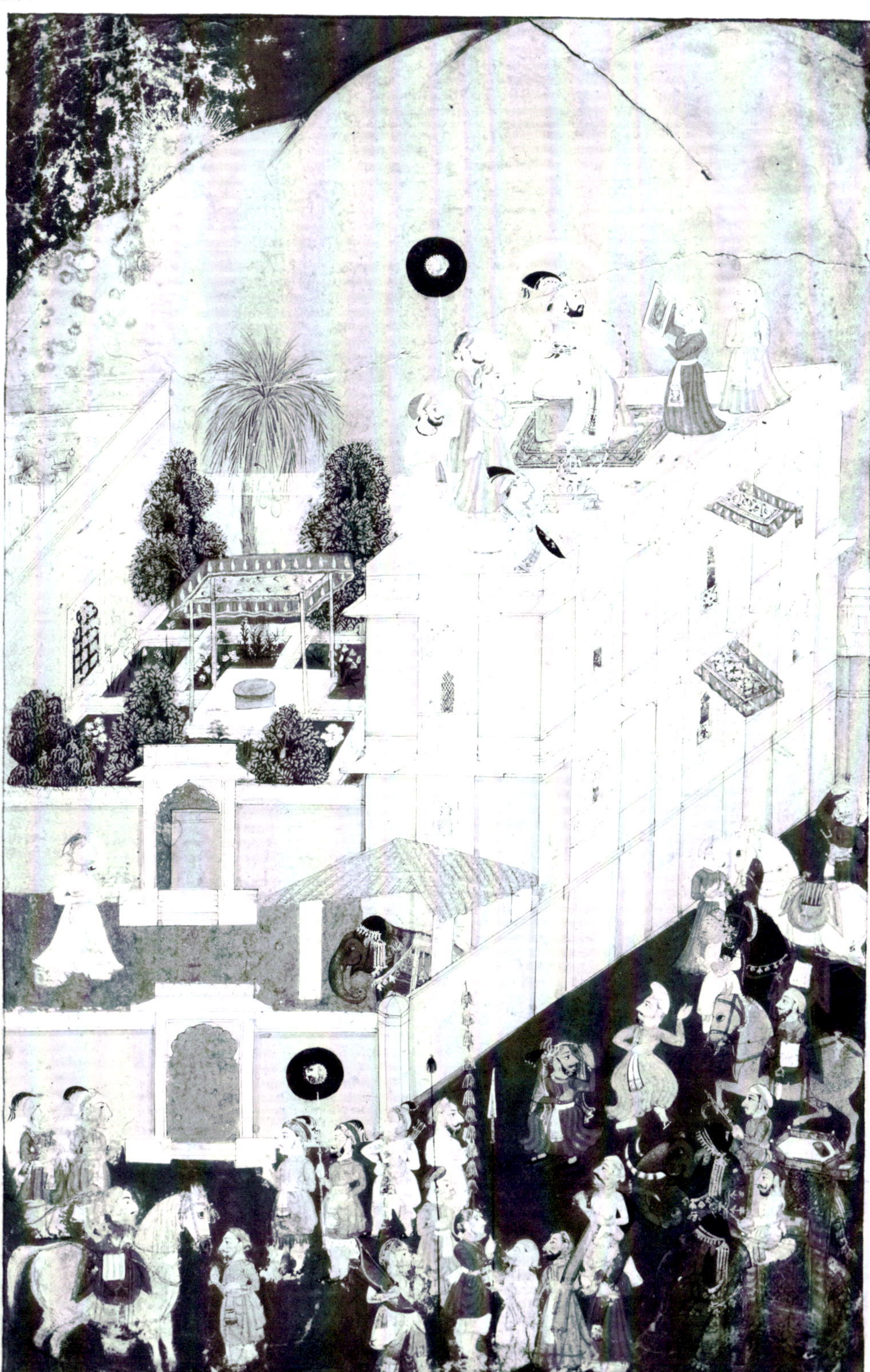

2.80 The Court of Aurangzeb

Not illustrated

On the right, a middle-aged Aurangzeb sits in a golden peacock-pavilion as a nobleman approaches offering a decorated manuscript. The surrounding courtiers include a scribe and a pair of figures waving peacock-feather fans. Elaborate, diverse costumes are worn by the courtiers who represent different age and ethnic groups. On the left, the outer court is occupied by approaching nobles, their attendants and mounts. A musician accompanies whirling dancers, one of whose sleeves stretches over his hands. There are no female participants at this public, courtly reception.

P. Chandra, *Indian Miniature Painting*, no. 50, black-and-white illustration.

2.81 Maharana Jagat Singh II (1734-1751) of Mewar at the Festival of Holi
Mewar, c. 1740
16¼ x 10½ in.

The subject of this painting is a public celebration of the festival of Holi. The nimbate Maharana, seated on the rooftop of his pink and white palace, is smoking a water pipe. He is about to bestow a flower garland on the nobleman who holds a mirror before the Maharana. The holding of a mirror before the ruler is a rather subdued Rajasthani custom tied to the spring festival of Holi, which includes joyous and playful sprinkling of colored water and powder and is intricately associated with the god Krishna (compare nos. 2.30 and 2.45). The inner courtyard of the palace reveals a garden with a gold and red rooftent, and the outer courtyard houses a stabled elephant. To the left are the inner quarters wherein the women reside. The attendant figures outside the wall are gaily dressed in red, yellow, orange, pink and blue. Some dance, while others attend to the horses and elephants of their masters. Courtly accoutrements such as fans, spears, fly-whisks, and rolled-up rugs add to the royal and festive tone of the scene. Two dervishes dance in celebration. The squat bodies and large heads are typical of eighteenth-century Mewar painting. A green hill rises in the background against a deep blue sky with the sun half-hidden behind the hill.

P. Chandra, *Indian Miniature Painting*, no. 93, black-and-white illustration.

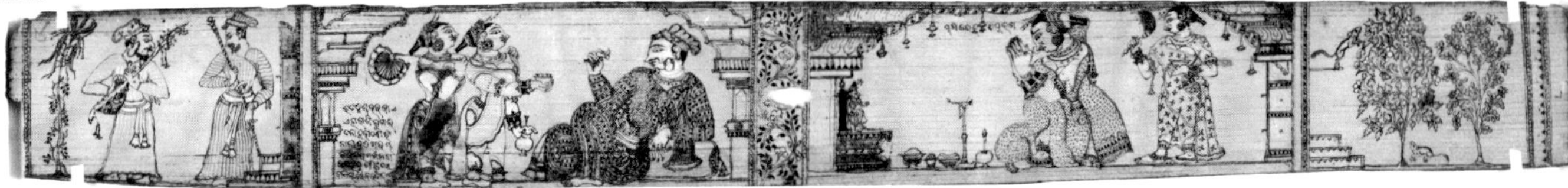

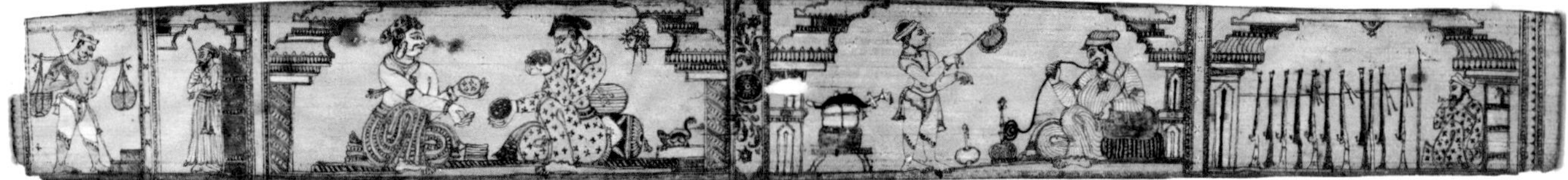

2.82 Court Scenes: Illustration of an Unidentified Manuscript

Orissa, eighteenth or
nineteenth century
1³/₄ x 16¹/₁₆ in.

The two sides of this palm leaf show various leisure activities in a palace. The obverse is divided into four compartments. The left panel shows a musician and a guard. The tree suggests an outdoor location. The next panel contains a lounging male figure approached by two women, one of whom offers a small incense bowl while the other holds a fan. The other central panel shows a woman worshipping a figure which is placed on a small altar. An attendant holding a fly-whisk stands behind the devout woman. The last panel returns to the outdoors, where a bird and two mongooses scamper between the trees. The reverse is divided into five panels. On the left a vendor balances his wares on one shoulder while carrying a staff on the opposite one. Next, a guard stands before an open door. The following large panel shows two men engaged in a game. Note the bird on a perch protruding from the wall, and the mongoose scampering on the floor. The next panel contains a lounging male figure who smokes a water pipe while an attendant waves a fan before him. The final panel shows an armoury with a row of rifles guarded by a single male figure. Inscriptions are in the Oriya script.

Red and yellow, with an occasional patch of green, supplement the black outlines constituting the main color-scheme in this style of painting The painting was part of a manuscript that was meant to be read by turning the leaves upwards, thus explaining the reversal in the top to bottom direction from one side to the other.

Elvehjem no. 66.13.2. This painting was not included in the original catalogue of the Watson Collection. It is very similar in style to no. 7 in Chandra's catalogue, and is probably from the same manuscript, according to Mrs. Watson.

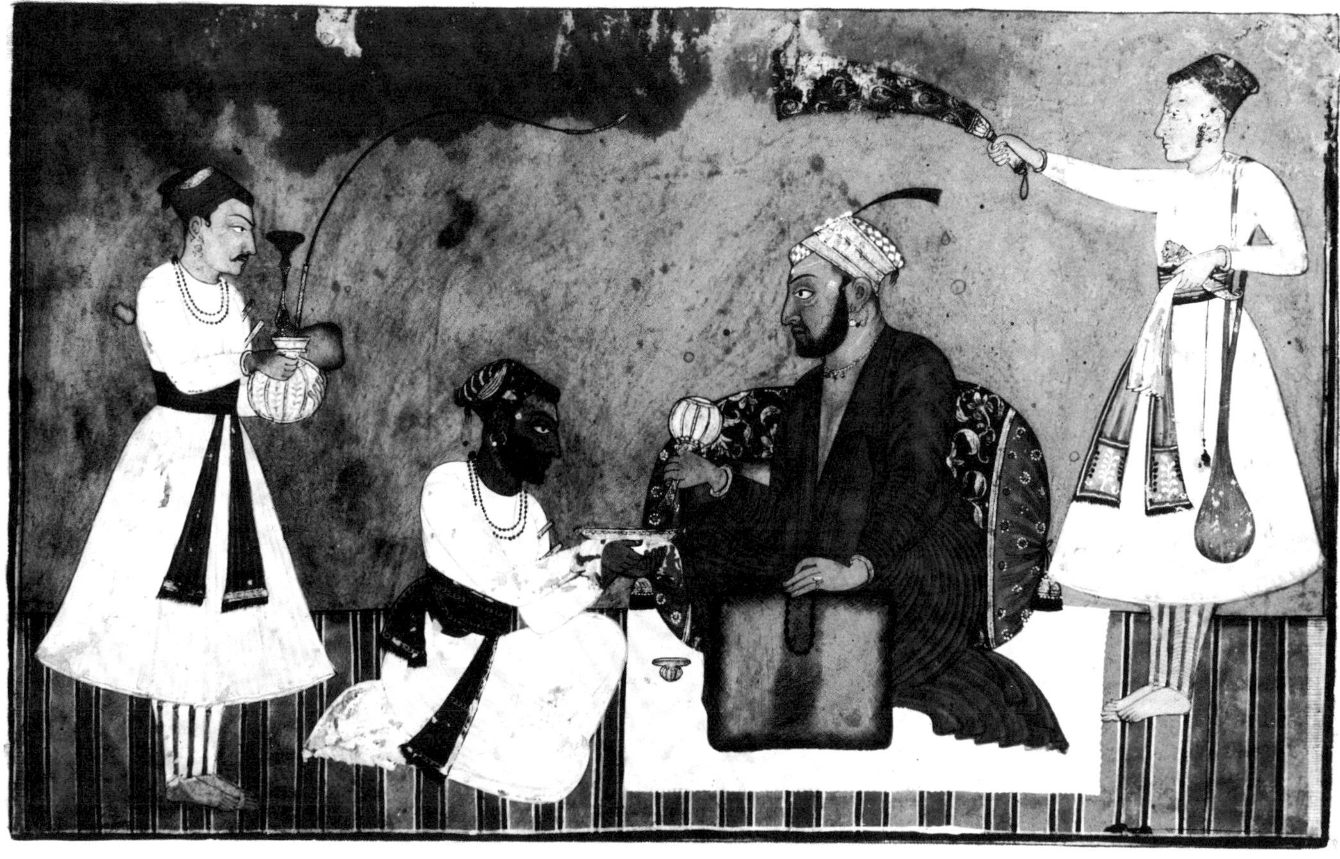

2.83 The Summer Season
Marwar, c. 1825
14 x 9³/₄ in.

Not illustrated

The emphasis of this painting is on the luxury and finesse of courtly life. A king, with a halo to corroborate his royalty, sits in a garden pavilion accompanied by a group of six women. All are dressed in gold-trimmed yellow clothes. Variously shaped fans and a flask of wine await the pleasure of the king. In the foreground, a lotus pond and rows of fountains beautify the garden setting. The trees are a dark mass interspersed with light green and golden banana leaves. Pink hills on a yellow ground stand against the blue sky at the top. An elephant grasps a snake in his tusk near a panting tiger who lies before the distant hills.

P. Chandra, *Indian Miniature Painting,* no. 154, black-and-white illustration; Chandra identified the king as Man Singh of Marwar (1803-1843).

2.84 Raga Shri:
Folio from a *Ragamala* Series
Bundi or Kotah, c. 1780
7 x 4⁵/₈ in.

Not illustrated

The setting for this musical interlude suggests the courtyard of a palace. The light clothing of the figures contrasts with the richly colored tiled area and background sky. The white tunic of the enthroned *vina* player subdues his bright orange pants. The old, gray-bearded musician who sits on the ground wears a pink tunic, while his companion who sings and claps hands is dressed in pale green. A fly-whisk-waving attendant, dressed in a yellow tunic and green pants and holding a shield and sword, stands behind the enthroned figure. The elegant blue-tiled garden, complete with fountain, and a shimmering orange-to-gray sky completes the picture. A line of *nagari* script on the red border identifies the subject as the metaphorical expression of a musical mode.

P. Chandra, *Indian Miniature Painting,* no. 118, color illustration.

2.85 Raja Chhatar Singh
(1664-1690) of Chamba
Basohli Style (Chamba),
early eighteenth century
6³/₈ x 10¹/₈ in.

Portraits of local rulers with courtiers were popular in eighteenth-century Punjab-Hill schools. In this painting, various amenities are offered to the seated Raja. One attendant stands holding a water pipe, another kneels holding a drinking bowl on a white cloth as the king pours from a slender carafe, and a third courtier waves a peacock-feather fan and holds a white cloth pendant in the opposite hand. The red-robed king sits on a small white embossed rug set atop a lavender, deep-blue and red striped rug. The attendants wear white tunics with striped pants and colored turbans. The background is a flat apple-green expanse.

P. Chandra, *Indian Miniature Painting,* no. 226, color illustration; he cites other known portraits of this king.

2.87

2.86 Raja Bir Singh (c. 1789-1846) of Nurpur
Kangra Style, late eighteenth century
7⅝ x 4⅝ in.

Not illustrated

The Raja relaxes against a large white bolster, smoking a water pipe of which only the slender, decorated hose of the pipe is shown. His dark blue tunic and turban is offset by his bright red Kashmiri-style shawl. The shawl is delicately edged with a white strip containing a pink and green pattern which suggests floral buds. The border of the shawl has a broad band with a stylized floral pattern. His retainer wears a pink tunic and orange shawl while holding a fly-whisk and white cloth. The fly-whisk, whose original purpose is described by its name, came to be a symbol of respect when used by the attendant of a king or deity. The use of the white cloth is more difficult to define, though respectful gestures such as the washing and drying of feet remain a part of many rituals in South Asia today. Fine cloth is a traditional offering in many secular and religious ceremonies in the Northern hill areas of the subcontinent.

The paint has been applied with a controlled hand which gives the unpatterned cloth a rich appearance. The fanciful shape of the ear and the curl of the Raja's hair as well as the sharp angle at the bridge of the nose are examples of the integral use of linear pattern and design in miniature paintings.

P. Chandra, *Indian Miniature Painting*, no. 240, black-and-white illustration.

2.87 Gulab Singh (1820-1857)
Pahari Style, mid-nineteenth century
6 x 3¾ in.

The ruler is wearing a black coat which is decorated with gold in the manner of an embroidered shawl. A white tunic trimmed in gold and yellow-striped pants complete his costume. He wears a rather soft, white-with-gold-trimmed turban, with a small black plume at the front. His right hand rests on a sword while his left holds a handkerchief. The gold chair on which he sits rests on a red and blue carpet with green trim. A low retaining wall separates his platform from an apple-green background. A thin, curved strip of blue and white indicates the skyline. A single attendant stands behind Gulab Singh. He is dressed in white with a red scarf and a bright orange turban.

P. Chandra, *Indian Miniature Painting*, no. 261; Chandra inadvertently described Gulab Singh's coat as red.

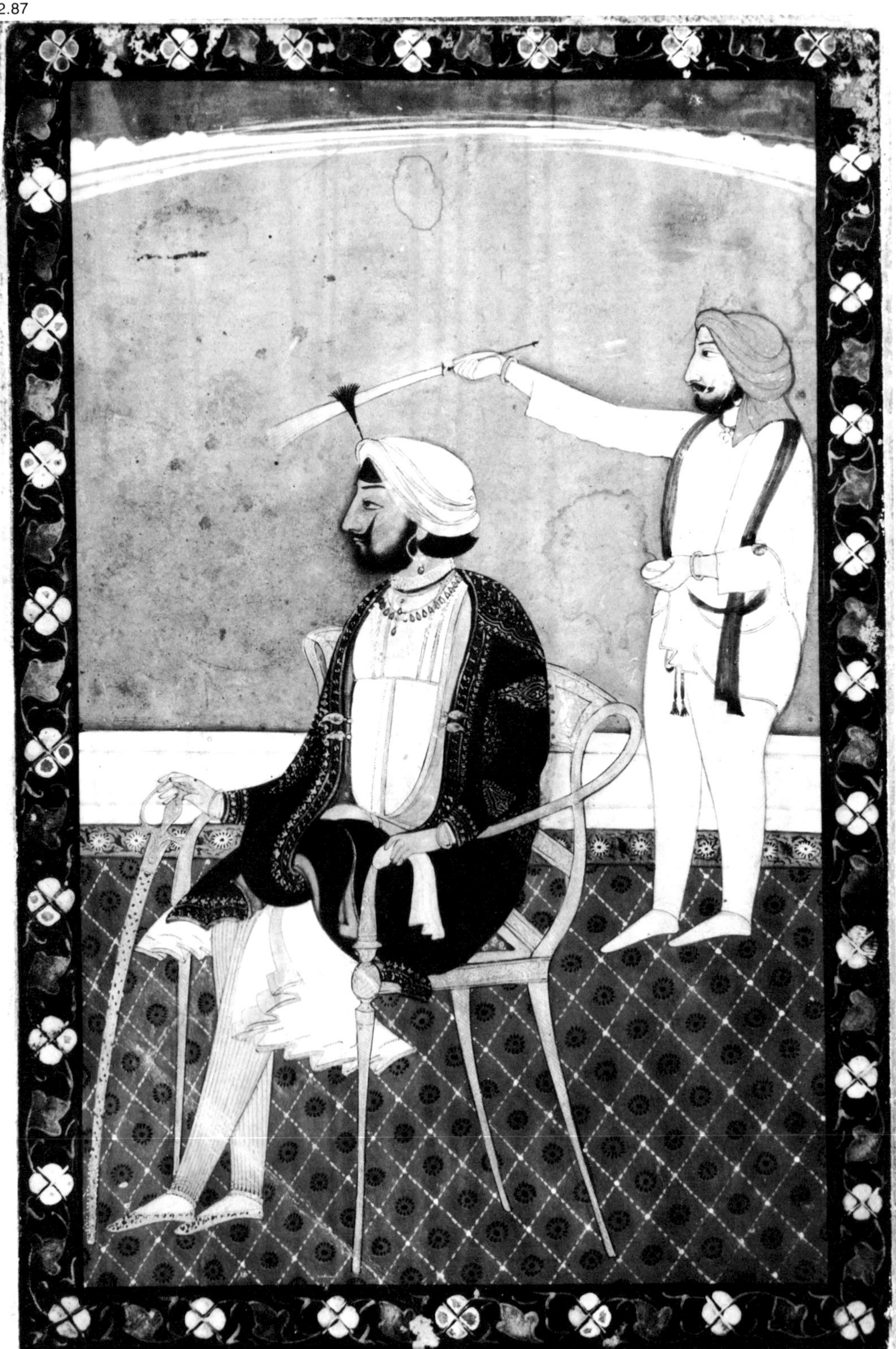

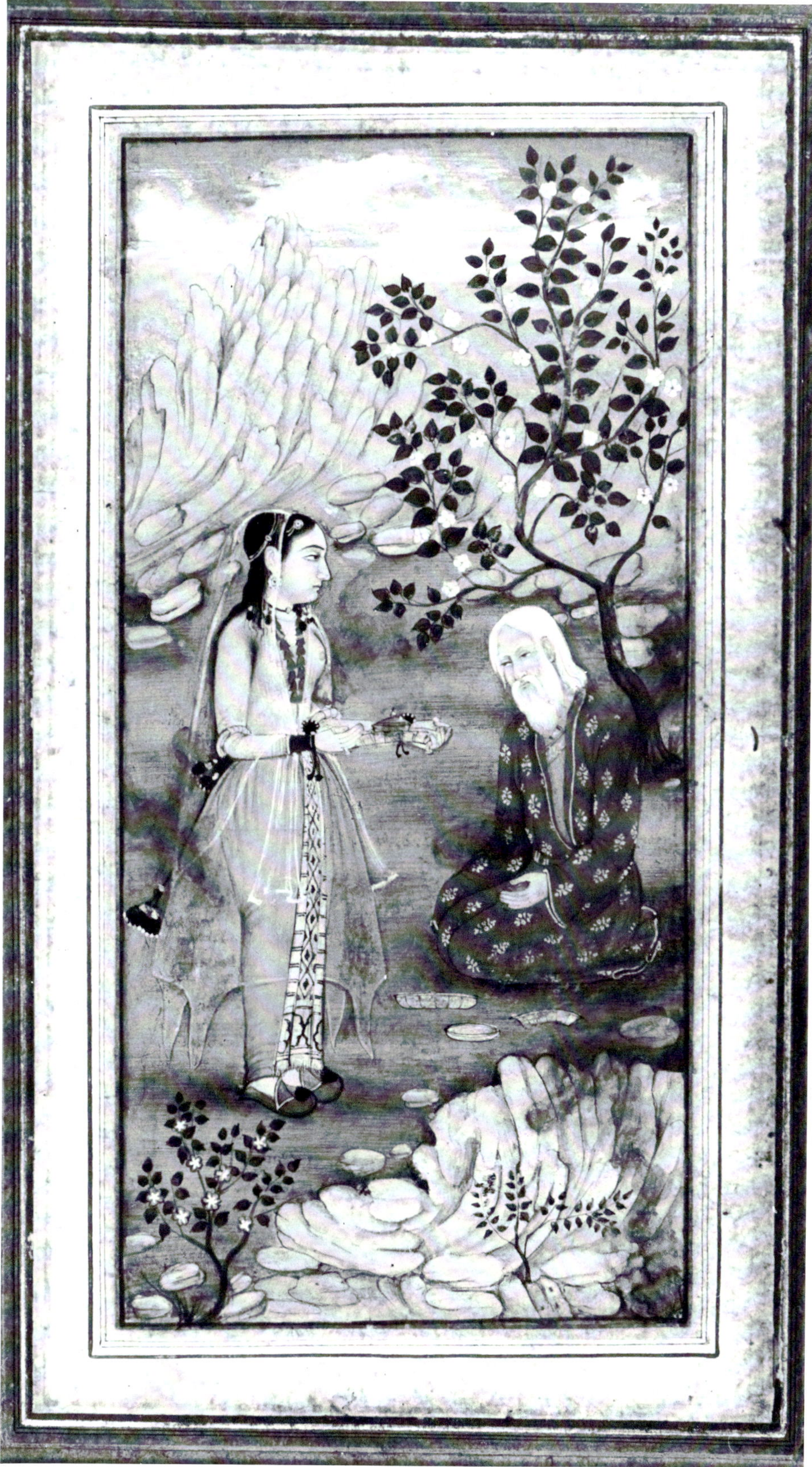

2.88 A Woman Visiting an Ascetic
Mughal Style, c. 1605-1610
5¾ x 3¾ in.

The world of women included presenting offerings to and seeking instruction
from religious adepts. A young woman,
wearing a white veil, a yellow jagged-
edged tunic, and orange pants accented by jewelry and a long golden
waist scarf, approaches an aged
ascetic who sits under a tree between
green and brown hills. She holds a
golden tray and box which she is about
to add to the other offerings on the
ground before the seated man. There
is a long inscription on the reverse in
Arabic script.

P. Chandra, *Indian Miniature Painting*,
no. 19.

2.89 Zulaykha in Deep Thought:
Folio from a Ms. Illustrating the
Story of *Yusuf and Zulaykha*
Mughal Style, c. 1610
4 1/2 x 2 3/4 in.

The inner quarters of the women are
the setting for this scene. Note the
male figure in the foreground, guarding
the entry to the courtyard. Zulaykha sits
in a decorated pavilion, head resting
on her hand in a pose of deep thought.
She is tormented by her infatuation with
Yusuf, a romance which is an allegory
for the relationship between God and
humankind. Her orange and gold
dress is set against a blue carpet and a
large, olive-green bolster. An attendant,
hands cupped in a gesture of respect,
approaches her. Three other attendants carrying flasks, trays and musical
instruments are in the foreground
which is a deep yellow expanse accented with delicate floral arrange-
ments. The attendants wear costumes
of light blue, pink, orange, deep blue
and green. Gold highlights many
details including the sky behind the
back wall. There are lines of script
above and below the painting as well
as on the reverse.

P. Chandra, *Indian Miniature Painting*,
no. 18, color illustration.

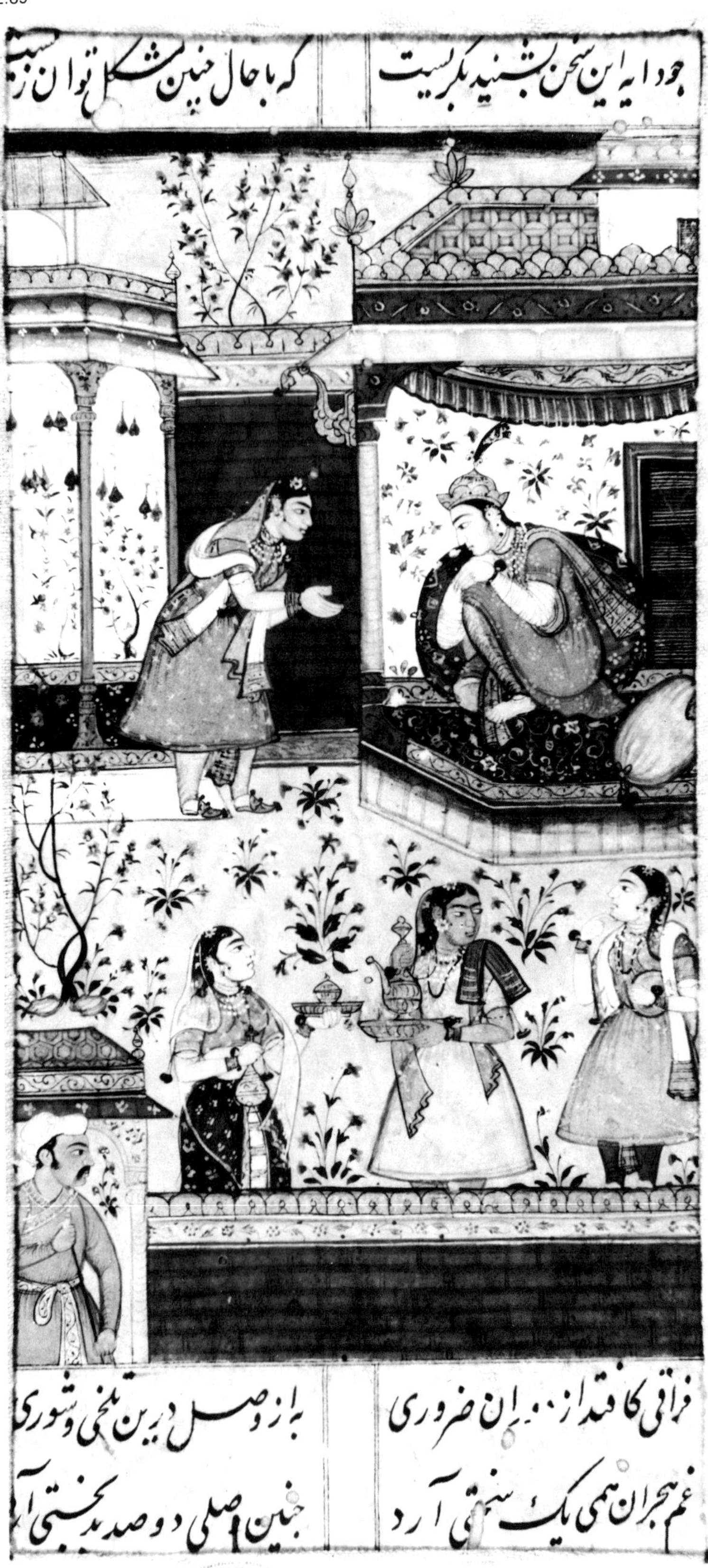

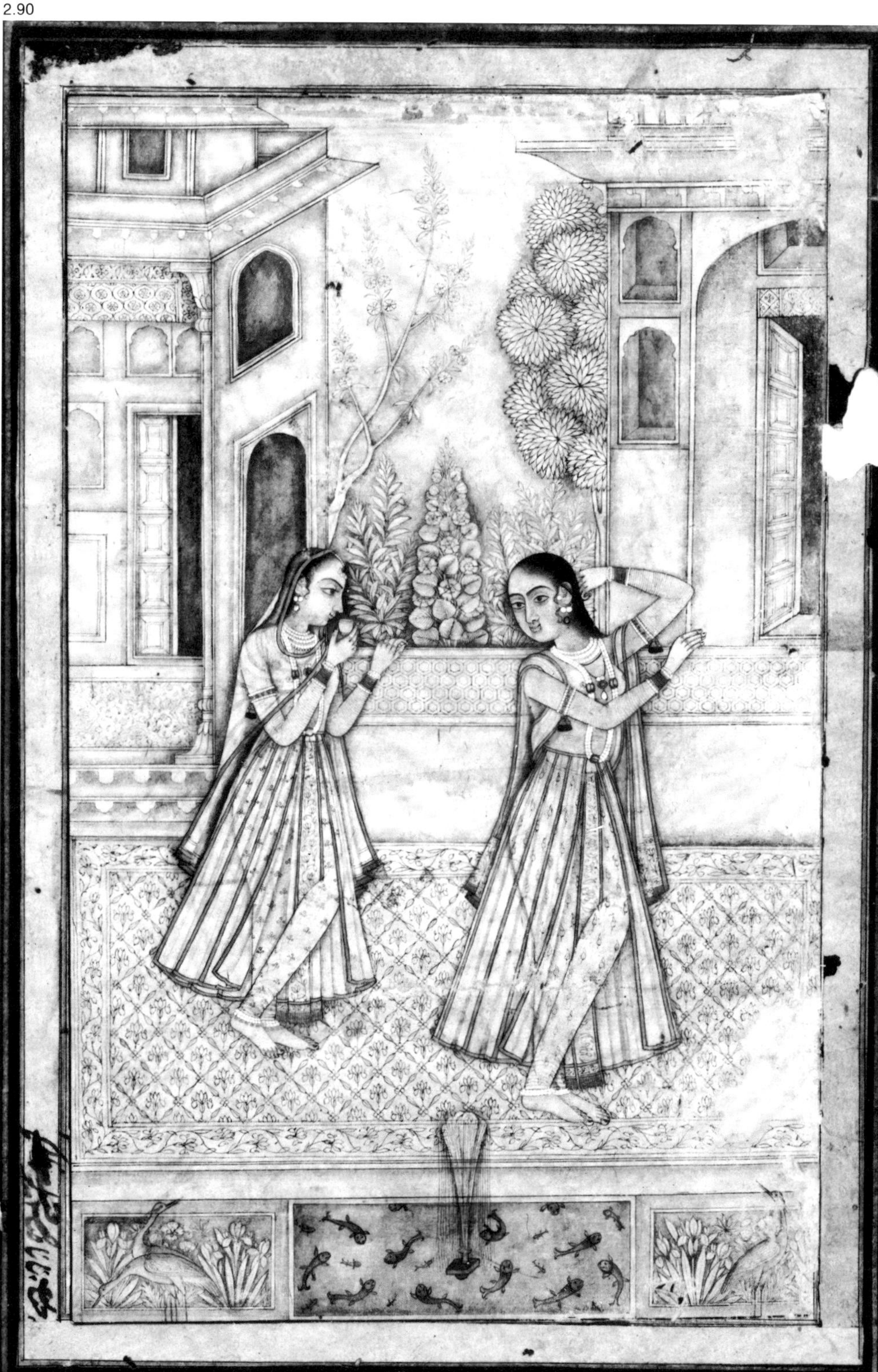

2.90 Ladies Relaxing on a Terrace
Deccani Style (Hyderabad),
early eighteenth century
9¹/₄ x 5³/₄ in.

Two woman relax within the confines of their quarters. The figure in the foreground in three-quarter profile has let her veil fall onto her shoulders as she runs her fingers through her long locks. Her companion drinks from a small cup. Both figures stand with crossed legs leaning against a grate that is usually quite low but here seems to surmount a solid expanse of wall. The drawing is meticulously executed. Only jewelry and the borders of the women's garments have been highlighted with paint. Attention to detail has been lavished on the floral patterns, background vegetation and architectural facade as well as on the figures.

P. Chandra, *Indian Miniature Painting*, no. 67, black-and-white illustration

2.91 Ragini Malashri:
Folio from a *Ragamala* Series
Probably Malwa,
early eighteenth century
9¹/₈ x 6¹/₈ in.

Not illustrated

The pair of beautifully dressed women depict the mood of the *Ragini Malashri*, a musical mode. The seated figure, dressed in yellow and gray cloth, which has a traditional pattern of white dots, holds a *vina* and a lotus, from which several petals fall. The standing figure, wearing a richly decorated green and red costume holds a garland and honorific white cloth. The terrace is above a geometrically shaped garden. In the background, monkeys, birds and peacocks are set in the trees and on the rooftop against a light blue sky. The identification is given in an inscription on the back of this painting (a single verse is written twice, each time by a different hand).

P. Chandra, *Indian Miniature Painting*, no. 135, black-and-white illustration.

2.92 Ladies at their Baths and at Leisure in a Palace

Rajasthani Style,
early eighteenth century
11 x 7⅞ in.

The everyday life of courtly women is the subject of this painting. In the stylized pool several ladies swim, using fired-clay pots filled with straw as their floats. At the edge of the terrace, near a garden with white flowers, a standing figure turns away from the playful splash of one of the swimmers. The standing figure on the right holds a small spouted jug. Two female musicians kneel at the opposite side of the pond. In the background, one woman receives a massage while another smokes a water pipe. The costumes are orange, green, pink and magenta. Similar colors decorate the background with a deep green forest outside the walls.

P. Chandra, *Indian Miniature Painting*, no. 212.

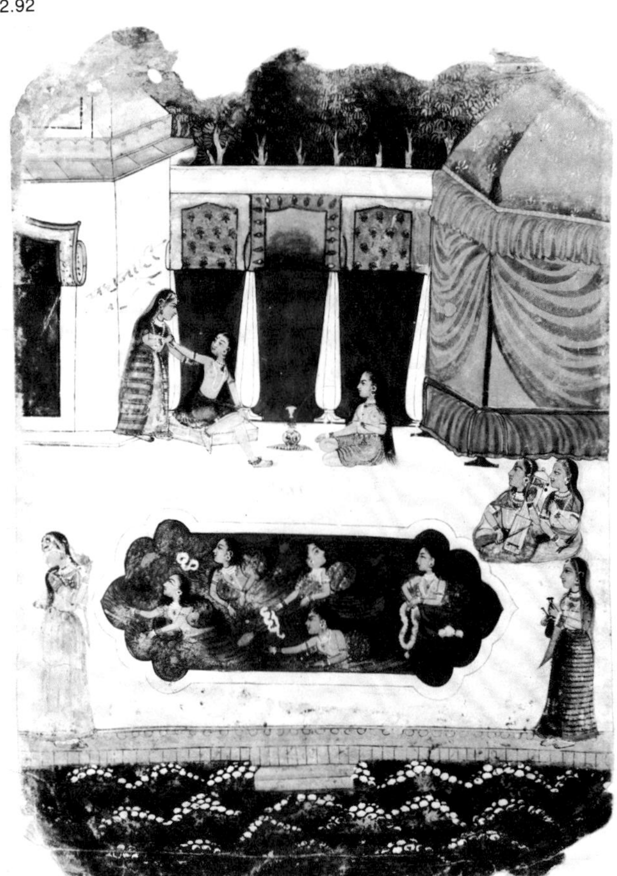

2.92

2.93 Ladies in a Landscape

Kishangarh, mid-eighteenth century
8⅝ x 12 in.

The world of women is relaxed and dreamlike in this painting. Six women in the foreground exchange tufts of grass as the lead figure effortlessly carries three small water pots on her head. The women scattered in the background are engaged in various activities, including playing in a pond, bathing, dressing, gossiping, filling water jugs, and venturing home with the jugs balanced on their heads. Parried against this slow-paced vision is the frenetic level of activity in the background where their male counterparts engage in hunting and marching amidst horses, elephants, running deer and a rhinoceros. The juxtaposition of energy levels describes the separate worlds of male and female activity.

Against a yellow-green background, the six main figures are engaged in one of village women's primary duties, carrying water. Gold trims their pink, red, blue, yellow and green costumes. The background figures on both sides of the river are hazily sketched with detail decreasing with increased distance from the central figures. Long boats float in the pond adjacent to the palace on the left as well as on the distant river.

P. Chandra, *Indian Miniature Painting*, no. 160, color illustration.

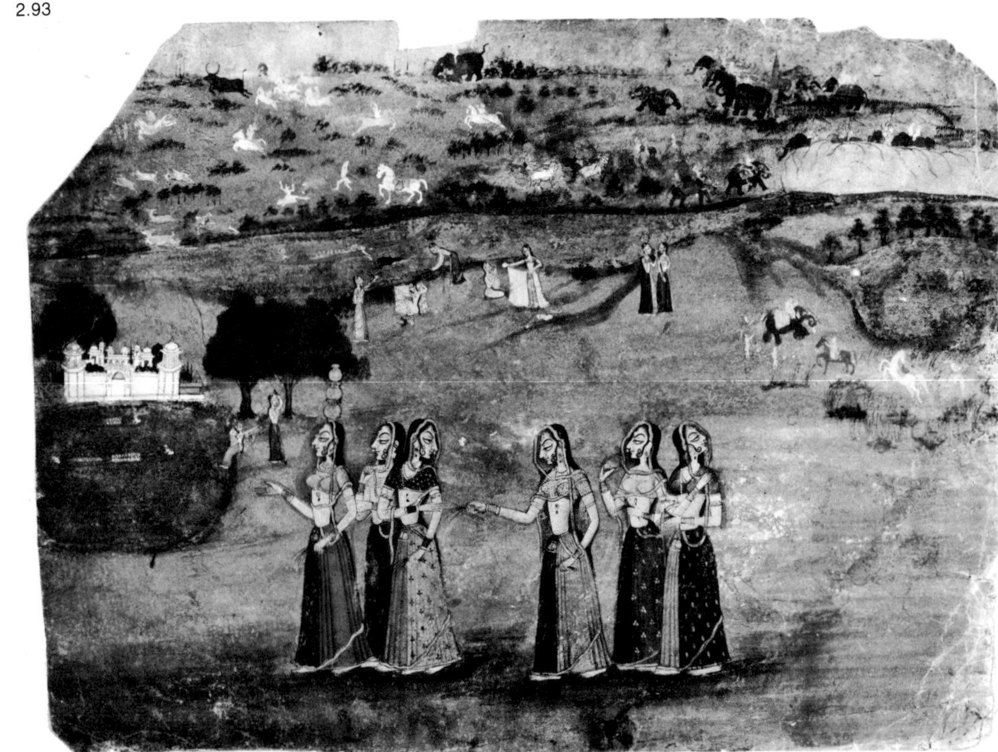

2.93

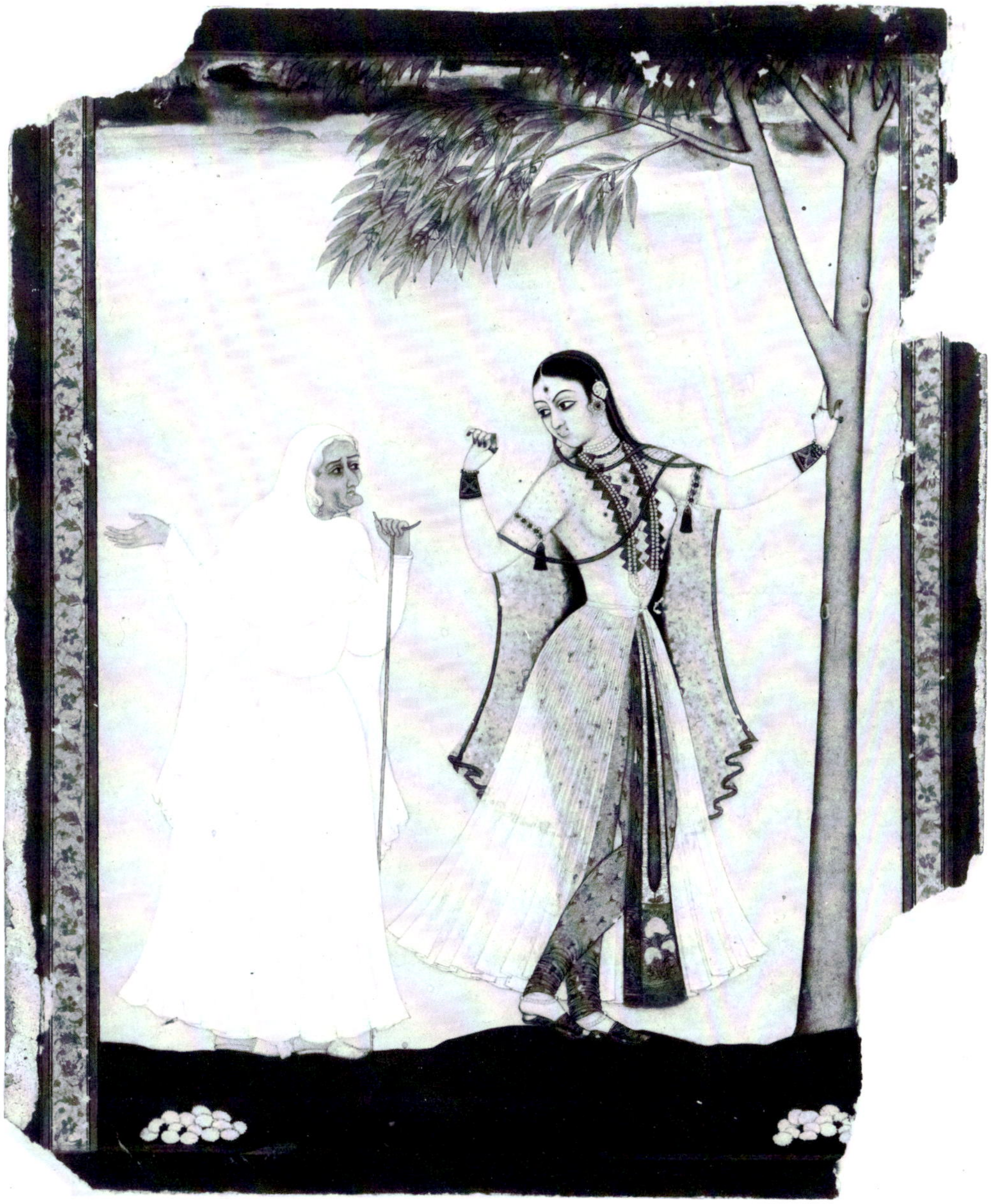

2.94 A Palace Scene

Mughal Style (prob. Lucknow),
late eighteenth century
10³/₄ x 8³/₄ in.

Color illustration

The foreground of this painting is set in
the women's quarters of a palace. A
woman sits on a yellow rug with attendants nearby, one waving a peacock-
feather fan while another holds a tray
with small decorated bottles. From
across a small patch of flowers, two
female musicians entertain the lady.
Other women relax on rug-covered balconies at various levels. The well laid-
out gardens contain fountains and
pavilions. In the distance a river with
swimmers, washermen, boats and a
makara (water monster), who is attack-
ing a horseman, winds toward a larger
river that crosses the entire horizontal
span at the top of the painting. Village
women carry water pots away from the
river. Rows of soldiers march in the
distance. This charming painting com-
pares the relaxed world of courtly
women with the active world of men as
soldiers. The difference in perspective
emphasizes the women in the foreground, making them the focal point of
a broader world.

P. Chandra, *Indian Miniature Painting*,
no. 42. black and white illustration.

2.95 Lady Conversing with a Duenna

Deccani Style, late eighteenth century
6⁷/₈ x 4⁷/₈ in.

The young, elegantly dressed woman
rests a hand on the apple-green trunk
of a tree with light green leaves and
yellow blossoms. Her golden pants
and gossamer blouse reveal the sump-
tuous figure of youth. She turns to greet
an old woman, dressed in white,
whose deeply lined face is a striking
study of old age. The difference between the two stages of life is further
emphasized by the walking stick upon
which the old woman leans as op-
posed to the ripe tree which the young
woman touches. The pale yellow background is edged by a strip of blue sky
with clouds. Deep green grass with
white and red flowering plants are in
the foreground.

P. Chandra, *Indian Miniature Painting*,
no. 69.

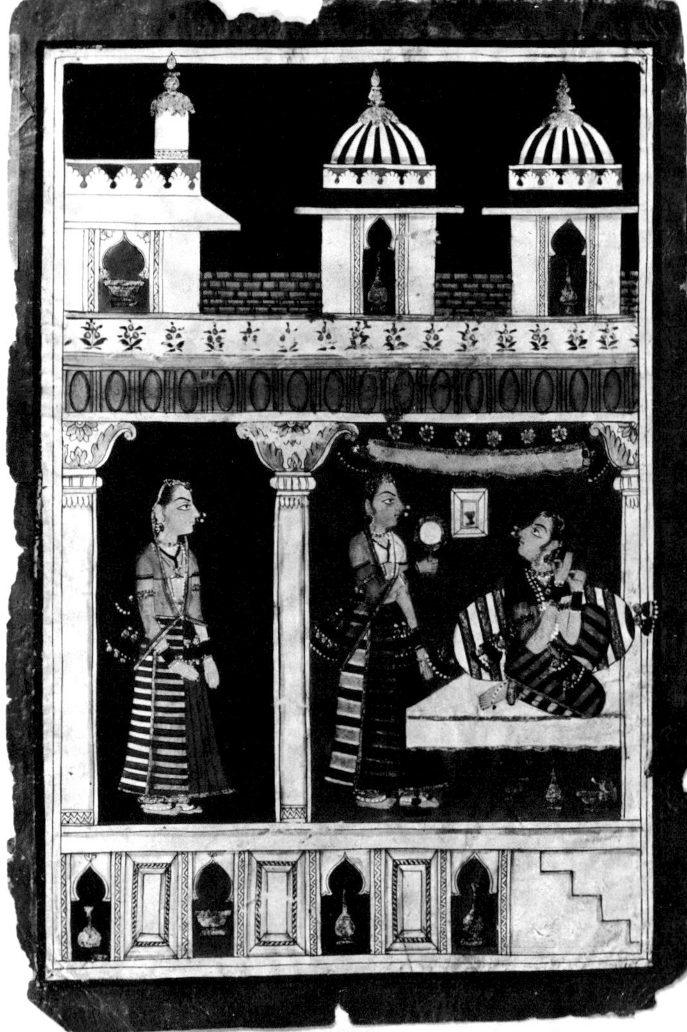

2.96

2.96 Ragini Vilaval:
Folio from a *Ragamala* Series
Malwa, late seventeenth century
7¼ x 5 in.

A young woman, who is preparing to
meet her lover, adjusts her earring
while a companion holds a mirror and
another waits outside the room. The
strong solid areas of color in the background, the compartmentalized composition and the striped domes are
characteristic features of the Malwa
style of the late seventeenth century.
The broad striped pattern on the cloth
skirts of the women is a typical textile
pattern.

P. Chandra, *Indian Miniature Painting*,
no. 133, black-and-white illustration.

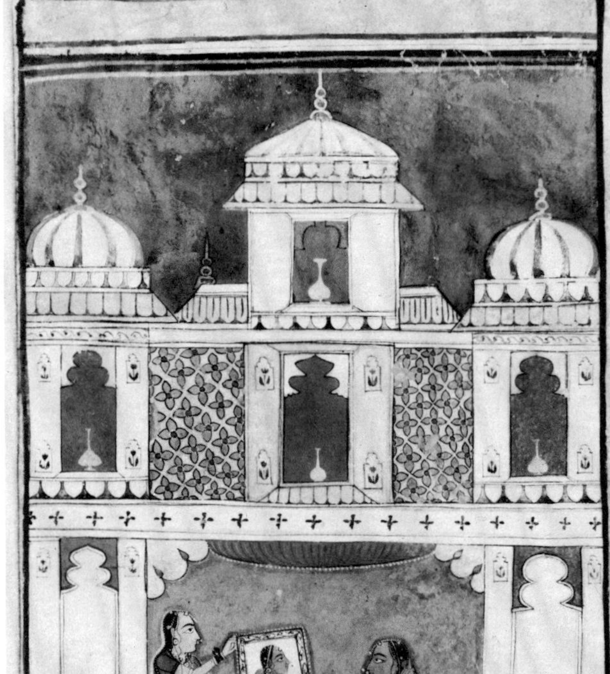

2.97

2.97 Ragini Vilaval:
Folio from a *Ragamala* Series
Malwa, c. 1700
8½ x 5½ in.

This painting depicts the same theme,
and is from the same school, as no.
2.96. Similarities include broad, flat
patches of background color, conventional architectural niches, and striped
domes. In this example, the artist has
painted the reflection of the lady in the
mirror held by her companion. The col-
or scheme is dominated by the gray-
blue background which appears
behind the figures as well as in the sky
and is repeated in the floral patterns
between the second story niches as
well as in the domes.

P. Chandra, *Indian Miniature Painting*,
no. 134, black-and-white illustration.

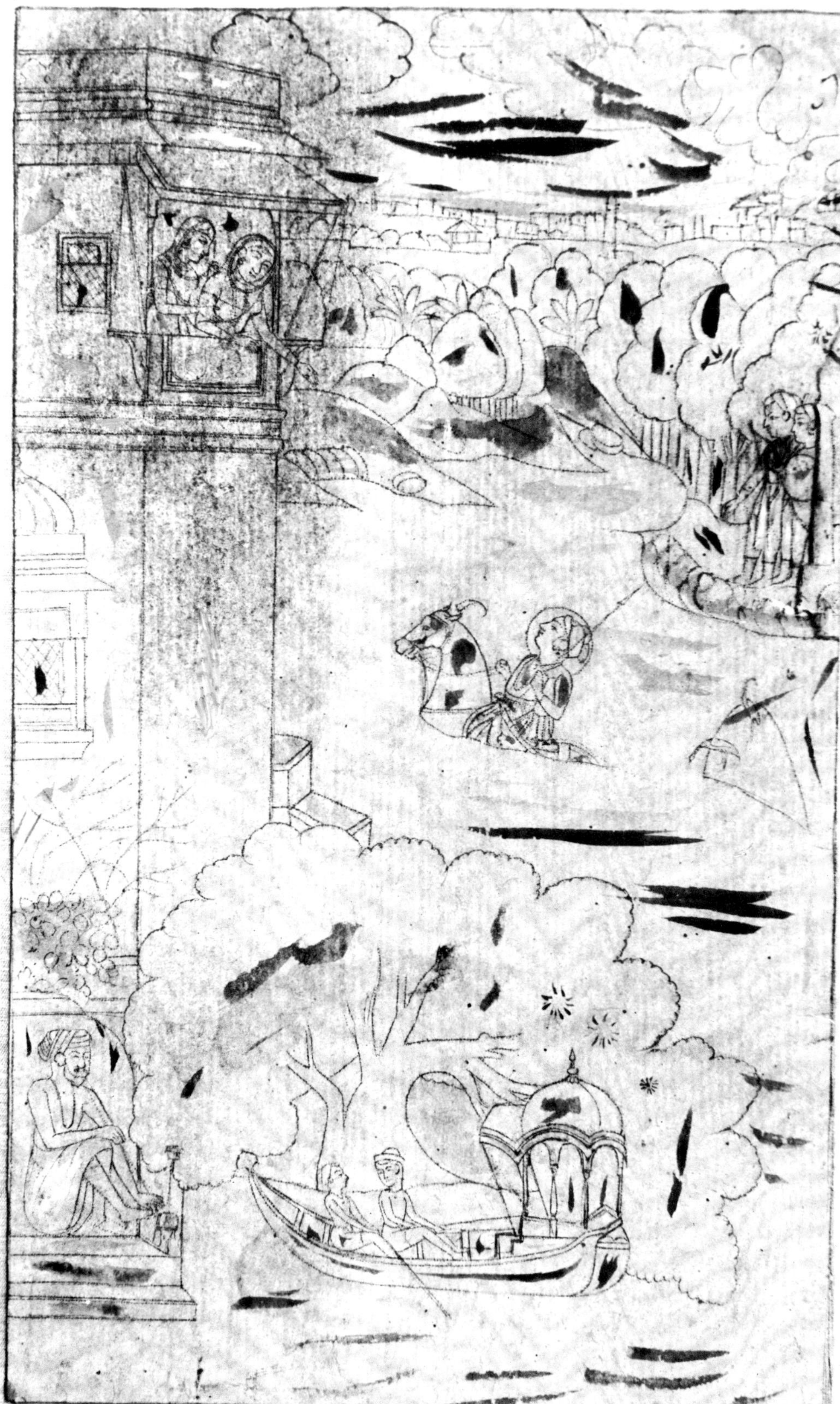

2.98 Ragini Lalita:
Folio from a *Ragamala* Series
Probably Bundi,
early eighteenth century
7⅞ x 4½ in.

Not illustrated

The lover turns back for one more
glance at his beloved as he steals
away in the early morning. The pattern
of the maroon and orange cloth which
covers the sleeping woman is of the tie-
dye type. The bold colors in the floor
tiles and in the decoration of the
pavilion stand out against the pale
early morning sky.

P. Chandra, *Indian Miniature Painting*,
no. 114, black-and-white illustration.

**2.99 A Prince Crossing a River
to Meet His Beloved**
Rajasthani Style,
mid-eighteenth century
8¾ x 6 in.

This sketch of a lover fording a river to
meet his beloved exemplifies an underlying characteristic of Indian painting. It
is a sketch of a well-known theme and
its repetition was viewed as a creative
opportunity for the artist. The life which
an individual artist could instill in a classic composition served as a testament
to his skill.

P. Chandra, *Indian Miniature Painting*,
no. 214.

2.100 A Lady on Her Way to a Tryst
Bundi or Kotah, late eighteenth century
7½ x 5⅛ in.

Color illustration

The twilight setting in a forest for the
tryst of two lovers enhances the danger
and excitement of the moment. The
woman, having left the safety of the city
walls, crosses a large grassy expanse.
Coyly, she raises her pink skirt and
holds her veil about her face. Her lover
appears amidst the trees in a fine white
tunic, delicately decorated in pink and
gold. His gold-encrusted black turban
stands out against the dark green
variegated foliage. Peacocks and other
birds peer out from the tree tops. In the
foreground, water from a light green
lotus tank spills onto a bed of gold-
tipped grass. The city walls in the background, approached by a bullock cart,
are set against a shimmering twilight
sky. A temple-tower within the city
pierces the border of the painting. The
outer border of the painting is an elaborate combination of lotus ponds,
birds and ducks in a variety of poses.

P. Chandra, *Indian Miniature Painting*,
no. 119, black-and-white illustration.

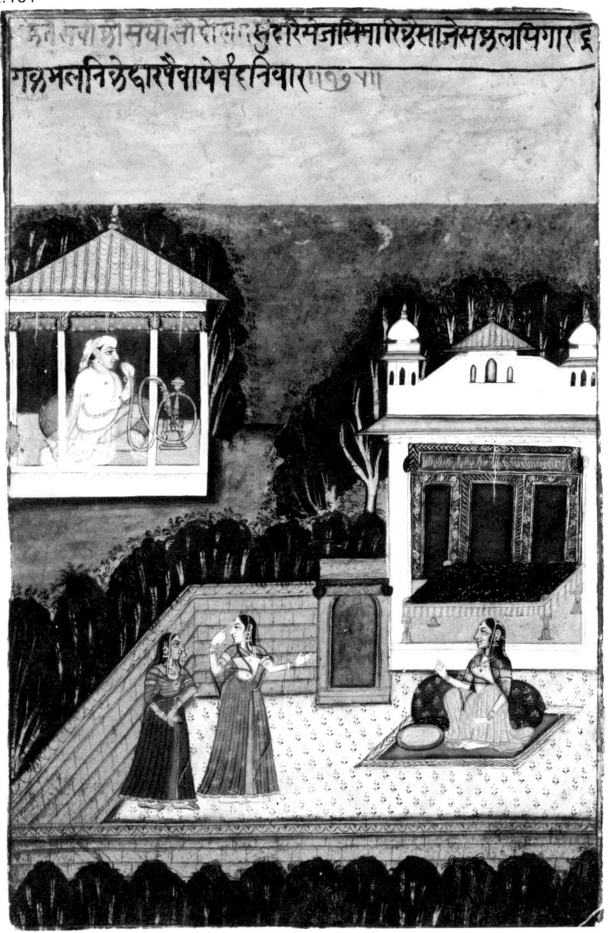

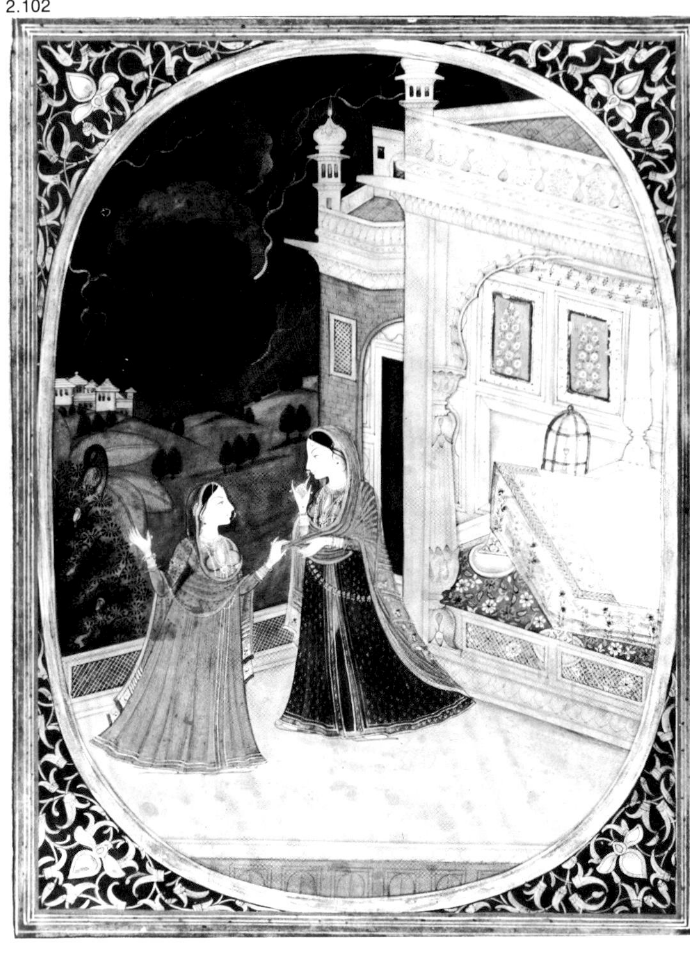

2.101 A Lady Waiting for Her Lover: From a Series Illustrating the Verses of Matiram
Bundelkhand, late eighteenth century
9 x 7¼ in.

Inside the pink walls of a tree-enclosed compound, a woman sits on an orange rug awaiting her lover. The courtyard is decorated in yellow with pink and green floral patterns. Two female attendants stand to one side, one of them pointing toward the waiting lady. Costume colors are pink, yellow, green, orange and blue. The empty bed in a pavilion above draws the viewer's eye to the female protagonist and highlights the theme of the painting—the absent lover. He is shown casually smoking a water pipe in a not too distant pavilion, located in a small clump of trees. A verse describing the scene is inscribed at the top on a deep yellow band.

P. Chandra, *Indian Miniature Painting,* no. 202; another folio from the same manuscript is in the Watson Collection, see, P.C. 203, black-and-white plate.

2.102. Waiting for the Lover
Kangra Style, early nineteenth century
8¾ x 6½ in.

This painting expresses a mood as much as a specific narrative though the love of Radha and Krishna is suggested. The lightning in the midst of thunderous clouds expresses excitement. Birds in trees near the balcony have tucked their heads under their wings. This pose suggests the night and the upcoming storm. The gray walls and the deeply colored clouds streaked with lightning confirm the idea of a stormy night. The woman waiting for her lover wears her finest clothes, a deep blue dress with olive-green border highlighted in gold. Her sheer golden veil has a large border of pink floral buds. Like her companion, she wears delicate jewels around her face, neck and arms. Made secondary by her diminished size, the companion is dressed in a green-colored dress and wears a gossamer veil. Both figures wear bright orange slippers. The red rug inside the pavilion offsets the pale pink floral-pattern, pink walls and

yellow bedspread with delicate touches of green and pink. The empty bed in the palace room and the countryside bereft of any human movement create a mood of solitude and anticipation rather than union. In the Kangra area the oval frame was a popular alternative to the typical rectangular format.

P. Chandra, *Indian Miniature Painting,* no. 252.

Select Bibliography

Part I: Textiles of South Asia

Alemchiba Ao, M: see *Census of India 1961* v. XXIII pt. VII.

All India Handicrafts Board. *Indian Kalamkari*. New Delhi, Government of India, Ministry of Industry, n.d.

Arness, Judith Russell. "Tie-Dyeing in India." *Handweaver and Craftsman* v. 14, no. 1(1963): 6-8, 37.

Barbier, Jean Paul. *Art du Nagaland*. Geneva, Musée Barbier-Müller, 1982.

Bareh, H. *Gazetteer of India, Nagaland, Kohima District*. Kohima, Government of Nagaland, 1970.

Barkatari, S. *Tribes of Assam*. New Delhi, National Book Trust, 1969.

Bühler, Alfred. "Dyes and Dyeing Methods for Ikat Threads." *CIBA Review* no. 44(1942): 1597-1603.

———. "The Ikat Technique." *CIBA Review* no. 44(1942): 1586-1596.

———. "The Origin and Extent of the Ikat Technique." *CIBA Review* no. 44(1942): 1604-1611.

———. "Patola Influences in South East Asia." *Journal of Indian Textile History* no. IV(1959): 4-46.

Bühler, Alfred, *et al. Patola und Geringsing*. Basel, Museum für Völkerkunde, 1975.

Bühler, Alfred and Eberhard Fischer. *The Patola of Gujarat*. Basel, Krebs AG, 1979.

Butler, Major John. *Travels and Adventures in the Province of Assam*. Smith, Elder & Co, 1855.

Census of India 1961 v. III Assam, pt. VII-A Selected Handicrafts of Assam. Compiler, E.H. Pakyntein. Delhi, Manager of Publications, 1966.

Census of India 1961 v. XXIII, Nagaland, pt. VII, Handicrafts of Nagaland. Text, M. Alemchiba Ao and H. Zopianga. Kohima, Census Office, 1964.

Chandra, Moti. "Kashmir Shawls." *Bulletin of the Prince of Wales Museum*, no. 3(1953): 1-24.

Choudury, P.C. *History of the Civilization of the People of Assam to the Twelfth Century A.D.* Gauhati, Department of Historical and Antiquarian Studies in Assam, 1959.

Corrie, Rebecca Wells: see Yale University Art Gallery 1975.

Crill, Rosemary: see Victoria & Albert Museum 1982.

DeBone, Mary Golden. "Patolu and its Techniques." *Textile Museum Journal* v. IV, no. 3(1976): 49-62.

Dhaky, M.K: see Nanavati, J.M. 1966.

Dhamija, Jasleen. "The Survey of Embroidery Traditions." In *Marg, Textiles and Embroideries of India,* 1965.

Devi, Pria (ed.), Jyotindra Jain, *et al. The Master Weavers*. London, Festival of India in Britain, Royal College of Art, 1982.

Elson, Vickie. *Dowries from Kutch: A Women's Folk Art Tradition in India*. Los Angeles, Museum of Cultural History, University of California, 1979.

Elwin, Verrier. *The Art of the North-East Frontier of India*. Shillong, Sachin Roy Publishers for NEFA, 1959.

Emery, Irene. *The Primary Structures of Fabrics*. Washington, D.C., The Textile Museum, 1966.

Erikson, Joan. *Mata Ni Pachedi*. Ahmedabad, National Institute of Design, 1968.

Fischer, Eberhard, *et al. Orissa, Kunst and Kulture in Nordost Indien*. Zürich, Museum Rietberg, 1980.

Fischer, Eberhard, Jyotindra Jain and Haku Shah. "Matano Candarvo: Textile Pieces for Goddess Worship in Gujarat." In *Homage to Kalamkari. Marg,* v. XXXI, no. 4 (September 1978).

————. *Tempeltücher für die Muttergöttinen in Indien*. Zürich, Museum Rietberg, 1982.

Frater, Judy. "The Meaning of Folk Art in Rabari Life." *Textile Museum Journal* v. IV no. 2(1975): 47-60.

Fürer-Haimendorf, Christoph von. *The Naked Nagas*. Calcutta, Thacker Spink & Co, 1933.

Gandhi, M.P. [Manmohan Purushottam]. *How to Compete with Foreign Cloth*. Calcutta, G.N. Mitra, 1931.

Gittinger, Mattiebelle. *Splendid Symbols, Textiles and Traditions in Indonesia*. Washington, D.C., The Textile Museum, 1979.

————. *Master Dyers to the World*. Washington, D.C., The Textile Museum, 1982.

Goody, Esther N., ed. *From Craft to Industry: The Ethnography of Proto-Industrial Cloth Production*. Cambridge, Cambridge University Press, 1982.

Gulati, A.N. *The Patolu of Gujarat*. Bombay, Museums Association of India, 1951.

Hacker, Katherine F. "Bandha Textiles, India's Ikat and Plangi Expression." *Arts of Asia* v. 12, no. 4(1982): 63-71.

Hacker, Katherine F. and Krista Jensen Turnbull. *Courtyard, Bazaar, Temple*. Seattle, University of Washington Press, 1982.

Hutton, J.H,. *The Sema Naga*. London, MacMillan and Co, 1921. Reprinted Bombay, Oxford University Press, 1968.

————. *The Angami Nagas*. Bombay, Oxford University Press, 1921. Reprinted 1969.

Irwin, John. *Shawls*. London, Victoria & Albert Museum, 1955.

————. *The Kashmir Shawl*. London, Victoria & Albert Museum, 1973.

Irwin, John and Margaret Hall. *Indian Painted and Printed Fabrics* (*Historic Textiles of India at the Calico Museum*, v. I). Ahmedabad, Calico Museum of Textiles, 1971.

————. *Indian Embroideries* (*Historic Textiles of India at the Calico Museum*, v. II). Ahmedabad, Calico Museum of Textiles, 1973.

Irwin, John and Babette Hanish. "Notes on the Use of the Hook in Indian Embroidery." *Bulletin of the Needle and Bobbin Club*, v. 53, nos. 1-2 (1970).

Jain, Jyotindra. *Folk Art and Culture of Gujarat: Guide to the Collection of the Shreyas Folk Museum of Gujarat*. Ahmedabad, Shreyas Folk Museum, 1980.

Jain, Ramesh C. *Catalogue of Ruth Reeves Indian Textile Collection*, 2 v. Unpublished MS, 1968.

Jayakar, Pupul. "A Neglected Group of Indian Ikat Fabrics." *Journal of Indian Textile History* no. I(1955): 55-65.

Karpinski, Caroline. "Kashmir to Paisley." *Metropolitan Museum of Art Bulletin*, November, 1963: 116-123.

Larsen, Jack Lenor, *et al. The Dyers Art; Ikat, Batik, Plangi*. New York, Van Nostrand, Reinhold, 1976.

Marg. Textiles and Embroideries of India, 1965.

————. *Homage to Kalamkari*. v. XXXI, no. 4 (September, 1978).

Mehta, R.N,. "Bandhas of Orissa." *Journal of Indian Textile History* no. VI(1961): 62-74.

Mills, J.P. and J.H. Hutton. *The Ao Nagas*. London, Macmillan and Co., 1926. Reprinted Bombay, Oxford University Press, 1973.

Mittal, Jagdish. "Telia Rumal of Pochampalli and Chirala." *Marg* v. 15, no. 4(1962): 26-29.

Mohanty, Bijoy Chandra and Kalyan Krishna. *Ikat Fabrics of Orissa and Andhra Pradesh*. Ahmedabad, Calico Museum of Textiles, 1974.

Murphy, Veronica: see Victoria & Albert Museum 1982.

Museum of Modern Art. *Textiles and Ornaments of India*. Monroe Wheeler, ed.; texts by Pupul Jayakar and John Irwin. New York, MOMA and Simon and Schuster, 1956.

Nanavati, J.M., *et al. The Embroidery and Beadwork of Kutch and Saurashtra*. (Ahmedabad,) Department of Archaeology, Gujarat State, 1966.

Pauly, Sara Buie: see Yale University Art Gallery 1975.

Ripley, S. Dillon. "Roaming India's Naga Hills." *National Geographic* v. CVII, no. 2 (February, 1955): 247-264.

Robinson, W. *Descriptive Account of Assam*, 1841.

Rossbach, Ed. *The Art of Paisley*. New York, Van Nostrand, Reinhold, 1980.

Roy, Nilima. *Art of Manipur*. Delhi, Agam Kala Prakashan, 1979.

Silverstein, John. *Woven Winds: The Art of Textiles in India*. Stratford, Ontario, The Gallery Stratford, 1981.

Singh, Prakash. *Nagaland*. Second ed. rev. New Delhi, National Book Trust, 1977.

Singh, R.K. Jhalajit. *Manipur*. New Delhi, Government of India, Ministry of Information and Broadcasting, 1975.

Skelton, Robert: see Victoria & Albert Museum 1982.

Thomas, Mary. *Dictionary of Embroidery Stitches*. New York, William Morrow and Co, 1935.

Victoria & Albert Museum. *The Indian Heritage: Court Life & Arts under Mughal Rule*. London, The Museum, 1982.

Watt, Sir George. *Indian Art at Delhi*. Calcutta, 1903.

Waugh, Nora. *The Cut of Women's Clothes 1600-1900*. New York, Theatre Arts Books, 1968.

Yale University Art Gallery. *The Kashmir Shawl*. New Haven, The Gallery, 1975.

Zopianga, M.: see *Census of India 1961*, v. XXIII pt. VII.

Part II: Paintings of South Asia

Archer, W.G. *Indian Painting from the Punjab Hills*. Two volumes. London, New York and Delhi, 1973.

Archer, W.G. *The Loves of Krishna*. London, 1954.

Archer, W.G. *Rajput Miniatures*. Portland, 1968.

Barrett, D. and Basil Gray. *Painting in India*. Lausanne, 1963.

Beach, Milo Cleveland. *The Grand Mogul*. Williamstown, 1978.

Beach, Milo Cleveland. *The Imperial Image*. Washington, 1981.

Beach, Milo Cleveland. *Rajput Painting at Bundi and Kota*. Ascona, 1974.

Chandra, Moti. *Jaina Miniature Painting from Western India*. Ahmedabad, 1949.

Chandra, Moti. *The Technique of Mughal Painting*. Lucknow, 1946.

Chandra, Pramod. *Indian Miniature Painting*. Madison, 1971.

Chandra, Pramod. ''An Outline of Early Rajasthani Painting.'' *Marg* 11, no. 2 (1958): 32-37.

Coomaraswamy, A.K. *Catalogue of the Indian Collection in the Museum of Fine Arts, Boston, Part 5, Rajput Painting and Part 6 Mughal Painting*. Cambridge, Mass., 1926 and 1930.

Coomaraswamy, A.K. *Rajput Painting*. Oxford, 1916.

Das Gupta, Rajatananda. *Eastern Indian Manuscript Painting*. Bombay, 1972.

Gangoly, O.C. *Ragas and Raginis*. Bombay, 1945.

In the Image of Man. New York, 1982.

Khandalavala, Karl. *Pahari Miniature Painting*. Bombay, 1958.

Krishna: The Divine Lover: Myth and Legend Through Indian Art. Ed. by Enrico Isacco and Anna L. Dallapiccola. Boston, 1983.

Lee, Sherman. *Rajput Painting*. New York, London, 1960.

Rawson, P.S. *Indian Painting*. London, 1962.

Sivaramamurti, C. *South Indian Paintings*. New Delhi, 1968.

Skelton, Robert. *Indian Miniatures*. Venice, 1961.

Skelton, Robert. *Rajasthani Temple Hangings of the Krishna Cult.* New York, 1973.

Welch, Stuart Cary. *The Art of Mughal India.* New York, 1963.

Welch, Stuart Cary. *Room for Wonder.* New York, 1978.

Welch, Stuart Cary and Milo Cleveland Beach. *Gods, Thrones and Peacocks.* New York, 1965.